Lines in the Sand

Lines

Timothy James Lockley

The University of Georgia Press // *Athens & London*

in the Sand

RACE AND CLASS IN

LOWCOUNTRY GEORGIA,

1750–1860

University of Georgia Press paperback edition, 2004
© 2001 by the University of Georgia Press
Athens, Georgia 30602
All rights reserved
Designed by Walton Harris
Set in 10.5/14 Sabon by G & S Typesetters, Inc.
Printed and bound by Thomson-Shore

The paper in this book meets the guidelines for
permanence and durability of the Committee on
Production Guidelines for Book Longevity of the
Council on Library Resources.

Printed in the United States of America
08   07   06   05   04   P   5   4   3   2   1

The Library of Congress has cataloged the cloth edition
of this book as follows:

Library of Congress Cataloging-in-Publication Data
Lockley, Timothy James, 1971–
Lines in the sand: race and class in lowcountry Georgia,
1750–1860 / Timothy James Lockley.
p.   cm.
Includes bibliographical references (p.) and index.
ISBN 0-8203-2228-8 (alk. paper)
1. Georgia — History — 1775–1865. 2. Georgia — Race
relations. 3. Georgia — Social conditions. 4. Social
classes — Georgia — History — 18th century. 5. Social
classes — Georgia — History — 19th century. 6. Slaves —
Georgia — Social conditions. 7. Afro-Americans —
Georgia — Social conditions. 8. Rural poor — Georgia —
History. 9. Whites — Georgia — Social conditions.
I. Title
F290 .L63 2000
975.8 — dc21   00-036461
ISBN 0-8203-2597-x (pbk. : alk. paper)

British Library Cataloging-in-Publication Data available

For my father, Sidney Lockley,

August 18, 1927–January 20, 1983

CONTENTS

ACKNOWLEDGMENTS

THE PRIMARY RESEARCH for this book was conducted in archives in North Carolina, South Carolina, and Georgia. I am indebted to the staff at all the libraries I visited for their helpfulness in guiding me through their collections and dealing patiently with my endless requests for photocopies, especially those at the Georgia Historical Society in Savannah and at the Department of Archives and History in Atlanta. I would also like to thank those who housed me during my six-month sojourn in the South: Genie Jensen, Ada Thomas, Ruth Smith, Sue Nauright, and John Howard. Their hospitality made being so far away from friends and family easier to bear. Special thanks must go to Norman Owens, who has entertained me royally with true lowcountry hospitality on several of my return visits to Savannah.

Many scholars have honored me with their advice, for which I am very grateful. I particularly thank Alan Day for introducing me to American history while I was an undergraduate at Edinburgh University. Connie Schulz, Mark Kaplanoff, Tony Badger, Peter Parish, Sylvia Frey, and Bill Dusinberre have all given me the benefits of their insights into the field, and Christopher Stanton patiently proofread several drafts of this book. Since moving to Warwick University I have benefited from the advice of many colleagues, particularly Roger Fagge and Chris Clark. Malcolm Call, Jennifer Comeau, Trudie Calvert, and the anonymous readers of the University of Georgia Press have also been very helpful in guiding me through the publication process. Above all, I thank Betty Wood for her wit, intelligence, and scholarly humor, which have made this task thoroughly enjoyable. For her careful understanding and judicious advice, even after I had passed beyond her official care, I shall always be grateful.

ix

This project would never have been started without the financial support of my mother, Margaret Lockley, and my brother, Simon Lockley. My family have always encouraged me in my work, and I hope that this book is worthy of their confidence in me. I would also like to acknowledge the financial support of the Research Institute for the Study of Man, the Ellen McArthur, Prince Consort, and Thirlwall Funds of the History Faculty of Cambridge University, Queens' College, the Cambridge Historical Society, the Economic and Social Research Council, the British Academy, and Warwick University.

Part of chapter 3 appeared as "Trading Encounters between African Americans and Non-Slaveholders in Savannah, 1790–1860" in the *Journal of Southern History,* 66 (February 2000), 25–48. I would like to thank the editor of the journal, John B. Boles, for granting his permission for me to reproduce the material here.

Finally, I thank my wife, Joanne. Over the last eight years she has always been ready with advice and understanding. Her support has gone way beyond the call of duty, proofreading various pieces of work, encouraging me with her comments and criticisms, and keeping me sane during the completion of the manuscript. Yet she still found the time to give birth to our beautiful baby daughter, Alice.

To all of the above and unmentioned friends, colleagues, and family, I owe an enormous and unrepayable debt.

INTRODUCTION

THE LOWCOUNTRY of Georgia and South Carolina was a unique society in the colonial and antebellum South. In no other location in mainland America was there such a massive concentration of wealth in the hands of the small slaveholding elite coupled with the oppression of an overwhelming black majority. The obvious contrasts between the privileged lives of elite white slaveholders and the meager existence of black slaves have encouraged both contemporaries and some later scholars to overlook the thousands of lowcountry whites who did not own slaves. What was the status of nonslaveholders in lowcountry society, and how can we characterize their relationship with the large enslaved population? Indeed, it is ironic that we know far less about the largest social group in the South, namely nonslaveholding whites, than we do about slaveholders or slaves.

In recent years there has been something of a renaissance in plain-folk studies as scholars attempt to redress this historiographic imbalance. I hope that this book contributes to the quest to uncover more about the everyday lives of ordinary Southerners in the years before the Civil War. The plain folk have never been totally anonymous in the historiography of the antebellum South, but it is obvious when one looks at the large volume of material published on the lives of the white elite and on slaves that nonslaveholders have been neglected in historical research. In part, this neglect stems from the widespread perception, which existed even before the Civil War, that the antebellum South was a society of "cavaliers, poor whites, and slaves" and that poor whites were nothing more than "trash" who could safely be ignored.[1] Despite the best efforts of some contemporaries such as Daniel Hundley, a native of Alabama, to dispel this notion by pointing to the social, economic, and political importance of the Southern middle classes, neglect of them persisted long into the twentieth century.

The lack of scholarly insight into the lives of nonslaveholders has meant that one of the most important historical questions about them has been seriously addressed only in the last twenty years. Why did nonslaveholders remain loyal to the Southern ethos and support the Confederacy in 1860? Contemporaries varied in their responses to this question. Hinton Rowan Helper, writing in 1857, called on nonslaveholders to unite with Northerners to overthrow the plantation regime, believing that the South's peculiar institution condemned poor whites to "a second degree of slavery" and that they had little reason to support it.[2] Among the many responses Helper's book elicited among Southerners, two stand out. Virginian Samuel Wolfe claimed that the "upright poor man" fared far better in the South than in the North and that working whites would never be degraded "to social or political equality with the negro."[3] Daniel Hundley argued that, far from feeling aggrieved toward slaveholders, most nonslaveholding whites had a great deal in common with the elite, of which race and a shared "Southern" identity were most important. Hundley drew an important distinction between the vast majority of nonslaveholders and the "separate class of poor whites who traded and socialized with slaves.[4] While all of these views of Southern class relationships contain elements of truth, they by no means tell the whole story.

Historians have only gradually reassessed the extreme perceptions of nonelite whites left over from the nineteenth century. The "father" of slavery studies, U. B. Phillips, paid scant attention to nonelite whites in his exploration of the antebellum South, commenting only that the numerous travel accounts that portrayed ordinary nonslaveholding whites as degraded, pathetic creatures were perhaps exaggerated.[5] Other early-twentieth-century articles by Paul Buck, Avery Craven, and A. N. J. Den Hollander generally accepted the accuracy of the stereotype of the lazy, illiterate, racist nonslaveholder but made important distinctions between the desperate poverty of some whites and the relative prosperity of yeoman farmers.[6] By the mid-1940s most scholars had come to accept that antebellum white society was far more complex than previously had been supposed.[7]

Much of the most recent work on the plain folk acknowledges a debt to the work of Frank and Harriet Owsley in the 1940s at Vanderbilt University which did much to bring the yeoman farmer to the attention of historians.[8] While building on the conclusion that white society in the South was finely gradated, they offered explanations about the historic anonymity of nonslaveholders, pointing, for example, to the so-called hidden wealth of the yeomen, namely livestock that would have been allowed to roam wild, thus not being particularly visible to travelers who described yeomen as poor. The Owsleys' research did not win wholehearted support from all sides. Fabian Linden, for example, criticized their narrow focus on the yeomen (and the more prosperous yeomen at that) to the detriment of the true "poor white."[9]

Much of the next generation of Southern scholarship ignored the plain folk. It was not until 1979 that a leading historian again explored the world of the South's nonslaveholders. J. Wayne Flynt saw the term "poor white" as essentially sociological, defining a type of person as much as his or her status.[10] Flynt applied this term to the lowest groups in society, not the yeomen, and characterized them by their illiteracy, their economic and geographic isolation, and their inability to improve their situation. In contrast, he perceived yeomen as semiprosperous farmers, primarily self-sufficient, and with the potential to move into the planter class. On the issue of planter hegemony, posited so comprehensively by Eugene Genovese with regard to slaves, Flynt suggests that planters had little to do with real "poor whites" and could usually ignore them.[11]

The issue, touched on by Flynt, of how far the plain folk internalized the elite social ethic, has become central in nearly all studies of the plain folk published since 1983. Steven Hahn has suggested that in backcountry areas, where nonslaveholders predominated, yeomen were able to impose their own community-based ethos in the face of planter opposition.[12] In contrast, J. William Harris has argued persuasively that, despite the involvement of nonslaveholders in local government, members of the plantation belt elite used their racial, economic, and kinship ties with nonslaveholders to impose their own social ethic on society.[13] Seeking a middle way, Lacy Ford argued in his study of the South Carolina upcountry that racial and economic ties between the elite and nonslaveholders did not constitute formal hegemony, and in fact the nonelite strongly resisted any attempts to curb their political and social independence. In a recent article, Ford has argued that the political ideology of the plain folk emphasized the equality of all white men, elite as well as nonelite, and their collective elevation above the rest of society.[14]

Two studies of plain folk in North Carolina by Bill Cecil Fronsman and Charles Bolton offer fairly similar views of the relationship between the elite and the nonelite. Fronsman argues that links among whites were racial as much as economic and were further bolstered by kinship ties. Thus the attacks on slavery in the 1850s were perceived by nonslaveholders as attacks on white society as a whole.[15] Bolton suggests that members of the elite actually went out of their way to cultivate this perception among nonslaveholders but paid heed to the views of the plain folk only when forced to.[16] The most recent contribution to this debate has come from Stephanie McCurry, whose study is the only one to explore the social milieu of the lowcountry. She argues that yeomen and the elite in coastal South Carolina shared a common evangelical culture, one that stressed the role of all white men as "masters" of their own households and brought them together to defend slavery.[17]

The historiographical consensus therefore seems to be that more forces acted to unite than to divide white society. No book-length exploration of the relationship between slaves and nonslaveholders exists, however. Central to such a discussion must be an assessment of the degree of racial prejudice felt by nonslaveholders toward slaves and how their interaction affected each group's relationship with the white elite. Of course, some historians have examined this relationship, in varying degrees of depth, but, as yet, no systematic exploration of the mentality of nonslaveholders has been offered to try to explain why they acted in the variety of ways that will be described in this book.

Those historians who have attempted to discuss the relationship between nonslaveholding whites and African Americans usually conclude that they could not coexist harmoniously. Indeed, U. B. Phillips's "central theme" of southern history, delineated in the early years of the twentieth century, was that the ethic of white society was based on racial solidarity and suppression of the Negro and that this ideology was subscribed to by all white people.[18] W. O. Brown, a generation later, went so far as to say that, apart from sporadic urban interaction, racial tensions prevented any relationship at all between nonslaveholders and African Americans.[19] Eugene Genovese concluded that planters went out of their way to encourage a mistrust and hatred of "poor white trash" among their slaves. This view fits neatly with Genovese's concept of paternalism, whereby slaveholders believed themselves to be the best guardians for African Americans, whom they regarded almost as members of their own family in need of the same correction or guidance given to children, and that slaves, to a certain degree, internalized this ideology.[20] Unfortunately, the theory of paternalism tends to deny the independent agency of slaves in the formation of social relationships, a major theme in this book. Modern scholars have been willing to challenge Genovese's theories, but even those historians who do not completely subscribe to the concept of paternalism and planter hegemony fail to appreciate just how far nonelite whites and African Americans permeated each other's worlds, arguing instead that relations between these two social groups were often casual.[21] Indeed, in their attempt to explain white solidarity in the 1850s and 1860s, scholars have often overlooked the shaky commitment of some nonslaveholders to Southern society during the early years of the nineteenth century.[22]

A generation ago Barbara Fields argued that the concept of race existed only in the mind and was not a genuine reflection of biological differences.[23] Consequently, the main question to be answered is the extent to which ordinary nonslaveholders internalized an ideology of race and racial difference, which they believed distinguished them from African Americans. In what ways were the racial self-perceptions of nonslaveholders different from those of the elite? What impact did the range of biracial interactions, social, religious, criminal, and economic, have on racial ideology? In sum, were racial boundaries nothing more than "lines in the sand," barriers that were readily overcome by the "waves" of everyday contacts between white and black? This is not to deny that the "lines" existed but merely to suggest that they were not as strong and impervious as once thought. Finding answers to these questions is the purpose of this book.

Examining the lives and thought processes of ordinary Southerners forces historians to try to define them as a social group. Scholars who have explored the lives of nonelite whites rarely agree on definitive parameters.[24] The obvious problem is that generalized terms such as "poor white," "common white," "plain folk," and "yeoman" are riddled with inconsistencies. Bill Cecil Fronsman, for example, prefers to use the term "common white" because it encompasses both poor whites and yeoman farmers. Charles Bolton seems to define "poor whites" as landless laborers, while Stephanie McCurry's definition of yeomen as "self-working farmers" owning up to ten slaves, though appropriate in the lowcountry, would not fit elsewhere in the South.[25] The pitfalls of relying on generic terms are exposed once we realize that, for example, artisans fit into none of these groups, for some were nonslaveholders barely making a living, while others owned several slaves.[26] Equally, there would have been few practical economic differences between small farmers who owned one slave and those who owned none.[27] I do not wish to suggest that all non-slaveholders should be perceived as one single group, with an identical racial ideology. In fact, this book will show that nonslaveholders' inter-actions with African Americans were extremely varied. Even though non-slaveholders constitute a heterogeneous socioeconomic status group, my main purpose is to assess the relationship between African Americans and those white people who did not own slaves, and in that endeavor economic differences between individual whites are of only peripheral importance. The term "non-slaveholder," which I use in this book, natu-rally has its own problems and inconsistencies because not all nonslave-holders belonged to the same economic or social class, but the term suits my purpose well. Of particular interest is how white people reacted to African Americans in situations in which they held no formal jurisdiction over them. Were their encounters always characterized by a deep-seated racism or were they more pragmatic? Did the fact that interactions be-tween white nonslaveholders and African Americans were usually volun-tary, not coerced, test the racial barriers of the lowcountry? What was the attitude of members of the elite to biracial interaction? Did they employ a variety of stratagems to split nonslaveholders from African Americans, and, if so, how successful were they? While not denying that racial iden-tity permeated every aspect of Southern culture, I posit that their actions show that the white nonelite believed that the ideological constructs sepa-rating black from white were flexible and permeable.

I decided to study the society of lowcountry Georgia in part to offer a contrast to the several studies of the backcountry which appeared during the 1980s. Unlike the upcountry, the coastal plain contained a large black majority population, as well as urban centers where interracial interac-tion could flourish. By the nineteenth century, the lowcountry in both South Carolina and Georgia was dominated by a small merchant-planter elite, engaged principally in the cultivation of rice, whose intensive labor demands were met by a large number of bondspeople.[28] The coastal areas were also the only locations that supported both a metropolis and a group of smaller towns. By 1800, Charleston and Savannah were the largest cities in their respective states and the largest ports between Balti-more and New Orleans. To some extent, many of the conclusions offered here are applicable throughout the lowcountry; after all, lowcountry

Georgia and South Carolina were acknowledged by one resident to be "strikingly alike."[29] Indeed, the residents of coastal South Carolina were, in many respects, responsible for the socioeconomic development of coastal Georgia after 1750. The influx of planters with their slaves from the northern side of the Savannah River created a society in Georgia fundamentally constructed on the South Carolina model.[30] South Carolina, however, was already on its third generation of settlement by the time General James Oglethorpe arrived on the *Anne* to settle Georgia. South Carolina also does not provide an example of a clear legal transition to slavery; for some years in the seventeenth century the status of black workers in the province was unclear. In contrast, when Georgia permitted slavery in 1751, all but a handful of African Americans entering the state were enslaved.

This book examines four separate, but interlinked, spheres of biracial interaction: social contacts, economic networks, criminal encounters, and shared religious experiences. I will examine race relations in both private and public spheres, showing how African Americans and nonslaveholding whites responded to each other when interacting in different forums. Although my research suggests that we should not merely accept the previous conclusions of historians that relations between nonslaveholding whites and African Americans were highly antagonistic, I will not ignore areas of conflict between these groups. Ultimately I offer an explanation for why nonslaveholding whites and African Americans were willing to cross the racial divides of Southern society, what implications their interactions had for race relations generally, and how important racial ideology was to the ordinary nonslaveholder.

During the 110 years from the introduction of slavery to the onset of the Civil War lowcountry Georgia matured into a highly complex society. Within that society, multiple threads united the lives of lowcountry African Americans and nonslaveholding whites, and biracial interaction sometimes blurred the strict boundaries of race. By grouping all white people together regardless of status, early historians assumed that the two halves of the resident lowcountry white population shared common racial prejudices. Yet it will become apparent that the elite constantly tried, and consistently failed, to prevent biracial interaction. As I will demonstrate, the socioeconomic position of nonslaveholding whites in this society led them into various spheres of voluntary and involuntary proximity with African Americans, which could not have flourished if their actions were determined only by racism. The attitudes this proximity engendered in the minds of nonslaveholding whites and African Americans form the ultimate focus of this book. I seek to establish that, within certain limitations, race could defer to self-interest, friendship, cooperation, and brotherly or sisterly solidarity in the minds of the poorer black and white members of lowcountry Georgia society.

Lines in the Sand

I Nonslaveholders in the Georgia Lowcountry

THE COLONIAL AND ANTEBELLUM SOUTH was dominated economically, socially, and politically by a small planter elite, some of whose wealthiest individuals inhabited the fertile coastal lands of Georgia and South Carolina.[1] Their spectacular wealth was founded principally on the production of rice and sea island cotton. The lowcountry encompasses a 250-mile strip of coastline from Georgetown in South Carolina in the north to St. Marys on the Florida border in the south. The six Atlantic counties on the Georgia side of the Savannah River encroach between 30 and 50 miles inland, are characteristically flat, and are crossed at regular intervals by river systems. This book is not about the rich and powerful individuals who inhabited coastal plantations but about white people who had to work for their subsistence either as artisans, on their own farms, or as wage laborers.

Only in Georgia among the mainland American colonies was there a clear legal transition from a free to a slave society. Before 1750, few white people had to concern themselves with the effect of slave labor on their lives. After 1750 the social upheaval engendered by the introduction of slavery into Georgia radically changed both the new colony and the socioeconomic life of every inhabitant. Although differences in status had existed among the early colonists, dependent on birth, political position, and economic function, no settlers before 1750 owned slaves.[2] The abrogation of that basic equality after 1750 fostered a rapid expansion in slave importation and the development of a plantation economy, which increasingly economically marginalized those poor Georgians who could not afford slaves. Conversely, slavery permitted wealthy planters to prosper and institutionalize their new sociopolitical dominance.

1

From the late colonial period onward enslaved Africans outnumbered whites in the lowcountry, whether slaveholding or not, by a factor of between two and three to one.[3] Neither race, however, was evenly distributed in the coastal plain. The vast majority of lowcountry bondspeople lived in rural areas rather than in the urban centers of Savannah, Darien, Jefferson, and St. Marys.[4] In contrast, more than a third of the white population and nearly all lowcountry free blacks were urban residents.[5] Most bondspeople resided on plantations, producing the rice and cotton that financed the luxurious lifestyle of the white elite. Conventional wisdom dictates that, apart from their owners, and in stark contrast to backcountry areas, the only other white people with whom lowcountry bondspeople came into contact were overseers. The myth that the lowcountry population consisted only of planters, overseers, and bondspeople, however, has been thoroughly exposed by the work of Stephanie McCurry.[6] Her study of yeoman farmers in the South Carolina lowcountry has demonstrated that the planter/slave typology is false and that the farms of nonslaveholders intermingled with the plantations of the elite, even in this wealthy society. McCurry argues persuasively that the gentility myth arose because planters portrayed their society to outsiders as the ultimate republican ideal of equal citizens with no wealth inequalities among whites.[7] As I will show in this chapter, there is ample evidence that, just as in lowcountry South Carolina, nonslaveholding whites resided in every corner of coastal Georgia, which facilitated their formal and informal interactions with African Americans.

The ultimate problem faced by social historians of the plain folk in colonial and antebellum Georgia is the high level of illiteracy among nonslaveholding whites. Very few wrote letters or kept diaries, and what little is known about their everyday existence is often filtered through elite or non-Southern sources.[8] The anonymity of nonslaveholding whites also extends to official records, ensuring the imprecision of all contemporary estimates of the size of slaveholding in the lowcountry. Poor and geographically isolated people could often be overlooked by census enumerators or tax collectors. By working with a variety of sources, spread over more than a century, however, it is possible to trace the changing structure of the nonslaveholding population.

The colony of Georgia was founded primarily to give a secure buffer to the southern frontier of British North America, threatened by the Spanish in Florida and the French in the Mississippi Valley, and also to fulfill the philanthropic aims of the Trustees. The original charter stipulated both of these aims, declaring that the settlement south of the Savannah River would provide a "comfortable subsistence" for poor families from Europe "but also strengthen our colonies and increase the trade, navigation, and wealth of these our realms."[9] The Trustees for Establishing the Colony of Georgia in America, to whom was entrusted the charter for a period of twenty-one years, quickly came to believe that slavery would hinder both of these aims. A colony with several thousand slaves but few white people was believed to be hard to defend against attack. Equally, a colony using African slave labor would not encourage white people to work for themselves but would indulge their idleness.[10] The exclusion of slavery from Trustee Georgia in 1735 was clearly not motivated by a deep hatred of the system of African bondage in America.[11]

The Trustees were firm believers in the cathartic nature of work and especially in its capacity for improving the moral self.[12] They envisaged the creation of a society of contented small landholders in Georgia. Therefore, those poor farmers, debtors, and artisans who were sent to Georgia "on the charity" were carefully screened to weed out those who would fail to strive for the economic development of the colony.[13] The events of August 1733 strengthened the belief of Oglethorpe and the Trustees that the widespread use of slave labor would foster laziness among white people. On his return from a visit to Charleston, Oglethorpe found the white settlers idle and dissolute, prepared to sit and watch the slave sawyers, lent from Carolina, work in the oppressive summer heat, while doing nothing themselves.[14] Clearly some early settlers did not share the perceptions of the Trustees regarding the beneficial nature of manual work, and episodes such as these prompted the legal prohibition of slavery from Georgia in 1735.[15]

The formation of a prominent proslavery faction among the English and lowland Scots in Georgia, who argued vociferously in both America and London that "nothing but Negroes will do," eventually wore down the resistance of the Trustees.[16] Yet, while a majority of Georgia's inhabitants supported the introduction of slavery, a significant minority did not, most notably the Salzburgers at Ebenezer and the Scottish Highlanders at Darien. The Salzburgers suspected that the introduction of slaves would encourage the establishment of large rice-producing plantations, which would result in the reallocation of land originally intended for poor people.[17] The Highlanders were more practical, stating that "we are not rich, and becoming debtors for slaves in case of their running away, or dying, would inevitably ruin the poor master, and he become a greater slave to the Negro merchants, than the slave he bought could be to him."[18] These representations are significant because they defended the cause of poor white people in Georgia—those who would never be able to afford slaves—against the interests of merchants and planters. Although their protestations were ultimately ineffectual, the issues they raised about the effect of slave labor on the poorer inhabitants of Georgia resurfaced periodically throughout the colonial period.

Despite the views of the settlers at Darien and Ebenezer, many poor people supported the malcontents in their attempts to legalize slavery in Georgia. In 1739 General Oglethorpe claimed that many of the poorer people supported the petitions for slavery because they believed it would result in their receiving more credit from planters and merchants.[19] Oglethorpe characterized these people as having spent all their money in taverns and sold the rights to their white servants, and as now hoping to live off the labor of slaves they could not hope to pay for.[20] Oglethorpe's view may be extreme, but it is certainly possible that some people in Savannah, depressed by the lack of economic progress under the Trustees and conscious of their own poverty, hoped that the introduction of slavery would be matched by a new wave of Trustee philanthropy in the form of credit for slaves. Oglethorpe perceived other malcontents as being unwilling to exert themselves to improve their land without the use of coerced labor.[21] Hence "the idleness of the town of Savannah is chiefly owing to their seeing the Negroes in Carolina as the industry of the Southern division of the province."[22] As Thomas Christie freely admitted to the Trustees, Georgia was poorly developed precisely because the white people "would not be slaves" in a region of America where manual labor was traditionally seen to be the proper employment of the African.[23]

Some poorer people, however, may have genuinely shared the belief enunciated by the more vocal malcontents that the introduction of slavery would engender inward migration, increased trade, and general prosperity. The introduction of slavery clearly made Georgia an attractive investment opportunity to planters from South Carolina and the Caribbean islands because of the availability of high-quality agricultural lands. The more people in the colony, the more demand there was likely to be for handicrafts. In the Petition for Negroes of 1738, the malcontents had claimed that the use of slaves would "occasion great numbers of white people to come here."[24] Thus, in part, their petition was intended to stop the hemorrhaging to South Carolina of both ordinary settlers and servants who had completed their time.[25] Propaganda like this was increasingly common in Savannah in the 1740s, no doubt encouraging some poorer whites to believe that slavery could engender general economic benefits, even for nonslaveholders.

The Trustees took little notice of these arguments, preferring to believe that allowing Africans into Georgia "would thereby discourage and drive away white servants."[26] In rejecting the petition, the Trustees reaffirmed their commitment to a colony in which industrious white people could prosper; indeed they informed John Martin Bolzius that their paramount objective was to ensure "the happiness of the subjects."[27] Their rejection of the Petition for Negroes in 1738 was no doubt also motivated by suspicions that the malcontents had little if any regard for the effect slavery would have on poor white people. One Charleston merchant, a Mr. Crockat, admitted to the Trustees that nonelite whites would find fruitful employment in a slave society only as "overseers to the Negroes of the richer men," if not in Georgia then in Carolina, hardly the gainful employment the Trustees envisaged for white settlers.[28]

Although slavery was not officially permitted in Georgia until January 1, 1751, slaves were illegally employed on several plantations from as early as 1746.[29] These infractions of the law clearly increased in frequency so that by 1750 the Trustees were effectively recognizing de jure what had long been practiced de facto. As the long-heralded legalization of slavery approached, fears grew among those who believed that slavery would harm the poor white population. Chief among the champions of the poor was John Martin Bolzius.[30] As early as 1747, Bolzius had predicted that the introduction of slaves into Georgia would place poor Georgians at the mercy of South Carolina slave traders, who would buy the best lands and encourage people to borrow money beyond their means to finance the purchase of slaves. Bolzius also recognized the threat slave artisans posed to white skilled workers. He argued that planters would find it cheaper to train and employ slave rather than white artisans and thought this would lead to the emigration of white workers who would otherwise be unable to support themselves.[31]

Yet the poor inhabitants of Georgia lost none of their enthusiasm for slavery during the 1740s. Indeed, the evidence from both the President and Assistants, who desired the introduction of slaves, and Bolzius, who did not, seems to indicate that people from all social classes in Georgia before 1750 supported the use of slaves. In 1748, after being instructed by the Trustees to seize any slaves found in Georgia illegally, the President and Assistants reported that their actions had caused "general consternation and uneasiness . . . among the inhabitants in all parts of the colony."[32] Later the same month Bolzius lamented that none of the politically or socially important residents of Savannah supported his position on slavery.[33] In the same letter he noted that "all from the highest to the lowest vote for Negroes" and that only his opposition prevented the immediate introduction of slaves. By the end of 1748 Bolzius reported the euphoria in Savannah at the news that the Trustees were considering the repeal of the law of 1735; "even the poorest and lowest sort of people are happy about this prospect and want it to happen soon."[34]

The Trustees, together with the President and Assistants, did not seem too interested that the "lower sort" supported their decision to introduce slavery into Georgia. In August 1748 Benjamin Martyn wrote to the President and Assistants asking them to consult only with the "principal people of the province" when framing a set of regulations to govern the use of slaves.[35] These "principal people" included the President, William Stephens, the four Assistants, leading planters such as Noble Jones and Henry Yonge, and merchants such as James Habersham and Francis Harris.[36] John Martin Bolzius, whose opposition to slavery was well-known, was also invited to attend this meeting. He later took comfort in the fact that he had been able to include stipulations in the regulations that all slaves were to receive religious instruction on Sundays and that miscegenation was to be outlawed.[37]

Three of the regulations eventually agreed upon by the elite colonists and the Trustees related to poorer white people. To counteract the possibility of Georgia becoming a colony like South Carolina with an overwhelming black majority population, the Trustees insisted that a proper ratio of white people to slaves must be maintained. Therefore they required planters to employ one white man on their plantations for every four slaves.[38] There is evidence that this regulation was widely ignored. In 1755 (the first full year of royal rule in Georgia), 114 migrants to the colony were granted land by the governor and council. They brought with them 971 slaves but only 32 white servants. Eight planters complied with the ratio of 4:1 stipulated in 1750; only another six complied with the higher ratio of 20:1 outlined in the 1755 slave code. Clearly, by 1755 these regulations were so poorly enforced that the vast majority of immigrating planters could disregard them.[39]

To protect white artisans, slaves could not be employed by their masters in craft work, and white artisans were prohibited from taking on slaves in preference to white apprentices. The only exception permitted slaves to pack barrels of rice for export because there did not seem to be enough whites to accomplish the task.[40] These regulations were supposed to ensure that most bondspeople brought into Georgia were principally employed on plantations to engage in staple-crop production rather than in more varied economic capacities. In contrast to the expectations of some settlers, the elite had no intention of allowing poor whites to purchase slaves on credit. By preventing most artisans from owning slaves, planters and merchants secured for themselves a new status symbol, the slave, and the new title of "master." Thus slave ownership rapidly became the principal means of social differentiation in colonial Georgia. Owning slaves guaranteed a degree of acceptance among the highest ranks of white society. Conversely, nonslaveholders' reliance on their own labor for subsistence would have engendered an obvious association with laboring Africans in the minds of the elite.

Certain of Georgia's inhabitants expressed apprehension regarding the nature of landholding following the introduction of slavery, believing that the growth of large plantations would confine the small farmer to the poorest and most isolated lands. Recent research has confirmed that small farmers were indeed marginalized away from main rivers by planters from South Carolina.[41] The Salzburgers were the first to express their fears to their pastor in early 1749.[42] They believed that lands near Ebenezer would be granted to planters entering the colony with large numbers of slaves. Bolzius resolved to petition the council, asking that the land around Ebenezer be reserved to them or to other nonslaveholding farmers. Bolzius's petition clearly went unheard because in January 1750 a planter "with many Negroes" was granted a large piece of land near Ebenezer "in the area where our young people wish to take up their land." When he made further representations to the council, Bolzius was told by James Habersham that without slaves the Salzburgers could not realistically hope to receive large land grants.[43] The council and other merchants and planters were obviously not prepared to permit a continuance of the Trustees' original policy of granting fifty- or one-hundred-acre tracts, which was intended to encourage the settlement of small independent farmers. Coupled with the decision to introduce slaves was a reform of the land policy of the colony to grant five-hundred-acre tracts to those with the manpower to exploit them. Indeed, an analysis of the governor's land-granting policy in the mid-1750s supports the conclusion that although petitions from slaveholders were likely to be accepted, few large land grants were made to nonslaveholders.[44] Therefore, with an abundant (if expensive) labor force to work these large acreages, the merchant-planter elite prepared to turn Georgia into a plantation province on the South Carolina model.[45]

It was not only the Salzburgers who protested about the tendency of the President and Assistants to grant five-hundred-acre tracts to planters from South Carolina.[46] In July 1750, the inhabitants of the village of Abercorn complained to the Trustees that they were being "eaten up" by the five-hundred-acre grants now surrounding their settlement, and that "being confined to our 50 acre lots we shall have but little range or food for our few cattle."[47] The settlers of Abercorn petitioned that they be granted an island in the Savannah River for their own agricultural use, coupled with a bounty on silk culture. The influx of wealthy South Carolinians into their colony, eager to make quick profits, obviously raised fears among the poor rural farmers of Georgia for their own economic prospects.[48] The experience of the leading signatory of this petition, Isaac Gibbs, illustrates the marginal existence of poor migrant farmers. Gibbs had arrived from England with his wife and two sons in January 1738.[49] As a paying settler he received fifty acres at Abercorn, but within ten months of arriving he petitioned the Trustees for emergency supplies from their store. Apparently loss of property on the voyage from Europe together with the death of his wife and the difficulty of clearing the ground without oxen had hampered his agricultural efforts. Gibbs subsequently lost "a great deal of my crop" during the panic over the Spanish invasion, and in 1742 he was granted thirty shillings as recompense by the provincial government to buy replacement supplies. Therefore, despite having had "about £100 of my own which I thought would have done pretty well," less than five years of mishaps in Georgia had made him penniless.[50] To farmers such as Isaac Gibbs, whose lives had not been easy under the Trustees, the introduction of slaves was a new and ominous threat to their subsistence existence.

Contrary to the fears of Bolzius and some of the Trustees, however, there is little evidence that the introduction of slaves into Georgia precipitated a departure of white working people. Although land was increasingly concentrated in the hands of the white elite—more than half the land sold by artisans between 1750 and 1761 went to planters or merchants, whereas only a quarter of the land sold by planters and merchants went to artisans—the possibility of quick profit did not lead to the wholesale disposal of land by poor people.[51] A comparison of royal land grants made in 1755 with Colonial Conveyance Book C-1, shows no evidence that people who received land from the governor and council sold it for profit.[52] Apparently, white people of all social classes hoped to benefit from the introduction of slavery, retaining their land in the hope of becoming slaveholders themselves.

Nevertheless, once it was assured that slaves would eventually be permitted in Georgia, the economic avenues open to poor people became increasingly limited. The lack of opportunity available to disbanded soldiers from Oglethorpe's regiment initiated a wholesale desertion of Georgia for other colonies, despite the soldiers' original promises that they would remain in Georgia.[53] Some small farmers perhaps attempted to join the ranks of the slaveholders: credit was available at a price from merchants in Savannah and South Carolina toward the purchase of slaves, but bondspeople remained a risk-laden investment for the poor.[54] Bolzius recorded that the demand for new slaves in Charleston had recently pushed up the price for young male Africans from £20 to £40. As he pointed out, "Who, except the very rich, could risk that amount upon an unproven and still inexperienced slave?"[55]

Slaves were clearly an expensive commodity in colonial Georgia. The farmer who believed he could profit by the use of a slave needed supreme confidence in his own ability either to spend or borrow the amount needed to purchase that slave. If the slave escaped, the farmer faced almost certain ruin. The cost of slaves was easily the highest expense for a planter when setting up a plantation in Georgia. Bolzius estimated that the purchase of slaves could absorb more than 60 percent of the cost of setting up a standard plantation in South Carolina.[56] For many poorer Georgians the high risks of slaveholding would have outweighed any potential benefits. The cost of being a planter did not become any cheaper when the plantation economy became established in Georgia. In 1773, William De Brahm believed that forty slaves for a two-hundred-acre plantation would cost £1,800, or 72 percent of the total outlay of £2,476.16.0.[57] Such sums were clearly beyond the resources of the average inhabitant of colonial Georgia.

Excluded by their relative poverty from owning slaves, ordinary whites in Savannah survived either by selling goods, using skills they possessed, or doing day labor. Those lucky enough to possess a valuable skill, especially in the construction trades, were able to command high wages, something viewed with particular disgust by Pastor Bolzius.[58] As the main colonial settlement, Savannah was home to most Georgian artisans, and they had the advantage of trading with the ships from the Northern colonies, South Carolina, and the West Indian islands which regularly docked in the town.[59] Apparently certain goods could be purchased directly from the ships at significantly lower prices than were usually charged by merchants in Savannah. In return, the crews of these ships would purchase goods from artisans and small farmers "at very good prices."[60] Yet everyday life in Savannah still remained expensive in comparison with the rest of the colony. An empty house lot in Savannah cost in the region of £20 sterling, and Bolzius believed that nonslaveholding whites living there needed to master several skills to survive because not enough money could be made from one trade.[61] Many colonial artisans would not have had the opportunity to practice the skills they had acquired before emigrating. Bolzius stated that while "there is still a shortage of carpenters, turners, brickmakers, carriage builders and potters in Georgia, weavers, hosiers, knitters, needlemakers, bakers, millers and so on are not necessary here."[62] Some artisans were so disillusioned with craft work that they turned their hands to agriculture, but up to a tenth of colonial mechanics determined to learn two or more trades in their quest for competency. Jacob Holbrook and George Peters were two such versatile men. Each listed himself in Colonial Conveyance Books as both a carpenter and a cabinetmaker. Carpentry would provide regular work, while more profitable cabinetmaking commissions were available only occasionally.[63]

Not all mechanics were wooed by the charms of Savannah, however. One builder sought to move to Ebenezer in 1750 to "enjoy the quietude" and the relaxed atmosphere of that small settlement. His motivation may have been more economic than spiritual. Bolzius noted that there was plenty of work to be done in Ebenezer, and the Salzburgers were able to pay cash rather than offer goods in exchange or credit.[64] Indeed, the willingness of the Salzburgers to employ white artisans and their relative reluctance to become slaveholders made them a profitable source of income for white workers struggling in Savannah. Bolzius recorded that even day laborers and carters could earn substantial amounts in Ebenezer.[65] It seems clear that any artisan involved in a building trade such as carpentry, bricklaying, or the lumber business could find plenty of work. But artisans in more specialized trades, especially the clothing industry and the production of specialized foods, found economic conditions in Georgia in the 1750s harsh, and many were forced into subsistence farming to survive.[66]

A rapidly expanding population in Georgia between 1750 and 1775, which needed housing both in Savannah and on the plantations, ensured work for carpenters, brickmakers, bricklayers, and plasterers. In the year that Georgia permitted slavery, the Trustees reported that there were seventeen hundred white people and four hundred African Americans in Georgia. In the last colonial census taken in 1773, De Brahm counted sixteen thousand white and thirteen thousand black inhabitants.[67] Thus in twenty-two years, Georgia's population had increased by an average of more than twelve hundred people per year and its racial makeup had altered significantly. In 1751 four out of every five Georgians were white; by 1773, more than 40 percent were black. As a consequence, not only did white residents of Savannah need housing, but the several thousand bondspeople now inhabiting the coastal plantations also needed domiciles built for them. No doubt most of the construction of slave huts would have been done by bondspeople themselves, although white artisans may well have been employed in the final stages of construction. South Carolina planter Henry Laurens engaged several white artisans to work on his plantations on the Altamaha during the 1760s, evidently trusting them above local enslaved artisans to repair his plantation buildings.[68]

The growth of Savannah as both a commercial port and an administrative center also created employment for artisans involved in the construction industry. The humid and hot summers of Georgia took their toll on the fabric of buildings, necessitating regular repairs of important public buildings. During the colonial period the Tybee lighthouse, the council meetinghouse, and the Savannah city jail all required repairs.[69] In 1773 John McIver, a carpenter employed by the provincial government, informed the House of Commons that the jail was irreparable and was about to fall down.[70] No doubt many white artisans were employed in the construction of its replacement. It seems that construction artisans found ample work both inside and outside the towns of colonial Georgia, despite the introduction of enslaved labor.[71]

White people employed in the service sector—most notably those providing food and clothing—were also ensured a steady business. Residents of Savannah, Darien, Frederica, and Sunbury provided bakers, fishmongers, shoemakers, seamstresses, tailors, and butchers with reasonably good business. Occasional references in the colonial records show that the food business employed white women as well as men, although the sources do not tell us how many women earned their living in this way. For example, in 1773 Elizabeth Anderson petitioned the House of

Assembly for payment for providing bread to the prisoners in the Savannah jail, and one of only two women accredited with an occupation in the Georgia Colonial Books described herself as a victualer.[72] While the provision of food was the only livelihood for many white people, it was also the source of income for some bondspeople. Bondspeople grew crops both for their own use and for sale from the early years of slavery in Georgia. By the 1770s they had established their own Sunday market in Savannah, selling homegrown produce and livestock to residents, much to the disgust of the Provincial Grand Jury.[73] The livelihood of white providers of food would eventually come under serious threat as a result of this competition.[74]

In Savannah and along the main roads in the province, poor white people could find employment in several taverns and boardinghouses catering to travelers. One such establishment was the stopping point in 1750 for John Martin Bolzius, who had sympathy for the "destitute Englishman" who owned the "very poor little inn."[75] In 1763 a total of twenty-eight licenses were granted either to retail liquor or to operate taverns. Of those, seventeen were in Savannah and another five were located on roads leading into the town.[76] Only three women held tavern licenses in their own right, but it is likely that many other taverns operated as family businesses and that wives, sisters, and daughters were employed in their day-to-day management. Aside from working in the service sector, an unknown number of nonelite white women found work as domestics to the planters and merchants resident in Savannah. For example, in 1761 a housekeeper, Elizabeth Bough, was recorded as having borrowed £150 from her employer, the leading merchant Edward Summerville.[77] As the colonial period went on, however, white women were increasingly replaced as cooks and housekeepers by bondswomen, and for a time after the Revolution the opportunities for white women to work as domestics were limited.[78]

The manufacture of clothing and footwear provided a livelihood for many white urban residents.[79] After about 1750 the rapidly expanding enslaved population helped to boost demand for homemade rather than imported clothes and shoes. Many planters simply refused to pay European prices for slave apparel. Bolzius noted that cheap cloth could be had in Georgia for as little as eight pence per yard, whereas high-quality material sold in Charlestown cost as much as one shilling and eight pence per yard.[80] In 1768 Governor James Wright stated that of the meager amount of manufacturing in Georgia, most significant were "trifling quantities of raw hides and tanned, which are made up into coarse shoes chiefly for our Negroes and possibly our poor families [who] may make their own coarse clothing of a mixture of cotton & wool."[81] Therefore, the introduction of slaves into Georgia helped to secure the economic well-being of at least some poor working white people. All artisans knew, however, that occupational flexibility and geographical mobility were vital to their success. In late 1752, shoemaker Jonathan Groll moved from Ebenezer to Savannah because while there was a surplus of shoemakers in the village Savannah, at that time the biggest settlement in Georgia, supported only one shoemaker. Bolzius noted that Groll, like many other newly arrived settlers, was particularly unsuited to the pastoral way of life in Ebenezer, for he had settled on bad land and been unable to grow any crops.[82] For many immigrants their lack of agricultural experience quickly dashed any hopes of making a fortune from planting.

Some poor white men were employed as overseers on the plantations of the elite. Their social position may be estimated from the correspondence of South Carolina planter Henry Laurens to his overseers on his plantations on the Savannah and Altamaha Rivers in Georgia. These letters reveal that overseers who were "tolerable good rice planters" were highly valued in the lowcountry, whereas "common mercenary overseers" received little respect or job security from the elite.[83] Constant interference from employers concerning the treatment of slaves, planting techniques, and the propriety of sexual dalliances with bondswomen clearly undermined the effective authority of overseers on absentee plantations.[84] For some white men, however, a reputation as a productive and fair overseer would have offered a far higher social status than performing manual labor for hire. Daniel Ross, the only overseer to leave a will in the colonial period, even owned two slaves, demonstrating that for a select few, overseeing could be an avenue to the junior ranks of the slaveholding elite.[85]

The network of rivers and streams throughout the coastal area, combined with poor land communications, ensured that one of the commonest occupations for poor white men was to transport goods by boat from the plantations to the main ports of Savannah and Sunbury.[86] The growth of the plantation economy placed a great premium on lands situated on rivers because planters could use the river network to get their produce to market in Savannah quickly.[87] Many bondsmen were used as oarsmen on these boats, but the 1755 slave code prohibited slaves from owning or manning boats without a white person to supervise.[88] Consequently, while some planters knew that their bondspeople were "capable enough" to man boats themselves, the assumption that "it would be highly improper as well as illegal to put such confidence in a Negro" ensured that many white men earned their living in this manner.[89] The development of the plantation economy as far south as the Altamaha during the period of royal government provided employment for those who made canoes and other small craft as much as for those who made larger vessels. Boatmen and shipbuilders were therefore another group of artisans who directly benefited from the economic growth engendered by the introduction of African enslaved labor.

Those artisans who provided luxury goods found economic opportunities somewhat limited in the infant colony. The undeveloped nature of society in colonial Georgia meant that few except the very rich could afford to commission work from silversmiths, goldsmiths, chair makers and cabinetmakers.[90] During the colonial period most highly specialized artisans remained in Charleston, no doubt undertaking occasional commissions for those few Georgians who could afford their services. Some Charleston luxury-good makers were themselves wealthy men. In 1768, the cabinetmaker Thomas Elfe estimated his personal fortune at £37,230.14.6, of which more than £7,000 was invested in slave labor.[91] So much wealth for an artisan was unheard-of in colonial Georgia. Indeed, the only evidence of the property of a luxury-good maker in Georgia is the will of the cabinetmaker James Love, who died in 1768, leaving three slaves, three town lots, and 250 acres of land.[92] Although the introduction of slavery, if anything, helped artisans who provided luxury goods as the increasing profits enjoyed by successful planters could be spent on luxuries, there were relatively few artisans willing or able to undertake this type of work when other occupations offered far more regular employment and potentially higher rates of return.

The one luxury craft that was officially encouraged and was pursued with alacrity by the poor in Georgia was silk-making. The bounty offered to silk producers was not originally intended by Whitehall to be a means of government support for poor people in Georgia but rather to offset Great Britain's reliance on Spain and Italy for silk and to help her balance of trade.[93] The bounty offered for silk was clearly not sufficient for planters to take the trouble of teaching their slaves the intricacies of caring for silkworms. To poor people with time on their hands, however, especially for poor white women, silk-making was one of the few pursuits that could offer a means of support for those usually unable to earn money in the fields.[94] Spinning and weaving remained traditional female occupations in English societies, and gender conventions prevented women from undertaking most other artisan or laboring work. The production of silk in Georgia therefore was almost entirely the preserve of poor white women by the mid–eighteenth century. The gendered nature of silk production was clearly recognized by the colonial government. In 1750 the council approved the construction of homes for people making silk and agreed to supply ten machines for their use. As an added incentive, the council offered to give a bounty of £2 to each young woman who was willing to start learning the art of silk-making.[95]

Yet silk-making was not a sure route to wealth and security; indeed, it remained a precarious business in colonial Georgia. Poor weather could blight the silkworms at a crucial stage in their development, thus impoverishing those who cultivated the worms, as well as those who wove the silk. Still, the potential rewards were great for those for whom luck was combined with skill. In 1751 Bolzius reported that a shoemaker named Zettler together with his wife had earned enough from silk production to purchase a pregnant slave from Carolina.[96] Unfortunately, the unreliability of silk-making and the view of many people that it was only a minor player in economic terms—continually failing to compete with rice and indigo in profitability—ensured that it never became a major factor in the economic development of Georgia. In a memorial to the Board of Trade in 1758, William Little highlighted some of the troubles associated with silk production.[97] Part of the problem, as he saw it, was the lack of an experienced and constant workforce. The women who worked at silk-making were constantly being distracted from work by child rearing or by caring for livestock or crops. The women engaged in silk production generally worked at home in rural areas, and they often struggled to get to Savannah or to a river to ship their produce to Savannah. According to Little, these factors, combined with less than prompt payment of the bounty, fostered the decline of silk culture in Georgia. The same conclusions were also reached by Governor Henry Ellis, who believed that silk-making was retarded because of its questionable profitability, the lack of poor white people willing to undertake the task, and the decision of most planters that silk-making was not worth the effort of their slaves when rice and indigo offered more appealing prospects.[98]

The governorship of James Wright heralded a new era of silk production in Georgia. By 1762, William Knox, Georgia's agent in London, was thanking the Board of Trade for continuing the silk bounty, stating that nearly half of the white inhabitants of Georgia were engaged in silk manufacture of some sort.[99] But with the bounty under threat in 1765, James Wright wrote to the board pointing out that its removal would not only end the involvement in silk production of the few planters who bothered with it but would also ruin the poor people, who "would have nothing to depend on." He also clarified the supposed reason behind the maintenance of the bounty, stating that the Trustees had implemented it "to assist the poor people in Georgia, who at that time labored under many difficulties."[100] According to Wright, only the bounty on silk kept the industry going, and unless the cost of living in Georgia fell substantially, people would not continue production for a lower price.[101] The bounty on silk continued in Georgia until the Revolution, and during its existence it provided an economic lifeline for hundreds of the colony's poorest and most disadvantaged citizens. Many of these people were forced into silk culture because they had no other means of support once slave labor had replaced white labor.

The use of bonded labor in Georgia most immediately imperiled the livelihoods of laborers who relied on being paid for carrying, delivering, and collecting goods around Savannah and who made a little extra money helping local farmers at harvest time. John Martin Bolzius believed that it was precisely these people whose economic subsistence would disappear if slaves were introduced into the colony.[102] Before 1750, all of the labor needs of planters had supposedly been met by white indentured servants. The unreliability of these servants, their high rate of absenteeism, and their small numbers no doubt figured in the quest for slave labor. The arrival of a new group of indentured servants in 1749, located principally in Savannah and Ebenezer, illuminates the reaction of white servants to slaves, as well as to the changing status of manual labor in a colony where field work was rapidly becoming the preserve of the African.[103] Although problems with servants were nothing particularly new, the turmoil experienced by those who used white indentured servants in the late 1740s and early 1750s far exceeded earlier troubles.[104]

The newly arrived servants caused problems from the outset. Disputes over length of service arose almost immediately as servants who remained in Savannah were promised only one or two years' service, while those going to Ebenezer could expect to serve the full three years and five months. The loophole allowed by the Trustees, permitting servants to be redeemed within three months of their arrival, even deprived the Salzburgers of one of their new servants only forty-eight hours after he was allotted to them.[105] Less than a week after their arrival in Ebenezer, servants were complaining about the long terms of service and the expectation that they would undertake field work, rather than practice their respective trades, and they began to talk of flight to Carolina.[106] Yet the first group of runaways from this transport of servants came not from Ebenezer but from Savannah. Two of these runaways were indentured to minister Zouberbuhler, and the example they set was not long in being followed: by the end of October 1749 the first two Ebenezer runaways had fled to South Carolina.[107] Bolzius was at a loss to explain these flights, for he believed the servants were well fed and were not expected to do more strenuous work than the Salzburgers themselves. As the remaining servants in Ebenezer became more restless after hearing unconfirmed reports that newly arrived white servants in Charleston were being settled on their own lands with provisions supplied by the South Carolina government, Bolzius struggled to keep order in Ebenezer.[108]

Reports that German settlers across the Savannah River in Purrysburgh, South Carolina, had helped the Ebenezer runaways led Bolzius to write to Governor James Glen of South Carolina seeking his assistance. In this letter Bolzius revealed that the two Ebenezer runaways were bakers by trade and had made their way quickly to Charleston following their escape in a canoe across the Savannah River.[109] Evidently these artisans were not willing to labor in the fields but preferred the more secure urban opportunities available in South Carolina to comparable ones in Savannah. Help from the governor of South Carolina was not forthcoming; Bolzius remarked that Governor Glen was evidently seeking to repopulate his colony with as many white people as possible to offset the growing number of slaves there.[110] The willingness of the South Carolina authorities to ignore or even encourage the settlement of white people there did not go unnoticed by the servants in Georgia. By April 1750, the President and Assistants were pointing out to Governor Glen that the continuation of his policy had encouraged more indentured servants from Georgia to desert to South Carolina.[111]

It seems clear that white servants coming into Georgia around 1750 were almost immediately dissatisfied with their social position. Although the lack of primary sources written by them makes it difficult to determine the reasons for the servants' attitudes, conclusions may be tentatively drawn about their views on field labor from the testimony of others. John Martin Bolzius remarked in late 1750 on the difference in attitudes of servants with some years to serve and those who had managed to purchase their freedom early. He praised the "great service" done by artisans who were free to pursue their own trades; conversely, indentured servants believed "it hard & unjust to serve for their passage some years."[112] This was the fundamental dichotomy between free and unfree labor. Those who worked for themselves inevitably worked harder and more thoroughly both for their own benefit and for that of the wider community, whereas those forced to labor for others with no real advantage accruing to themselves for good work learned quickly that it was not worth their effort to be diligent. Yet it is also intriguing to think that with more than three hundred working slaves in Georgia by mid-1750, field work and manual agricultural labor were becoming increasingly associated with Africans and slavery.[113] Judging from its frequent mentions in contemporary correspondence, slavery was a topic much discussed in Georgia around 1750. Indentured servants were no doubt aware that the only other unfree people in Georgia were African slaves. By running away to South Carolina, where they enjoyed "an equal share in the province's encouragements & in the tenure of lands," servants elevated themselves above the African slave in both wealth and status.[114] It is certainly possible that the flight of servants from Georgia in 1749 and 1750 was partly motivated by the rapid immigration of slaves and a subsequent decline in the status of field labor in the eyes of poorer whites.

Those indentured servants who remained in Georgia were in direct economic competition with slaves after 1750, and it is clear that the poor reputation of white servants as a result of their shoddy work, their unwillingness to undertake physical labor, and the ease with which they found safe havens in South Carolina led planters and others to prefer slaves. Even the Salzburgers overcame their hatred of slavery to employ bondspeople instead of white servants, whom they found too unreliable.[115] Ralph Gray and Betty Wood have established statistically what was suspected by planters and others at the time, that slaves were more profitable than white servants despite the high initial investment. Less spent on food for slaves, rather than higher output, was the principal reason for this discrepancy.[116]

Despite the problems they had experienced previously, the Salzburgers at Ebenezer continued to receive servants until the mid-1750s.[117] Five months after the arrival of a new group of servants in 1751, Bolzius praised them as being "better than any servants before."[118] This group of servants is the only one to be described in detail, including information about family status, age, and gender. Of the thirty servants listed in Bolzius's letter as living in Ebenezer, there is an even division between genders and an emphasis on family groups. Only seven of the thirty were single, two of whom were children. The rest migrated in family groups and were employed in a variety of occupations. Two were assigned to the sawmill at Ebenezer, two to the public filiature, one was apprenticed to the schoolmaster, and two set up a tanning business. Eight were involved in agriculture, either renting land from an established settler or sharecropping. Occupations were not given for the other servants. The servants who had previously joined the Salzburgers were permitted to pursue a trade if they so chose, and those who engaged in agriculture benefited from their labor in proportion to the work they completed.[119]

By late 1752, however, Bolzius was complaining that these servants were "unhelpful and ungrateful" and generally unwilling to work. This second failure with white servants eventually led even the Salzburgers to endorse the idea of enslaved labor.[120] The catechist Joseph Ottolenghe reported similar antipathy toward manual labor. He complained of those building his house in Savannah that "ye working people are all girls, who love play better than work, & no soon my back is turned, but a cessation of hands immediately ensues."[121] This attitude was related to white servants' perception of work in a slave society. Like their predecessors who had fled to South Carolina to escape the stigma of laboring, the typical servant in Ebenezer desired to be "a gentleman, master and householder" rather than a "servant, apprentice, or hired hand."[122] Bolzius attributed this attitude to the social fluidity of America, which encouraged the new migrants to think that there was no caste and class in Georgia, only endless opportunity. The social mobility of a fortunate few in the New World was obviously a radical departure from the social rigidity of the Old World, yet it was not the norm.[123] Bolzius realized that without their own industry, new settlers would become "poor and physically ill."[124] The unwillingness of new settlers to believe in the work ethic held so dear by both the original Salzburgers and the Trustees ensured that many of them slid into debt and poverty. In July 1753, Bolzius commented that new Swabian immigrants did not understand how to farm and were unwilling to learn and so "they are becoming poor."[125] The attempt to continue with white servants after 1750, in competition with African slaves, clearly failed.

The migration of white servants to the rest of Georgia did not entirely cease after 1750, however. White servants were still sent by the Trustees or brought over from Europe by immigrating planters. In 1751, for example, Richard Oswald and a group of Glaswegian merchants received grants of five hundred acres each after they promised that they would bring white servants to the colony.[126] Yet the number of indentured servants brought into Georgia declined rapidly in the late 1750s. In 1755 planters brought thirty-two white servants into Georgia. This number fell to seven in 1756, rose slightly to eleven in 1757, but the last case of a new white indentured servant coming into Georgia was recorded in 1758.[127] These figures show that white indentured servitude barely survived a decade following the onset of African slavery in Georgia.

Despite the limited economic opportunity offered to nonelite white people in colonial Georgia, new settlers still arrived in the colony, and Ebenezer was only one settlement augmented by immigrants. In 1765 a group of French immigrants received £14 from the Commons House of Assembly to pay for the survey of a tract of land near the Great Ogeechee River, "by reason of their extreme poverty."[128] The settlement of Queensborough was greatly enhanced by Ulster Protestants who migrated between 1769 and 1770. These poor farmers received a grant of £200 from the Commons to set up their agricultural endeavors and to defray the cost of their migration.[129] From the evidence available, it seems likely that many of the fourteen thousand new white settlers between 1750 and 1775 were poor farmers without slaves rather than planters with many slaves.[130] Indeed, Betty Wood has estimated that by the end of the colonial period only about 5 percent of Georgians were slaveholders.[131]

Governor Henry Ellis perhaps somewhat prosaically characterized the migrants to Georgia after 1750 as primarily poor people, often from other colonies in British North America, who gradually paid off their debts through hard work.[132] Not that all people who settled in rural areas engaged in farming. In 1759 an expedition to a settlement south of the Altamaha River, at that time outside the control of Georgian authorities, found that many of the inhabitants "subsist chiefly by hunting."[133] Rural itinerant traders and workmen could also find occasional employment on coastal plantations. Henry Laurens employed two such men on one of his Georgia plantations although neither secured more than a temporary contract; Mr. Duke was replaced by a professional carpenter, while Mr. Rhetson was dismissed for general incompetence.[134] The total number of unsettled people in Georgia is difficult to determine, but considering the growth in legislation concerning poor relief, transient poor people, and vagabonds, destitution was a growing problem in the 1760s.

In 1764 the legislature passed a law intended to control the number of "idle and disorderly persons" entering Georgia. Those who lacked any means of subsistence and attempted to live off the land faced a prison term of ninety days. Persistent offenders were impressed into the British navy.[135]

The vagabond law clearly failed to stem the influx of poor people into Georgia. The formation of several new charitable associations such as the Union Society and the implementation of a colony-wide poor law based on the parish system were other attempts to alleviate the distress of growing numbers of "poor and indigent" people in the colony. Much like early modern England, poor relief in Georgia was organized around the parish system, with churchwardens empowered to levy a local tax on parishioners to fund poor relief activities.[136] In 1767 the churchwardens of Christ Church in Savannah petitioned for an extra grant from the Commons House of Assembly to fund poor relief in the town. If the money was not forthcoming, the wardens believed that they would have to put the poor out onto the streets.[137] The growth of poverty in the late colonial era was perhaps in part a result of Georgia's reputation as a land of opportunity, which encouraged poor people, both from Europe and from other parts of America, to flock to this new frontier colony in the hope of creating a better future for themselves and their families. Rather than having a detrimental effect on poor white migration into Georgia, the introduction of slaves actually seems to have been something of a stimulus. Yet while the economic growth which Georgia experienced in the late colonial era, built on the back of slave labor, encouraged the immigration of white people, it did not necessarily provide them with gainful employment after their arrival.

In colonial Georgia, social mobility was possible, usually through credit, but it relied heavily on the skill and determination of the particular individual, combined with fortune.[138] Most poor people in the colony found themselves unable to secure the economic advances they desired. The influx of planters from other British colonies, especially South Carolina, helped to create a two-tiered society of "indigent subjects" and "men of some substance."[139] The small elite group of men who sat on the council also sat in the assembly, judged in the courts, acted as justices of the peace, and served as royal commissioners.[140] The surviving records indicate that their political control of the colony was almost total. The planter-merchant elite also dominated the capitalist economy. By the late 1760s, artisans were purchasing lands only about half as frequently as they had done twenty years previously. In addition, there was also a marked increase in the amount of land being sold by mechanics to planters and merchants and a fall in the corresponding trade from the elite to artisans.[141] Records of colonial land grants during royal government reinforce this impression. Of more than a thousand individuals granted land in the three coastal parishes of Christ Church, St. John, and St. Andrew, the richest fifth owned nearly half the total acreage, holding on average more than a thousand acres each.[142] Even less social mobility is documented for indentured servants who completed their time. Of the thirty servants named individually by John Martin Bolzius in 1751, only five were subsequently granted land by the provincial government.[143]

The colonial elite also dominated the internal trade in slaves. In the decades following the onset of royal rule in Georgia, artisans were twice as likely to sell slaves than to buy them. This trend became even more marked as the colonial period went on, suggesting that artisans who had bought slaves in the early days of slavery were increasingly willing to divest themselves of an unnecessary burden.[144] Thus, although some artisans experienced a growth in demand for their work during the late colonial period, they also found that the economic hegemony of the elite increasingly marginalized them in the deeply unequal slave society which Georgia had become.

The records and impressions of colonial Georgia reveal that nonslaveholding whites could, and did, survive despite the influx of several thousand African slaves. The increased economic activity and general prosperity engendered by the introduction of slavery permitted some artisans to flourish. Yet poor farmers and laborers often found themselves economically marginalized, forced by slavery into a subsistence existence. Although the techniques of survival differed for each nonslaveholder depending on individual economic function and ability, slavery manifestly affected all nonslaveholders to some extent, forcing them to be more competitive and to prove their worth in a manner that had not been needed under the Trustees.

Although we can talk in general terms about the lives of nonslaveholders in colonial Georgia, no accurate estimates of the size of the nonslaveholding population can be made because of the confused nature of colonial statistics. We know that slaves were usually held in large groups; indeed, one historian has calculated that up to half of the thirteen thousand bondspeople resident in Georgia in 1773 were owned by just sixty planters—less than 1 percent of white people.[145] Yet many nonslaveholders would have resided in backcountry inland areas that were an integral part of colonial statistics, rather than in the lowcountry. The first federal census provides a clearer picture of coastal social structure. In 1790 fewer than one in ten white Georgians resided in the lowcountry, while more than two-fifths of the African American population lived and worked on coastal plantations.[146] The clear geographic and demographic differences that divided lowcountry and backcountry permitted the emergence of an ideology which claimed that few, if any, nonslaveholders resided in wealthy coastal counties. Thus the economic and social dominance of the elite began to be perceived by visitors, and promoted by native elites, as demographic exclusivity. This perception is wrong.

The destruction of the Georgia federal manuscript census returns for 1790, 1800, and 1810 in the burning of Washington during the War of 1812 makes it almost impossible to ascertain exactly how many of the 4,000 white people in the lowcountry in 1790 owned slaves and how many did not. We know from the extant returns of other states that had these returns survived they would have listed the names of heads of households and the racial composition of each household. The only part of the census that has survived enumerates the total population for the counties in 1790, broken down by gender and race. The 2,456 white people who resided in Chatham County in 1790 collectively owned 8,201 slaves; what is missing is the precise number of slave owners and the size of their slaveholdings. A reconstructed estimate may be obtained from an examination of the Chatham County Tax Digest for 1793. In that year the slave-owning taxpayers of Chatham County paid tax on 6,439 slaves, owning on average 17 slaves each.[147] A third of taxpayers were nonslaveholders, and if those who defaulted are included, then as many as half of the households in postrevolutionary Chatham County were nonslaveholding.[148]

Similar conclusions can be drawn from Savannah city tax records in the nineteenth century. The wide employment opportunities offered in Savannah and its status as an entrepôt for white immigrants ensured that the coastal city retained a highly visible nonslaveholding population. In contrast to rural areas, artisans in Savannah could find employment in many different trades, for the population growth of the city enhanced the economic demand for various goods and services.[149] Seven times as many white people worked in manufacturing in Chatham County than in the rest of the lowcountry put together.[150] In the 1848 city census, the first to document comprehensively the professions of the male inhabitants of

Savannah, mechanics and artisans constituted the largest white social group in the city.[151] When in 1860 the occupations of white women were noted for the first time, domestic service and cloth working dominated, though some women worked in traditionally male trades as doctors and as brass and iron founders.[152] These nonslaveholding whites came into regular contact with urban slaves, rural slaves visiting the weekly markets, and the larger concentrations of free blacks.[153] Indeed, the greater freedom permitted to urban slaves, for example over self-hire, enabled them to encounter white nonslaveholders outside the supervision of their masters.[154]

Tax digests from 1809 onward provide some insights into Savannah's social structure. Despite small fluctuations, nonslaveholders maintained their numerical majority in the city throughout the antebellum period, even though the total number of taxpayers doubled between 1809 and 1860. They were able to do this partly because of the immigration of large numbers of nonslaveholding laborers from Europe, especially Ireland, and the Northern states.[155] The other significant conclusion to be drawn from the Savannah tax digests is that slave owners were increasing the average size of their human property holdings, from under three slaves to over five slaves per slaveholder. Thus the numerical majority of nonelite people in the city and their vital role in the urban economy did not prevent the socioeconomic domination of the white elite. This hegemony curtailed the ambitions of nonslaveholders to become members of the slave-owning class in marked contrast with the social mobility documented for the Georgia upcountry.[156] A study of two randomly selected groups of nonslaveholders over five-year periods suggests that basic competency was the general lot of the Savannah nonelite.[157] Only a few managed to earn enough money to enter the slave-owning class or were lucky enough to inherit slaves. The purchase of a slave was evidently something most nonelite whites could only aspire to.

That the social structure of Chatham County was not typical is borne out by statistics from the rest of the lowcountry. A series of tax digests from Liberty County permit an assessment to be made of the changing social structure of a rural area of the lowcountry. In 1785, only two years after the Peace of Paris, more than 85 percent of white inhabitants of Liberty County were slave owners.[158] This situation changed rapidly. By the turn of the century, not only had nonslaveholders doubled as a proportion of the total white population from 15 to 30 percent, but they had also formed their own neighborhood near the Cannochie River in the interior of the county.[159] This area was the most remote and undeveloped part of Liberty County and thus was ripe for the influx of small subsistence farmers. These tax digests allow two further conclusions to be drawn. Nonslaveholders were steadily increasing as a proportion of the total white population so that by 1860 they amounted to nearly half of all whites.[160] But the wealth differentiation between slave owners and nonslaveholders was also widening. While the ratio between the races remained fairly constant at about three African Americans to every white person, slaveholders in 1860 owned, on average, twice the number of slaves they had owned a generation before.[161] Yet in contrast to Savannah, social mobility was comparatively easy in Liberty County. Judging from tax records, nearly half of those who resided in the county between 1785 and 1800 improved their economic standing, and only a fifth saw it decline.[162] Evidently the increase in the number of nonslaveholding whites in Liberty County during the antebellum period was the result of inward migration rather than an impoverishment of certain existing residents. Despite the large number of new migrants, nonslaveholding whites remained economically marginalized in their own neighborhoods in the rural parts of the lowcountry.

The concentration of wealth in the hands of a relative few is attested to by other lowcountry tax digests. The richest 20 percent of planters and merchants usually paid roughly three-quarters of the total tax bill.[163] Early national tax laws were not designed to be income progressive; in fact, an individual's income was not taxed at all. Tax assessments were based on property holdings, including slaves, merchandise, and land. Thus those with the most land and the largest labor force paid the most tax. It was even significant what type of land was owned, with tidal swamp used for rice cultivation being taxed far more heavily than pine woodland.[164] That such a small group of planters and merchants paid the most taxes reflected their relative wealth in this overwhelmingly agricultural society.

The social geography of the Georgia lowcountry also reflected the power and prestige of the elite. Although they were in a minority, slaveholders in Glynn County in 1794 owned two-thirds of the total sea island acreage and nearly all of the most productive corn land.[165] Of nonslaveholders in the county, half owned no land at all, and a further quarter owned only a few acres of pine barren.[166] Therefore, not only were nonslaveholders disadvantaged by their inability to pay for bonded labor, they were also unable to afford the best lands—a situation that did not improve over time. The changing social geography of the lowcountry is demonstrated by the case of Camden County. In 1794 four-fifths of the taxpayers of this southerly outpost of the continental United States were nonslaveholders. They owned nearly three-quarters of the best quality swampland in the county, reflecting their numerical dominance.[167] The situation was markedly different fifteen years later. Economic and demographic growth, principally engendered by slaveholders, led to the socio-geographic marginalization of nonslaveholders to poor quality lands. By 1809 more than 80 percent of tidal swampland was owned by slaveholders, and a quarter of nonslaveholders owned only pine woodland.[168] As Camden County entered the mainstream of the lowcountry economy, it had evidently become a popular investment opportunity for the planter elite. All but six of the hundred or so new slaveholders in Camden County in 1809 had not been resident in the county fifteen years before.[169] The growth of social inequality in Camden County during the nineteenth century was entirely characteristic of the lowcountry.

While we may be able to demonstrate statistically the existence of a large nonslaveholding population in the lowcountry, such abstractions do not tell us much about their daily lives. For that information we must turn to more subjective sources. Despite the highly visible lifestyle of the elite, visitors to coastal Georgia were often intrigued by the existence of "white trash" in proximity to the lowcountry plantations. The specific needs of rice production had imposed severe geographic limitations: only on tidal rivers or inland swamps could it be successfully cultivated, leaving large areas of land between river systems devoid of staple production.[170] These less accessible lands were often occupied by smaller farmers who concentrated on pastoral rather than arable farming, thus taking advantage of poorer quality lands.[171] The least productive areas in this region were the so-called pine barrens, sandy soils mainly supporting coniferous forest and characterized by low fertility. Much of this land was settled by squatters, hunters, and drifters unable to afford either the cost of a farm or the rents in Savannah.[172] In 1783 Anthony Stokes suggested that Georgia was attractive to migrants from other states because "the winters are mild, and the man who had a rifle, ammunition, and blanket, can subsist in that vagrant way which the Indians pursue."[173] Although Stokes's observation is hard to substantiate, a generation later Fanny Kemble was to characterize rural nonslaveholding whites as those who, "too poor to possess land or slaves, and having no means of living in the towns, squat (most appropriately it is so termed) either on other men's land or government districts—always the swamp or the pine barren—and claim masterdom over the place they invade till ejected by the rightful proprietors."[174] Evidently some whites declined to participate in the lowcountry economy, preferring lives of subsistence to the disciplines of the market.[175]

Visitors to the lowcountry frequently remarked on the tattered appearance and hand-to-mouth existence of rural nonslaveholders. J. B. Dunlop was astonished at the "sickly yellow complexions" of a family of poor white people whom he encountered on his way overland from Savannah to St. Marys.[176] The miserable everyday life of many poor whites is also attested to by Henry Ker, who believed that their children "had not the appearance of cleanliness which is the sure preservative of health."[177] The yellow complexions of rural poor whites was caused by the chronic eating of clay and would have occasioned an obvious comparison with the paler mixed-race slaves in the minds of visitors.[178]

While the pejorative perceptions of many visitors are neatly summarized by John Palmer, who in 1808 described those who lived in the pine woods as "generally an idle set of people," not all observers were so harsh.[179] Some authors highlighted the difficulty rural poor people experienced in making ends meet and praised the fact that even though the country was "wild [and] sparsely settled," the poorer inhabitants did not shrink from "toil or hardship."[180] The continual struggle for economic competency was hampered by poor-quality soils because even "after toil and anxiety, nature refuses to pay the industrious." Indeed, the social marginalization of many of these people was complete: often the only visitors were "families moving to the western country, or the wagons passing down to the city with their crops."[181] Aside from squatters and small farmers, some rural nonelite whites subsisted by shopkeeping and peddling, providing much of the household goods to the plantations and the slaves. For those who resided too far from a city market, the local country stores were often the only place to barter or retail goods. Other rural whites found employment as boatmen and wagoners transporting bulk crops to market. John Lambert described these wagoners as "crackers (from the smacking of their whips, I suppose). They are said to be often very rude and insolent to strangers, and people of the towns, whom they meet on the road."[182] It was mainly these varied and disparate types of nonslaveholders who came into contact with the ordinary plantation slaves of rural lowcountry Georgia.

Lowcountry bondspeople were also aware of the existence of a local poor white population. Charles Ball believed that it was a "great error" to perceive that coastal society was separated into only "white and black, freemen and slaves." He argued that any visitor to the lowcountry would immediately be aware of "a third order of men located there," namely "the white man, who has no property, no possession, and no education." According to Ball, "the contempt in which they are held . . . by the great planters, to be comprehended, must be seen."[183] Bondspeople were perfectly aware that on particular occasions the elite made little distinction between them and poor whites. One former slave recalled that when the president visited Savannah, only "the great gentlemen and the rich folks" were allowed access to him and that "negroes and other poor folks" were kept at a distance.[184]

A sizable portion of the white population, probably as much as half in lowcountry Georgia as a whole, and more than that in Savannah, did not own slaves. Nonslaveholders in this slave society lived a wide variety of lifestyles as they sought to provide a subsistence for themselves and their families. It is the myriad of relationships that artisans, farmers, shopkeepers, and other nonslaveholding whites—the forgotten half of the white population in the lowcountry—formed with African Americans that is the focus of the rest of this book.

2 Working, Drinking, and Sleeping Together

THROUGHOUT THE COLONIAL, early national, and ante-bellum eras, lowcountry nonslaveholders and African Americans met and socialized in numerous ways. Some biracial social encounters were informal, unstructured occasions, others were formalized, and some were even orchestrated by the elite. In this chapter I describe everyday relationships between nonslaveholding whites and African Americans in the Georgia lowcountry. I question how accurate are the historians who have argued that these two groups existed in a state of permanent antipathy and that the racial barriers between whites and blacks and the racial ties uniting nonslaveholding whites with the white elite prevented the formation of any common biracial, lower-class culture.[1] Or does the concept of racial solidarity overlook different relationships between white and black?[2] I argue that in areas such as the workplace, dramshop, and brothel, where there was no reason for maintaining racial distinctions, racial lines could become blurred and permeable. This is not to claim that social relations between white and black were entirely harmonious. Tensions certainly existed, especially when nonslaveholding whites were employed as patrollers and overseers. Yet the fact remains that nonelite whites regularly interacted with African Americans, often on terms of parity, in the social sphere. The idea that their interaction was one only of conflict ignores the rich variety of lowcountry social relations.

That white Southerners lived lives of leisure and that nonelite whites also shunned the Northern work ethic, while only blacks worked, was a popular nineteenth-century misconception. Nevertheless, white manual laborers in the South often faced community prejudice as wage labor was often described as "Nigger work."[3] Fanny Kemble believed that poor white people in the lowcountry had internalized elite concepts regarding manual labor, holding it "nobler to starve" than to work alongside African Americans. She stated that the elite cultivated a view among bondspeople that "it [is] the lowest degradation in a white to use any exertion."[4] Even some bondspeople believed that nonslaveholding farmers would not stoop to work for hire on the plantations of the elite because "they are too proud to work with the Negro slaves."[5] Yet available evidence shows that many white people, including women, worked manually at a variety of tasks in the antebellum South. By bringing white people into close and regular contact with African Americans, these arrangements created a relationship that scholars have yet to explore fully.

In the lowcountry towns of Savannah, Darien, and St. Marys, the smaller shops and offices employed both whites and blacks in a variety of menial jobs. Certainly some employers were unconcerned about the race of their employees. During the Revolutionary War Mr. McCulloch advertised for several tailors "white or black" who would meet "with immediate employment" from him, and in 1825 Joseph Singer sought "two first rate journeymen" together with "a free colored apprentice" to work at his boot-making business.[6] White women as well as African American women answered job advertisements. In 1819 those advertising for a female servant declared that they were "not particular to age or color," requiring only that applicants should be "of good disposition, and accustomed to children."[7] Other employers who did not specify race in their advertisements would have received applications from both white and black women.[8] White workers could not be sure that they would receive higher wages than African Americans. Reuben King in Darien paid both the black and white employees at his store a flat rate of two dollars per day.[9] That some white people were willing to work on the same terms as African Americans most likely demonstrates their overwhelming need for paid work, a need that overcame in their minds any stigma of working alongside an African American. For those whose very survival depended on bringing in a wage, maintaining some mythical racial boycott on hard work evidently held marginal significance.

Industrial businesses in early national Savannah were among the most willing to employ both black and white workers. The federal manuscript census of manufacturing for Chatham County in 1820 enumerated several industrial businesses that employed workers from both races.[10] Many of the African American workers listed were slaves, but it is possible that some free African Americans were employed in jobs deemed particularly hazardous. The social position of white workers in each individual business is difficult to determine. It is not known, for example, whether the three white men employed at the Chatham Steam Saw Mill held a supervisory role over the eight bondsmen, two bondswomen, and four slave children also employed there.[11] Certainly some white people were engaged specifically on the understanding that they would serve as overseers. Daniel Heyward employed a white couple to supervise the thirty slaves working at his cotton mill, and in 1779 William Panton advertised for "two white coopers, who are willing to take charge of a number of black coopers under them."[12] White artisans knew that this managerial role was highly prized by employers, and when looking for work they would occasionally state that they had experience supervising African Americans.[13] It is also unknown how much, if at all, African Americans were paid for their work and how their pay compared with that of white people. Baldwin & Company, candle and soap makers, paid their one black and three white employees a total of $1,450 annually but did not give individual amounts paid.[14] Although one might expect white workers to receive more than blacks, on several occasions one Savannah carpenter paid his black employees more than his white ones.[15] Numerous other white apprentices, both male and female, worked side by side with African Americans in retail stores in the city.[16] After 1790 shopkeepers in Savannah were required always to have a white person present if they employed slaves in their businesses or pay a fine of up to five pounds.[17] Clearly, a large proportion of the workplaces in Savannah and other lowcountry towns were biracial to some degree.

In rural areas it was fairly common for planters to employ local slaves and free blacks together with a white artisan for short periods of time. A Bryan County planter, Richard James Arnold, employed a white carpenter to assist his slave artisans in the completion of "negro houses" on his Cherry Hill plantation.[18] Another planter, Alexander Telfair, instructed his overseer in 1832 that if there was any work the enslaved blacksmiths could not do, "you will employ John Wilson to do at two dollars and fifty cents per day (he to feed himself)."[19] In addition, many of the boat captains trading up and down the coastal rivers employed mixed crews; Tyrone Power's boat crew consisted "of two fine white boys, apprentices, and a couple of stout slaves."[20] While the essential flexibility of the lowcountry labor market ensured that white people, men especially, found hired work in the coastal area forthcoming if not plentiful, nonslaveholders had to accept that they might be working alongside African Americans at any time. From their point of view, the better employers did draw a distinction between the wages of whites and their African American workmates. W. C. Blott, for example, paid his black workers only half what he paid a white man, but not all employers were so race conscious.[21] Working in such close proximity in all of these environments inevitably engendered a degree of personal familiarity between the races that may have weakened racial barriers and stereotypes.

Some nonslaveholding white people had vocations that would inevitably involve regular contact with African Americans. Overseers were often drawn from the poorest groups of white society and were in daily contact with the slaves under their control. South Carolinian David Ramsay declared that poor nonslaveholders in his locality "were of little account otherwise than as overseers."[22] Planters most often sought someone with the characteristics of "honesty and sobriety" and preferably without family distractions.[23] William Scarborough's study of overseers throughout the South contends that this occupation employed people from many different backgrounds but that they were all stereotyped by the cruel behavior of the poorest white men toward bondspeople. According to Scarborough, some owners found it necessary to warn against fraternization with slaves, as "an overseer ought to have little conversation with Negroes under his care."[24] One planter, after employing a series of unsatisfactory overseers, advocated that they be taken at an early age from the orphan house so that they would learn the appropriate deportment in front of slaves.[25] In this sense, planters had to tread carefully, simultaneously distancing themselves socially from overseers while instilling respect for all white people among their bondspeople. That this balancing act was not always entirely successful is evinced by the prevailing attitude of slaves toward their overseers, which indicated that many bondspeople were aware of their lowly social status. Former slave Alec Bostwick stated that his overseer had been "poor white trash, with a house full of snotty-nose chilluns."[26] Emily Burke knew one young overseer who labored "with his own hands" alongside slaves to bring the harvest in, "for the paltry sum of fifty dollars per year besides his board."[27]

The disdainful attitude of African Americans grew partly from the position of authority their overseers held over them and partly from a distinction made by slaves between "good white folks" and "white trash." Eugene Genovese has argued that slaves often perceived themselves to be above "white trash" in the social hierarchy.[28] But Genovese overlooks the possibility that bondspeople also distinguished between overseers and other poor whites such as farmers, shopkeepers, and artisans. In other words, bondspeople perceived white society to be more stratified than Genovese allows for. Overseers, unlike many other nonslaveholding whites, represented masterly authority on the plantation and had wide license to discipline unruly slaves. Their job was, after all, to obtain the best crop possible from the labor resources available. The license to whip slaves was generally intended to serve a corrective purpose, demonstrating that absenteeism or poor work would not be tolerated, not to indulge a penchant for violence. The paternalist ideology of owners clearly did not permit excessively violent overseers to go unchallenged, especially if such violence hampered the productive capacity of bondspeople.[29] Henry Laurens informed William Gambell, his overseer at Broughton Island, that after several slaves had absconded he would no longer "suffer acts of cruelty of unnecessary rigor and severity to be exercised towards those poor wretches."[30] Because African Americans' testimony was inadmissible in court, however, planters did not necessarily have any legal redress against acts of violence they personally disapproved of, except outright dismissal. Thus when Swinton, an overseer of General Carr "most dreadfully beat" Jack, who was on hire from Robert Allston, the lack of white witnesses to the attack meant that suggestions that Swinton should be prosecuted, "as nothing could justify it," came to nothing.[31]

Bondspeople often reacted with violence to the physical abuse of themselves and their families. A large proportion of the assaults committed by lowcountry bondspeople on white men were against overseers. Those bondspeople who struck against oppression by killing their overseers rarely found other white people sympathetic to their suffering. Harry, who murdered Lancelot Feay, his overseer, was tried by a court of Chatham County freeholders, found guilty, and executed.[32] John Melish viewed the remains of two slaves executed on the Augusta Road in 1806 for the murder of their overseer, who, in order to send a shockingly plain message to other bondspeople in the lowcountry, had been burned alive.[33] While the motivation for these killings usually involved redress for past abuse, this was not always the case. James Buckingham encountered two lowcountry bondsmen arrested for the murder of their overseer after he had caught them in the act of stealing cattle which they were using to provision local fugitive slaves.[34] The white elite feared that violence toward overseers might spill over and lead to wider killing. In 1774 the *Georgia Gazette* reported that "six new Negro fellows and four wenches" had murdered the overseer on Captain Morris's plantation near Darien. What made their crime particularly heinous was that after this murder, the slaves had killed Morris's wife and "dangerously wounded a carpenter named Wright."[35]

The tripartite relationship between bondsperson, overseer, and owner inevitably created a high degree of nonviolent tension. Some masters found it difficult to employ a satisfactory overseer who would refrain from entertaining "idle fellows" on the plantation.[36] Others found their slaves complaining of mistreatment or misbehavior by the overseer in an attempt to get him removed. J. B. Grimball attempted to defuse such a situation when one of his slave drivers came to Charleston to complain that he had been dismissed by the overseer, whom the driver alleged was helping himself out of the corn store. Three days later the overseer appeared personally in Charleston to put his case, which Grimball eventually accepted.[37] Not all owners sided with the overseer against the bondspeople. William Hoffmann, an overseer at the Retreat Plantation near Savannah, grumbled that the interference of George Kollock, the owner, would "ruin the Negroes and make the overseer a bankrupt."[38] Evidently some slaves believed that it was possible to influence the choice of an overseer and to mitigate any harshness in his behavior by appealing directly to their owner. One female slave on hire at Retreat was able to escape punishment after she "used violence" toward Hoffmann because she managed to obtain "a letter of pardon [from] . . . her master Houstoun." Hoffmann, recognizing the futility of his position, declared that Houstoun "dont ought to own a Negro."[39] In this sense the labor value of slaves made their well-being more important to the planter than the social standing of the overseer.

While white men encountered African Americans in a multiplicity of urban and rural workplaces, engendering differing responses depending on their precise role, white women had fewer opportunities to come into direct contact with working blacks. In a society where the economic opportunities available to women were severely limited, some women were forced into domestic or housekeeping vocations. White female domestics were employed to wet-nurse children in addition to cooking and cleaning, and newspaper advertisements from women show that versatility was the key to successful employment.[40] In the 1820s, a rash of ads appeared from local families in Savannah and Darien seeking white women as servant maids and governesses, perhaps suggesting that having a white female employee was a status symbol.[41] Increasingly as the antebellum era wore on, elite white women preferred to have white rather than black domestics. As one resident of St. Marys stated, "I could have black servants enough by hiring, but they have very little discretion and I do not feel easy when they are out of my sight."[42] No doubt these white women worked in households where the only other working people were African Americans. Although the status of working white women in these households is not clear, the white elite evidently had no social prohibition against poor white women earning wages, even working alongside African Americans. One visitor to Savannah in the 1850s believed that the white housekeeper employed by the Pulaski Hotel had formed such strong bonds with black employees that "she is very averse to reporting any of the darkies as requiring correction (alias a whipping)."[43]

By 1860 more than thirteen hundred white women were working in Savannah, principally in the cloth trades (dressmakers, seamstresses, mantua makers, and milliners) but also as domestics and servants. Younger women, especially those from Ireland, dominated the latter group, and older and native-born women were more likely to be found in the former group. White women in all but the most highly specialized jobs (such as teaching or managerial positions) competed with more than two hundred free black women and more than a thousand slave women for work. In many of the larger households and in the city market these women, black and white, slave and free, would have come into regular informal contact.[44]

Outside of the domestic and urban environments, nonslaveholding white women who were engaged in cloth production sometimes worked alongside African Americans. John Melish visited a lowcountry farm in 1806 where he observed "a black girl carding cotton, and a daughter of the landlord spinning . . . they were quite busy and appeared to be industrious and happy."[45] The new cotton mills of the nineteenth century also offered employment to women of both races. One visitor to such a factory observed "the white girls working in the same room and at the same loom with the black girls . . . working together without apparent repugnance or objection."[46] These had been traditional occupations for women in both England and Africa, thus it is not surprising that some women recreated these roles in the New World. What is intriguing is that white women were willing to work with African Americans on apparently similar terms of employment. Working together perhaps enabled some black and white women to form relationships within gendered spaces that crossed, and therefore undermined, racial boundaries.

While many whites, both skilled and unskilled, regularly worked alongside African Americans, some nonslaveholders were prepared to go one step further and violate the ultimate working taboo, field labor with slaves. It was common practice throughout the South for small farmers to work alongside their hired help on a Sunday to maximize productivity. One observer near Charleston noticed that poor white farmers and hired slaves worked together in the fields, "almost on the same footing."[47] Ten years later Basil Hall noted that only a few miles inland from the coast, white men were working in the fields with blacks, and he "more than once saw a black man seated in the same room with a free person."[48] Emily Burke observed "white women and black women" working in fields together "without distinction."[49] As Stephanie McCurry has pointed out, the employment of wives in their fields by yeoman farmers in the South Carolina lowcountry was the key to maintaining their political and economic independence.[50] Without the vital labor of women, occasionally in concert with hired slaves, many farms would have failed to produce enough for the family to survive or to pay their debts at the local store. More significantly, white people and African Americans working "on a similar ground of dependence and poverty," undermined theories of race supremacy.[51] The similar social condition of nonslaveholding whites and African Americans in these situations destroyed the concept of whiteness as a trait that naturally and innately elevated the European above the African. The willingness of some white people to accept this position suggests that they understood that whiteness alone was not necessarily a passport to economic security.

The immigrant European population of the lowcountry performed much of the unskilled laboring work in both rural and urban areas. After the devastating fire in Savannah on January 11, 1820, which destroyed more than a quarter of the city, for example, Irish laborers flocked in from Northern states, perhaps responding to ads in Northern newspapers.[52] During the 1820s and 1830s Irish immigrants helped to build the lowcountry canal and railroad networks, and it was there that many Irish workers first encountered slaves. In 1827 a correspondent to the *Daily Georgian* stated that "100 white and 200 black laborers" were employed on the Chatham County sections of the Savannah, Ogeechee, and Altamaha Canal. A report of the Board of Health to the Savannah City Council later that same year stated that most of the white people working on the canal were from "the Northern States of Ireland."[53] Similarly, in the late 1830s both Irish workers and slaves were employed in building the Brunswick Canal south of Savannah. In 1838 local newspapers carried ads seeking up to a thousand slaves for work on the canal, but within a year the Annual Report of the Brunswick and Altamaha Canal Company stated, apparently without irony, that the slaves found the work "too difficult for them, [since they] were only accustomed to the light labors of the cotton field." In their place two hundred Irish laborers had been employed, and more were being sought.[54] No doubt some planters believed that it was more economic to use Irish laborers who had no intrinsic value as property for the sometimes dangerous work on the canal rather than risk their own slaves.

Fanny Kemble noted in her journal the often tense relationship between Irish laborers and slaves employed on the Brunswick canal. Apparently local planters advertised for slaves and Irish laborers, offering wages of $20 a month together with food and housing.[55] Kemble declared that the two groups were not permitted to work on the same section of the canal because "the low Irish seem to have the same sort of hatred of Negroes which sects, differing but little in their tenets, have for each other."[56] This, however, should not necessarily be taken as symptomatic of Irish racism. The Irish workers, according to Kemble, disliked slaves not because of their color but because they themselves were considered "almost as a degraded class of beings."[57] The Irish were competing with slaves for unskilled laboring work throughout the lowcountry, and it seems to have been this competitive edge, as much as any racial element, that shaped their attitudes toward slaves working on the canal.

Unlike foreigners, immigrant white workers from the Northern states, who constituted nearly a third of the population of Savannah before 1832, were most likely accustomed to working with African Americans in some form. The situation in Savannah, where half the population was black, however, would have contrasted starkly with the ethnic divisions visible in New York, Boston, and Philadelphia. Of course, the use of immigrants was in some ways an economic necessity because they constituted a significant proportion of the urban unskilled labor force in the lowcountry.[58] Savannah death records between 1803 and 1832 indicate that 75 percent of those who died in the city were born outside of Georgia. A quarter of city residents in the early nineteenth century came from the British Isles, principally from Ireland.[59] As early as 1812 Irish immigrants in Savannah had formed the Hibernian Society, which supported destitute fellow countrymen until they found employment. By 1860 nearly a third of all Savannahians were Irish born.[60] Many arrived with few financial resources. Consequently, they sought semiskilled or unskilled work, either in shops or as day laborers, and they tended to work alongside African Americans at the bottom of the socioeconomic scale in the lowcountry.[61]

Although local planters and merchants may have thought little of the white people who worked voluntarily with African Americans, the elite often compelled these groups to labor together. During times of military uncertainty, for example, all males were required to work on the fortifications of Savannah. In the Revolutionary War and again in 1814–15, slave owners were required to provide slaves to build up the city fortifications against a possible attack.[62] Slave owners were compensated at the rate of three shillings per day, and white overseers were appointed to supervise their work. In 1815, in addition to the slaves, the City Council employed mechanics to labor manually on the fortifications, paying them over $300 for their services.[63]

Certain activities, most notably road duty, required the regular participation of all males, black and white, slave and free, between the ages of sixteen and sixty.[64] The inconvenience caused by this service eventually necessitated the exemption of Savannah and its hamlets and the substitution of an annual levy.[65] All local inhabitants, however, continued to work on rural roads.[66] Road duty outside of Savannah fell equally on both women and men. Although no record exists of women actually undertaking this task, the regulation requiring them to do so was not repealed until 1824.[67] The original proviso was probably a realistic assessment of the sparse settlement of some areas of the countryside: there were simply not enough men to complete the task. Road duty involved some slaves overseen by white people but also required manual labor by some poorer whites. Reuben King, for example, spent one period of road duty "trimming the trees and pileing bushes."[68] The letter of summons for Camden County required all men "to attend and perform labor on the main post road," the white men to be "armed and equipped as the law directs" while the slaves were to bring "hoes, axes or spades."[69] Most of the manual labor done by white people on the roads was done by the poorest members of society, and the road duty lists from Camden County in 1804 illuminate the class distinctions drawn by the elite. Slave owners were far more likely than nonslaveholders to be placed in a position of authority over workers.[70] Equally, nonslaveholding whites were three times more likely to be summoned to perform manual labor on the roads instead of being assigned a supervisory role.[71] In an obvious attempt to differentiate between free and slave labor, limits were placed on the authority of supervisors over white and free black laborers. Unlike slave workers, who could receive up to twenty lashes for "neglecting the work to be done," whites and free blacks were merely reported to the road commissioners so that they could be fined.[72] Some planters, and others who could afford it, exploited a loophole that permitted them to purchase their time to avoid serving, either by paying another person to replace them or the fine to the Inferior Court.[73] Reuben King, tired after having served "all the week" on the roads, purchased the rest of his time "for two gallons of poor brandy," presumably giving the liquor to another person to serve in his place.[74] It is not unrealistic to presume that the only people willing to engage in extra manual labor in return for alcohol would have been nonslaveholding whites or possibly free African Americans, though with only ten of the latter in McIntosh County in 1800, the former is more likely.[75]

In 1824 the Camden County Grand Jury protested that some planters had developed a method of avoiding sending their slaves to do road duty. Apparently the Inferior Court would give a dispensation permitting an individual to employ his slaves on the road leading to his own plantation rather than on the public highway. Some planters had obtained these exemptions for several years, "to the injustice of those individuals who are consequently obliged to do all their own public work and that also of the residents of these parts & districts."[76] As the Grand Jury tacitly recognized, these exemptions placed even more onus on the poorer members of society to undertake road duty alongside African Americans. Dangerous tasks such as dredging lowcountry rivers were not part of the normal duties for road gangs. In some districts nonelite whites may have been the only ones to perform this work regularly.[77] As one historian notes, nonslaveholding whites became more aware in the nineteenth century that working on the roads benefited primarily the elite, not themselves, and consequently they were increasingly unwilling to contribute their labor and their time to this work.[78]

Other encounters between African Americans and lowcountry nonslaveholders were sanctioned and organized by the elites. Fire duty, especially in the towns and cities, was the responsibility of black fire crews under white superintendents.[79] Fire crews in Savannah were paid 12.5 cents per hour for their time when on duty, which indicates that this function was highly valued by the civic authorities.[80] African Americans evidently enjoyed the responsibility of attending fires. In spring 1826 the *Georgian* reported that a fire in the Female Asylum had been extinguished only because of the rapid response of the congregation from the First African Baptist Church, who happened to be worshiping close by. Black fire crews were disproportionately supervised by nonelite residents. In the 1840s and 1850s many Irish immigrants became volunteer firefighters, sometimes competing with black fire crews to arrive first at a fire.[81]

Although it is impossible to quantify with accuracy, it seems that whites and blacks frequently worked alongside each other in the lowcountry from the introduction of slavery until its abolition. While some whites became more politicized over the issue of black labor from the early nineteenth century onward, large numbers of immigrant men and women took jobs that placed them on a par with slaves and free blacks. The racial boundaries separating whites and blacks evidently did not extend to most lowcountry workplaces.

Of course, not all social encounters between nonslaveholders and slaves were based around the workplace. Probably the most common nonwork activity in which nonslaveholders and African Americans interacted involved the patrol. Although officially the responsibility of all white adults, nightly patrols had always been the preserve of nonslaveholding whites in the Georgia and South Carolina lowcountry, and their reputation for violent conduct toward African Americans was often entirely justified.[82] In 1794 the Charleston Grand Jury complained that the patrol was "for the most part confined to overseers who frequently maltreat the slaves."[83] Shortly afterward the Chatham County Grand Jury complained that compelling people to perform patrol duty was increasingly difficult because most of the patrollers lacked the "visible property hereon to levy the fine imposed by law for default of duty."[84] Lowcountry patrolling, from its inception, was the exclusive domain of nonelite white people.

Some members of the elite went to great lengths to avoid doing patrol duty. When C. W. Jones, head of the local patrol, wrote to planter Louis Manigault requiring him to serve, he received a response that no doubt would have been familiar. Manigault refused to do patrol duty, decrying the "miserable little jurisdiction" of Jones, and, although he knew he would be fined for failing to serve, the amount would be so insignificant for someone of his wealth that "it wont be very killing to pay." Crucial to Manigault's response was the belief that patrolling was the proper duty of overseers and that it would be "very disagreeable" for planters.[85]

Clearly some elite citizens believed that patrol duty should be done by respectable yeomen rather than by "improper persons, and overseers, who are regardless of that propriety of conduct which ought to guide men in the execution of that important duty." [86] Complaints about the effectiveness of the patrols and their spasmodic occurrence were frequent, perhaps indicating a fundamental reluctance among nonslaveholders for this task. [87] Certainly some nonslaveholding whites believed that they were being duped by the elite into undertaking patrol duty which the elite benefited from but rarely did themselves. [88] One patrolman, William Smith, warned that it would be increasingly difficult to find men willing to do patrol duty unless the elite were seen to be helping to "protect [their own property] by doing patrol duty" rather than hindering the cause of controlling the activities of African Americans in Savannah. [89] Thomas Gibbons, the mayor of Savannah, to whom this letter was addressed, responded that he claimed "no exemptions [from patrol duty] because I possess more property [and] that my possessions in the city are additional inducements to watch over its safety." [90] Nevertheless, patrolling, both in Savannah and in rural areas, was generally done by nonslaveholding whites.

Despite attitudes such as William Smith's, not all nonslaveholding whites could afford to surrender the income patrol duty provided. When first formed in 1793, the Savannah watch required the voluntary appearance of citizens in rotation, as "the funds and revenues of the said city are inadequate to the support and maintenance of the [watch] on hire or constant pay." [91] The instigation of a paid watch during the early nineteenth century made watch duty an attractive source of extra income for the poorest members of society. Members of the city watch in Savannah in 1819 received one dollar for every evening they served, as well as part of any fines the City Council levied and a share in rewards paid by owners for the return of fugitive slaves. [92] Watchmen were apparently under contract to the council for a specific period. If they did not serve the full term, they were likely to lose all their wages. [93] A register of watch members from November 1819 lists forty men, of whom only eight were listed as taxpayers in the 1819 tax digest for the city of Savannah: six nonslaveholders and two slaveholders. [94] Thus more than three-quarters of the watch were marginalized or transient individuals who were missed by the tax collectors.

Patrol duty brought nonslaveholding whites into highly antagonistic contact with African Americans, and this may have limited the fraternization possible between them. [95] Patrollers in colonial Savannah had authority to inflict up to twenty lashes "on the bare back" of bondspeople taken without "a ticket or token from their respective owners or a white person in company with him or them," and some patrollers took their responsibility to protect lowcountry society seriously.[96] Once slaves had been taken up, the patrol was often unwilling to release them to their owners until proper procedures had been completed. William Davidson had such a problem in 1806. One of his slaves, a gardener, who had "only gone over to Mr. Boyer's for some rice & bread for his supper," was taken by the Charleston patrol. When Davidson located the patrol and asked for the return of his slave, he was "knocked down by a bludgeon over the head in a terrible manner" by several patrollers.[97] One cannot help suspecting that some patrollers delighted in exercising this authority over those who were normally their social superiors. To prevent similar occurrences in Savannah, the City Council was prepared to fine watchmen who illegally apprehended slaves in the company of their owner, and in 1854 it passed an ordinance stating that slaves could not be arrested "without good cause" during daylight hours.[98]

New regulations introduced in the late 1820s in Savannah, which provided for tickets to enable African Americans to pass after 10 P.M., caused much confusion in the city. The watch's interpretation of the ordinance of 1825 resulted in the arrest of many slaves whose owners believed them to be in possession of correct tickets.[99] Eventually, in an effort to reduce the "frequent disputes [which] have arisen between citizens of Savannah & the city watchmen," the council reinterpreted the ordinance to permit African Americans to travel after 10 P.M. providing the place to which they were going was inscribed on the pass.[100] These laws did not prevent bondspeople from going about their business in the normal way. In 1835 the council was forced to pass an ordinance preventing slaves from passing without any tickets at all, suggesting that the watch provisions were not strictly observed by slaves, owners, or the patrol.[101]

Nonelite members of the patrol evidently felt that they had sufficient authority to resist the hegemony of the elite. Being a member of the patrol in effect gave nonslaveholding whites the temporary status of master, permitting them to exercise undisputed authority over African Americans, and may well have determined their views on suitable contact with African Americans. William Craft knew that "the lowest villain in the county, should he be a white man, has the legal power to arrest and question, in the most inquisitorial and insulting manner, any colored person." If the African Americans in question proved recalcitrant, they "may be beaten

[and] . . . killed on the spot [while] the murderer will be exempted from blame." [102] Any white person, whether slaveholding or not, was likely to respond violently to a direct challenge from African Americans. [103] Although the elite may have disliked such sweeping authority over their property being granted to poor whites, the City Council felt obliged to support watchmen who came under attack from city residents while on duty. In 1826 the city paid the legal costs of watchman Andrew Parkhill after he was prosecuted by Levi D'Lyon for an assault on one of D'Lyon's slaves. [104] Four years later, the council resolved to prosecute two slaves for an assault on a member of the watch unless their owners "cause them to be whipped for said offences." [105] The council was also willing to punish those who attempted to prevent the watch from arresting slaves. In 1840 P. D. Woolhopter was fined $50 for trying to prevent the watch from dispersing an "unlawful assembly of negroes on his premises." [106]

While patrols brought African Americans and nonslaveholding whites into the familiar power structures of slavery, there is evidence that the violent reputation of patrollers stemmed more from the actions of yeoman farmers than those of the poorest individuals. Former slave Charles Ball stated that in central South Carolina it was the "man who is master of only four or five slaves, [who] is generally the most ready of all to apprehend a black man . . . and generally whips him unmercifully for this offence . . . [thus] the experience of all ages, that petty tyrants are the most oppressive, seems fully verified in the cotton country." [107] In contrast, Susie King Taylor recalled that many fellow slaves in Savannah "went out at any time of night and were never arrested, as the watchmen knew them so well he never stopped them, and seldom asked to see their passes, only stopping them long enough, sometimes, to say 'Howdy,' and telling them to go along." [108] Julia Harn confirms that the ticket/pass system was laxly enforced by lowcountry patrols and that "there was not likely to be any trouble if the negro behaved." [109] In 1851 the Chatham Grand Jury requested that shopkeepers be prevented from turning out as watchmen because they knew so many slaves personally as trading partners. [110] While it is unclear how frequent such genial encounters were, it is certainly possible that urban slaves out in the evening were known to many Savannah residents. [111] The legal authority given to nonslaveholders in this instance does not always seem to have altered their perception of racial boundaries. When African Americans remained submissive and aware of their subordinate racial position, the patrol generally did not bother them. William Grimes was never challenged by the watch, even late at night, though Grimes's light skin color may have created a doubt in the mind of the watch as to whether he was an African American.[112]

Nonelite whites would have interacted with African Americans when on road or patrol duty, but these encounters were sporadic. Far more frequent were the informal social contacts forged in the bars and taverns that clustered in lowcountry towns and on the principal roads. Often these taverns and bars were cited by grand juries for trading with slaves or "entertaining Negroes."[113] In 1811 the Camden County Grand Jury complained that the shops and tippling houses open in St. Marys for "trading with and harboring Negroes" were also the resort of "seamen and others in inebriety."[114] The larger ports of the lowcountry, Savannah and Charleston, also struggled to cope with the behavior of black and white sailors in the taverns and gambling houses. In 1770, the South Carolina Grand Jury complained that, not content with retailing liquor to slaves, tippling houses in Charleston also encouraged sailors "to neglect and desert their duty."[115] The meetings of seamen in "houses of entertainment for mariners," such as that owned by John Fleetwood in Yamacraw, aroused great alarm among Savannah's residents.[116] Disorderly assemblies of sailors regularly necessitated action on the part of city authorities, and one riot in 1811 between French and American sailors resulted in the arrest of more than 120 individuals.[117]

While ashore, many seamen frequented the taverns on the bluff in Savannah. One visitor to such a tavern observed that "here could be seen inebriety at every stage & here could be heard the ne plus ultra of blackguard & obscene language accompanied as usual by wrangling and fighting."[118] William Harden recalled seeing sailors "lying in the squares nearest the waterfront in a state of insobriety—some too far gone to be noisy, others in a hilarious condition."[119] Bondspeople also knew that alcohol was readily available, both at grocery stores and at dramshops, in this quarter of the city. William Grimes had little problem locating sufficient quantities of liquor on the bluff to make him forget about a painful toothache.[120] White people who frequented these dramshops seem to have cheerfully shared their bars with African Americans. Ann Catherine Harris, an innkeeper, stated in 1824 that it was common for whites and slaves to drink together in her establishment.[121] The enjoyment of alcohol by bondspeople does not seem to have been perceived as a threat to the social status of nonslaveholders, for it made slaves neither white nor free. While nonelite shopkeepers often encouraged African Americans to buy alcohol, most white customers were indifferent to black patrons. Indeed, the only people whose peace of mind was obviously threatened by intoxicated slaves were their owners.

The tippling houses and gambling haunts tended to be conveniently located for their clientele. Many tippling and gaming houses were located in town, but the more secretive ones were located just beyond or "near the city limits," often on main roads coming in and out of town.[122] The Chatham County Grand Jury protested that a "large portion" of the offenses it presented were "committed on the outskirts of this city & beyond its present boundaries."[123] Protests were still being made in 1855 about the volume of crime occurring in areas just beyond the city limits.[124]

Several offenses were associated with the racecourse near Savannah, which attracted gamblers from all over the state. Adam Hodgson encountered a coach full of disillusioned gamblers returning to Augusta after the cancellation of the races occasioned by the fire of 1820.[125] According to the Grand Jury, the races were characterized by disorder, and "drunkenness is encouraged by the tippling shops & booths that are erected in the vicinity."[126] Aside from the obvious attractions of alcohol, African Americans and nonslaveholders would also have socialized and traded at the race meetings. Similar encounters occurred whenever the circus visited Savannah.[127] Yet African Americans were seldom confined in the Savannah city jail for gambling and drunkenness. Between 1809 and 1815 only eleven slaves were imprisoned in the city jail for gambling and only a further two for drunkenness.[128] Those few slaves arrested for drunkenness in the 1850s never spent more than two or three days in the city jail, suggesting that slaves apprehended by the watch for these offenses were more likely to be sent back to their masters rather than being imprisoned.[129]

Many gaming and tippling houses in the city center supplied alcohol to the resident population of African Americans and nonslaveholding whites. In Savannah six white men were fined by the City Council for gambling with slaves, and those convicted for permitting illegal gambling in their establishments could receive in a thirty dollar fine or a jail sentence.[130] Gambling by slaves enriched those who provided the location for "cards, dice and other games in secrecy" who knew, as did the Grand Jury, that because of the agency of slaves "sufficient proof cannot be adduced to lead to a conviction of the guilty parties."[131] Easy and regular sociability flourished because it did not challenge the social or racial status of nonslaveholders in the lowcountry. Such racial barriers as existed in the lowcountry were loose enough to permit voluntary interactions. Slavery, as a sociolegal system, did not prevent ordinary whites from relating to African Americans in whatever manner they chose.

Biracial social interaction was facilitated by the residential proximity of nonslaveholding whites and African Americans in the poorer neighborhoods of Savannah. Yamacraw and the eastern and western suburbs offered relatively cheap rented accommodations, without the supervision of the city watch, which usually confined its activities to the city wards. Many slaves living in Yamacraw hired themselves out, which was the first step toward greater personal freedom in their lives. Less than twenty years after the introduction of slavery in Georgia, the provincial Grand Jury protested that many slaves in Savannah were allowed to live away from their owners "or any other white person" by which "many notorious offenders are encouraged and screened from publick justice."[132] The gradual formation of African American neighborhoods in Savannah, concentrated around Yamacraw to the west of the city, no doubt fostered many personal contacts between the bond and free African American communities. As early as 1798, when the first black census of the city wards was taken, African Americans congregated in Oglethorpe ward and Yamacraw in the west of the city.[133] Moreover, the register of free people of color reveals that a third of free blacks in Savannah resided in Yamacraw.[134]

Legally, slaves were not permitted to rent houses for themselves because such liberty was believed to encourage theft and intemperance.[135] But there is evidence that these laws were widely ignored. In 1800, in response to complaints from the Grand Jury, the City Council had imposed a fifty dollar fine on white people renting houses to slaves.[136] The council republished this ordinance four years later, which suggests that it was not being widely observed. Enslaved African Americans may have resided close to, or indeed rented from, nonelite whites, but the only evidence we have of individuals renting property to slaves involves the white elite. In a fascinating example of the economic enterprise of a bondsman, the Savannah Female Asylum first rented a lot and then a house to John Deveaux, a slave of Mary Bulloch. Deveaux erected the house himself while renting the lot and then sold it to the asylum for $140 with "the price fixed by him." As part of the deal, Deveaux remained as a tenant in the house, paying rent to the asylum.[137] Although restrictions on slaves renting houses had been in force from the colonial period, no such limitations were placed on free African Americans. In 1806, John Williamson sued a free black woman named Dolly Houstoun for $36 back rent on a house.[138] A year later, the City Council tried to close that loophole by ordering that no one could rent a house to a free African American without its permission.[139]

Despite legal sanctions, it is evident that African Americans continued to live apart from whites in the lowcountry towns. The Town Council in St. Marys ordered that slaves should not be allowed to meet "in the dwellings of servants who reside in buildings not in the premises of their owners."[140] In Savannah Charles Colcock Jones observed "hundreds of negroes . . . who go about from house to house, some servants, some house carpenters, etc., who never see their masters except at pay day."[141] Furthermore, the mayor protected the property rights of African Americans by jailing two white men for "breaking into a negro house."[142] Some African Americans took advantage of their independent living arrangements to make money. In 1858 John Krieke was assaulted in a house that "belonged to Mr. Robert Habersham, and was rented by negroes from him, and I rented it from them."[143] No doubt there was sufficient profit in the transaction to make the deal worthwhile for the African Americans concerned.

Surviving records document that poor white people also tended to reside in the west end of the city. Just under a quarter of nonslaveholding whites in 1826 owned property to the west of West Broad Street, constituting the largest concentration of nonslaveholders in a single suburb of the city.[144] Many more nonslaveholders may have lived in these areas, but more than two-thirds of people who did not own slaves also did not own any property in 1826—the residency of those white people who rented property is unknown.[145] Records from the Board of Health reinforce the impression that a large segment of the nonslaveholding white population of Savannah lived in the same wards that were popular with free and enslaved African Americans and even shared houses with them.[146] The ready mixing of black and white in these locales clearly unsettled the white elite. Emily Burke was warned that Bay Street and the bluff were "always so thronged by sailors, slaves and rowdies of all grades and color, that it is not safe for ladies to walk there alone."[147] Such a reputation ensured that nonslaveholders and African Americans in these neighborhoods were often left to interact how they pleased, away from the close scrutiny of the elite.

Many of the white residents of these mainly African American suburbs were immigrants to Savannah.[148] In 1838 Levi Russell reported that the transient labor force in Savannah amounted to roughly three thousand people annually; indeed, the continued growth of the nonslaveholding population in the city only made biracial social interaction more likely as the antebellum period wore on.[149] The cheap housing of the eastern and western suburbs would have been the only option available to immigrants with limited financial resources. Some residences in Oglethorpe ward were described by Charles G. Parsons as "low, dingy, squalid, cheerless Negro huts."[150] These residents clearly did not earn a higher standard of living or better social conditions than African Americans simply because they were white. Herbert Weaver has argued that these biracial suburbs existed on the periphery of many Southern towns, and in that sense Savannah was no different from many other places in the lowcountry and elsewhere.[151] The significance of residential proximity, admittedly a peculiarly urban phenomenon, is that it helped to foster personal contacts between the races in nonthreatening environments. Certainly, mixed-race groups were more likely to frequent the same taverns and form social bonds if they lived in the same immediate locality.

While many encounters between African Americans and nonslaveholding whites in the informal social sphere were unstructured or chance encounters, some poor whites were willing to hold more organized social events for local free and bond African Americans. While Emily Burke was resident on one lowcountry plantation, she attended a quilting organized by Caroline, the overseer's wife, for both male and female slaves. Burke was surprised that the invitation was extended to men but was informed "that among Southern field-hands, the women can hoe as well as the men and the men can sew as well as the women, and they engage in all departments of labor according to the necessity of the case, without regard to sex." What attracted the slaves, apart from the easy sociability of the occasion, was the food that Caroline provided, "pastry of various kinds and frosted cake . . . tea and coffee . . . fowls, ham and other meat most deliciously prepared."[152] In such encounters between nonslaveholders and slaves, racial barriers did not hamper mutual enjoyment.

Although this quilting was approved by the owner of the plantation, not all biracial amusements were so agreeable to the wider community. In 1801 a controversy erupted in Savannah over the activities of Adrian Boucher and Mayor Thomas Gibbons. According to a letter written to a Savannah newspaper by a member of the patrol, William Smith, Boucher had given a party for "upwards of forty" African Americans, supposedly sanctioned by Gibbons.[153] When the city patrol demanded to see authorization for the event, it was handed a ticket signed by Gibbons permitting the dance. In view of the potential for disorder, however, the patrol "thought it prudent for the city at large" to arrest all the people there, including Boucher. Boucher's wife notified Gibbons of his arrest, and Gibbons ordered his release the next day.

This was only the start of a greater dispute, which brought into question Gibbons's ability to authorize the dance or to order the release of prisoners from the city jail. Gibbons's response to Smith's attack appeared three days later.[154] He did not deny that he had given permission for the dance, stating that he and the captain of the guard, a Colonel Tattnall, had agreed that there was no reason to prevent a gathering of people. Gibbons claimed that the dance was orderly, and local residents afterward stated that they had heard nothing of the dance until the guard arrived. On the matter of Boucher, Gibbons argued that he had told the jailer to release him because there was no formal "written order or authority for the imprisonment." In Smith's repost, he stated that he had arrested the African Americans because "free Jim and Bouche [sic] had abused the confidence placed in them, and had admitted all Negroes indiscriminately with and without tickets."[155] He declared that Boucher was kept in jail because "he was impudent and insulting," while the more docile African Americans were released the following morning. Smith claimed that this was not the first time that Gibbons had given permission for dances to be held at Boucher's and that "the house has been complained of as a nuisance for some time past." Despite an attempt by Gibbons to persuade Smith to withdraw his complaint, Boucher was indicted before the Chatham County Superior Court in June 1801 for keeping a disorderly house. The prosecution was subsequently dropped without a trial.[156]

Boucher was an immigrant from France and had resided in New York before coming to Savannah. He was variously described as a carpenter, a bricklayer, and a builder and evidently made his living through skilled manual work.[157] Yet he clearly knew the mayor of Savannah personally and was also in regular contact with African Americans. Boucher's motivation for permitting this dance may have been financial: Smith alleged that Boucher made "three or four dollars" out of the entertainment.[158] Manifestly this nonslaveholder did not feel his social status to be under threat from social interaction with African Americans.[159] Perhaps Boucher enjoyed the music or the dancing, or possibly he was personally acquainted with the bondspeople and free blacks in question. Indeed he may have worked side by side with some African Americans on commissions in and around Savannah.

Those fraternizing improperly with African Americans were usually fined by the City Council. Charles Clark, a nonslaveholder resident in Yamacraw, was fined a dollar for "suffering Negroes to dance in his kitchen after 12 o'clock at night."[160] Otto Nienhaus was fined thirty dollars for letting "two parties" of African Americans play cards in his house.[161] The only Nienhaus living in Savannah around 1809 was an individual "professing himself a doctor," resident at Springhill, though it is not known whether he owned slaves.[162] These individuals clearly lacked "respectability" in Savannah. One lived in Yamacraw, the least genteel of all Savannah's suburbs, and the other was perceived as holding a dubious professional qualification. Their free association with African Americans completed their alienation from "polite" white society. White people who permitted such events on their property were permitting African Americans to enter their own private space—the home. By meeting African Americans in a private rather than a public forum, nonslaveholding whites were encouraging, and were seemingly unconcerned by, the violation of the most sacred of domestic racial barriers. Some nonelite whites did not perceive such encounters as undermining their status as white people because ultimately nothing could change the fact they were white and therefore free, while slaves were black. Nevertheless, polite society was mildly disgusted by interracial socializing. When, in 1861, Confederate soldiers in Camden County held a dance to which they invited female African Americans, Loulie Brown believed that "they must be very bad off for wives, to take the negroe girls to carry on such a caper with in public."[163]

Poor people were not the only ones who sponsored social events for African Americans. In 1795 a Charleston magistrate, Captain Cunnington, defended the rights of African Americans to hold an evening dance in the city without official permission.[164] Cunnington's authority to grant this permission was challenged first by two local residents, Peter Ryan and James McBride, who were members of a "small patrole" set up to "watch their property." Around midnight on Tuesday, November 3, 1795, they heard music coming from the house of the recently deceased Julius Smith. When Ryan questioned its origin, McBride informed him that "there was a Negro dance to be there."[165] Ryan summoned the watch, who attempted to enter the house but were initially refused "by some Negroes." On forcing the door, the watch was met by Cunnington angrily demanding who dared to force such an entry. On being informed that the watch wished to search the house for African Americans, Cunnington claimed that "there was none in the house but friends within the circle of the neighbourhood who were amusing themselves." The guard persisted and was eventually permitted to enter, finding inside "a number of mulatto & black wenches, & some Negro fellows" though others, including one white man, escaped out of a second-floor window.

It is not clear why Captain Cunnington was willing to lie to protect African Americans. The watch also found "a variety of delicacies" being served on "china," which was displayed to the neighbors as an example of "their extravagance."[166] The watch recorded the violent manner of Cunnington's vocal defense of the African Americans, declaring that those who had entered the house were "house robbers" and that he used physical force to defend the house. Clearly Cunnington knew several of the African Americans personally. One African American woman, on being arrested, "delivered to Capt. Cunnington her head-dress & bonnet, and desired him to take care of it for her," suggesting that she trusted Cunnington to respect her request.[167] This evidence hints that, contrary to his claim, Cunnington had not just happened to arrive at the dance "to look on."[168]

There are several unusual facts about this event which require explanation. The dance took place on a Tuesday night and continued until almost six o'clock the following morning, which suggests that the participants were not field slaves or from out of town. Most likely these African Americans were either free or able to hire their own time without the close supervision of their owners. There may well have been a sexual motive behind Cunnington's reluctance to permit the guard to enter the house. The only people mentioned as attending the event were African American women and men and white men: no white women were present. It is possible that this house was being used as a brothel and was frequented by white and black men alike. Certainly the owner of the house, the recently widowed Mrs. Julius Smith, was not on the premises because Cunnington had obtained the key from her to enter the house. Without more evidence, however, this remains a hypothesis.

Biracial sexual contact was, of course, a frequent occurrence in the lowcountry. The mulatto population of the South is testimony to a significant degree of mixed-race intercourse, with many sexual encounters involving the abuse of black women by white men.[169] Yet there are examples of sexual contact between the races that did not involve either rape or coercion. Intimate relationships between white women and black men were highly secretive, most likely because of the prevailing attitudes of white society toward the sexuality of black men, who were supposedly filled with desire for white women.[170] Accusing a white woman of sexual contact with an African American was a dangerous thing to do. When John Smith declared to several onlookers that he believed Mrs. Clara Powell to be a "damn'd whore" for sleeping with "a mulatto fellow by the name of Wilson," Mrs. Powell's husband physically assaulted Smith, "but not in a cruel manner," because of the accusation. At his trial for assault Mr. Powell was so determined to expunge the slur on his name that he brought seventeen character witnesses to court to attest to his wife's fidelity.[171] The disgrace attached to a white man if his wife engaged in sexual activity with an African American was sufficient to persuade some men to divorce their spouses and seek the vengeance of the lynch mob.[172]

White women were occasionally willing to flaunt openly their relationship with African American men. Martha Bells, a propertyless white woman in Charleston, was registered as being married to Henry Bells, a thirty-five-year-old free mulatto, by whom she had five children.[173] Relationships involving white women and black men obviously encountered a high degree of social resistance. In 1751 Pastor John Martin Bolzius was disgusted to learn that "2 white women, one French and one German, have secretly disgraced themselves with Negroes and have borne black children."[174] These relationships usually involved free African Americans and poorer, almost certainly slaveless, white women. Poor white women who violated social and racial norms in this manner effectively lost their racial privileges. Judges and juries throughout the South were reluctant to condemn black men for "rape" when the moral character of white female plaintiffs was questionable. Indeed, it was only in the later nineteenth century that all white women, regardless of status, were regarded as sexually inviolate.[175]

Violent rapes of white women by African American men were extremely rare in the antebellum lowcountry. The case of George Flyming, a slave convicted in Savannah in 1820 of attempting to rape a poor white girl, Eliza Hand, aged about fourteen, shows the severity with which such crimes were viewed. Despite a recommendation of mercy by the jury, Flyming was sentenced to die five weeks after his conviction.[176] A petition to the governor by several prominent citizens of Savannah obtained a stay of execution. The petitioners claimed that "the evidence [presumably Eliza's] upon which he was convicted is doubtful and uncertain" and asked for his sentence to be commuted to transportation because execution would perhaps kill "an innocent human being."[177] Similar gender affinities between black and white men elsewhere in the South were studied by Martha Hodes and Diane Sommerville.[178] White men were reluctant throughout the South to convict any other male, white or black, of rape unless the case was completely clear-cut, for example, the white woman concerned was of absolutely irreproachable character.[179] Although it is likely that George Flyming was ultimately executed, the final outcome of his case is not known.[180]

The only other interracial rape case in the Georgia lowcountry occurred during the tense years of the Civil War. One Sunday in January 1862, Amelia McGuire, a thirty-three-year-old seamstress, was raped at Canal Bridge in Yamacraw by a black man. Four slaves, Edward, Edwin, Thomas, and York, were quickly arrested and indicted before the Superior Court. One might think that with racial tensions running high in Savannah little attention would be paid to due process; however, each slave received a proper trial. The charges against Edward were quickly dropped, as were those against York, following a direct representation on their behalf by McGuire. Ultimately Edwin's and Thomas's cases came to trial, but only Edwin was convicted.[181] Instead of summary execution being carried out, legal arguments brought the case back before the court in January 1863. According to the court record, Edwin had an alibi that was corroborated by both white and black witnesses. In a significant new development, the court heard that on the day the rape was committed the members of the First African Church had seen a slave named Allin running past them, armed with a knife, and jump into the canal where they were holding baptisms. Other African Americans testified that Allin and Edwin looked alike (the judge recalled that McGuire's identification had been tentative at the outset), and as a result the judge ordered a new trial. Edwin was still awaiting this trial when General William T. Sherman's army marched into Savannah in December 1864.[182] The doubts about this case, as well as prevailing gender prejudices of Southern society, surely saved the life of this slave, despite the offense with which he was charged. The measured, even calm, response of Savannahians to this case is in marked contrast to a similar case in Harris County in 1861. A bondsman named George, accused of raping a white woman, did not even get to have a trial before being taken from the county jail by a lynch mob and burned alive.[183]

Of course, sexual relationships between white men and black women were more frequent. Pastor Bolzius knew that "an abomination more common . . . is that white men live in sin with Negresses and father half-black children who walk around in large numbers to the shame of the Christian name."[184] Charles Lyell, however, believed that "the colored women who become the mistresses of the white men are neither rendered miserable nor degraded."[185] His observation is reinforced by the comments of William Craft, an escaped slave. He remarked that while "a great majority" of white men involved with black women "care nothing for the happiness of the women with whom they live . . . there are those . . . who are true to their pledges [of love]."[186] For these individuals, the race of their partner was unimportant.

Sexual relationships could, and did, occur between overseers and the slaves in their charge. Owners often went to considerable lengths to discourage these relationships, perhaps feeling that they distracted the overseer from his role as manager of the plantation and its labor force. Despite the efforts of planters, many overseers took black mistresses, some willingly, many unwillingly.[187] Other nonslaveholding white men formed casual relationships with free African American women. A twenty-seven-year-old ship carpenter, George Miller, was evidently closely associated with a free French mulatto woman in whose house he died of fever in 1815, though it is not known if they were married.[188] Some, such as John Smith, a thirty-five-year-old North Carolina sailor, received medical attention from free black women resident in Savannah. Rebecca Thomas, described as "a free wench," nursed Smith for eight days before his death.[189] It is possible that she did so because of a personal relationship between them. The lack of records makes it impossible to determine accurately the number of mixed-race relationships in Savannah.

Sexual encounters between the races in the lowcountry probably occurred most frequently in the unofficial brothels frequented by African American and white men, which employed women of both races. These "disorderly houses," like the taverns and tippling houses, tended to be on the outskirts of cities such as Charleston and Savannah. Robert Boyd's disorderly house was situated in Oglethorpe ward, home to the largest concentration of African Americans in the city.[190] The death of three mariners from out of state in the house of "Looie" in Yamacraw in the early nineteenth century strongly suggests that either she herself was a prostitute or that she operated a brothel for visiting seamen.[191] In 1855, when the Savannah police chief compiled a report on the city, brothels were a fixture in Yamacraw, Trustees' Gardens, and Currytown.[192]

Authorities in Savannah viewed interracial sex with some severity, and those convicted of keeping a disorderly house could expect prison terms. Mrs. McLean was sentenced in 1789 to forty days' imprisonment in the common jail for "keeping a disorderly house"; sixteen years later, Sarah McBride received an even longer prison term for a similar offense.[193] McBride's confinement marked the start of a crackdown on such persons in Savannah. In April 1805 five people were indicted for keeping disorderly houses, although only one conviction resulted.[194] The remarks of the Grand Jury revealed that this crackdown resulted from the "exertions of the chief magistrate" to weed out "every species of vagrants."[195] Efforts to eliminate city brothels were not completely successful. In both 1808 and 1809 the Chatham Grand Jury cited "houses of ill fame" which "are suffered to be kept in the very centre of the city" and where "the sacred ties of marriage are forgotten, and the foundation of diseases laid."[196] A correspondent to the *Georgian* believed that it was the easy availability of liquor that caused African Americans to become involved with "improper association and . . . debauchery."[197] Nor were rural areas exempt from the "dissipated conduct [of] persons of little standing." Brothels and "disorderly houses" were evidently established wherever African Americans and poor whites congregated.[198]

Women were far more likely than men to be indicted for sexual offenses, either by the City Council or by the Chatham County courts. Only one of those charged with "keeping a riotous and disorderly house" between 1790 and 1848 was male.[199] In addition, the only people to be charged with "keeping a house of ill fame" and "keeping a lewd house or place for fornication" were women.[200] The jail sentences handed down to prostitutes were often long and made worse by a frequent inability to pay jail fees when the sentence was officially completed. In 1820, three prostitutes in the Savannah city jail petitioned the City Council for release because the heat of the summer was making them ill. The council recommended that the governor pardon them because each of the women had already served a lengthy period in jail.[201]

Women were traditionally associated with this type of business, and there is no reason to believe that Savannah should be any different from other localities. In the early national South, however, such biracial liaisons were not meant to occur, especially if they involved the willing participation of white women.[202] The marginal social status of women who violated Southern racial and gender barriers is clear: indeed, as one Southern court stated, white prostitutes "yielded their claims to the protection of the law by their voluntary associations with those whom the law distinguishes as inferiors."[203] For some women, however, prostitution was a necessary way of earning a living, especially for young immigrant women who may have lacked the sexual prejudices of their Southern counterparts. Contact with African Americans was evidently insufficient incentive for white women to abandon this line of work.[204] Color norms for these women were evidently irrelevant.

Despite the best efforts of the civic authorities in Savannah and the constant complaints of lowcountry grand juries, biracial brothels continued to exist until the Civil War. In part they thrived because elite male Savannahians showed by their behavior that even they were incapable of resisting the charms of black prostitutes. But it is also evident that nonslaveholding white men and women continued to see little wrong in choosing a black partner. In the face of the actions and personal choices of both nonslaveholding men and women and African American men and women, those who sought to suppress interracial sexual activity were doomed to failure.[205]

Nonslaveholding whites and African Americans interacted in many different social spheres. Personal daily contacts, either through the workplaces, the tippling houses, or the brothels of Savannah, engendered a breakdown in mutual suspicion and hatred—it was hard to believe in stereotypical pictures if regular interaction continually disproved them. To the nonslaveholding whites who resided in Yamacraw, for example, African Americans were neighbors and perhaps friends. Most nonelite whites did not feel themselves under threat from the freedom African Americans gained from alcohol and entertainment. It was only in more formal environments, such as the patrol, that African Americans could be treated with suspicion. Social encounters between white and black, providing they remained informal and unstructured, could encourage biracial toleration and almost wash away the "lines in the sand." The social contacts described in this chapter undermine the theory that all white people based their worldview on race and that the poorer white people were the most racist of all. Evidently some white people carried on a normal day-to-day existence with African Americans that was not characterized by hatred and suspicion.

3 Competition and Trade

BETWEEN THE INTRODUCTION of slavery and the onset of the Civil War, a variety of economic relationships developed between nonslaveholding whites and African Americans in the Georgia lowcountry. This chapter details the growth of independent production by slaves in the lowcountry, the marketing strategies pursued by individual bondspeople, and the consequent development of a trading relationship with white shopkeepers, most of whom were nonslaveholders. Economic interaction between nonslaveholders and African Americans in this environment can be described as symbiotic but only when nonslaveholders remained sure of their superior social status. Petty capitalist economic encounters, which were detrimental only to the interests of the elite, evince a biracial relationship frequently based more on trust and mutual advantage than on economic exploitation. Shopkeepers were able to look beyond their racial ties with the elite, and indeed one can detect something of a class antipathy toward elite views as to the suitability of economic contacts with African Americans. Trading, however, was not the only area of biracial economic interaction. The vocal reaction of nonslaveholding whites to African American competition suggests that economic encounters were sometimes antagonistic, and nonelite whites could identify with the elite, especially if their livelihood and social status were threatened. The response of the elite to these representations was, at best, ambivalent.

Obviously, the basic purpose of slavery was to get work from African Americans. Only relatively recently have the independent economic activities of slaves attracted scholarly attention. Sidney Mintz was the first to stress the economic importance of slave gardens and to examine the marketing systems through which slave produce was sold. He argued in his study of British Jamaica that these informal economic systems were firmly established by the early nineteenth century and that bondspeople saw growing and retailing produce as a right rather than a privilege.[1] Philip Morgan, Loren Schweniger, John Campbell, and Betty Wood have argued that the informal economy, especially in the Georgia and South Carolina lowcountry, held great "political and psychological meaning." Moreover, the market activity of bondspeople was the cause of a constant battle between owners and slaves over free time and self-determination.[2] What is less well understood is that some, if not many, of these market interactions brought rural slaves into contact with urban bondspeople, free people of color, and white shopkeepers.

Economic transactions and the power dynamics they reveal hold a special significance in any society. Who one traded with was almost as important as what was traded. Trade indicated trust, regardless of race or class. Economic confidence could be eroded by faulty or overpriced goods, thus personal trust was a central element to the renewal of economic contacts between individuals.[3] It is highly unlikely that Dandy, a slave belonging to Pierce Butler, returned to the Darien store where he had been given "miserable material" by a storekeeper in return for "a quantity of moss and eggs [and] . . . who refused him payment in any other shape."[4] When Shadrack Winkler, who was frequently prosecuted by the Savannah City Council for trading with slaves, lost one of his buildings through arson committed by a bondswoman, some citizens may have interpreted it as an act of revenge by a disgruntled customer.[5]

The idiosyncratic nature of African slavery in the Georgia and South Carolina lowcountry undoubtedly facilitated the trade that developed between slaves and nonslaveholding whites. Rice production used task labor rather than the gang system.[6] Each slave was given a specific task to do each day, on a set piece of land (usually a quarter of an acre), and once that task was completed the slave was officially finished with work for the day. As one observer commented, once a task had been finished, "his master feels no right to call on him."[7] The task system was a reciprocal arrangement whereby slaves who completed a task quickly and satisfactorily were free to engage in their own pursuits. Planters found this system to their advantage because it encouraged efficient and accurate work by bondspeople anxious for their free time at the end of the day. By far the most important consideration for some planters was that the work be completed satisfactorily. One planter declared that "we don't care what they do once their tasks are over—we lose sight of them till the next day."[8] Bondspeople also seem to have made the most of the opportunity to gain time for themselves. Basil Hall, while visiting a plantation on St. Simons Island in 1828, observed that "active hands get through their proportion generally by the middle of the day, others in two-thirds of the day, after which, they are left to the employ the balance."[9] In 1853 Richard Arnold informed Frederick Law Olmsted that "during a large part of the year all the industrious hands finish the regular tasks required of them by one or two o'clock in the afternoon and during the remainder of the day are at liberty, if they chose, to labor for themselves."[10]

Other sources confirm that many slaves completed their workload under the task system before sunset. Adam Hodgson believed that lowcountry slaves usually finished their work by midafternoon, a conclusion supported by Fanny Kemble, who spent six months on a coastal plantation in the late 1830s.[11] Not all observers agreed with this portrayal of the task system. Former slave John Brown denied that the task system gave any free time to slaves as "he never gets done till night-fall, and often cannot finish his task at all"; freedman Harry McMillan agreed, stating that lowcountry slaves worked from "daylight and continuing till 5 or 6 at night."[12] Nevertheless, most lowcountry slaves generally managed to get at least some free time at the end of the day. In addition, slaves were not required to work on Sundays, a right established and maintained in all the Georgia slave codes, nor were they usually forced to work at Christmas.[13] Some planters also gave their slaves holidays during the planting year, perhaps to reward hard work during the harvest or to allow slaves to finish planting their own crops.[14] Betty Wood uses the term the "right of free time" to define the ability of slaves to secure for themselves, first as a privilege, later as a customary right, their own time to spend as they pleased. Wood argues that once planters had granted this right, they found it hard to revoke and, for example, would offer free time in compensation for work on a Sunday.[15] Planters who hired slaves were expected to follow certain conventions allowing extra payment for special days. Allard Belin, a South Carolina planter, was informed by one hired slave that "New Year's day his mistress allowed him as his day & I must pay him for that day's work which I did."[16]

How slaves occupied themselves during their free time varied enormously. Some slaves, exhausted by daily toil in the hot sun, would have enjoyed the chance to rest from physical labor. Others, knowing that this time provided their only opportunity to mitigate the material harshness of their lives, undertook a wide variety of pursuits intended to improve the day-to-day existence of their families. Probably the most common occupation for those slaves motivated to work in their free time was in the gardens provided for them on most plantations.[17] Barbara Bodichon met one slave who hired land on which to grow maize and melons and, in response to her inquiry, he proudly declared that the profits were "for myself."[18] Charles Ball recalled that slave gardens were often situated on unprofitable and distant parts of the estate, yet the slaves traveled to toil there because the vegetables they grew supplemented their meager diets.[19]

Ball's observation reveals why some planters were perfectly willing for slaves to conduct these activities. If slaves grew food for their own consumption, the planter could reduce his ration provision for them, thus making each slave cheaper to keep. By making slaves responsible for their own diet, planters believed—or hoped—that they would become more dependent on the plantation. As one slave owner stated, "No Negro, with a well stocked poultry house, a small crop advancing, a canoe partly finished, or a few tubs unsold, all of which he calculates soon to enjoy, will ever run away."[20] This interpretation of the informal economy as a method of slave management is supported by some scholars, and it is certainly possible that it was a concept accepted by many planters.[21] Yet the obvious willingness of bondspeople to undertake responsibility for this part of their lives gives weight to the argument that many slaves enjoyed growing their own food. In a work system in which nearly everything was decided by their owners, slaves apparently grasped any chance for self-determination, however small. Ironically, while planters may have intended to offer a degree of economic freedom on their own terms, the determined actions of bondspeople effectively robbed them of that control.[22]

Vegetables were not the only commodity produced by slaves. Although several observers believed that "slaves rarely tasted flesh," too many accounts exist of slaves supplementing their diet through hunting or the raising of domestic livestock for their own consumption to be discounted. Georgia Bryan Conrad remembered that the slaves on her father's plantation "always kept chickens," and on Argyle Island the overseers were expressly denied the right to raise chickens to avoid disputes with slaves over ownership. William Bartram, while visiting Jonathan Bryan, observed a group of slaves returning from a neighboring swamp with "horse loads of wild pigeons" they had just caught. The lowcountry river system, where "oysters, fish, crab and shrimp were abundant and could be had for the taking," also provided many opportunities for slave fishermen to catch food. Charles Ball managed to secure substantial provisions for other slaves in this manner, ostensibly on his master's time. Indeed, Daniel Lord believed that the main occupation of lowcountry slaves in their free time was fishing.[23]

As well as foodstuffs, some slaves made handicrafts for their own use. On most plantations at least some slaves were trained in a craft such as carpentry, blacksmithing, or cooperage.[24] Planters reaped a twofold benefit from artisan slaves. First, odd jobs around the plantation could be completed by slaves rather than white artisans who charged fees.[25] Second, as former slave William Craft acknowledged, slaves with knowledge of a trade were potentially more valuable than field slaves, and many were taught a skill precisely for this reason.[26] On one St. Simons Island plantation visited by Basil Hall, thirteen of the fifty-seven slaves possessed an artisan skill.[27]

Slaves were often able to satisfy their immediate economic needs through hunting and craft work. But certain articles could not be grown or made and had to be purchased. Several masters encouraged their slaves to sell their produce to them in return for cash, credit, or goods, perhaps viewing it as a method of controlling the economic activities of their slaves. Henry Laurens and Thomas Ravenal both purchased items from their slaves, giving them clothes, foodstuffs and credit in return.[28] Such a relationship was apparently common: Georgia Conrad recalled that her father's slaves "constantly" sold produce to the family.[29] Richard Arnold declared that "his family had no other supply of poultry and eggs, except what was obtained by purchase from his own Negroes." Arnold himself acted as factor for his slaves, supplying them with goods in return for their produce or giving them credit notes, which in 1853 amounted to more than $500.[30] Some slaves were able to build up enough credit with their owner to purchase their own freedom.[31] Most bondspeople, of course, would not have had access to such large sums of money. Anna King never paid her slaves more than twenty-five cents per item for providing fowls and ducks to her St. Simons Island plantation.[32] Although planters could be a significant source of cash for slaves, it was mutually understood that if masters were unwilling to pay a fair price for produce, the slaves were "at liberty to carry their poultry to a better market if they can find one."[33] Some owners no doubt found it in their own interest to give high prices for goods to prevent their bondspeople from trading with white shopkeepers.[34]

Of course, many trading activities were conducted without the involvement of the elite. An obvious way for bondspeople to obtain items not produced domestically was to sell their surplus goods and produce for cash to a shopkeeper or trader, spending the proceeds in the lowcountry towns or at the local country store. Fanny Kemble noted that her slaves collected the Spanish moss that flourished in the humid air of Georgia, hanging in abundance from the branches of oak trees, and sold it to local shopkeepers. This moss was used as stuffing for mattresses and upholstery. One shopkeeper in Darien told Kemble that "in the course of a few years, he had paid the Negroes of this estate several thousand dollars for moss which is a very profitable article of traffic with them." [35] These economic transactions, which took place in towns and at country stores, were at the heart of the trading relationship between nonslaveholding whites and African Americans. Without the cooperation of white shopkeepers, tavern keepers, and boatmen, bondspeople would never have been able to purchase the range of goods they did, nor would they have had access to alcohol.[36] By trading with African Americans, white shopkeepers and peddlers frequently broke the law but, more significantly, they also contravened the racial norms and color barriers of the society in which they resided.[37]

Naturally, there were gender differences in the independent economic concerns of slaves, which to some extent dictated the nature of their economic encounters with nonslaveholders. On the plantations, bondsmen either hunted or made handicrafts, whereas bondswomen were expected to tend to the garden and perhaps engage in some cloth work. Bondsmen seldom did domestic chores, while bondswomen were "obliged to do all the household work, and to weed and cultivate the family garden." [38] Fanny Kemble, who was particularly aware of the role of women in Southern society, concluded that "the principal physical hardships . . . fall to the lot of the women." [39] Bondswomen did not, of course, have the same occupational opportunities as bondsmen, though Barbara Bodichon encountered one lowcountry bondswoman who was hired out in Savannah to a white washerwoman and returned to the plantation only to have children.[40] In her analysis of runaway slave advertisements in Georgia, Betty Wood has established that while male fugitives had many different occupations; female fugitives were described only as domestics or retailers. Indeed, most of the public market trading in the Savannah City Market was undertaken by women—just as it was throughout the Caribbean Islands and in West Africa.[41] Emily Burke observed that owners and bondswomen alike placed great importance on brightly colored clothing "to make her as conspicuous as possible that she may be successful in trade."[42]

The dominance of bondswomen in the city market is also shown by the number of licensed vendors who were slaves. In 1801, the Savannah City Council granted thirty licenses to slaves to work out, twenty-five of which went to bondswomen.[43] Civic authorities were aware of the gender divisions in slave occupations. During one attempt to control the independent economic activities of bondspeople in the city, the mayor specifically ordered the arrest of "all colored females, who may be selling in and outside the market, with or without badges when not authorised by the ordinance regulating badges."[44] Much trading among bondswomen relied on personal contacts, often to the exclusion of white people, rich and poor alike. This is not to say that white people did not purchase at the market. The City Council itself, when trying to regulate Sunday trading in 1829, acknowledged that it was customary for "the poorer class of white persons who generally receive their wages in the evening of Saturday [to] . . . require a short time on Sunday morning to preserve the usual food for their families."[45] Much of the best farm produce was apparently sold before the Sunday market officially opened, and attempts by the City Council to control it met with only limited success.[46] In 1814 the Chatham County Grand Jury presented slave vendors for "forestalling in purchasing large quantities of eggs, poultry, etc. and vending them at a higher rate to the inhabitants."[47] The Grand Jury's plea that the City Council prevent this activity was not heeded. Four years later, the Grand Jury again presented "colored and black women" who "monopolise in divers ways, many of the necessaries of life, which are brought to our market, by which the price is greatly enhanced, and the poor inhabitants of our city, proportionately distressed."[48] The independent economic role of bondswomen evidently caused some concern to Savannahians, but probably more disquiet was engendered by the free time activities of urban bondsmen.

Bondsmen often journeyed to Savannah with their wives, bringing produce to town to be sold, a journey also undertaken by many poor white families coming to the city to trade.[49] Bristol, a slave of James Martin Gibbons, transported a wide variety of garden vegetables to Savannah during several weeks in April and May 1786, during which time he could hire himself out for portage and carting work and purchase goods for himself and his family.[50] African Americans dominated the transportation of goods up and down the bluff and through the streets of Savannah, and had their economic ambitions ended there, they would probably have caused little controversy.[51] Some slaves, however, were highly skilled painters, butchers, barbers, bricklayers, and plasterers.[52] One slave, described as a "master craftsman," was hired illegally by Joseph Habersham, earning the latter a $5 fine.[53] In 1848 the Savannah census reported that 126 enslaved tradesmen were registered as working in the city; doubtless they were joined by numerous unregistered colleagues.[54] Male slaves living in urban areas could be hired out by their owners for a weekly $3 fee.[55] Such hiring arrangements were sometimes left to the discretion of the slave, and self-hire in Savannah and Darien created many opportunities for bondspeople to forge social and economic relationships of which their owners would have disapproved.

For many urban bondspeople self-hire was an obvious step toward economic independence. Slave hire, with the appropriate ticket or badge from the owner or employer, had existed for as long as slavery had been permitted in Georgia.[56] Yet in Savannah the hiring of slaves was not closely regulated until the last years of the colonial government. In 1774 the annual cost of a badge from royal officials was set at ten shillings. Owners who allowed their slaves to work out without badges would be fined ten shillings for each offense; for those hiring a slave without a badge the fine was five shillings.[57] Slaves who were to be hired out were to go to the public market every morning to accept whatever commission came their way. Standard rates were established for the daily hire of slaves, depending on weight of load, distance covered, and length of time involved. This law remained substantially the same until 1790, at which time the newly incorporated City Council found it necessary to differentiate between slaves engaged in artisan work and those doing manual labor.[58] Badges for slave artisans cost twenty shillings, compared with ten shillings for slave carters and seven shillings and sixpence for slave porters, effectively recognizing that the occupations of some urban bondspeople were becoming more diverse. Further refinements to the badge regulations in the 1850s saw rates tiered among skilled, semiskilled and unskilled slaves and a new distinction between city slaves and country slaves, with the latter paying double for the privilege of hiring themselves in the city.[59]

This ordinance and others that both preceded and followed it increased the fines for employing slaves who had no badges. The original five-shilling fine stipulated in 1774 was doubled to ten shillings in 1787, doubled again to twenty shillings in 1790, and doubled again to forty shillings in 1792. By 1857 those who allowed their slaves to be hired without badges and those who hired them were liable for $50 fines, half of which went to the informant. The reason for continually increasing these fines must have been that those who hired slaves illegally were not discouraged by the fines already in place. In other words, slave hire was profitable for both whites and blacks.[60]

The regulations stipulated between 1774 and 1792 considerably tightened the rules governing slave hire in Georgia. Between 1755 and 1774, slaves were allowed to hire themselves out providing they had their owner's ticket and did not keep the proceeds from the work for themselves.[61] Yet, despite the new regulations, abuses of this system were rife by the early nineteenth century. Owners avoided purchasing badges for their slaves, while slaves kept as much of their wages as they dared for themselves. James Silk Buckingham observed that several African Americans in Savannah had progressed so well with their trades that they "had acquired property" and could be termed "rich."[62] William Grimes and Charles Ball each testified that the $3 weekly fee usually demanded by masters did not consume all the wages earned by bondspeople in Savannah.[63] After the Civil War, the Southern Claims Commission dealt with many suits from lowcountry slaves, most of which were for property worth several hundred dollars destroyed during Sherman's march to the sea. Usually this property had been obtained through self-hire as draymen, carpenters, and hucksters; one bondswoman even operated a boardinghouse.[64] Adam Hodgson believed that owners permitted hired slaves to keep any money earned above the stipulated weekly rate as an incentive to work hard.[65] Dimmock Charlton, working as a stevedore in Savannah, earned enough by self-hire to purchase his freedom.[66] Occasionally the City Council clamped down on owners who did not buy badges and on nonslaveholders who employed slaves without their owner's permission.[67] But the problem of the self-hire of slaves was probably too big to be controlled by the legal system. Neither masters nor bondspeople had an incentive to curtail it. Self-hire gave masters a steady income without any of the responsibilities of caring for the slave, and it provided bondspeople with opportunities for self-advancement and greater control over their own lives than they could have secured on the plantations or as domestics.[68]

Like many other bondspeople, Charles Ball was not insensible to the attractions of self-hire. In 1807, while in Savannah, he observed "many black men, who were slaves, but who yet acted as freemen so far, that they went out to work where and with whom they pleased, received their own wages, and provided the means of their own subsistence."[69] The same was true in Charleston, where slaves could hire their own time without their master's knowledge and presumably keep the proceeds. In 1772, David Rhind publicly warned "cabinet-makers, house-carpenters, and joiners" not to employ his slave York without his prior approval.[70] Obviously York was accustomed to hiring out his own time, thus gaining a degree of freedom over his working life usually denied him. It is also clear, however, that the system of self-hire permitted many fugitive slaves to earn an illicit living in Savannah. The collusion of nonslaveholding white people in employing African Americans who were obviously escaped slaves is a prime example of a biracial alliance that worked to undermine the authority of the elite.[71]

The widespread hire of slaves naturally involved them in contact with nonslaveholders. Outside of Savannah, nonslaveholding farmers occasionally paid local slaves to work for them on a Sunday, especially if they were unable to afford the capital outlay to purchase a slave. John Brown knew one local poor white man, John Morgan, who hired both races.[72] Occasionally overseers hired the slaves on their plantations to cultivate their own fields on Sundays. Charles Ball recalled that twenty of his fellow slaves were paid "fifty cents each" to do so.[73] Similar hiring arrangements occurred in urban areas. Reuben King, who was involved in a variety of artisan trades, hired "a Negro boy to roll durt [sic]" on Sunday, September 19, 1802.[74] Planters were often willing to hire some of their slaves to locals. At Brampton plantation, slave hire brought in nearly 15 percent of the total yearly income.[75] The widespread hire of slaves on Sundays permitted nonslaveholding whites to obtain the benefits of extra labor and the qualified status of master—qualified because on Sundays slaves worked voluntarily and could refuse to work if they so chose. The power relationship between nonslaveholding whites and hired slaves thus rested not on coercion but on contract: on Sundays bondspeople were remunerated for their labor, just as white artisans and laborers usually were. The fundamental difference between free and bond labor, and, indeed, between white and black—the ability to choose their employer, how often they worked, and on what terms—disappeared for one day in the week. For the other six days nonslaveholding whites had to rely on their own and their families' labor. As one observer put it, nonslaveholders were their own "shoemaker, tanner, tailor, carpenter, brazier and, in fact everything else."[76]

Slaves were not the only African Americans who came into economic contact and competition with nonslaveholding whites. The relatively large numbers of free people of color in Savannah pursued a wide variety of jobs and occupations. In 1828 the register of free black people for Chatham County listed 246 individuals, and for 178 of them occupations were listed.[77] There was a clear gender division of work, with free black women mainly pursuing retailing, domestic, washing, or seamstressing work and free black men doing a variety of handicraft jobs.[78] Thirty years later, in 1860, the federal census showed that free black men continued to follow a variety of trades, but free black women specialized in a small number of occupations.[79] In contrast to all other lowcountry counties, Chatham County had a clear female majority in its free black community.[80] Perhaps the urban work environment was particularly suited to the flexibility of women, while men found it difficult to prosper in competition with white and slave artisans. No doubt some of these free black workers would have come into contact with slaves coming to town to trade produce and with permanently resident urban slaves. For example, ten free black women listed their occupation in 1817 as "huckster"— selling goods on the streets, in direct competition with the licensed slave vendors.[81] By 1860 no free black women were registered as vendors of small wares, signifying either that any trading activity was done unofficially or that slave retailers had driven them out of business.[82] A slightly different pattern emerges from Camden County in 1819. The particular circumstances of the county, with its rural character and dependence on maritime industries, is reflected in free black occupations. More than a third of working female free African Americans were laborers, and a further fifth were house servants. Male occupations were more diverse, encompassing laboring, artisan work, and maritime professions, and one man was described as a merchant.[83]

The variety of trades pursued by both free and enslaved African Americans brought them into competition with white artisans. In the early colonial period mechanics had increasingly turned to the law to protect them from what they perceived as the unfair competition of slaves. The slave regulations imposed by the Trustees in 1750, which had prevented bondspeople from working in most trades, were supplanted in 1755 with a new slave code based on that of South Carolina.[84] This new code placed some restrictions on the employment of slaves in artisan trades, confining them to carting, porting, and fishing but effectively ended the privileges artisans had enjoyed for the previous five years.[85] Planters of course found that to train their own slave craftsmen as sawyers, coopers, and carpenters rather than employing white mechanics was "very lucrative" and increased plantation profits.[86]

Georgian artisans were not content merely to accept this as a fait accompli. On January 28, 1758, a law was proposed to the provincial legislature to "prevent Negro slaves from working at handicraft trades in the several towns within this province."[87] It is not known who proposed this law, but it is likely that artisans in Savannah combined to put forward a bill that directly addressed their economic concerns. Ten days later the bill was introduced into the Lower House of Assembly and passed its second reading; two days later it passed its third reading and was sent to the Upper House for consideration.[88]

On February 11, 1758, the Upper House took up the "Act to encourage white tradesmen" and ordered that a copy of the bill be published.[89] The publication of the bill brought a rapid response from interested parties. Local merchants, most notably Edmund Tannat, Alexander Wylly, and Lewis Johnson, argued that the premise of the bill was "specious."[90] They complained that it was motivated by "the greediness and insatiable thirst after gain of a few tradesmen of the town of Savannah" and argued that the high wages permitted under the bill would reduce the amount of work available and consequently discourage, rather than encourage, white immigration. In addition, the law would deprive slaveholders of the privileges granted in every other British colony—namely the right to use their property in whatever manner they saw fit.[91]

Local artisans in Savannah were not prepared to let planters have their say unchallenged. In a corresponding petition, an unspecified number of "inhabitants, freeholders and handycraft tradesmen" in Savannah described the bill as "a most salutary and beneficial law [which] would greatly tend to the further increase and more advantageous settlement" of Georgia. Knowing that the bill would be fiercely debated in the legislature, the tradesmen requested that they be heard "before this honourable house in support of the said bill."[92] Three days later both the merchants and the tradesmen got their chance to put their case to the legislature, raising unspecified issues that were debated throughout the day.[93] A week later the Upper House again considered the bill, inserting a clause that those who already owned slaves with a trade should be allowed to continue to use them, "for their own use and benefit only."[94] When the bill finally came for its third reading, there was a last-minute attempt to ruin it by exempting all slaves who had lived in Georgia for six months, but this proviso was defeated, and the bill was passed.[95] In a free conference of the two houses of the legislature, agreement was reached on which amendments to the bill should stay, though these are not recorded, and the bill was forwarded to the governor, Henry Ellis, who had already expressed his belief that the law would be "attended with public utility."[96]

The new law stated that after September 13, 1758, it would be illegal to employ a slave in Savannah, Augusta, Frederica, or Ebenezer in a handicraft trade, on pain of a ten shilling fine for every offense. But the final form of the bill, which was signed by the governor on March 15, 1758, was not entirely to the original wishes of white artisans.[97] Unlike the 1750 act, which merely prevented slaves from undertaking artisan work, the 1758 act to encourage white settlement prevented white artisans from exceeding stipulated rates set by council-appointed commissioners for their goods and services. Thus while white artisans were reserved the right of first refusal at a job, planters and merchants were allowed to employ any slave they chose if, after advertising for three days, they were unable to find a white person to employ at the set rate. Moreover, by limiting the act to the larger towns in Georgia, lawmakers were recognizing the impracticality of trying to enforce a law requiring rural planters not to use their own trained slaves if they desired. Legislators evidently intended to respect the power of masters over their slaves. Thus a law that was supposed to restrict the competition white artisans experienced from slaves exempted slaves who had been trained in a profession for more than a year and placed no restrictions on slave hire. With such limitations, this law could have had only a limited impact. Of course, measures to encourage white artisans to settle in Georgia helped to ease fears concerning the exposed nature of the colony after the outbreak of the French and Indian War in 1754. Yet the ability of mechanics to persuade the colonial assembly to pass a measure so contrary to the interests of planters is a testament both to their political influence in the 1750s and to their dedicated pursuit of a class issue.

The act of 1758 was to be in effect for seven years, but there is no record of its renewal in 1765 or later. The failure to renew the 1758 act can perhaps be explained by the changing political situation in North America. Victory over the French and the Spanish in 1763 had effectively ended the threat of invasion, thus obviating one of the main reasons for attracting poor white people and tradesmen into Georgia, namely, the need to man numerous forts in the remoter areas of the colony. Another possible reason for the ending of legal support for white artisans was the consolidation of political and legislative power in the hands of the planter elite. Planters who had been unable to prevent the passage of the 1758 act were now able to ensure its lapsing. To prevent a shortage of skilled labor, however, legislation was introduced in the year the 1758 act lapsed to encourage the immigration of people "male and female, of what nation or color soever being born of free parents."[98] The granting to free blacks, Indians, and foreigners of the same rights of settlement enjoyed by white working people forever broke the white monopoly on free labor.[99] By ending the stranglehold of white mechanics, members of the elite made their skilled slaves more valuable. James Habersham ruefully noted that though planters disliked having their bondspeople evangelized, most trained them to be "ingenious mechanicks, [as] making them good tradesmen is immediately profitable."[100] Of course, any restriction on the use of slaves violated the sanctity of the relationship between master and slave. The ending of legal protection for white mechanics and the encouragement given to free blacks, combined with the lack of enthusiasm for manufacturing in the colony, demonstrated that white artisans could expect their livelihoods to remain under constant threat from African American competition.

The situation did not improve for white artisans after the Revolution. Indeed, if anything, the competition from slaves and free blacks actually intensified. Increasing numbers of bondspeople were trained in a trade, were hired out, or were allowed to work out. The number of fines levied by the City Council of Savannah for letting a slave work out without a badge tripled in the first decade of the nineteenth century in comparison with the last decade of the eighteenth century.[101] The expanding free black population in lowcountry Georgia, swollen by natural increase as much as by immigration from places such as San Domingo, further threatened the economic subsistence of white workers. Between 1790 and 1860, the free black population grew at twice the rate of the enslaved population of the lowcountry, though the absolute numbers remained small.[102]

The constant struggle for economic supremacy between white workers and African Americans, both slave and free, therefore became a recurrent theme in the early national lowcountry. Because white mechanics had only limited employment opportunities, their precarious financial position made them extremely vulnerable. In the day-to-day life of lowcountry towns and cities, white and black laborers were in constant economic competition. White laborers were usually more expensive to hire than their African American competitors, and some lowcountry mechanics thought that lowcountry planters were more willing to employ free blacks than white artisans because the fees for hiring them were lower. Such a policy would lead to the elimination of white workers as a class because the free black artisan "has very often no family to support, his wife and children are slaves. He lives on the promises of their owner, he has no house rent to pay, no clothing or food but his own to purchase, his expenses are almost nothing, and he can therefore labor for almost nothing."[103] Free African Americans in the lowcountry apparently could undercut some of their white competitors, though, as one historian has noted, free blacks were sometimes considerably more skilled than their white competitors.[104]

Competition from slaves also aroused the ire of white artisans. Charleston mechanics protested about the incursions African American artisans were making into the business of white workers both "as contractors and [as] masters" and noted that tight legal restrictions on the pursuits open to African Americans limited their employments to ones that directly clashed with white artisans.[105] Somewhat radically, these artisans argued that if slaves or free African Americans had the capacity to master a difficult mechanical trade, they also surely had the capacity to become shopkeepers and merchants—trades to which they were denied access.[106]

Naturally, these artisans were not advocating the relaxation of laws to permit African Americans greater economic freedom and flexibility; rather, they sought to foster a racial affinity with the elite. African Americans, whether slave or free, were barred from most elite professional occupations, most notably mercantile, medical, and legal positions.[107] By seeking job protection similar to that routinely offered to the elite, mechanics were asserting what they believed to be their rights as independent white men, regardless of social status. The artisans thought it was perfectly logical for merchants, lawyers, doctors, and clerks not to have to face competition from African Americans, but neither should they. Rather ominously it was supposed that the only reason for the current discrepancy was that "the law and the law-giver intend to declare the mechanic is not the equal of the merchant, the lawyer, the doctor, the wharfinger, the tradesman, or the shopkeeper." Therefore, this petition for redress included a warning that continued discrimination would "tax the loyalty of the working poor man . . . to the institution which he is educated to defend, and in defence of which he is always the foremost."[108]

These petitions were, in effect, demanding that mechanics be given the privileges of race enjoyed by other white people. By forcing white artisans into an economic dependency similar to that usually experienced by African Americans, the elite were perceived to be drawing a parallel between the social status of free and slave and therefore between white and black working people. As white mechanics noted in 1811, the economic prosperity of black mechanics weakened the social distinctions between the races so much that some African Americans attained an "equality of skin" with white artisans.[109] To these artisans, their race clearly and unambiguously differentiated them from African Americans. They perceived that their superior status was under threat from economic competition and needed to be defended.

Many artisans suspected that free and slave African American artisans obtained an unfair advantage because "by undertaking [work] for very little more than the materials would cost . . . it is evident the stuff they work with cannot be honestly acquired."[110] Grand juries sympathized with the plight of urban artisans, noting that the employment of slaves in "various handicraft trades" injured the "poor mechanics of this city."[111] Mechanics also highlighted the role of bondswomen as employers by proxy. It was apparently common practice for "the most opulent inhabitants of Charleston, when they have any work to be done . . . not [to] send it themselves, but leave it to their domestics to employ what workmen they please; it universally happens that those domestics prefer men of their own color and condition; and as to a greatness of business thus continually passing through their hands, the black mechanics enjoy as complete a monopoly, as if it were secured to them by law."[112] Indeed, the racial bonds that seemingly united African Americans in this respect were precisely those demanded from the elite by white artisans. It would become clear, however, that members of the white elite were far more interested in economic than in racial criteria for employment.

White mechanics throughout the lowcountry suspected, with some justification, that the white elite—the planters and lawmakers—had no desire to assist them. On one occasion the elite defended the rights of African Americans to undertake mechanical work, lauding their "industry, sobriety, and irreproachable conduct."[113] Free African Americans were apparently "indispensable" workers, who would labor during the hot summer months, unlike their white counterparts, who were often perceived to be unreliable, sometimes leaving a job half finished. The geographic immobility of most free African Americans ensured that they could not afford to be unreliable employees.

In Savannah the greatest conflict between white artisans and African Americans arose over the retailing of meat. In 1822 several white butchers petitioned the City Council to limit the competition they experienced from enslaved and free African American butchers. This petition not only cited the economic hardship of white butchers but reminded the City Council that much of the meat sold by bondspeople was likely to have been stolen. In a calculated attempt to appeal to the sensibilities of the elite, the butchers also claimed that many of the slaves retailing meat in the market were keeping the profits for themselves instead of turning the money over to their owners. The committee appointed to investigate the butchers' petition recommended that an ordinance be introduced to curb the market activities of free blacks and, especially, to prevent African Americans from retailing meat. This first reading was passed, but at the second reading two weeks later, Alderman Davis managed to strike out the third and fourth sections of the ordinance and then postpone further debate on the measure. It was never reconsidered.[114]

The white butchers' problem was highlighted in a letter to the *Savannah Republican* in 1820 in which the correspondent counted twenty-two African American men retailing meat in the market, most of which, he claimed, had been stolen "from the respectable inhabitants of the city." According to this author, many of these retailers had previously been "following different grades of profession, particularly that of dray-men, coopers etc.," but the easy profitability of the meat trade and the fact that all work was over by 9 A.M. meant that they had more time and money "to indulge themselves in every species of gambling, drunkenness etc." Yet even this writer distinguished between "trustworthy" free black butchers of long standing, such as Joshua Bourke and Adam Whitfield, and those seeking quick profits, suggesting that white butchers would find it almost impossible to stop all African Americans from selling meat.[115]

White butchers in Savannah tried again in 1825, 1829, and 1842 to bar African Americans from the meat trade, with similar results. Even though they described the competition they experienced from African Americans as "a very great and evil grievance," all of the butchers' petitions were eventually shelved. In 1842 the council's decision was apparently influenced by a counterpetition from "many citizens," unfortunately unnamed, who remonstrated against the passage of any ordinance that would restrict the rights of African Americans to sell meat. With secession looming, white butchers tried one final time to prevent African

Americans from selling meat, but the City Council remained true to its historic stance, on this occasion believing that white butchers would take "great advantage" of any monopoly granted them.[116]

Competition between white and black workers continued into the late antebellum period. In the 1850s African Americans were used as scab labor to end strikes initiated by white workers. One such strike in 1856 by several hundred white men who loaded and unloaded ships at the city wharves resulted in their sacking and the employment of African Americans in their place.[117] On other occasions white workers were simply replaced by slaves on hire to lower costs.[118] Increasingly white mechanics in the late antebellum lowcountry attempted to assert what they saw as racial privileges. In 1851 Savannah mechanics met to send delegates to a state convention in Atlanta. Their stated aim was to try to limit the employment of African Americans in artisan trades, though they hotly denied charges of abolitionism. At the heart of their action was the concern that if whites worked alongside African Americans, as they did in many Savannah businesses, "either one must be elevated or the other degraded by this proximity." Clearly preserving their distinctiveness in more than just racial terms was perceived as vitally important by most Savannah mechanics.[119]

White women also faced competition from African Americans. White female domestics, for example, sometimes struggled to find work in a city like Savannah, where many domestic jobs were filled by bondswomen. House servants often worked long hours, and it was no doubt easier for owners to use older female slaves, who were no longer productive in the fields, rather than pay white women. One visitor to Butler's Point remarked on Fanny Kemble's "good fortune in having a white woman with my children." Such a sight was something of a rarity in the South by 1838.[120] Even those who hired rather than purchased domestics frequently employed African Americans. William Curry negotiated with "black Betty" to cook for him for a weekly wage.[121] Charles Cotton was clearly an exception in preferring a white housekeeper to an African American, and even he recognized that this choice incurred "further heavy expense." [122] By 1860 more than a thousand white women competed with a similar number of bondswomen and about two hundred free black women for a variety of skilled and unskilled jobs in Savannah. A detailed analysis of female occupations shows that social status for working women in Southern society depended as much on age, nativity, and family status as on race.[123]

Although the economic competition of African Americans could engender antagonistic responses from mechanics and artisans concerned both with their own economic prospects and the erosion of their racial privileges, not all nonslaveholding whites shared these sentiments. Indeed, nonslaveholding whites who had profitable economic contacts with slaves, such as shopkeepers and peddlers, keenly defended the economic enterprise of slaves in the face of stiff elite opposition. The government of Georgia had attempted to exercise control over the trading activities of slaves from the inception of slavery in the colony in 1750, most specifically what and to whom they sold, fearful of the consequences to their own security if African Americans were permitted too much freedom to travel and form independent social relations. The slave code of 1755 limited slaves to trading garden produce, fruit, and fish.[124] Yet slaves who possessed tickets from their owners were not limited in what they could trade, providing a loophole for slaves and white traders alike. Tickets giving permission to trade could be, and often were, forged and used as proof that trade between slaves and others was legitimate.

The ticket system, in use throughout the Georgia and South Carolina lowcountry, was evidently not perfect. Many owners either failed to write tickets or to buy badges for their slaves. White shopkeepers were certainly not overly concerned that slaves lacked the proper documentation to trade, knowing that prosecutions were unlikely to result in a hefty fine. Between 1790, when civic government was first instituted in Savannah, and 1848, when records of fines ceased to be noted in the council minutes, the City Council, acting as the Mayor's Court, handed down more than fifteen hundred fines to nearly nine hundred individuals convicted of violating the trading ordinances.[125] The offenses included retailing liquor without a license, keeping a shop open after official hours, trading with slaves, and, after 1829, violating the prohibition against trading on Sunday.[126] These records probably include only a portion of those who were dealing with bondspeople illegally. William Craft believed that prosecutions of white shopkeepers would be difficult to achieve because slave testimony was inadmissible in court, thus barring the only witnesses.[127] The law preventing African Americans from bearing witness against a white person in the South worked against elite interests in these cases. Frederick Law Olmsted realized the irony that "the law which prevents the reception of Negro evidence in courts, here strikes back with a most annoying force upon the dominant power itself."[128]

In an attempt to limit economic interaction between the white shop-keepers and bondspeople in Savannah, the market for slaves' produce was customarily held on a Sunday, the only day of the week when all white businesses were supposed to be shut. Some prominent white people were unhappy even with the existence of this Sunday market, believing it gave slaves too much freedom.[129] The 1762 act for "keeping holy the Lord's day" imposed a ten-shilling fine on any person who worked in any business on Sunday. The act specifically named tippling houses and taverns and made innkeepers liable to a five-shilling fine for every customer found on their premises. The only exceptions to this act permit-ted the retailing of fresh fish and milk before nine o'clock and after four o'clock.[130]

White shopkeepers regularly disregarded these Sunday trading regu-lations. As early as 1766 the Grand Jury highlighted "that mischievous kind of commerce too frequently carried on by petty shopkeepers on Sun-days with Negroes."[131] Subsequent Grand Jury presentments frequently mentioned the Sunday trading activities of African Americans and white shopkeepers.[132] Reuben King stated that Sunday was the busiest day of the week at his store in Darien, where he would spend "all day tradeing with Negroes."[133] Evening trading also aroused the ire of grand juries. Just as Sunday was the only day when slaves from plantations from sev-eral miles around Savannah, Darien, and Sunbury could make the jour-ney into the towns, evenings were the only time when slaves in the im-mediate proximity of a town could sell their produce.

Evening trading at "unseasonable hours" was thus a point of conflict between shopkeepers and the elite.[134] Slaves coming into town in the hours of darkness were a perceived threat to the peace and security of the city. The "idle and dissolute" slaves in and around Savannah on weekday evenings and all day Sunday altered the racial balance of Savan-nah from relative equality to black majority. The encouragement given to these slaves by white shopkeepers thus amounted to a rejection of the authority of the elite. Successive pieces of legislation attempted to tackle the problem of trading with slaves first by limiting the range and number of goods to which slaves had access and then by trying to prevent white shopkeepers from violating regulatory standards to trade out of officially sanctioned hours or purchasing illicit goods. In 1786 trading with slaves earned a ten-pound fine, which was increased just two years later to fifty pounds.[135] By 1818 white people convicted of trading with slaves could receive a $500 fine and up to six months in jail.[136] Courts were willing both to convict and imprison those who were intentionally purchasing items from slaves without tickets, especially if the commodity traded was a crop such as cotton, corn, or rice. In 1826 Elizabeth Dobson received a $100 fine and a thirty-day prison term for buying rice from a slave named Wallace, though the fine was later remitted "on petition of a number of respectable citizens." [137]

Rural storekeepers also dealt with slaves from the plantations who lived too far from a town to be able to market their produce there. These stores often monopolized the local market in household goods and food-stuffs.[138] Planters' efforts to prevent their slaves visiting and trading at these stores usually failed.[139] For slaves living on plantations where either necessity or choice dictated that trading with owners was not possible, these stores were the only source of goods that could not be produced at home. On Charles Ball's plantation, the local store was one of the few options open to slaves wanting to trade. For a white person and an African American to establish and maintain a relationship that contravened the law, the parties involved had to trust each other. That such trust existed is revealed in the details of an encounter between Ball and a passing boatman. In the contract negotiations, determined by the white man, one hundred pounds of bacon were sold to Ball in return for three hundred shad. Ball knew that he was not getting the full value of the fish, but he recognized and accepted the fact that the boatman "ran the hazard of being prosecuted for dealing with slaves." Yet the boatman clearly wished to maintain regular contact with his new criminal partner, furtively suggesting that the trading relationship be renewed in a fortnight's time when he was next down on the river. This man hoped that in future Ball could supply him with cotton (presumably stolen), stating he would give him half the going rate in Charleston for it. Manifestly, a potential 50 percent profit margin was worth the relatively small risk of prosecution for this boatman. In a parting shot, the boatman told Ball to "take care and do not betray yourself." [140] To this boatman, trading in stolen goods with African Americans was an acceptable method of socioeconomic advancement, despite its wider political significance. The fact that trading with African Americans empowered them was evidently less important than the maintenance of financial and political independence in a slave society.

Ball and the other slaves knew that white shopkeepers cared little whether they had their owner's or overseer's consent to trade. He believed, with some justification, that the income brought in by slaves was very important for storekeepers as much for the type of payment as for the amount. According to him, "storekeepers are always ready to accommodate the slaves, who pay cash, whilst the white people require credit."[141] The financial argument, of course, goes to the heart of the trading relationship between nonslaveholding whites and African Americans. The cash economy was limited in the lowcountry. Rural areas throughout South Carolina and Georgia still depended on barter in the nineteenth century. Daniel Turner estimated that even rich planters had less than a hundred dollars in cash at any one time.[142] Small farmers had ready money only immediately after the sale of the harvest in late summer. Paying off debts to local shopkeepers was probably not the most pressing call on their limited finances.[143] His continual problems collecting debts led Reuben King to resolve to "trust no person in this years book account," as he had previously been duped by "vagabonds that git thare living by swindling."[144]

Bondspeople who could obtain small but regular amounts of cash tended to spend it on the goods sold in these stores, "tobacco, clothes, and other articles of use or luxury."[145] Fredericka Bremer stated that slaves spent their money on "treacle or molasses (of which they are very fond), biscuits, and other eatables."[146] Jeremiah Evarts, however, said that "everything which they can carry to market, is sold for liquor."[147] Betty Wood pointed out that in 1800 the nine thousand lowcountry slaves could each spend up to a dollar a week in shops in and around Savannah.[148] Therefore, the ability of large numbers of bondspeople to supply small amounts of cash all year-round was a highly prized, indeed vital, contribution both to the functioning of the capitalist market economy and to the individual finances of lowcountry shopkeepers.

In areas where shopkeepers were few and far between or where slaves did not believe they were obtaining the best prices for their goods, rural nonslaveholding farmers sometimes conducted trade with slaves. Stolen goods were probably more difficult to resell from an official store, where a planter might well come looking for goods missing from the plantation. Neighboring poor white farmers were willing to purchase goods from slaves because, if questioned, they could plausibly claim ownership of farm goods or produce. Nevertheless, planters often suspected poor farmers of being involved in trading in stolen goods with slaves and dealt with them in an appropriate manner. One such poor white man, who lived in a hut three miles from Charles Ball's plantation, was suspected of dealing with slaves over a number of years. Eventually local planters, together with their overseers, joined forces to search the man's hut, afterward burning it to the ground.[149]

Much of the time of lowcountry superior courts outside Savannah was taken up with cases of whites trading illegally with slaves. In Liberty County, for example, similar problems of evidence and witnesses to those seen in the city resulted in few convictions. Even those convicted knew they would escape with little more than a slap on the wrist. William Thompson of Walthourville was fined only $10 for "furnishing ardent spirits to a negro without a pass," and the $30 Zachariah Johns was fined after conviction for "trading with a slave without permit" was not an effective deterrent.[150]

The inability of the court system to control illegal trading forced planters to take matters into their own hands. The Savannah River Anti–Slave Traffick Association was formed in November 1846 to combat "the extensive and growing traffick unlawfully carried on with slaves by white persons and chiefly by retailers of spirituous liquors." According to lowcountry planters, slaves were becoming unmanageable and whereas "formerly slaves were essentially members of the family to which they belonged . . . now masters and slaves are beginning to look upon each other as natural enemies." In this sense trading with slaves struck at the heart of owner-slave relations and challenged the very fabric of Southern society. Savannah River planters did not acknowledge that many of the goods traded to shopkeepers were in fact the product of African American ingenuity and industry, preferring to believe that all trade goods were stolen. While some goods were no doubt purloined for sale, the fact that owners believed that all trade goods were stolen is more an example of their disbelief that slaves could be commercially aware than a reflection of reality.

While attacking the "Negro-trafficker" whose activities undermined the traditional patterns of race subordination, planters were at pains to deny that their association was "a combination to oppress the poor." Indeed, planters went so far as to encourage a racial solidarity with nonslaveholders, claiming that slaves stole from nonslaveholders and slaveholders alike, with a disproportionate impact on the poor. The regulations adopted by the association, though designed to bring "Negro-traffickers" to justice, were more concerned with limiting the independent economic activities of slaves. The association resolved to prevent slaves from hiring their own time and to purchase themselves, at market rates, any produce the slaves had to sell. This was a realistic assessment of their ability to halt the supply of goods sold by slaves, though it had little chance of reducing the demand from the shopkeepers.[151]

Frederick Law Olmsted recognized the futility of such arrangements. One such association near Savannah had managed to bring "several offenders to trial, but as it was a penitentiary offence, the culprit would spare no pains or expenses to spare himself from it, and it was almost impossible, in a community constituted as theirs was, to find a jury that would convict."[152] Nonslaveholders, by acting as jurymen, were thus able to impose their own social ethic on the wider community. Unable to eliminate "Negro-traffickers" through prosecutions, some planters perhaps turned to extralegal actions such as framing those suspected of illicit trading in order to reassert their control over slaves.[153]

Trading with another man's slave seems to have been viewed as a personal insult by planters. Their often violent responses, combined with a willingness to prosecute those who violated the sanctity of the master-slave relationship, reveals to some extent a hatred of those who traded with slaves. Not only was trading with a slave often a criminal act, it also undermined owners' household relations with their "family"—white and black. In 1784 a local Georgetown justice, Peter Horry, had to deal with a disgruntled slave owner, John McCartey, who proclaimed that John Car had been trading with his slaves without his permission.[154] To add insult to injury, when confronted, Car had struck McCartey with a stick. McCartey had Car arrested and bound over to keep the peace, but Car managed to escape, and he presumably evaded justice.[155] Planters of a less violent nature could bring civil prosecutions against those they believed to be trading with their slaves. Jacob Rice brought one such case against John J. Eiffort in 1815, though the outcome of the suit is not known.[156]

The one commodity which slaves were believed to desire the most, and the one which many planters went to the greatest lengths to deny them, was alcohol. The provision of alcohol to slaves was banned by the 1755 slave code, on pain of a twenty-shilling fine for offenders.[157] This regulation was shown to be "ineffectual" in the tavern law of 1757, which admitted that taverns and tippling houses were the constant resort of "lewd idle & disorderly people . . . servants and slaves."[158] This law stipulated a three-pound fee for liquor licenses and prohibited artisans or tradesmen from selling alcohol to the negligence of their usual trade. While the 1757 law reaffirmed the ban on selling alcohol to slaves, it apparently did little to limit the consumption of liquor by slaves in the twenty-eight licensed, and numerous unlicensed, dramshops in colonial Georgia by the mid-1760s. By 1768, fines had been increased to five pounds for retailing liquor to slaves, with the added threat of a three-month jail term for repeat offenders.[159]

The willingness of some planters to pay African Americans with liquor complicated attempts by the authorities to control shopkeepers' trade in alcohol. Peter Gaillard, for example, paid black carpenters with demijohns of rum while they worked for him in 1804.[160] It is not known whether these carpenters were bondspeople or free blacks, but they worked alongside white carpenters, who were also paid in rum. Even the Savannah City Council was not totally blameless in the provision of alcohol to African Americans. In 1796 the city treasurer settled the accounts of Humphry Murphy and Ebenezer Balwin "for rum supplied the Negroes working on the town & common."[161] Perhaps it was standard practice to reward bondspeople for their work on public facilities in this way, but all attempts to prevent shopkeepers from selling alcohol to slaves would have seemed hypocritical thereafter.

In the temperance fervor that swept the South in the late antebellum era, the consumption of liquor by African Americans gained further condemnation. A heated exchange of letters published in the *McIntosh County Herald* in 1839 illustrates the divisions caused by temperance in lowcountry society. Those supporting temperance specifically stated that grogshops spread "the cause of inebriation among our negroes" and led to the "subversion of good order." Other correspondents claimed that those advocating temperance were "fanatics" trying to subvert republican democracy. Indeed, one author derided the women leading the temperance cause, stating that "it is more fitting for them to attend to domestic matters. . . . Nature never intended them to mingle with the affairs of state."[162] Despite the growing spirit of temperance, lowcountry grand juries continued to complain about the retailing of liquor to slaves. The Chatham County Grand Jury declared that "the practice opens the door to evils of great magnitude, injures the master, and demoralizes the slave. . . . The returns they most generally receive, intoxicating liquor, only add to the evil, by fastening on them the habits of drunkenness, exciting them to further depredations and sinking them lower in vice. . . . All slaves are interested in this matter & all should unite in endeavours to stop this fruitful source of mischief & danger."[163] Such activities were therefore perceived by the elite as not only harmful to their property but also as a threat to their very peace and security.

Small fines imposed by the City Council were clearly no deterrent to white shopkeepers in Savannah. Fines for retailing liquor without a license or for entertaining Negroes outside of hours averaged about $15 between 1790 and 1848.[164] Indeed, average fines for "entertaining Negroes" generally decreased between 1830 and 1848.[165] This decline was partly a response to concerns among city councilmen about the ability of offenders to pay their fines, but it also reflected the control which "Grocers" periodically exerted over the council from the mid-1820s onward.[166] Whatever the cause, the fact remains that fines were insufficient to prevent shopkeepers from trading with African Americans.

The inability of the civic authorities in Savannah to control the activities of dramshops was a source of constant irritation to grand juries. In 1783 the Chatham County Grand Jury presented as "a great grievance, the number of tippling houses in and about Savannah, where liquors are sold to and a villainous traffick carried on with the slaves, to the detriment of their owners and the community."[167] Five years later ninety Savannah residents petitioned the Grand Jury to include in its presentments a diatribe against "the traffick carried on by Negroes with a number of people keeping tippling houses." The Grand Jury went on to warn all the citizens of Savannah to "be vigilant" and to report any people retailing liquor to slaves to the Board of Wardens.[168] The pleas of the Grand Jury went unheeded by shopkeepers involved in the liquor trade. In 1794 the Chatham County Grand Jury again cited the retailers of liquor for keeping their shops open in the evening and on Sundays "by which practice, the Negroes are induced and encouraged to steal and pillage and commit other enormities to the injury of our citizens."[169] It was widely believed that there was a link between retailers of spirituous liquors and theft by slaves. Grand Jury members suspected that the promise of alcohol and other goods encouraged theft. White shopkeepers apparently rarely questioned the source of articles slaves sold to them, not caring that planters and merchants suffered because of the trade in stolen goods.[170] One Grand Jury rather charitably believed that the trade between white shopkeepers and African Americans arose out of ignorance of the law on the part of shopkeepers. It recommended that the City Council publish the relevant law and then enforce it more stringently.[171]

Minutes from the City Council reveal that one-fifth of the people granted liquor licenses before 1820 were at some time prosecuted for trading with slaves, keeping their shops open late or on Sundays, or "entertaining Negroes."[172] Fines were evidently not a sufficient incentive to stop this highly lucrative trade because a fifth of all people fined were recidivists.[173] The council concluded from the large number of applications for liquor licenses (by 1855 more than two hundred liquor shops existed in the city) that retailing liquor must be "sufficiently profitable."[174] Indeed, the large amount of money which the combination of liquor licenses, fines for retailing to slaves, and trading without a license brought into the city treasury may well have discouraged stringent action against the taverns by the civic authorities. In 1814 fees for liquor licenses brought in more than $6,000—nearly a quarter of the total revenue of the city in that year.[175] In 1855 the combination of licenses and fines still contributed more than 10 percent of the city's revenue.[176] The Grand Jury was also aware of the economic necessity that occasioned the licensing of tippling houses, lamenting the "misfortune when governments cannot be supported without legalising vice, and we would seriously recommend a resort to other modes of increasing the financing of our city than by throwing open the flood gates of excess and riot."[177]

City tax records reveal more about the social status of those violating trading ordinances. From 1809 onward the city treasurer constructed a tax digest, itemizing the property of heads of households such as real estate, merchandise, and slaves and calculating their tax bill. Just over a third of those appearing before the council for violating trading ordinances also appear in the city tax records.[178] Considering that more than a hundred offenders committed their offenses before tax records began to be kept in 1809 and that one in ten offenders were women who were not usually taxed separately from their husbands, this third is a respectably large sample.[179]

The tax records show that only a quarter of those trading illegally were slaveholders and even among those, extremely few might be considered as verging on elite status.[180] There are significant differences between males and females who violated trading ordinances. Slaveholding women were a majority of the women who traded illegally with bondspeople, whereas their male counterparts were in a small minority.[181] But the slaveholding women who violated trading ordinances were not members of the Savannah elite. Only three owned more than one slave, and ownership of one slave may have made little difference to the material life of the owner, depending on the age and gender of the slave. Bondswomen in town frequently acted in a domestic capacity, which was not an income-producing activity.[182] Bondsmen may have been hired out to third parties, but the income from such arrangements, rarely more than $3 per week, was hardly enough to live on if there was no other source of revenue. To the women violating trading ordinances, many of whom were probably widowed, the quick and easy profits to be made by trading illegally with slaves clearly overrode any racial sensibilities or identification they may have had with the slaveholding elite.[183]

Nearly a third of the three-quarters of offenders who did not own slaves paid tax on merchandise, denoting that they owned a store or were merchants. Several of the nonslaveholding women were married to shop-keepers, and the actions for which they were convicted most likely occurred when they were left in charge of the shop. For example, immigrant Irish shopkeepers Bridget and Dominic Gilligan were both fined by the council for violating the Sabbath ordinance in 1844; similarly, Mary Prendergast was fined for trading on Sundays three years after the council had fined her husband, Edward, for the same violation.[184] Another third of taxpaying offenders paid nothing more than a poll tax, denoting that they were a head of household but owned no property. Of course, this category could include the several hundred offenders who were not located in the tax records. These individuals were either dependents in households where only the head of the household was taxed or were transients not normally resident in the city. The remaining offenders owned some property, usually a dwelling place, and little else. Of the slaveholding quarter, a minority owned several slaves (only five owned more than five slaves), owned substantial amounts of other property, or were members of the legal or medical professions. In general, therefore, while there were significant differences among those who violated regulatory standards to trade with slaves, they generally belonged to the nonelite class.

All attempts by the city authorities and the grand juries to control the dramshops and tippling houses in and around Savannah failed. By 1804 the Grand Jury was complaining of the increase in the number of dram-shops "and other disorderly houses in this city," which "encourage Negroes to plunder their owners" and were therefore "public nuisances in society."[185] The primary cause of the "amazing increase" in the number of retailers selling alcohol to slaves was its obvious profitability.[186] Slaves were clearly willing to sell goods cheaply in return for liquor. As an example of the amounts of money trading with slaves could bring in, Charles Manigault recorded in 1845 that the purchaser of a $4,000 property near his own on Argyle Island was a Mr. Dillon, who "has been keeping a grog shop in Savannah for several years, & made his money by trading with Negroes & has already established a grog & trading shop on his new purchase."[187]

A brief survey of those most frequently fined by the City Council for offenses involving trading with slaves illuminates how several nonslaveholders availed themselves of the money to be made from African Americans to become slaveholders themselves. Most strikingly, Mary Garnett, widowed in 1815, was fined $335 for sixteen separate citations between April 17, 1823, and November 8, 1827. Despite these fines, Garnett made sufficient profits to purchase several slaves.[188] Shadrack Winkler bought a country plantation together with more than twenty slaves because of the profits from retailing to slaves on Sundays.[189] As a sign of his family's respectability in Savannah society by the late 1820s, Winkler's wife, Jane, was a member of the prestigious Independent Presbyterian Church.[190] Perhaps the ultimate irony of the trade with slaves was that it was the purchasing power of African Americans themselves that allowed some nonslaveholding whites to enter the ranks of the slave-owning class.

Persistent offenders who did not purchase slaves with their profits were sometimes denied the opportunity to do so by an early death. Bernard McGran was fined more than $100 in late 1820 and early 1821 for five separate instances of "entertaining Negroes." Although the profits from his business had enabled him to obtain more than $200 worth of stock-in-trade, his death in September 1821 prevented any further economic advancement.[191] Others left Savannah shortly after their appearances before the City Council. Peter Carre most likely left Savannah in 1811 after being fined more than $140 between 1809 and 1811 for "entertaining Negroes" and retailing liquor without a license.[192] Some offenders, however, chose not to purchase slaves with their ill-gotten gains. Pierce Howard appeared a record thirty-eight times before the council between 1824 and 1845, paying an enormous $586 in fines. Howard was an Irish immigrant who arrived sometime in the 1810s or early 1820s, evidently penniless, for whom trading with slaves was an obvious way to make money. By 1829 he had amassed property worth $400 and his shop held $2,500 worth of merchandise, and soon he began to make enough money so that he no longer needed to break the law by trading illegally. But for some reason Howard's business declined, and by 1832 he had no property whatsoever. It is surely no coincidence that he began trading with slaves again shortly afterward.[193] What brought many of the most regular and chronic offenders together was a common Irish heritage. No less than six of the ten most frequently appearing before the council were born in Ireland.[194] Quite likely making money in this way was frequently discussed in the Yamacraw dramshops and gambling haunts popular among Irish immigrants. In addition, Irish immigrants, having little knowledge of the slave system or of the Southern social hierarchy, would probably not have been overly concerned with the racial propriety of trading illegally with African Americans.[195]

In an attempt to limit the number of people permitted to retail liquor in Savannah, licenses were supposedly granted only to people incapacitated from other employment. Yet the Grand Jury was well aware "that too many persons capable of obtaining their living by labor, with others; are in the habit of selling spirituous liquors."[196] Clearly the profitability of retailing liquor attracted laboring people "without the habits of industry" into the business.[197] In an effort to keep their illicit Sunday trading activities secret and thus avoid fines, some tippling houses had "private doors for the admission of Negroes on the Sabbath day (as is evidenced from the many we see inebriated)."[198] The City Council attempted to shame those fined for trading with slaves by publishing their names in the *Georgia Gazette.*[199] Few names were publicized in this manner until the 1820s, when the Sabbatarians brought the issue of trading with slaves to the forefront of the political agenda. By 1808 grand jurors had become exasperated at "the little attention heretofore paid to the presentments of the Grand Inquest of this county. . . . Every man of observation must see with deep regret, the multiplied offences which flow from our tippling shops, and tho' these have been frequently complained of, the morals of the people continue to grow more corrupt. Let those whose duty it is, look to this sink of corruption, and apply the cleaning hand er it is too late."[200]

Shopkeepers in Savannah were not the only ones who cared little for the law concerning opening hours and the racial propriety of trading with slaves. The Grand Jury of Camden County found it necessary to complain about the activities of shopkeepers in St. Marys who ignored the "decorum of the Sabbath day" by "trading with and harbouring Negroes."[201] Even jurymen in mainly rural Liberty County cited the trade between shopkeepers and their slaves, describing it as "a practice manifestly destructive of the good morals & best interests of this community."[202] As in Savannah, courts usually lacked "sufficient evidence to convict" shopkeepers, despite seeing slaves "in a state of intoxication."[203] The inability of the elite to control the economic activities of nonslaveholders and African Americans demonstrates that their social ethic did not permeate all classes. So exasperated did the Charleston Grand Jury become that it ridiculed the "equality of sociability" between slaves and shopkeepers, no doubt in hope that traders would be chastened by the comparison.[204] But the fact remains that it was fundamentally in shopkeepers' interests to continue trading with slaves, despite both the law and the economic empowerment such trade gave African Americans.

Several shopkeepers located their businesses precisely where bondspeople tended to congregate in Savannah. In 1812 the Grand Jury presented "as nuisances, two houses, situated a short distance from the S.E. of Carpenter's Row, the resort of Negroes on Sundays & other days, and generally scenes of drunkenness and disorderly behaviour."[205] Carpenter's Row was situated to the east of East Broad Street, in the residential neighborhood known as the Trustees' Gardens. In 1817 twenty-five free African Americans listed Carpenter's Row or Trustees' Gardens as their residence.[206] In 1798 John J. Gray advertised his new liquor store on the market square, where a large number of bondspeople gathered, either to sell goods or to hire their time.[207] Mrs. Falligrant petitioned the City Council in 1818 for a permit to retail goods on a Sunday in the market square.[208] Although her request was not granted, it is likely that the only people to frequent this establishment would have been slaves selling their produce in the Sunday market.

During the 1820s, grand juries repeated their presentments against tippling houses and those who traded with slaves. For example, in 1823 they complained of "the continued practice of opening shops for trade on the Sabbath day, which we consider as opposed to the laws of God and the statutes of the state."[209] The grand juries had probably noticed a marked increase in the number of prosecutions for "entertaining Negroes" appearing before the council in the 1820s.[210] In 1824, as a sign of the increased Sabbatarianism in the city, the Grand Jury railed against the "many interests [which] combine in opposition to the entire suppression of the Sunday trade, and how difficult it is to enforce the law to its fullest extent."[211] Unfortunately, the Grand Jury did not outline exactly which interests opposed attempts to control the trade with slaves. Certainly other grand juries suspected that the City Council itself, mindful of the revenue from licenses and fines, was lax in preventing the trade between shopkeepers and bondspeople in Savannah.[212] Indeed, in 1824 the council passed an ordinance that permitted a market to be held in the city "on each day of the year," a regulation the councillors would live to regret.[213]

One resident even claimed that no regulation of Sunday trading was forthcoming, despite "the prayer of two hundred and sixty of the citizens," because the council relied "upon the votes of shop-keepers" and was thus unwilling to "put in force their own violated ordinances" or take "the least notice . . . of the offenders."[214]

By 1826 grand juries in Savannah were advocating practical steps to control the trade between shopkeepers and slaves, for example more rigorous inquiry into the character of those applying for licenses and an increase in the license fee to $100.[215] Although license fees were raised in that year, a swift protest from Savannah grocers and their political mobilization brought a rapid retreat by local officials.[216] In 1826 the white elite evidently could not ignore the political influence of white males, whether slaveholding or not. Indeed, the grocers regarded attempts to raise license fees as an attempt to control the activities of African Americans without tackling the root of the problem, namely the slave owners' inability to discipline their own "idle and disobedient" slaves.[217] Petitions from the "Sabbath Union," formed by evangelicals in Savannah, to have market trading on Sundays prohibited were twice rejected by the "Grocers' council."[218] In 1827 the committee appointed to examine the petition from the Sabbath Union stated that the Sunday market was necessary to enable all Savannahians, not just African Americans, to purchase fresh food. The committee pointed out that without the trade shopkeepers carried on with African Americans, planters would have to provide more food for their slaves. In the committee's opinion, prohibition of the Sunday market would not end trading with slaves but merely necessitate more secrecy on the part of shopkeepers and bondspeople alike. Complaints the following year that bondspeople sold not only in the morning but "during the whole of the sacred day" and that those "sequestered in the temple of the most high" were compelled "to listen to the rude cry of the blacks offering their articles for sale, under the very windows of the churches," were ignored by this committee.[219] Evidently many aldermen in the 1820s suspected that attempts to limit Sunday trading would simply be disregarded by large sections of the populace, both black and white. By 1828, even though the grocers no longer controlled the council, the city aldermen were moving generally toward a more pragmatic policy in which fines for illegal trading were based on ability to pay rather than on making examples of penniless offenders. In this sense, the nonelite was winning the battle with slave owners over their relationship with African Americans. To many planters, the trouble associated with enforcing the trading regulations was simply not worth the effort involved.[220]

Betty Wood argues that by 1829 the City Council was split between those who desired the stricter regulation of the Sunday market in Savannah and those who believed that any change in the law was unenforceable and unnecessary.[221] Newspaper articles make it clear that splits among councilmen merely reflected those in wider society. Certainly the Sabbath Union had its supporters in the lowcountry. Patrick Houstoun chaired a meeting of White Bluff residents who offered their wholehearted backing to the Sabbath Union—and in the late summer of 1828, a meeting of the union lauded "the favorable effect already produced upon the community by the exertions of this Union."[222] The defensive tone of one correspondent to the *Georgian,* however, indicates that many Savannahians found the activities of the union distasteful. This "Member" attempted to alleviate fears regarding the impact of the union on daily life: "We do not wish to signalize a revolution in society. We do not wish to aggrandize a particular sect or party. Nor would we bring the requirements of religion to bear *too* strongly upon the temporal interests of men."[223] Whether these concerns had been raised by the nonelite is not known. But certainly some Savannahians viewed the activities of the Sabbath Union as a direct assault on their privileges as independent white men.

In 1829, the Sabbath Union tried once more to change the city ordinance that permitted retailing on Sundays. Its case was strengthened by a recent Superior Court decision against Mr. Whiting, a nonslaveholding retail grocer, for the violation of a state law prohibiting any trade at all on Sundays. According to a report in the *Georgian,* this was a test case, designed to obtain "an authoritative statement of the law," and was presumably brought by the Sabbath Union.[224] As one supporter of the Sabbath Union wrote to the *Argus,* slaves knew that the main consequence of putting an end to Sunday trading would be to prevent them purchasing whiskey from the grocery stores in Savannah. Such stories only served to fuel the call for reform.[225] The council committee appointed to examine the new petition of "a numerous and respectable body of the citizens of Savannah" reported that proper observance of the Sabbath should ultimately override concerns about the ability of residents to purchase food on Sundays. The committee claimed that local planters were willing "to allow a portion of their slaves to visit the city of Savannah in weekly rotation in order to obviate the inconvenience at present resulting from their trading on the Sabbath." Above all, the retailing of liquor to slaves by shopkeepers who were not deterred by "occasionally paying a fine of $5 or $10" would be prevented by the strict application of the new ordinance.[226] According to a correspondent to the *Georgian,* there was "no subject of more vital importance to the inhabitants of Savannah" than stopping the retailing of liquor to slaves. Since this council was unwilling to make a decision on the new ordinance until after the annual elections, Sunday trading became the prime issue for the city electorate.[227]

Nonslaveholders were not willing to permit the elite to reduce their economic freedom without a fight. In a series of letters written to the city newspapers, supporters of Sunday trading attacked the stance of the Sabbath Union from a variety of angles. Most potent was the charge that the union was trying to "mingle religion with politics," despite its denials. As one correspondent asked, "Would you willingly submit to be the slaves of a code of religion, framed by one sect for its own benefit—its own interest?"[228] By drawing a direct parallel between slavery and the intended actions of the Sabbath Union if its supporters were elected, non-elite whites were revealing their innermost fears. In a slave society, where just earning enough to survive was a daily struggle for many nonslaveholders, any attempt to reduce still further their ability to make ends meet provoked an understandably vigorous response.

Those who stood for election to the council that September cannot be split between elite and nonelite or between planters and shopkeepers. Most of those putting themselves forward for election owned substantial property of some sort, though not all owned slaves.[229] When the votes were counted, neither the People's Ticket, in favor of regulating Sunday trading, nor the Independent Ticket, that supported the liberal laws then in force, won outright. Those elected were a mixture of the two tickets, though, confusingly, some individuals stood on both tickets. The first issue to come before the new council was the Sunday trading ordinance. The five aldermen elected solely on the People's Ticket voted four in favor of change, one absent; the three elected solely on the Independent Ticket voted two against and one in favor of change; and the six elected on both tickets voted two in favor, two against, and two absent.[230] Of the four who voted against reform, William Waring and Moses Sheftall were doctors and, though slaveholders, had long argued that changing the Sunday trading law was hypocritical and unenforceable; J. B. Gaudry and George Shick were storekeepers, and of all the aldermen Shick was the most likely to oppose tightening the trading ordinances, having been himself fined $15 for "entertaining Negroes" ten years previously.[231] The heterogeneous mix of the antireform camp is matched by those in favor of reform, a group that included a mason, Thomas Clarke, a merchant, Francis Welman, a saddler, Jacob Shaffer, a planter George Anderson, and a shopkeeper, Charles Gildon. What linked these reformers, as Betty Wood has shown, was religious idealism. All but one of the seven supporting change were regular churchgoers, three attending the Baptist church, which spearheaded the Sabbath Union's assault on the ordinances. Two were Episcopalians and one belonged to the Presbyterian church.[232] None of those opposing reform belonged to an evangelical church.

The Sabbatarianism that arose in Savannah quickly spread to the rest of the lowcountry. In Bryan County the Grand Jury requested that slave owners be prevented from giving out weekly rations on Sundays. In 1835 a new ordinance was passed in Darien along the lines of that in Savannah, ordering fines of up to $50 for trading on Sundays; simply being seen in a shop was taken as prima-facie evidence of trading. Similar ordinances were also passed in Brunswick and St. Marys.[233]

The slave owners serving on the Chatham County Grand Jury in 1830 initially welcomed the new ordinance in Savannah: "The act to prohibit slaves from trading with white persons, is founded not less in a state of mercy to them, than of safety to society and taken in communion with the extended jurisdiction of the city, must by the combined efforts of the county and city officers, have the desired effect and prove a benefit to all."[234] But perhaps because of pressure from local planters, the ordinance closed only the shops, not the Sunday market operated by slaves in Savannah.[235] The fact that African Americans still came to the city to trade on Sundays was an obvious temptation to shopkeepers to trade illegally with them. In 1833 the council deliberated whether to close the Sunday market, most likely aware that since bondspeople still came to Savannah to trade, white shopkeepers would secretly trade with them, but on this occasion the council took no action.[236] Consequently, the new ordinance did not immediately reduce the number of black and white people trading on Sundays. In the decade following the enactment of the ordinance, more than three hundred people appeared before the council to be fined for trading illegally, more than double the average number of prosecutions during the 1820s.[237] The deterrent effect of the ordinance was further dampened by the small fines that were imposed despite continued protests from the Chatham County Grand Jury.

In 1836, a number of "Grocers and Traders" in the city petitioned the council to reform the Sunday trading law. They pointed out that since bondspeople were permitted to come to the city to trade on Sunday in the market, while all other retailers were "forbid under severe penalty to sell," slaves were effectively given privileges denied to white shopkeepers. The shopkeepers knew that slaves would make only one visit per week to Savannah to trade, and therefore the bondspeople would trade with each other to the exclusion of whites. Two alternative solutions were proposed by the grocers: first, that the market be closed on Sundays and that slaves be permitted by their owners to come to town on Saturday afternoons, or second, that shops be allowed to open on Sundays.[238] But while the council acknowledged that the law as it stood seemed to suggest that it was "morally right to sell on Sunday in the public market, and morally wrong for the Grocer to sell from his store on that day" so divided were the aldermen on the issue that no revision to the ordinance could be agreed on. What angered white grocers more than anything was not that African Americans held a Sunday market or that they were allowed to trade but that the city gave "one class of citizens privileges to the exclusion of others." The shopkeepers noted that the only reason that slaves came to Savannah to trade in the first place was because owners denied them "the necessaries and most of the comforts of life." But because most of the city aldermen in the mid-1830s were slave owners, they had little financial incentive to restrict the independent economic activities of their bondspeople, nor did they wish to facilitate the disruption to plantation life that would inevitably have followed the curtailment of trading privileges.[239]

After two weeks of deliberation, the committee appointed by the council to examine the petition reported that the aldermen had a "difference of opinion," with some advocating a liberalization of the law while others wished for more concrete enforcement. Aldermen D'Lyon and Shaw argued that shops should be allowed to open for the same number of hours as the market on Sunday. This would avoid any major disruption to the plantation routine while permitting white people who were not paid until the end of the week to continue to purchase their groceries on Sundays. More significantly, these aldermen recognized that the 1829 ordinance was in "complete conflict with public opinion [and] cannot be enforced without great difficulty." Part of the problem facing the council was that so many white people violated the current ordinance, "since they can realise great profits on their goods," that only light fines were inflicted from fear of public disorder. This proposal would have revived the ordinance of 1817, which had been surpassed by that of 1829. Alderman Purse pointed out, however, that by permitting shops to open on Sundays the council would be violating a state law, which would make the alder-men individually liable for prosecution. The mayor agreed and stated that just because an ordinance was unpopular and poorly enforced did not mean that council should repeal it. After much discussion, the recommen-dation of the committee to alter the ordinances was rejected.[240]

The council's resolve to do nothing received scathing criticism from some sections of the press. "Spectator," writing in the *Georgian,* con-demned the council for encouraging the local slave population to come to Savannah on Sunday "when our own colored population is idle and at leisure to plot mischief with them if disposed to do so." Stung by this and other attacks, in July 1836 the council passed an ordinance closing the Sunday market, allowing it to stay open late on Saturday instead.[241] How much impact this change had on the behavior of either the African Ameri-can or the white community is questionable. Prosecutions for violating the Sabbath ordinances ran at roughly the same rate after the passage of this ordinance as they had done before it, though average fines were significantly higher.[242] In 1838 the council reaffirmed its commitment to the Sunday trading laws, especially concerning the activities of African Americans. It acknowledged that there was no specific law prohibiting African Americans from trading on Sundays but believed that existing ordinances relating to Sunday trading were sufficient to check the trade. As if to clarify the situation further, two new ordinances were passed in 1839; the first enforced the observance of the Sabbath, and the second restated that the market was to be closed on Sundays.[243] The class divi-sions in white society (and nothing divided whites in Savannah as much as this particular issue) therefore contributed to the functioning of the informal economic contacts between nonslaveholding whites and African Americans. The elite was unwilling to end the trading privileges of slaves and unable to prevent shopkeepers from selling to them. The shopkeepers knew that bondspeople desired to trade and chose to ignore the wishes of the elite in favor of asserting their political and cultural independence by serving their own class interests. African Americans got the best of both worlds: the elite did not prevent them from trading, and the shopkeepers were willing to deny their racial ties to accommodate bondspeople for economic gain.

Illicit Sunday trading continued between African Americans and non-slaveholders in the city right up to the Civil War despite increasing social pressure to curb it. The city elections frequently rested on the issue of illegal trading, and civic power changed hands many times between those supported by the elite and those backed by shopkeepers.[244] In the 1840s the Chatham County Grand Jury, while urging strict enforcement of the Sabbath ordinances, was "happy to see the vigilance of our police, bringing up offenders."[245] By 1850, however, the shopkeepers had managed to persuade Dr. Richard Wayne, the mayor, to pursue a policy of nonimplementation of the Sabbath ordinances. When fellow medic (and former and future mayor) Dr. Richard Arnold stood against Wayne in 1850 his ticket was defeated by more than three hundred votes. Arnold complained that Wayne was able to "regulate the shopkeepers politically by not regulating them as to the law" and that the voting was marked by intimidatory bands of "Irishmen with shillalahs, who raised a shout and blocked up the way whenever one of our men was bringing up a voter, but whenever one of theirs came along the waves were stilled and he was pushed along quietly." Apparently Wayne had told the shopkeepers that, if elected, Arnold "would fine every shop-keeper a hundred dollars who might be convicted of breaking the ordinances."[246]

The stranglehold of the shopkeepers on the city government did not prevent the local elite from protesting about the violation of city ordinances through the Grand Jury system. In 1852 the Grand Jury publicly complained that "the ordinance forbidding the sale of liquors or trading on the Sabbath, is habitually violated the more bold do not hesitate to open their doors publickly on that day, while the more timid evade the law by admitting their customers in a private manner."[247] Later the same year, the jury declared that the council under the shopkeepers' friend, Richard Wayne, was not doing its duty in suppressing this trade.[248] The new council elected in 1853 again attempted to end the Sunday trade between nonelite whites and African Americans by the passage of new market and Sabbath ordinances.[249] The elite also appealed to the racial and religious sentiments of the jurors serving in the courts that year. Judge George T. Howard solemnly declared that it was their "duty to put a stop to a practice which is so utterly inconsistent with the character and professions of a Christian community."[250] He knew, as did council members, that efforts to limit biracial trading were often hampered by juries who were unwilling to convict shopkeepers indicted for trial.[251]

These tactics seemed to be having some effect—the council had gone so far as to declare itself content with "the working and efficiency of the new police system"—when the yellow fever epidemic of 1854 struck.[252] On the recommendation of the Board of Health, the mayor, Edward Anderson, suspended the operation of the Sabbath ordinances, "for the convenience of the sick and destitute." Clearly the desperate situation in Savannah, where up to one hundred people were dying each week, made the implementation and enforcement of such ordinances impractical. The depopulation of the city occasioned by the fever meant that most of the regular civic functions were also suspended.[253] The ordinance was enforced again after only a month's respite, which upset certain Savannahians who clearly wanted the nonimplementation of trading laws to be more permanent. By early 1855, even the *Daily Morning News,* which had hitherto supported the council's Sunday trading policy, pressed for reform. It declared that although most citizens supported measures to uphold "public morals," these ordinances had caused "great hardship and injustice to the citizens, while it has brought ridicule upon the authorities."[254] Even the newest paper in Savannah, the *Daily Journal and Courier,* derided a policy that permitted residents to drink on Sundays as long as they purchased on Saturdays.[255]

The return of Dr. Richard Wayne to the mayoralty in 1857 ensured once again that shopkeepers would not find themselves under pressure from the City Council to curb their trading with African Americans, despite angry letters appearing in the city press denouncing liquor shops that entertain "a large body of negroes" even after bell ring.[256] Those seeking stricter implementation of city ordinances believed that holding the annual council elections in October was detrimental to their cause because "four-fifths" of native-born Americans were absent from the city at that time of the year. Consequently, voting was often left to "foreigners," and election leaflets were printed in a variety of languages by those supporting lax policing.[257] Fed up with the "peculiar privileges" given to the shopkeepers and "injudicious and inefficient" implementation of the ordinances, elite Savannahians mounted a concerted campaign to win the council election of 1859.[258] Charles Colcock Jones explained exactly why the elite felt it was necessary to take this stand: "Under the present administration the Sunday ordinance has become almost a dead letter; the police is unsustained in executing the internal regulations affecting public peace and order. They may report offenders, but the cases are not infrequently, even after they are placed on the Mayor's docket, *never called.* The rum shops are filled with Negroes drinking at all hours of the day and night. Gambling is rampant. *In fine,* the present condition of the city is anything but desirable."[259] The ticket led by veteran antishopkeeper Richard Arnold won the election, and the following January the council passed a new ordinance giving the police extra powers and responsibilities. Within six months of the election Arnold was able to impose fines of up to $150 per offense for trading illegally, finally starting to hit shop-keepers where it really mattered, in their pockets.[260]

Charles Colcock Jones, mayor of Savannah in 1860–61, made prob-ably the most concerted effort to control the trade between shopkeepers and slaves, yet even he could not prevent "those offenders of foreign birth, the rum-sellers . . . demoralizing our servants and ruining them."[261] As the Grand Jury of Chatham County ruefully noted, most of its pre-sentments of the past thirty years regarding the "grievous injuries result-ing from the selling of spirituous & intoxicating liquors to our slaves . . . are merely published—then entirely forgotten, & never afterwards al-luded to or acted upon."[262] Despite all the attempts of the elite over sev-eral decades to control the economic activities of nonslaveholders and African Americans, the battle was never won. No matter what ordinances were passed, the resourcefulness of both groups, either through political action or by simply ignoring the law, meant that attempts to control their trading activities were doomed to failure.

The economic relationships between nonslaveholding whites and Af-rican Americans in the Georgia lowcountry are therefore twofold. De-spite the status differences that divided white and black, mutual depen-dency and joint advantage persuaded poor white people and slaves that economic contacts could improve both of their material lives. Indeed, they found that their economic sufficiency was in many cases dependent on the choices of the other race. Without white traders, bondspeople out-side of Savannah may have struggled to find outlets for their produce. Without bondspeople willing to retail goods to them at cheap prices and in exchange for comparatively little, white shopkeepers may not have been able to survive. Their relationship was in many respects symbiotic. To the average slave and the average shopkeeper, biracial trading con-tacts were an important part of everyday life. The key difference between shopkeepers on the one hand and artisans and mechanics on the other was that economic competition eroded the racial status of nonslave-holders so much that some artisans feared that African Americans could obtain "an equality of skin" with them. Trading contacts empowered Af-rican Americans but always maintained them in their dependent status, never explicitly threatening the social status of shopkeepers. Because trading also empowered and enriched the nonelite, it was vigorously de-fended against all regulatory attempts by the white elite. In this sense, slaves themselves helped nonslaveholders to preserve their idea of republican democracy and independence. Faced by this alliance of petty capitalist convenience between nonslaveholders and African Americans, the white elite was powerless to prevent economic encounters between slaves and nonslaveholding whites.

4 Violence, Theft, and Plots

CRIMINAL INTERACTION between nonslaveholders and African Americans in the lowcountry can be separated into two broad and distinct themes. First, assaults by poor whites on blacks, and vice versa, were fairly commonplace, demonstrating that race relations could be violently antagonistic. Second, poor whites and blacks occasionally combined to commit crimes that adversely affected the interests of the elite, suggesting that under certain circumstances class alliances could overcome racial prejudices. In this chapter I attempt to account for the differing interactions between white and black in the criminal world. Were nonslaveholders prepared to ally with African Americans only when it was fundamentally in their interests to do so, or did they attempt to define themselves as completely independent individuals by defying the social mores of the elite? Biracial criminal activities were probably the most threatening sphere of interaction to the peace and security of Southern society. Certain members of the elite were extremely concerned by it; they were right to be so.

Criminal activity was not simply the preserve of the poor. Rich and privileged people did break the law, but few, if any, were imprisoned for their offenses. Very few of the antebellum inmates listed in the Georgia State Penitentiary had occupations common to the elite. Farmers, laborers, artisans, and the unemployed were far more likely to be imprisoned.[1] Moreover, once again illuminating the marginal position of immigrants in Southern society, more than a quarter of those sent to the penitentiary by lowcountry courts were born in Europe, and a further fifth were from Northern states.[2] The most common crime to be committed in the lowcountry, and in the South generally, was assault. Historians of criminal behavior in the antebellum South agree that the culture of male personal honor regularly involved violence and, as a study of the life of the murderer Edward Isham has shown, personal violence in the South was both socially acceptable and to some degree expected as a normal part of lower-class white male culture.[3] Assault cases often dominated the time of the Southern criminal courts. For example, of nearly five hundred white people imprisoned in the Savannah jail between 1809 and 1815, most had committed a violent offense and less than a fifth were jailed for larceny.[4]

Clearly, property crimes did not overly occupy the time of any lowcountry court, yet thieves tended to spend longer in jail than other criminals. The 69 white people confined in Savannah for theft between 1809 and 1815 spent an average of twenty-five days in jail; two pickpockets languished there for more than four months.[5] Conversely, those confined for assault averaged only ten days in jail and rioters only three days.[6] State penitentiary records confirm the impression gleaned from local jails that property crimes were more severely dealt with than violent crimes: less than a fifth of the 222 lowcountry residents confined between 1817 and 1865 had committed violent crimes.[7] But whereas those convicted of assault served an average of three to three and a half years in jail and those convicted of manslaughter only six months more, thieves and burglars served roughly four and a half years.[8] Theft was clearly perceived as posing the greatest threat to society. Only particularly vicious assaults were punished by jail, and even fatal attacks were sometimes overlooked by juries steeped in the culture of personal honor.[9] In part this was because larceny tended to be committed by the poor against the politically and judicially influential propertied classes, whereas assault could be committed by anyone and often involved privileged members of the lowcountry elite. In 1804, among fifteen men fined between $150 and $500 for an assault on Emmanuel Coryell were notable Savannah merchants such as Joseph Arnold and Samuel Howard.[10]

The antebellum South was evidently a violent place where individual assaults were commonplace. But whereas assaults by whites on whites were regarded fairly leniently by the criminal courts, violent acts that crossed the race divide were treated much more seriously. Physical violence carried out by nonslaveholding whites against bondspeople, and vice versa, merited intense scrutiny. Bondspeople were, of course, property, and injured or maimed slaves were temporarily or permanently unable to fulfill their normal duties. Because work was the main purpose of slavery, unfit slaves became a financial burden to their owners. Thus white people who had altercations with bondspeople could expect to be prosecuted to the limit of the law.[11] Still, the interests of owners in protecting their bondspeople did not stretch to defending them from the consequences of attacks on whites. Indeed, owners usually attempted to instill in their slaves the idea that assaults on whites would be punished.

In early 1806, a sixteen-year-old immigrant Irish laborer named William Moore appeared before Chatham County Superior Court charged with "maliciously shooting at, and maiming a Negro."[12] After Moore was found guilty, the judge told him that nothing "could justify or extenuate the offense with which you stood charged, you appeared to be influenced by a cruel and mischievous disposition." It was only luck that Moore's shot had not fatally wounded the bondsman in question. The judge cautioned him that if he had killed the slave, he "might stand in that bar now to receive a sentence of death."[13] The severity with which the elite dealt with poor white people who made unprovoked attacks on African Americans is evinced by cases such as William Moore's. His sentence of four months in the county jail of Chatham County, on top of a $50 fine, was above average for assault in the early nineteenth century.[14] William Moore was certainly not a member of the Savannah elite. In 1806 he paid just 62.5 cents in tax, placing him in the bottom fifth of resident taxpayers in Savannah.[15] We do not have enough evidence to assess Moore's motives. Perhaps he was drunk, or he may have been responding to a perceived insult from the slave. It is certainly possible that his only motive was race hatred. Nevertheless, Moore found some friends in Savannah who defended his actions.

In February 1806, fourteen citizens wrote to Governor John Milledge seeking clemency for Moore. They based their petition on two points. First, they believed Moore's "tender years" should have been taken more fully into account. Second, with Moore in prison, his parents were placed in a position of "extreme poverty and penury" because they "were dependent mostly on his labor for their daily bread."[16] His supporters petitioned for a remittance of the fine and his immediate release from prison, but the eventual outcome of the petition is not known. Apparently, most, if not all, of the petitioners were workingmen who did not own slaves. Only three were listed in the tax digest for 1806, and they numbered among the poorest third of Savannah taxpayers.[17] Information about six of the others was gleaned from their death records, which usually listed age, place of birth, and occupation. Only one man held a position of responsibility: William Pinder was the keeper of the county jail, who left "some property" when he died shortly after signing this petition.[18] Other friends of Moore included mariners, shopkeepers, cigar makers, and clerks. They owned little or no property and resided in poor neighborhoods of Savannah such as Yamacraw or Oglethorpe ward.[19] Only one of the six was born in Savannah, and even he was of French parentage.[20] This petition illuminates a network of working people that crossed the boundaries of age, trade, and ethnic background and remained outside the scope or control of officially incorporated societies such as the Savannah Mechanics Association or the Grocer's Society.[21]

These white men were evidently unconcerned by the random violence Moore exhibited toward an African American. As nonslaveholders themselves, the loss occasioned to the owner of the slave was less significant than the principle they felt this judgment articulated: that the authority of all white men over African Americans, or any other dependent, was not complete. The petition tacitly asked the governor to acknowledge the privileges of gender and race, despite the consequences for the property of a member of the elite. How far this belief in their innate racial superiority was typical of nonslaveholders generally is difficult to determine, but what is clear from the extant criminal records is that white violence toward African Americans was significantly more common than black violence toward whites. The evidence that is extant demonstrates that on average a white person in Chatham County was either indicted or jailed for physical violence toward African Americans once every two years. By contrast, available figures suggest that African Americans in the same county were prosecuted for violence toward whites only about once every four years.[22] Of course, this may just reflect the fact that the consequences for slaves who assaulted white people were far more severe than those for comparable assaults on bondspeople by the white nonelite and that slaves understood this truth and behaved accordingly.[23]

Nonslaveholding whites who assaulted African Americans had various motives. Irish-born artisan Samuel Patterson, for example, spent a year in the Georgia State Penitentiary because he chose to defend his honor from the slight of an African American. During his trial at Chatham County Superior Court in early 1821, witnesses recounted that Patterson had attacked a free black named Caleb Reed with a dirk, supposedly in a response to an insult made by Reed.[24] This was not a one-sided battle. Daniel Coyle testified that Reed had exchanged blows with Patterson and was so angry that he "took no advice to go away."[25] Evidently this attack was the culmination of a long-standing dispute between the two men. Patterson stated that he had been angered because on a previous occasion Reed had "raised an axe on him in the river and called him (prisoner) a dam'd liar." [26] While this insult may have caused ill feeling, what actually caused the fight was alcohol. Justice Russel, who took possession of the dirk, stated that "at the time of the affray [he] thought the prisoner in liquor." [27] Reed's blackness was perhaps only of secondary consideration; the insult provoked Patterson, though Reed's color no doubt made the insult more serious in Patterson's eyes, and he clearly felt that he had to defend his honor from the insults of a supposedly "inferior" African American. So common were assaults ostensibly in defense of personal honor in the South that had Reed not been seriously injured, it is likely that Patterson would have escaped jail. [28]

We know relatively little about the life of Samuel Patterson except that he was born in Ireland in 1791 and declared his occupation to be a turner. [29] He does not appear in any of the extant tax digests for Chatham County or the city of Savannah, implying that he lacked the property on which tax would be paid. It is highly probable that he formed part of the trickle of Irish migrants from the Northern states who made Savannah their home in the 1810s. Daniel Coyle, who testified at the trial, was also an Irish immigrant, working as a shopkeeper, and may have been acquainted with Patterson. [30] Of all those who testified, Coyle's evidence was the most favorable to Patterson, probably signifying an ethnic solidarity between two Irishmen of comparable age. What Samuel Patterson and William Moore also shared was their Irish nativity. [31] Most newly arrived Irish settlers in the lowcountry were nonslaveholders, and their social status was usually dictated by their birth and their Catholicism, rather than by ownership of bondspeople. Unlike native poor whites, who were accustomed to black slavery, the Irish settlers may have assumed a superior attitude toward African Americans because, almost for the first time, this was a group beneath them in the social scale.

Occasionally, violence toward bondspeople was used by poor whites as a method of inflicting financial losses on the propertied classes. Disabling or killing the chattels of a slaveholder who had offended the sensibility of a nonslaveholder was an easy way to damage the latter economically. This was the motivation behind the attack on James Hibben's slave Bob. According to Hibben, Bob was "attending to his business on Marskins wharf" in Charleston when he was attacked by Spencer Morrison, Thomas Holliwell, and Job Selb. The three later threatened "to beat and disturb his Negroes whilst they are attending to the deponents business." These men obviously felt that the best way to harm Hibben was to injure his slaves, knowing that it was unlikely that the slaves would respond with force, though the cause of their original dispute with Hibben is unknown.[32]

Almost all of those convicted by the Chatham County Superior Court for crimes against slaves and free African Americans were poor, marginalized individuals. William Clements and John B. Gabriel, who were convicted respectively for the murder of a slave and an assault on a slave, both later died at the Savannah Poor House and Hospital in Yamacraw.[33] Clements was sufficiently indigent that the judge ordered him to be enlisted as a soldier in a frontier garrison if he proved unable to pay the $340 restitution owed to James Jackson, the owner of the slave, with any wages he received being appropriated for his debt.[34] Others convicted of violence toward African Americans included a carpenter, John Stilwell, and James Ventres, who worked as an overseer on a Chatham County plantation.[35] Benjamin Killchrist, indicted for an assault on a slave in 1806, was not even able to afford his son's funeral expenses, which were eventually paid by the public.[36] Of course, it was precisely the nonslaveholders' slaveless status that ensured that their violence toward bondspeople would be prosecuted. Owners responsible for the death or injury of their own slaves were not prosecuted and could always claim that a slave had been harmed under "moderate correction," which was permitted under the law.[37] Nonslaveholders had no such immunity from prosecution.

White people convicted of willfully killing a slave without a proper reason were potentially liable to capital punishment.[38] In 1824 a shopkeeper, Thomas Franklin Hall, was sentenced to death for the murder of a slave named Dick, the property of William Williamson. No motive for the crime was given at the time, although perhaps "he had been drinking."[39] Ann Catherine Harris believed that Hall and the slave were social acquaintances and drank together regularly at her bar.[40] Yet the unprovoked and deliberate nature of the attack sufficiently shocked the judge and jury at his trial to earn him the maximum penalty allowed under law. Twenty-one-year-old Thomas Hall had powerful and influential friends to save him, however, and the legislature subsequently granted him a full pardon.[41]

While Thomas Hall may have escaped his proper punishment, James W. Wilson, convicted of fatally shooting a slave in 1854, was not so fortunate. Wilson, a thirty-four-year-old bricklayer from New York, lived in Yamacraw on the corner of Bryan and Fahm Streets. According to the testimony at his trial, he was employing several slaves under the general direction of Sam, owned by Mrs. Bell Cohen, to renovate his store. Apparently Wilson was dissatisfied with the quality of the timber that was delivered and summoned Sam to ask why secondhand, instead of new, lumber was being used. Sam responded that this lumber was perfectly good for the job, but Wilson became irate, believing that Sam thought him unable to afford the price of new lumber. Sam pointed out that since Wilson had not yet paid for the timber, he was not in a position to complain about it and immediately took his workers off the site until the matter was resolved. Wilson then took his pistol and, following Sam out into Fahm Street, threatened to blow Sam's brains out unless the workers returned. According to Wilson's neighbors, Sam's retort was, "Blow away!" At this Wilson shot Sam and, walking over to where he fell, shot him again, this time in the head, killing him. For Wilson, the perceived insult offered by Sam, combined with his public defiance of a white man, could not go without a violent response. Wilson proved that he could uphold his white masculinity. The jury at his trial understood this and instead of accepting the original charge of murder convicted him of the lesser charge of manslaughter, which meant that he would be released from jail after only three and a half years.[42]

On occasion biracial assaults crossed gender boundaries, but rarely, if ever, was the perpetrator a white woman. Indeed, white women committed few acts of violence in the early national lowcountry. This may have been related to social prohibitions on women visiting Savannah's dramshops, but it is no doubt significant that poor white women generally interacted with bondspeople either in the city market or in church, environments where violence was not generally expected or tolerated. Above all, the culture of personal honor in the South, which encouraged and condoned violence among white men, did not extend to white women.[43] More typical in the criminal courts were cases such as that of a thirty-year-old farmer, Levi Cobb, who had migrated to Georgia from Virginia in the early nineteenth century and who received a four-year prison sentence in 1826 for stabbing a bondswoman.[44] His assault on a slave named Mary arose out of an argument between the two over unloading a canoe on the Savannah wharves that ended with Cobb chasing Mary with his paddle and beating her with it before stabbing her.

Levi Cobb's paranoia is revealed in his comment to the constable William Barton that "the Negroes wanted to kill him, damn them." Certainly Cobb's attitude toward African Americans was deeply suspicious and fearful and appears to be fundamentally based on race. In many respects the assault on Mary was a method of asserting Cobb's white male identity. Despite his own apparent poverty, Cobb certainly believed he had the same supervisory rights over African Americans as the white elite. Hence the slightest perception of resistance from an African American, especially a woman, challenged his status as a white male and provoked a violent response.[45] The problem for Cobb and for other nonslaveholders who assumed a disciplinary role without proper authority was that they laid themselves open to charges of excessive violence and abuse. It is highly unlikely that any of the cases mentioned so far would have been prosecuted except that owners believed their slaves had been harshly treated. Although owners sometimes had no redress against the actions of nonslaveholders serving on the patrol, the violence of individual non-elite white men toward bondspeople outside of that sphere was not tolerated. Not only did violent assaults incapacitate a valuable economic asset, they also disrupted paternal relations between bondspeople and their owners. Paternalism brought African Americans under the protection of their owners' family, thus assaults by third parties were, in essence, an attack on the family honor of slaveholders that could not be ignored.[46]

Nonslaveholding white men were occasionally imprisoned for assaulting African Americans, but there are no records to suggest that any were ever actually executed for the murder of a slave. Nevertheless, the consequences for African Americans convicted of assaulting or murdering white people were often fatal.[47] Turner Smith, a free African American, was remanded in the Savannah City Jail after stabbing a visiting Spanish seaman named Antonio Silvers, presumably to await Silvers's recovery or death.[48] Nothing more is noted about this case, but in the death records of the city, Anthony Silvers is recorded as dying from "the stab of a sword" only ten days after Turner Smith was remanded.[49] Twenty-four-year-old Silvers served aboard the *Saucy Jack*, and it is likely that the fight leading to his death occurred in one of the several pubs in Yamacraw frequented by sailors and African Americans. The immediate cause of the fight may have been alcohol-related or racially motivated, though it is difficult to be sure. Although we have no clear evidence of what happened to Turner Smith after Silvers's death, he was recorded as leaving the city jail in May of the following year, perhaps indicating that he was given into the hands of the city executioner.[50] In a similar case, a Liberty

County slave, Jim, was executed for the attempted murder of a white man, Elisha McDonald, though sufficient doubts emerged about this case to drag it out for more than a year.[51]

White authorities were invariably keen to arrest and punish African Americans who murdered whites. When in March 1861, on the eve of Georgia's secession from the Union, an Irish laborer, Patrick Brady, was murdered in Yamacraw by a slave, no pains were spared to bring the culprit to justice. City newspapers carried graphic accounts of the murder, supposedly by a runaway slave whom Brady was trying to arrest, and of the pursuit by the city police. Although it was originally thought that the murderer escaped on a riverboat, he was found three days after the crime within a few hundred yards of the scene, harbored by fellow slaves. During his arrest the slave, Paul, was shot in the leg, and the city watch and later the county militia struggled to prevent Brady's "friends and countrymen" from lynching him. Their efforts were ultimately in vain; Paul died from his injuries two days after being arrested.[52]

Although the standards of justice in the lowcountry were appreciably harsher for African Americans than for white criminals, justices and magistrates often went to some lengths to secure proper convictions. In 1824 a slave named Ben was put on trial for "striking and cutting James Dent a white man," but at his trial by a court of magistrates and freeholders of Chatham County Ben was acquitted.[53] In 1815 the Charleston jailer actually upheld the rights of a free black prisoner of war to defend himself against blows from two white citizens. Apparently this particular African American accidentally jostled two white men, John Tiller and John Hughes. They felt that their honor had been infringed, and the ensuing exchange of blows was halted only by the arrival of Mr. Hefferman, the jailer. Instead of arresting the black man, as was perhaps expected, he told the white men that as the African American was both free and a prisoner of war he was "as good as any of you, and he can whip you both, and I wish he had done it and black'ned your eyes." Much to their astonishment, the two white men found themselves spending a night in the jail and having to pay $3.50 to be released the next day.[54]

According to the Georgia Penal Code, an African American could escape punishment for striking a white person only if he or she acted under the direct orders of an owner or employer.[55] The clearest case of this kind occurred in 1795, when a free black named Lewis was ultimately excused from punishment for the confinement and beating of James McCabe.[56] McCabe was the customs house officer for the port of Savannah and was seized by Lewis and a group of other Africans on suspicion of trying to steal a slave when he boarded their schooner, the *Nancy*.[57] Although there was no real dispute about the facts of the case, namely that Lewis had imprisoned McCabe, probably struck him, and released him the following morning, the question of whether Lewis acted properly was hotly debated. As the customs officer, McCabe had the right to enter any ship in the port at any time.[58] Once his guilt had been established, Lewis was sentenced to receive four hundred lashes. After the trial, it emerged that Lewis had been acting under the strict orders of the white captain of the *Nancy*, Vincent Hyer. Hyer subsequently petitioned Governor George Mathews to pardon Lewis, who had, after all, been acting on his authority. Lewis and several other crewmen were not Americans but Africans employed on a slave ship as a result of illness and desertion of white crew members when in Africa. On arrival in Savannah, Hyer together with the rest of his white crew had been forced into quarantine, necessitating his leaving Lewis, as the most senior seaman, in charge. On their first night in port an attempt was made to steal some of the slaves on board the ship. Consequently, Lewis was given clear instructions by Hyer the following morning that if the attempt was repeated he was "to confine such person on board the schooner until morning."[59] On finding James McCabe acting suspiciously around the wharves after midnight, Lewis naturally apprehended him.

Further intercessions to the governor on Lewis's behalf took place in the following days. William Wallace argued that McCabe was at fault because he had apparently "endeavored by the offer of some money, a handkerchief &c to get one of the new Negroes to go with him." Wallace believed that had Lewis been a white man, no prosecution would have taken place, but because he was black, and "the minds of people are much governed by prejudice," he received a sentence "which in justice ought to be inflicted on his accuser."[60] Thomas Cumming also believed that Lewis's race had determined his judicial treatment. He argued that, as an African, Lewis could not be expected to "understand so clearly, the distinctions our laws have created between people of his color (tho' freemen) and white men."[61] By far the most telling intervention came from the solicitor general of Chatham County, George Woodruff. He argued in logical legal terms that Lewis should not be punished for his actions because he was acting on the orders of his employer. The slave code of 1770 had exempted slaves (and by implication all African Americans) from punishment when they were acting under the express authority of their employers or owners. Woodruff pointed out that "humanity should dictate the most humane construition" of the law in this case.[62] The fact that McCabe was white and Lewis black should thus not have any bearing on the outcome of the case. Governor Mathews evidently agreed with Woodruff that McCabe was not entitled to the privileges of race in this instance, and Lewis was pardoned.

Physical altercations between African Americans and nonelite whites invariably occurred in typically lower-class environments where violence was commonplace such as the dramshop. They were often engendered by the racial attitudes of nonslaveholders, who occasionally interpreted the actions of African Americans as a direct infringement on their own racial privileges. Other types of criminal interaction, especially property crime, sometimes involved biracial cooperation. The often contradictory nature of biracial interaction, involving conflict as well as cooperation, demonstrates that race relations are complex and difficult to pin down. We should not expect lower-class Southerners, black or white, to have a coherently structured set of views. If anything, criminal relationships between nonslaveholders and slaves show just how flexible and adaptable racial attitudes could be.

People usually committed property crimes for financial gain. Stolen goods could either be sold or used as raw materials in the fabrication of other items. The lowcountry residents who suffered most in this primitive form of wealth redistribution were the economically privileged, usually planters and merchants. While it is perhaps no surprise that the poorest white people committed property crimes, the often willing involvement of African Americans with white people in acts of theft and robbery is more difficult to explain.[63] Chattel slavery and racial oppression combined to ensure that few African Americans, even those who were free, were able to acquire substantial property apart from their own dwelling.[64] Bondspeople rarely viewed thefts, often committed against their masters, as a real crime. Alex Lichtenstein has branded this attitude the "moral economy" of slavery, whereby slaves viewed their master's property as "theirs," to be taken without moral qualms.[65] One visitor to the lowcountry understood this dictum as "I belong to massa, all massa has belongs to me," and thought that security for whites would be achieved only by "keeping the darkies well employed."[66] Stealing food or other items from one's master, however, is highly distinct from engaging in theft from third parties. I am not concerned with crimes that were executed solely by slaves, but rather with the motivation of those African Americans who joined with white people in committing criminal acts.

An investigation of the motivation of white people who combined with African Americans to commit criminal acts against the established authorities offers insights into the class consciousness of whites. Were crimes committed with African Americans part of a biracial class identification, or were they merely alliances of convenience? Did nonelite whites see criminal activity as a way of expressing their independence of the elite? Although there are only a few clear-cut cases in which African Americans partnered with whites in criminal activities, this is most likely owing to the scarcity of trial transcripts rather than the lack of such crimes. No distinction, for example, was made by the clerks of the superior courts between those prosecuted for theft when acting alone or with an accomplice. Only those few trials for which the full testimony has survived reveal a biracial criminal relationship.

The best example of biracial cooperation in a criminal endeavor comes from the late 1830s, when, on the night of Saturday, February 5, 1838, a slave named George and a white youth named Henry E. Forsyth perpetrated a theft from the workshop of Isaac Morell, where they were both employed.[67] After breaking in, the pair took $118 and escaped on the Augusta road. Within a week of the theft, however, George and Henry had been tracked to Augusta, arrested, and returned to Savannah; it was not long before Forsyth confessed. Forsyth was arraigned before the May session of the Chatham County Superior Court, found guilty of larceny, and sentenced to three years' hard labor at the state penitentiary in Milledgeville; no records survive showing what punishment if any was given to George. By his criminal involvement with an African American, Henry Forsyth had crossed the racial lines that divided Southern society.[68]

George and Forsyth were obviously acquainted from their joint employment in the workshop of Isaac Morell. Eighteen-year-old Forsyth "was in the employ of Mr Morell but was not an indentured apprentice," and it is certainly possible that this job, working for an important cabinetmaker in Savannah, was Forsyth's first employment. During the trial, several witnesses testified that Forsyth was unhappy in Savannah, stating that he quarreled frequently with his brother (who apparently also worked for Morell) and that a desire to leave the city was the motive for the theft.[69] Forsyth's obvious problem was that relocation would cost money, which he apparently lacked. Thus it was most likely in an attempt to solve his financial problems and facilitate his migration that Forsyth turned to theft.

Isaac Morell was clearly a man of some substance. In 1837 he paid tax on merchandise valued at $11,000 and recorded his personal property as one slave (presumably George), a dog, and a house in Liberty ward worth $1,250.[70] In his own testimony, Morell stated that his employees were paid on Saturdays and that any money left over was kept in his desk in the store until Monday. As employees, both George and Forsyth would have been aware of this fact. Clearly the pair knew each other fairly well, and it is certainly possible that a friendship had developed between them. In his confession, Forsyth stated that the original idea of the theft had been George's because the bondsman knew where the key to the store was kept.[71] George's motive for participation in the theft is more difficult to determine. That he traveled to Augusta with Forsyth rather than seeking to escape to freedom in the Northern states would seem to suggest that George's paramount objective was to leave Morell's service. By traveling with Forsyth, he received the protection afforded by any white person to an African American, while enjoying the freedom that being "owned" by Forsyth would have entailed. To undertake this risk, George must have trusted Forsyth not to abuse their relationship.

George and Henry Forsyth are just one example of a nonslaveholding white person interacting with a slave in ways that contravened the usual patterns of race relations in a Southern city like Savannah. Their relationship as outlined in the trial documents was clearly not one of domination or subordination based on race. Rather, two people, who worked together on a daily basis and most probably lived similar lives, were able to overcome the status differences between bondsman and freeman to form a mutually advantageous partnership.

The case of Henry E. Forsyth does not in itself prove that African Americans and nonslaveholding whites interacted criminally any more than sporadically. Unfortunately, detailed reports of other somewhat similar crimes involving partnerships between nonslaveholding whites and African Americans have not survived. A report in the *Savannah Republican* in 1819 noted that a wagon belonging to Jonathan Robinson had been "robbed by a party of Negroes, and supposed some white men, at or near the seven-mile-house."[72] The report of this crime suggests that the participants were members of a gang engaged in a life of regular crime, rather than casual acquaintances, but there is insufficient evidence to speculate on precise power relationship between gang members.

Not all biracial crimes involved the direct participation of white people. For example, Frederick Miller was indicted by the Charleston District Court for inciting a female slave named Dinah to steal items from Henry Ryer.[73] The items stolen included a gold watch and a spyglass as well as bank bills and coins worth nearly $4,000. Miller and Dinah were apparently well acquainted because she immediately brought the goods she had taken to him and received payment for them. It is not recorded how much Miller gave Dinah, though it was possibly only a small sum. In some respects, Miller was exploiting Dinah, using her to steal for him while not exposing himself to the full risks of getting caught. But the fact that he was indicted by the court shows that this operation was not entirely risk-free for him. Dinah's motivation for committing the theft was probably financial gain. Maybe Miller had paid her for stolen goods before, and their relationship was characterized not only by a motive of mutual profit but also a high degree of trust. Such trust did not necessarily extend to include an "honor" code among thieves. When bondsman Charles was convicted by the Chatham County Inferior Court of stealing shoes from David Dillon, he was quick to name a white man, John Sehnaars, as an accessory to the crime.[74] Similarly, when the watch apprehended two slaves in the process of stealing cigars from the store of W. Lippit & Company, the slaves pleaded in mitigation that "they had been induced to commit this act by an individual who had promised to purchase from them the fruits of their villainy." The editorial in the *Georgian* commenting that "if there were no receivers, there would be no thieves" accurately reflected contemporary attitudes among the elite.[75]

Of course, not all the trade in stolen goods involved theft from unknown third parties. The easiest place for bondspeople to obtain stolen goods for sale was on their own plantation. According to grand jury presentments, a significant part of the trade between rural bondspeople and white shopkeepers involved goods stolen from the plantation or the mansion house. Many of these goods were highly unlikely to have been legitimate trade goods in the possession of bondspeople. In 1824 the state legislature prohibited bondspeople from selling cotton, tobacco, rice, corn, and poultry, in fact all articles "except such as are known to be usually manufactured or vended by slaves," meaning fish, milk, and vegetables.[76] Planters most likely heeded these regulations. In 1818 Ebenezer Kellogg visited one lowcountry estate where bondspeople had grown and sold cotton to the value of $50.[77] Yet by 1832 Alexander Telfair specifically ordered his overseers not to permit his slaves to plant cotton.[78]

This, of course, did not end theft by bondspeople of plantation crops, goods, or supplies. One of the slaves on Argyle Island was apprehended in Savannah by the city watch trying to sell "eight or nine bushels of rough rice" purloined from the plantation.[79] By April 1826 the Chatham County Grand Jury was complaining of "the trade in old iron recently commenced in this city, which holds out a temptation to our slaves to render articles of value useless and purloin plantation tools always certain of finding a ready sale for such articles."[80] Such articles were clearly not the usual property of slaves, which would have been known to white shopkeepers. In an effort to disprove a charge of accepting stolen iron from African Americans, ironmonger William Williams published fourteen affidavits attesting to his honesty.[81] Among the testimonials were several from white employees stating that Williams had told them not to purchase items from slaves without tickets.[82] Other citizens recorded that Williams had kept watch for items stolen from them in case they were offered to him.[83] The specific allegation Williams was attempting to refute pertained to a barrel screw belonging to Josiah Davenport. Williams claimed that one of his clerks must have purchased it when he was not at the store and rested his claims for innocence on the fact that he made no attempt to conceal the screw—in fact, it was on open display. Williams was eventually acquitted of all charges relating to this affair, despite an extremely zealous prosecutor. Nevertheless, African Americans knew they could sell stolen items to white shopkeepers relatively easily.[84] That some nonelite whites were willing to enter into such class conspiracies illuminates their instinct for profit and self-advancement regardless of the social consequences.

It was not only shopkeepers who purchased stolen items from the plantations. William Grimes mentioned that his overseer, who was "very poor . . . secretly bought things from the Negroes which they had stolen from my master."[85] Grimes's testimony suggests that the extant prosecutions for trading in stolen goods are probably only the tip of a very large iceberg and that slaves, overseers, and local nonslaveholding farmers often colluded to defraud the elite.

Contemporary court records document the difficulties associated with prosecutions for receiving stolen goods. Between 1782 and 1865, the Superior Court of Chatham County dealt with forty-one such cases, resulting in only four convictions, the last of which occurred fifteen years before secession.[86] Not all these cases involved African Americans. Some concerned only white people, but without further details it is impossible to determine precisely which of these cases involved biracial contact and which were racially separate.[87] Several of those arraigned for receiving stolen goods had been, or were to be, the subject of a separate prosecution by the City Council of Savannah. Peter Coleman, charged in 1796 for receiving stolen goods, had, for example, previously been fined $5 for retailing liquors without a license and $10 for entertaining Negroes on Sunday.[88] Francis Foley, against whom charges of handling stolen goods were eventually dropped, was fined more than $100 in the 1830s and 1840s by the City Council of Savannah for retailing on Sundays and "entertaining negroes."[89] The individuals who dealt in stolen goods, whether purchased from an African American or from a white person, were what can generally be termed the "criminal sort." Most of those receiving stolen goods seem to have been nonslaveholders. James King, for example, who served four years in the state penitentiary for receiving stolen goods, was a twenty-eight-year-old farmer born in England.[90] Buying stolen items from slaves was a gendered activity—all but two of these indictments were of men rather than women. While one of these women, Elizabeth Dotson, received a thirty-day jail term and a $100 fine for purchasing rice from a slave without a ticket, receiving stolen goods seems to have been the preserve of nonelite white men rather than women.[91] Few women, especially if they were married, would have had ready access to the cash needed to purchase stolen goods. If, however, the trade in stolen goods was a gesture of defiance toward the white elite, whereby poor white men were asserting and maintaining their independence by whatever means were available, then the gendering of this activity becomes clearer. Nonelite white men were more able to assert their social independence than white women, who were usually not assigned a public role in lowcountry society. The willingness of white men, sometimes in partnership with African Americans, to break the law can thus be seen not only as an attempt to obtain a financial advantage but also as a highly politicized action.[92] By joining with African Americans in subverting the social ethic of the elite, nonslaveholders indicated that race was not of prime importance to their social ideology and that racial boundaries were flexible and permeable enough to permit individual nonslaveholders occasionally to identify a class solidarity with African Americans.

Bondspeople stole, whether food or trade goods, for a wide variety of reasons. Certainly it would be wrong to assume that all goods stolen by slaves were sold to white traders. In 1802 Reuben King noted that he had lost "one short coat, one stieped vest and one pair of Nankeen over-halls" when Mr. Holzendorph's store in Darien had been broken into by "Mr Couper's Negroes."[93] Goods such as these were probably stolen for personal use. An example is the trial of two bondsmen named Frank and Abram in 1797. The pair were convicted of robbing the house of William Moubray in St. Marys and then heading for Florida. When Frank was apprehended, Moubray saw that he "had on his waistcoat" and had other personal items in his bag.[94] In other cases, the destination of stolen goods is harder to determine. In 1792 a bondsman named James Cook, belonging to the blacksmith Abraham Leggett, was convicted of stealing money and shoes from William Vanderlocht.[95] After his apprehension, Cook took Vanderlocht to several locations in Savannah to recover his property. It is unlikely that the white residents of these dwellings had bought stolen items from Cook. Among those visited were local notables such as Sir George Houstoun, James Mossman, and Francis Courvoisie, who among them owned more than two hundred slaves.[96] It is therefore probable that Cook was supplying their slaves with merchandise he stole.

Although slaves sometimes stole goods for their own use, more expensive items such as plantation crops and tools held little intrinsic value to bondspeople; they were desirable for their resale value. The complicity and encouragement of white shopkeepers was of vital importance in enabling slaves to retail stolen goods. Lack of effective security measures often made it easy for bondspeople to purloin goods both on and off the plantation. "Sundry wharf owners and residents of the city of Charleston," for instance, knew that the security of their goods "lying upon the wharves" was not thorough. They were fully aware that their cotton was easy prey for the "continual depredations" of bondspeople who found a ready market in white people "without property or character." As both the slaves and the white traders knew, "it is impossible to determine to whom [the cotton] belongs," and therefore "prosecutions are so easily defeated." As a measure of the scale of this traffic, the elite petitioners believed that they had lost five hundred bales of cotton in this manner.[97] Similar complaints were heard from Chatham County in 1825. The Grand Jury stated that the usual method of stealing prebagged cotton was for slaves to take "from each bale a part, not possible to be missed by the owner at the time." This cotton was then "carried constantly to shops for sale . . . [and] amounts to a heavy loss." What most irritated the jury was that the proceeds obtained by bondspeople were invariably spent on alcohol. Thus "some of the best servants in town have become . . . worthless." In an attempt to weaken the class alliance evinced by this relationship, the jury highlighted that "the seller of the cotton to the shop-keeper gets but a mite for his share of the robbery;" it is clear, however, that this "mite" was sufficient to make the theft of cotton by African Americans worthwhile.[98]

Lowcountry grand juries document the general disquiet and consternation among slaveholders about the effect that the trade in stolen goods was having on their slaves. The Chatham County Grand Jury contended several times that the trade in stolen goods undermined the relationship between owner and slave and that it was "demoralizing to the black population, ruinous to their health, and destructive of their usefulness as laborers." A slave should see "his master as his best friend instead of his dreading him, as the punisher of the faithless and the robber."[99] It was for this reason that slaveholders in Georgia and South Carolina formed the Savannah River Anti–Slave Traffick Association in 1846.[100] Grand juries almost always laid the blame for the trade in stolen goods on shop-keepers, preferring to believe their slaves were "misguided victims [of] mercenary individuals."[101] But the willing complicity of slaves in this "devious conduct" proves that the trade in stolen goods required ongoing cooperation between supplier and receiver.[102]

Charles Ball's narrative provides a valuable insight into the treatment nonelite white people could experience at the hands of elite planters and their overseers if caught or even suspected of trading with slaves. Ball believed that his master was predisposed to think that anyone who had regular contact with African Americans in an unofficial capacity must be holding "criminal intercourse with them." After terrorizing one particular forester who was believed to be buying stolen items from bondspeople, Ball's master burned his house to the ground, rejoicing that "he had routed one receiver of stolen goods out of the country." Indeed, the planters with whom Ball's master discussed this issue agreed that there were "many white men who, residing in the district without property, or without interest in preserving the morals of the slaves . . . [carried] on an unlawful and criminal traffic with the Negroes." As he listened to this conversation, Ball "began to suppose the losses of the planters in this way must be immense [because] so many white men were referred to by name as being concerned in this criminal business."[103]

The network of rivers in the lowcountry, principally the Savannah, Ogechee, Newport, Altamaha, and St. Marys, facilitated the trade in stolen goods between nonslaveholding whites and African Americans. Boats of all sizes transported goods and people up the main thoroughfares of the lowcountry and along the coast. Most of the sea island plantations had several different points at which boats could land or pick up goods, often well away from the main house and thus far from the gaze of either owner or overseer. State authorities were well aware that goods were being smuggled on the river system. In 1815 boat captains were required to complete a certificate stating the cargo transported and were subject to fines of $50 for any discrepancies found.[104] The amendment of 1816 was even more explicit, prohibiting boats from carrying any items to be sold by slaves because it had "been found, by fatal experience [to be] an encouragement to theft."[105]

Although some of the river trade was between white people and slaves, on other occasions the trade between the plantations and the boats was carried out by African Americans alone. In these encounters, slave rowers and sailors would trade with personal contacts on the plantations, using the mobility afforded them by their employment to provide goods to the slaves in return for homemade or stolen articles. White boat captains colluded in this trade. It was highly unlikely that the white captain of a small boat would have been ignorant of what his crew were doing or that he would not see the new cargo they were carrying. The willingness of some white boat captains to permit this trade suggests that they received a financial return from it. Certainly the Georgetown Grand Jury believed that the trade from boats was possible only because it was "under the protection of white men of no character."[106] Bonded rowers performed the actual trading to exploit their personal contacts on the plantations. A mutual profit motive of captain, crew, and plantation slaves thus combined to inform their criminal behavior.

Geography and laziness also worked to defeat attempts to prevent trade from the boats in the coastal area. Although bondspeople were forbidden to own boats and canoes, they made or bought such vessels. Fanny Kemble recorded that two of the slave carpenters at Butler Point spent their free time making a boat which they sold for $60 to a neighboring planter.[107] Kemble also saw her slaves rowing to Darien on market day to sell their produce in "their slight canoes, scooped out of the trunk of a tree."[108] It was widely acknowledged that slaves could not be prevented from using boats, and "in this way the vigilance of the patrole is defeated."[109] This trade was not confined to the distant corners of plantations. In Georgetown, for example, the Grand Jury protested about boats trading at night with slaves in the harbor and wharves of Georgetown itself.[110] Similarly, the Savannah Grand Jury pleaded for the institution of a river patrol to combat "midnight depredations . . . [and] for the protection of the rice, cotton, lumber and other property of the community."[111]

The general ineffectiveness of the patrol and the lax implementation of the laws governing illegal trading was a frequent topic of complaint. The Chatham County Grand Jury of 1845 was not alone when it opined that the law would continue to be broken "as long as our citizens are indifferent to its existence and our magistrates delinquent." According to jurors, "in several districts there is no organised militia company and therefore no regular patrol duty is performed in them."[112] Six years later, in an attempt to make the patrol more effective, the jurors requested that shopkeepers be disbarred from serving on the city watch, presumably out of fear that they would not prevent thefts by slaves from which they would later profit.[113] In 1855 the Grand Jury attempted to get the city watch to patrol outside the city limits and so arrest those purchasing stolen goods in areas under county rather than city jurisdiction.[114] On the eve of the Civil War, the Grand Jury complained that the "culpable indifference, inactivity or collusion of those officers who would detect and expose those gross violations of law" was responsible for many of the worst criminal offenses in the county.[115]

Of course, not all African Americans were aware that they were participating in criminal activities with white people. In January 1824 various leather articles were stolen from John Gardner by a white employee named Clark.[116] Clark subsequently sold them to George W. Jennings before absconding. Gardner immediately suspected that Jennings was involved, perhaps because he had had previous dealings with him, or because he knew that Clark and Jennings were acquainted. When Gardner arrived at Jennings's house, he found Jennings and an African American loading a cart with trunks that were later found to contain articles from Gardner's workshop. On seeing Gardner approach, Jennings fled, leaving the cart and the African American behind. Jennings was apprehended within an hour "in a small house on the Augusta road." Gardner was a tanner, Jennings a shoemaker. The principal article stolen was "undressed leather," which, according to Gardner, was not sold to the public but used to produce finished leather goods. He knew the leather to be his because "no one else tans in Savannah."[117] Jennings's landlady, Mrs. Bailly, stated that she saw the various trunks labeled "Augusta," suggesting that Jennings intended to set up a new business there with these stolen raw materials.[118]

Jennings received a four-year prison sentence. Clark apparently was never caught. The state penitentiary recorded the arrival of Jennings on February 28, 1824, and his release four years later. Jennings does not appear in the tax digests from the early 1820s, signifying that he owned little if any property. Jennings, only twenty-two years old at the time of his crime, had migrated from Virginia to work as a shoemaker in Savannah.[119] It is almost certain that Jennings did not own slaves. The African American who was seen helping him load the cart is not identified at the trial as belonging to Jennings and may have had no idea that the goods were stolen. The two may well have been acquaintances or neighbors, or Jennings may have hired the African American. After being discovered by Gardner, Jennings ran up West Broad Street so he apparently lived in the vicinity of African Americans, who were concentrated in the western suburbs of Yamacraw, Ewensburgh, and Oglethorpe ward.

Thefts certainly were a problem for individual slaveholders but, they never seriously undermined the institution of slavery itself, despite some fears. Probably the most emotive and subversive crime Southern whites could commit was to help a slave escape from his or her master or from slavery completely. Helping slaves to escape transgressed every concept of the sanctity of property, the rights of masters, and the propriety of African bondage. Some white people who helped slaves escape genuinely wanted to help them, though some cared little for bondspeople and even less for the system that enslaved them, and others saw an escaped slave as a means to personal economic advancement. It is sometimes difficult to determine from extant criminal records the exact nature of a crime. The people who wrote down charges and indictments believed that those caught in possession of a fugitive slave had stolen the slave for their own use. To contemplate that a white person was actually assisting a slave to escape from slavery, with no ulterior motive, would have seemed implausible. Yet although official court records are obscure about the motivation of white people toward fugitive bondspeople, the narratives of slaves who made it to freedom sometimes indicate that white people, usually the poorest individuals, assisted them in their flight.

It seems that white people were helping slaves to escape from the very onset of slavery in Georgia. In 1757, the patrol had been given "full power" to enter and search the house of anyone they suspected of harboring fugitive slaves. Those attempting to hinder the patrol in the execution of its duty were liable to a fine of twenty shillings, and those convicted of harboring fugitives faced a thirty-shilling fine for the first day the slave was missing and three shillings per day thereafter.[120] In the colonial period, more than a fifth of the newspaper advertisements for runaway slaves mentioned the possibility, or certainty, that someone was harboring them.[121] The advertisements make it clear that those suspected of being harbored were more likely than other fugitives to be described by their owners as "well-known in Savannah," indicating that many fugitives used their familiarity with the city to secure employment, accommodation, or a passage to the North. Harbored slaves were also more often believed to be heading toward Savannah than those who were not harbored. Of course, the motives for absence varied enormously among bondspeople. Joseph Gibbons believed that his slaves Santee and Jemmy had been stolen and subsequently sold in Florida by Simon Bradley and Samuel Cruse.[122] Others fled with a hope of eventual freedom. One fugitive named Billy had, following a previous escape, worked for two years on a ship under a Captain Simpson, presumably with the captain's knowledge.[123] Elizabeth Deveaux's slave Flora was "supposed to be harbored under the bluff by sailors, as she has been frequently seen about the wharves and the shipping."[124] Clearly Flora hoped she might escape on one of the numerous ships arriving in the city, and another ad from her mistress a year later indicates that she succeeded in her attempt.[125]

Data from the 1820s both confirm and challenge some of the impressions from the colonial era. Harbored fugitives were still more likely than other runaways to be described as "well-known," and the most popular destination remained Savannah. Yet, whereas less than a quarter of runaways in the colonial period were believed to be harbored, nearly half were thought to be so in the 1820s.[126] In the colonial era many fugitives were newly arrived in America and thus had few contacts off the plantations. Consequently, they were more likely to seek freedom in the interior of the colony or at sea.[127] The closing of the external slave trade in 1808 meant that by 1820 more lowcountry slaves than ever before were native born and had had the opportunity to cultivate contacts with those willing to harbor them. Male fugitives still constituted a large majority of those sought in newspaper ads, yet among those believed to be harbored a gender difference is evident. Nearly two-thirds of all female fugitives between 1822 and 1829 were suspected of being concealed, compared with only a third of fugitive men. Some women were harbored by African American acquaintances or relatives in Savannah.[128] Others sought their freedom in the company of whites. In 1825, S. Kearsey advertised for Peggy, whom he believed had been "enticed away from him by Samuel Townsend, Patrick Monroe, Joseph Orston and others."[129] Two years later, Richard Byne believed that Mary Ann had been given a pass "by a white man."[130] The reason that proportionately more female than male fugitives were harbored may have been because more occupations were open to men.[131] Female runaways worked as seamstresses, vendors, and nurses, whereas men could hire themselves out for a wider variety of artisan or portering work.[132] In other words, female fugitives may not have been as able as males to support themselves without outside help. Perhaps also planters did not believe that bondswomen could survive without the help of others.

Savannah was the most popular destination for fugitives because it offered, for men especially, the best chance of blending into the urban African American population and the most opportunities for employment. More than a third of male fugitives who were listed with an occupation had some experience in making or manning boats.[133] Such skills would have been of little use outside a major port. Another third possessed a variety of artisan skills such as carpentry, shoemaking, and tanning and thus could find work from local employers. The final third consisted of domestic servants and a small group of entertainers: fiddlers, drummers, and actors, who perhaps found employment in the taverns and brothels in Yamacraw.

Many fugitives received help from free African Americans or other slaves in Savannah. John Brown was assisted by a free black barber in the city during one of his several escape attempts. Brown believed that he was "in safer hands with one of my own race," and although the barber did help him, it was only temporarily and he was told that if "it were found out I was helping you off, it would break me."[134] Three slaves were confined briefly in the city jail in the 1850s for helping a runaway slave before presumably being turned over to their owners for punishment.[135] Runaways were apparently regularly concealed in specially constructed cavities under the floorboards at the First African Baptist Church; small holes were punched in the floor so they could breathe.[136] Transient free blacks, especially those involved in the shipping trades, found several opportunities to help fugitive slaves. In 1799 a Chatham County jury wrote to Governor James Jackson asking for clemency for a free black sailor, Moses, from Philadelphia, whom they had condemned to death, as he was "unletter'd and was not knowing the consequences" of his actions.[137] Moses had concealed a female slave named Phillis, owned by David Manners, on board his boat, promising her freedom in Philadelphia as "all the

Negroes are free in that place."[138] Similarly, in 1822, Prince Champlain, a free black sailor from New York, was convicted of attempting to conceal two female slaves in the hold of the *Diana* from New York, on which he worked as a cook.[139] He was sentenced to four years in jail and perpetual slavery afterward but was apparently released after two years.[140] Clearly, free African Americans regularly harbored fugitive slaves.

More important in terms of racial symbolism were those sympathetic white people who were sometimes willing to help fugitive African Americans with food, clothing, employment, and even passes. In nearly all cases, those white people who helped African Americans to escape bondage were nonslaveholders.[141] For example, in 1814 William Hutson advertised for his slave Sam, whom he believed would "be found selling fish (being a great fisherman) in Savannah market, or skulking about Savannah, [and] probably may contract with some fisherman to sell for him."[142] The fact that Sam would have been known to the fishermen through his previous employment clearly helped him to remain at liberty. Similarly, in 1839 the sheriff of McIntosh County was keen to recapture "wild" William Green, "under sentence of imprisonment in the jail of McIntosh county, for harboring a slave," because his behavior threatened the normal pattern of race relations.[143]

Nearly 15 percent of fugitives between 1822 and 1829 were reported to possess a pass. No doubt some were forged either by the slaves themselves or by other literate African Americans, but others were almost certainly written for them by white people.[144] Personal acquaintances were often the source of passes for fugitive slaves. Christopher Hall believed that his slave John had been given a pass by a white man with whom "he was seen several times talking." Hall identified the man as being a late "companion with him [John] in gaol, and it is supposed has given him a pass to New Orleans."[145] Two employees of shipmaster Thomas Holding, a slave named Ned and a white man named Stephen Conyers, conspired to desert together from the schooner *Polly*. Holding believed that the pair were headed toward St. Marys or Charleston because they were familiar with both ports.[146] In 1789 Samuel Iverson advertised for his slave Isaac, who had worked as a barber in Savannah. Iverson "supposed he is harbored by some white person as he has been encouraged in making his escape by Mr Clark, a waggoner or barber."[147] Mr. Clark probably worked with Isaac. Personal relationships originating in the workplace could engender a biracial interaction that subverted the interests of the white elite.

Some African Americans purchased their passes. During one of his many unsuccessful escape attempts, John Brown "obtained a forged pass from a poor white man, for which I gave him an old hen." [148] The bartering of the hen for a pass was probably a symbolic act. Certainly the unnamed white man would have been aware of the consequences of his action if caught. His acceptance of the hen merely put the seal on a transaction that provided John Brown with one means toward a successful escape. Similarly, an ad for a bondsman named Cain in 1807 stated that he had worked as a boatman on the North Edisto River and had managed to obtain a pass from "some ill-disposed person." [149] Owners obviously viewed the granting of passes to slaves by nonslaveholding whites as an infringement of their masterly prerogative. By using phrases such as "ill-disposed," owners were expressing their belief that the action of a white person in giving passes to slaves was a personal insult to them rather than a more general assault on slavery as an institution. It was easier to conceive that someone who gave a pass to a slave did so out of personal rather than altruistic motives. Legislators classified improperly giving a pass to a slave in the same category as harboring a fugitive and liable to the same punishment. [150]

Other white people were duped by fugitive bondspeople into giving passes to ease their passage to freedom. William Craft managed to obtain a pass from his employer, a cabinetmaker, who even wished him a pleasant holiday. [151] Moses Roper practiced a similar deception on a family of poor white people he encountered near the Altamaha River. Knowing that he would need a pass to reach Savannah, Roper convinced a poor white couple that he had lost his pass, and although the white man professed himself illiterate, his son was instructed to write a pass. Roper proceeded to tell him exactly what to write, "having heard several free colored men read theirs . . . filling a large sheet of paper for the passport, and another sheet with recommendations." Not content with this pass, which he believed would carry only limited weight, Roper met with a group of cattle drovers who obtained the recommendation of a local planter for him. The drovers were also illiterate, and Roper acknowledged that he had got them "intoxicated" before they visited the planter. [152]

Naturally, historians should not read too much into the suspicions of owners as revealed in runaway notices. Some owners did believe that their slaves were being enticed away by "ill-disposed" white people, but this fear was out of all proportion to the number of prosecutions for slave stealing. Between 1782 and 1860 only forty people were indicted before the Chatham County Superior Court for inveigling slaves, aiding slaves to escape, or "Negro stealing." Because markedly fewer prosecutions occurred after 1810 and most cases resulted in acquittals, the inveigling of slaves by white people clearly did not reach epidemic proportions in the lowcountry.[153] Of sixteen people who were imprisoned for short periods of time in Savannah City Jail for inveigling slaves between 1809–15 and 1855–60, at least six were released after spending only few days in jail, presumably because they were innocent.[154] Yet those few who were actually convicted of "slave stealing" could expect a long term in the state penitentiary. John Fitzgerald received a twelve-year sentence in 1828, though he escaped after serving three years, and Allen W. Davies's ten-year sentence was cut short by his death in 1863. Most "slave harborers" were nonelite people: those convicted from Chatham County included farmers, sailors, and a barber.[155] In 1793 the judge of the Chatham County Superior Court acquitted James Cochran on a technicality, though considering him "a bad man, and . . . connected with runaway Negroes," and even excused his court fees as "he was not worth 5/- over and above his wearing apparel."[156]

Only two of those indicted or imprisoned for inveigling slaves were women. Although women may have assisted fugitive slaves who arrived at their homes asking for help, it is unlikely that their involvement would have gone further into the public sphere. Women rarely enjoyed the same freedom of movement as men and therefore had fewer opportunities to purchase from or even encounter slaves in informal environments.[157] The provision of temporary assistance such as food or drink was unlikely to be either noticed or prosecuted.

The motivation of the perpetrator in one case of slave stealing in Camden County in 1821 may be ascertained. Tapley Tullis, a twenty-eight-year-old farmer, was convicted of stealing a slave from his neighbor, Cotton Rawls.[158] Rawls testified at the trial that his slave Mingo had run away and had been found in the possession of Tullis in the backcountry. Tullis apparently confessed that he had come across the slave while conducting business in the upcountry and had intended to deliver him up to his rightful owner. Tullis was convicted on the crucial evidence that he had claimed title to the slave when speaking to Joseph Reed. Under the law, holding a fugitive bondsperson for more than forty-eight hours without reporting it to a constable was deemed prima-facie evidence of intention to steal the slave.[159] That Tullis fled once the slave was caught was seen as further evidence of his guilt. Tullis served the full four-year sentence for his crime in the state penitentiary.[160]

The motive for Tullis's action was most probably financial. A fugitive slave, especially when encountered far from home, would have seemed an easy way to make a profit. Although Tullis had been a slave owner in 1819, he no longer owned slaves by 1820. His own slave may have died or fled in the intervening period, making it harder to support his young family. The only land Tullis held in 1819 was 140 acres of unimproved poor-quality pine land; it would have been a struggle to make ends meet.[161] Tullis may have known Cotton Rawls's slave personally because the two white men resided in the same district of Camden County. Unlike Tullis, Rawls was engaged in manufacturing rather than agriculture, and in pursuit of his business he owned several slaves.[162] The personal relations between Rawls and Tullis may not have been cordial, and Tullis may have been maliciously attempting to deprive Rawls of his property.

The prospect of economic gain also motivated criminals such as Richard Francis. Just before his execution in 1816, Francis confessed that he had stolen three slaves from near the Altamaha River, later selling them in East Florida.[163] White people such as Francis would either take up African Americans whom they encountered wandering the highway or entice them away by promising to help them to freedom.[164] The white people involved were almost always nonslaveholders. Of three men prosecuted in Camden County in 1797 for inveigling slaves, two possessed no real property and the third only a hundred acres of pine barren.[165] The relationship of "slave stealers" with African Americans was exploitative and sometimes cruel. Some slaves wished to leave a particular locality or to change masters, but others were taken while visiting family members on nearby plantations or while working on distant parts of an estate. This relationship does not exhibit a class alliance between the races; rather it shows that nonelite whites could occasionally act in isolation, to the detriment of both African Americans and the white elite.

John D. Roche encountered a fugitive slave south of Savannah who claimed to have been visiting family further down the coast. Roche suspected that the slave, who called himself "Bob," was a runaway, yet when they arrived in Savannah, he permitted Bob to work for him. As a fugitive slave, Bob clearly had little to lose by falling in with somebody like Roche, who offered a measure of protection from the prying questions of the more suspicious minded of Savannah's citizens. Indeed, Thomas Wilson testified at Roche's trial for slave stealing that Bob had told him that he belonged to Roche. On his arrival in Savannah, Roche had apparently looked in the Savannah newspapers for an advertisement concerning this slave but found none.[166] As time went by, Roche no doubt began to believe that no one was going to claim Bob. Unfortunately for Roche, a Savannah magistrate, William Pittman, recognized Bob as a slave named January belonging to Colonel Stewart of Jonesville, with whom Pittman used to go hunting. He took January to Daniel Stewart, the colonel's nephew, who confirmed the identification. At his trial in 1839 John D. Roche was sentenced to five years' imprisonment for stealing January.[167]

The relationship between Roche and January was clearly not the usual one between master and slave. Roche no doubt knew that if January talked to the right person and claimed to have been stolen, he would be arrested. But Roche could easily have placed January in the Savannah workhouse to be returned to Colonel Stewart's plantation, something January evidently did not relish considering that he had originally fled from there and he had made no attempt to leave Savannah during the several months he lived there with Roche. As in the case of Henry Forsyth, a nonslaveholding white and an African American had managed to supplant the usual pattern of race relations with one based more on mutual advantage than on distrust and oppression.

State and civic authorities viewed the illegal taking of a slave as a very serious offense. In antebellum Georgia the punishment for taking a slave or helping one escape was four to ten years' imprisonment.[168] The average term served in the Georgia penitentiary for Negro stealing was just under five years.[169] In fact, antebellum laws were noticeably more lenient than colonial or early national laws regarding slave stealing. In 1783 Robert Lewis was sentenced to death "for stealing Negroes" in Georgetown. A petition to save his life stressed his "extreme youth," though the eventual decision of the governor of South Carolina, Benjamin Guerard, is not known.[170] The case of Robert Lewis was only one of many regarding runaway slaves during the Revolutionary period. The disputes between Loyalists and Patriots created a climate in which slaves were frequently taken and retaken by individuals laying claim to them.[171] More advertisements for more runaways appeared in 1781 than for any other year between 1763 and 1790.[172] The flight of slaves was even remarked on by the newly formed Grand Jury of Chatham County in 1782.[173] Such was the threat to Southern society posed by those who stole slaves that community sanctions against those suspected of concealing slaves could even stretch to lynching and mob rule. James Johnston quotes the case of James Allen, who was lynched in Virginia for such a crime, and in Darien three unsuccessful attempts were made to lynch a man charged with Negro stealing.[174]

Recaptured bondspeople were placed in the local jail to await collection by their owners.[175] Sometimes they stayed there for lengthy periods, leading some Savannah residents to believe that by permitting "a condition of positive idleness" to exist among slaves in the jail, civic authorities were providing "subsistence without labor [to slaves who] feel their situation infinitely better than if at work."[176] To expedite the process of returning runaways, imprisoned slaves were advertised in Georgia and South Carolina newspapers together with a note of "distinguishing brands."[177] After eighteen months, unclaimed slaves could be sold to defray the cost of their confinement. For a sixpence daily fee the Savannah workhouse would receive slaves whom their masters wished punished away from the home or plantation.[178] According to Emily Burke, a Savannah city ordinance prevented masters from publicly whipping their slaves within the city limits. Consequently, when a master "considers his slave deserving of punishment, he sends him to the jail with orders to have him whipped so many times a day for a certain number of days."[179] As Betty Wood has pointed out, this punishment was only temporary: the labor of bondspeople was far too valuable for owners to permit slaves to be confined for any length of time.[180]

Although the workhouse was intended only as a temporary receptacle for fugitive slaves, many of whom would be quickly returned to their owners, slaves convicted of more serious crimes were confined in the city or county jails. These jails also held white criminals convicted of a variety of offenses. That a relationship could arise between jailmates of different races is testified to not only by the reports of grand juries and newspapers but also by the memoirs of escaped slaves. Henry Bibb, an upcountry slave jailed for running away, formed an escape plan with the white inmates, both male and female. According to Bibb, the white criminals in the prison befriended him, expressing "sympathy" for his cruel treatment as a slave and suggesting that they could help him attain his freedom permanently. Bibb's role in the ultimately unsuccessful attempt was to obtain the prison keys from the white prison warden with whom Bibb had a rapport.[181] In this situation, race was subsumed under a common need for freedom in a situation in which normal barriers between white and black had been eroded by a joint confinement and predicament. The white inmates saw Bibb as a potential class ally in their struggle against the authority that had imprisoned them. A similar case of a biracial quest for freedom occurred in Darien in 1822. Jonathan Belton and John Clarke, confined for assault and burglary respectively, broke out of the Darien Jail together with a runaway slave named Prince.[182] It is unknown whether Prince was a co-conspirator in the breakout or whether he merely took advantage of it.

In many respects the escape attempts of criminals were assisted by the poor security measures taken by prison authorities. As early as 1769 the Georgia Grand Jury was highlighting "the insufficiency of the present gaol, in the town of Savannah."[183] The ineffectiveness of its successor, the Chatham County jail, was notorious and was frequently mentioned by the Grand Jury. In 1787 the "insecure state" of the jail led the Grand Jury to recommend that it was "not worth repairing."[184] In 1790 five citizens of Savannah reported the "rotten and decayed state" of the jail whereby "desperate men cannot be kept and confined therein with safety, as is sufficiently evidenced by the many escapes that have been made therefrom as [much] by Negroes as by white men."[185] Despite a new jail and reforms that tightened security procedures, escapes still occurred.[186] In 1826 a committee appointed by the Grand Jury declared the jail to be so "out of repair" that "the most secure room or cell [was] insufficient to confine a prisoner disposed to make an escape."[187] Savannah was not the only place where jail conditions left a great deal to be desired. In Liberty County the Grand Jury claimed that the jail was "not calculated to hold persons of any description."[188]

When space permitted, criminals in Savannah were racially segregated: African Americans went to the workhouse while whites were confined in a "white jail."[189] Often, though, sheer weight of numbers meant that African Americans and whites were "intermixed."[190] The new jail constructed in the nineteenth century was large enough for both races, and between 1809 and 1815 it housed a total of three thousand African Americans and five hundred whites.[191] On his visit to the Savannah jail in 1820, Adam Hodgson observed that "besides numerous pirates, there were many slaves in confinement for not giving their masters the wages they had earned."[192] The minutes of the City Council also reveal that up to a quarter of the jail population in the 1830s was free black sailors, imprisoned during their sojourn in Savannah.[193] In 1835 the jail committee characterized the population of the jail as "sailors and indolent people who are often intoxicated. . . . These people are generally paupers."[194]

Indeed, the poverty of inmates seemingly encouraged recidivism to obtain free food and shelter.[195] Even as late as 1855 the Grand Jury continued to complain about the city jail, where "the prisoners are brought into contact irrespective of their sex, color and condition."[196] Only when a new workhouse for African Americans was constructed did the racial makeup of the jail alter. In 1856 the jailer reported that "formerly the proportion of white and colored inmates were about one half of each, whilst the latter are now only in the proportion of one to about five or six of the former."[197]

It was not only in the prison environment that white people and African Americans conspired against the established authority of the elite. Occasionally white people were involved in slave revolts and rebellions through the provision of food, weapons, or passes. James Johnston has characterized the collaboration of white people in Virginia slave revolts as the ultimate denial of racial identity.[198] White people who were prepared to support slave revolts against white society generally were clearly identifying with African Americans on a class basis ahead of their own racial loyalties. Elite white society was concerned enough about the activities of slaves without the added fear that their attempts at controlling African Americans were being undermined by nonslaveholding whites who had little interest in maintaining the slave system. Scares over slave revolts were common in the lowcountry, especially following a revolt elsewhere, though bondspeople in lowcountry Georgia never actually rose against their owners on a large scale. During such times nonslaveholding whites came under particular suspicion—suspicions that were not always unfounded.[199] In 1749 the South Carolina authorities arrested some "white people taken up upon suspicion of being concerned with the Negroes in the supposed insurrection."[200] A century later, Emily Burke was told of one aborted rebellion in Camden County that was incited by lumbermen from Maine who visited annually to harvest the live oaks.[201] In Savannah, however, the authorities remained sufficiently dispassionate to acquit William McGuire of "attempting to excite an insurrection and revolt of the slaves," even though sectional tensions were running high in 1857.[202]

The most serious involvement of white people in a lowcountry slave revolt came during the Denmark Vesey rebellion in 1822. The evidence is limited, but both white and black sources show that at least one white man was involved in the planning and execution of the revolt. A Mr. Richardson wrote to his nephew James Screven reporting that the revolt in

Charleston had led to the execution of several slaves and that "one white man was found aiding & abetting the Negroes, he has been a pirate."[203] One of the slaves involved in the rebellion stated that a free black named Peter Poyas had told bondspeople in Georgetown that "many poor white people in Georgetown would join them" in their assault on the town.[204] While the word of a single individual should not be taken to mean that there were a large number of white people prepared to support the slave rebellion of 1822, the fact that at least some bondspeople found this idea credible suggests that it was not totally fantastic. After the rebellion was crushed, four white people were placed on trial charged with inciting the slaves to rebel.[205]

As the sectional crisis grew in the 1850s, the lowcountry elite became increasingly concerned about the criminal activities of poor whites and slaves. In 1856 a Liberty County planter railed against "vagrants, traveling as organ-grinders and show-masters, having frequently clandestine intercourse with our slaves, and infusing dangerous notions, telling them, amongst other things, that they ought to be free."[206] Three years later the Savannah City Council met in an emergency session to debate the "unusual excitement" prevalent in the city caused by the "improper and illegal intercourse held by certain persons with slaves." This interaction was particularly worrisome to the elite because some of the white people involved were "long residents in the city," not recent immigrants, and the council had heard reports about their "alleged unsoundness in reference to our system of slavery."[207] While nothing ultimately came of this scare, the loyalty of some nonslaveholders toward the slave regime continued to be questionable right up to secession.

The involvement of poor white people in criminal activities with African Americans demonstrates their general rejection of the elite social ethic. By operating their own social rationale based on self-interest rather than on abstract notions of race, nonslaveholders freed themselves from the elite's dogma of what constituted proper contact with African Americans. In this sense, criminal activity went hand in hand with biracial trading and social encounters. Where nonelite whites felt their social status was threatened by the actions of African Americans they were perfectly capable of reacting violently, asserting the "rights of free men," even if it led to a jail sentence. Nonslaveholders were also perfectly willing to commit crimes with African Americans, help them escape, and even assist in slave revolts against owners. Individual nonslaveholders clearly made up their own minds as to what interaction they wanted with African Americans. The ideology of racial difference did not prevent nonslaveholding whites from forming relationships with slaves. By acting against the interests of the white elite, nonslaveholders displayed a highly subversive class affinity with African Americans which rejected a social system that was designed to ensure their economic and social marginalization. As independent individuals, nonslaveholders were clearly not content to accept the vision of society laid down for them by the white elite.

5 Praying Together

THE HISTORY of Southern religious experiences, both before and after the Revolution, is one of regular biracial interaction. No other formal environment encouraged such a high degree of contact between the races as the evangelical church. During the late eighteenth and early nineteenth centuries, both African Americans and poorer white people found that their spiritual needs were best served by Baptist, Methodist, and Presbyterian denominations whose message of spiritual equality before God held obvious appeal to those suffering inequality in the temporal world. The degree and meaning of biraciality in individual lowcountry evangelical churches obviously differed: some churches were dominated by one particular race, while others maintained a degree of parity between the races. In this chapter I examine how the racial attitudes engendered in rural mixed churches differed from the spiritual culture prevalent in Savannah, where religious observance was frequently racially segregated. I also explore the religious life of the lowcountry population and argue that the evangelical environment, particularly in the early national period, was a vital forum for the interaction of African Americans and nonslaveholding whites. The biracial encounters in lowcountry churches demonstrated to African American members that race was not a bar to spiritual fulfillment. But though the spiritual fellowship encouraged between white and black members by evangelical denominations to some extent blurred the racial distinction between poor whites and African Americans, the support offered to established social hierarchies by all churches, especially in the last years of the antebellum era, ultimately limited biracial identification.

Historians of antebellum evangelicalism have always been aware of the existence of biracial churches but have only recently begun to explore the racial, gender, and class dynamics that made them unique institutions in the Old South. In the South as a whole, slaves attended biracial churches more frequently than they attended purely black churches, but this did not prevent the formation of a separate black Christian culture—indeed, the separation of the races within a church, with blacks usually seated at the back or in the gallery, facilitated such a formation. Still, the wider significance of biracial religious communities in the antebellum South, and especially in the Georgia lowcountry, remains to be uncovered. How did the meaning of biraciality change with the onset of the plantation missions in the 1830s? Were the elite conscious of the threat a common religious identification between black and white posed to the Southern social order, and did they work to suppress it?[1]

Church services had been racially integrated from the first days of slavery in colonial Georgia. As early as 1750, Bartholomew Zouberbuhler, the minister at Christ Church in Savannah, reported that at the opening of the new church he took "pleasure to see many Negroes decently join our service."[2] At Christ Church, African Americans would have encountered white people from all social classes, including artisans and non-slaveholders.[3] The attendance of African Americans at religious services in Savannah was evidently not a cause of concern for white members, although some slaveholders apparently were perturbed by the effect Christianity might have on their bondspeople. Zouberbuhler was well aware that many Georgians denied their slaves access to religion, as did fellow slaveholders across the colonial South. They feared that permitting African Americans to congregate in large numbers and hear the message of Christianity might undermine slavery by stressing a higher master than the temporal authority.[4] One minister found that only "some masters will suffer [their slaves] to come to me," and newly arrived slaveholders (especially those from the West Indies) disseminated the view that Africans "have no souls at all" and thus there was little point teaching them "what they must do to be saved."[5] Other planters apparently believed that "a slave made a Christian becomes free by the law of England," despite assurances from ministers that Christianity would "not undo the heavy afflictive burden of slavery [but] . . . afford them the strength to run with patience the race that is set before them."[6]

Despite elite concerns, an attempt to evangelize the newly imported

African American population in colonial Georgia was undertaken and financed jointly by the Associates of the late Dr. Bray and the Society for the Propagation of the Gospel in Foreign Parts (SPG). Together they appointed a converted Jew, Joseph Ottolenghe, "as a catechist for instructing the Negroes there."[7] Shortly after Ottolenghe's arrival, Zouberbuhler estimated that forty-one children were attending the catechist's Sunday school.[8] These first religious meetings were specifically aimed at a biracial audience. Ottolenghe stated that the largest room in his new house would be used "for ye instruction of ye Negroes, & such of ye white people who can neither read nor can give any account of their religion."[9] The instruction of less privileged whites together with African Americans had been encouraged by the Bray Associates. In 1752 they informed Ottolenghe that "they should be glad he would encourage white children inclined to partake of the same knowledge" because most white people in Georgia resided some distance "from all spiritual helps."[10] As a result, Ottolenghe "invited anyone that would come to me, & would as far as I could, give them all the instruction I was capable of."[11] Clearly religious instruction in the colonial period to some extent ignored the status differences between the races. In 1758 Ottolenghe took pride in the fact that he instructed those white people "who have neither leisure to attend a public schoole, nor money to procure private instruction."[12] By instigating biracial education, philanthropists like the Bray Associates showed that they valued spiritual fellowship above the normal distinctions between African American and white children.

The Episcopalian church was not the only religious denomination to attract African Americans in the colonial period. In 1771 Samuel Frink reported the denominational loyalties of all two thousand Savannahians to the SPG. More than half were Anglicans, though many did not attend regularly for Frink often found only sixty communicants at Christ Church. The next most popular church for both whites and blacks was the Independent Presbyterian Church, of which a quarter of residents were members. The remaining citizens were split between the Lutheran church and the Jewish community, and Frink noted that thirty individuals, including seven African Americans, had "no religion" at all.[13] The lack of records means that the status of the black members of these religious organizations and their interaction with white members are unknown, yet the churches throughout colonial Georgia were generally biracial and they allowed, even encouraged, blacks and whites to experience religion without regard for the racial norms of secular society.

Outside of Savannah, African Americans were some of the earliest members of the Congregational church at Midway.[14] Many of the white members of this church were leading planters in St. Johns parish and thus it was not a meeting place for ordinary white people and African Americans.[15] Yet John Osgood, the preacher at Midway, instructed all the members of his church to treat each other, rich and poor, black and white, with respect. The rich were told to "be humble and don't think yourselves the better for your riches," while the poor were exhorted not to be "apt to think yourselves slighted for your poverty."[16] Osgood counseled leniency in slave discipline as "much correction seldom answers any good purpose," and ultimately "you and your meanest slave must stand together at last before the righteous judge of all, [as] death will shortly lay your head as low as theirs." Above all, white members were encouraged to "remember [that] your servants are your fellow creatures."[17] African American members of the Midway church would no doubt have absorbed, and been encouraged by, the basic notion of spiritual equality with whites expounded by preachers such as Osgood. Nevertheless, because of the lack of preachers, "many hundreds of poor people . . . [had] no opportunity of being instructed in the principles of Christianity" in colonial Georgia.[18]

Of course, Christianity was not confined solely to formal church environments where blacks and whites were preached to by white ministers. Informal plantation preaching was increasingly common in Georgia as the Revolution approached, and by the 1770s black preachers were carrying the message of Christianity to lowcountry plantations. Philanthropists had a hard time finding suitable white preachers because few candidates offered themselves for ordination. The dangers in using black preachers to evangelize the slaves became apparent when David Margate, a black Briton employed by the Countess of Huntingdon, preached to a biracial audience that "God would send deliverance to the Negroes, from the power of their masters, as he freed the children of Israel from Egyptian bondage." James Habersham, the Countess's proxy in Georgia, was forced to act quickly to prevent Margate from being lynched by local slaveholders. As he ruefully noted, "his [David's] business was to preach a spiritual deliverance to these people not a temporal one."[19]

But the spark of Christianity had been lit among the enslaved population in Georgia, and as it spread among bondspeople on Savannah

River plantations during the Revolutionary period, it led to the formation of the first black church in America at Silver Bluff in South Carolina. The precise date of its foundation is not known, but members from this church were responsible in 1788 for the establishment of the First African Baptist Church in Savannah.[20] Not surprisingly, the enslaved and free black members of this church came under much suspicion from the white citizens of Savannah, despite having the support of such influential individuals as Jonathan Bryan, who originally provided the land for a meeting place at his Brampton plantation. On several occasions church services were broken up by the city watch and the members "severely whipped." Yet Andrew Bryan, the black minister, continued to preach and "to exhort his black hearers, with a few whites."[21] Jonathan Clarke, the Savannah city treasurer, stated in a letter to the leading English Baptist John Rippon that Savannah's black preachers were admired by "a number of white people."[22] Although this admiration did not extend to actual membership in the First African Baptist Church, Clarke believed that Bryan had "been instrumental in the . . . converting of some whites."[23] Andrew Bryan himself noted that before the founding of the white First Baptist Church in 1800, African Baptists had received "the approbation and encouragement of many of the white people" who lacked their own minister or meetinghouse.[24] Henry Holcombe recalled that the "eight or ten" white Baptists in the city during the 1790s were "with one or two exceptions, low in their circumstances."[25] These early Savannah Baptists were actually more cosmopolitan than Holcombe remembered. Among the first fifteen members of this church were a local justice of the peace, Elias Roberts, and Eunice Hogg, who owned ten slaves, as well as a shopkeeper, Peter Robert, and a carpenter, Thomas Clubb's widow, Elizabeth.[26] The preaching of Andrew Bryan, the only ordained Baptist in the city before 1800, reached all social classes and was especially important to older white women.[27] Several of these women brought their husbands with them to join the congregation and reinforce the familial nature of worship—indeed, the first four male members of the church, including Holcombe himself, had wives who were members.[28]

The early history of the First African Baptist Church illuminates wide divisions among whites over whether to permit or suppress the independence offered by an autonomous black church. Attempts by the City Council of Savannah to close the African church on the basis that it encouraged dangerous gatherings of several hundred African Americans in the city "under a pretence of public worship" were met by two petitions from religious-minded white Savannahians.[29] During the 1780s Lachlan McIntosh led a petition seeking religious toleration for the African church, citing the orderliness of its members and the beneficial effects of Christianity on slave discipline.[30] Evidently this petition did not give the African Baptists the freedom they desired. In 1790, sixty leading merchants and planters gave permission for their own bondspeople to attend religious services. Some such as George Houstoun and William Moore stipulated that these meetings should take place only on Sundays and in daylight, while others like Thomas Pitt, Thomas F. Williams, and Mordecai Sheftall stressed the rights of all individuals, regardless of status, to religious toleration.[31]

The fears of some members of the white elite concerning large gatherings of African Americans were heightened by the San Domingo rebellion of 1793. The uprising of Caribbean slaves evidently caused concern throughout the mainland slave states, especially in Savannah, which became the refuge of many free black *émigrés*. The City Council even ordered that Andrew Bryan be silenced in an attempt to prevent African Americans from meeting in an environment in which white people would be unable to control them.[32] The planters' petition failed to convince the council to lift restrictions it had placed on the religious meetings of African Americans, and by 1795 no gatherings were permitted "unless they have a white preacher."[33] Christian slaves testified that a significant proportion of the white elite viewed slave Christianity as an excuse for mischief. To control religious meetings of African Americans, the Savannah city guard was given orders to arrest any slave found out at night, even those who were returning from one of Henry Kollock's late night prayer meetings.[34] Yet as time went on, increasing numbers of white people began to believe that Christianity did not pose much of a threat to the security of Savannah. White ministers from South Carolina, including such luminaries as Richard Furman in Charleston and Henry Holcombe, then minister at Euhaw, devised a rota system whereby they would visit Savannah to minister to the white and black Baptist congregations. Simultaneously a subscription was launched to fund a new meetinghouse for African Americans in the city. Among the trustees of this fund were three slaveholders who had given their bondspeople permission to attend Bryan's services.[35] Several elite citizens must have supported the rights of African Americans to religious toleration: Morgan Rees believed that the fund would raise more than £200 from Savannah residents alone.[36] The close association of at least some citizens with the establishment and maintenance of a black church in Savannah shows how far religious sentiments crossed racial boundaries. In 1797 the completed church was held in trust by four white men because free African Americans were restricted from holding property. All four of these men had some prior religious association with Andrew Bryan. Major Thomas Polhill had been converted by Bryan's preaching at Newington in 1789, as most likely had David and Josiah Fox, both residents of nearby Little Ogechee. Indeed the preaching of black ministers in the surrounding county as well as in Savannah was fairly common in the 1790s.[37] The fourth trustee, William Matthew, later became a member of the First Baptist Church in Savannah.[38] Some of the trustees were slaveholders, but David Fox was not, demonstrating that Bryan's religious influence not only spread many miles outside of Savannah but also encompassed all white social classes.[39]

The religious independence offered to bondspeople by the African churches in and around Savannah resulted in the rapid expansion of congregations, despite the restrictions imposed on them.[40] The most important reason for the success of the First African Baptist Church was that it employed black preachers. Unlike their white counterparts, black preachers regularly used the imagery of Moses leading the children of Israel out of slavery in Egypt to illustrate the comparable position of bondspeople in Southern society. White ministers preferred to reinforce the social order by expounding on the duty of obedience bondspeople owed to their owners. The millennial vision offered by African American preachers clearly struck a chord with, and engendered genuine piety in, those bondspeople seeking spiritual as well as temporal freedom and salvation.[41] Thus it is not surprising that bondspeople were invigorated by the spiritual message offered by African American preachers.

The success of the African churches in and around Savannah would seem to confirm the general impression that those African Americans who became members of white churches did so only when there was no black church in the immediate locality.[42] The First African Baptist Church was a member of the Georgia Association until 1803, and annual reports of its membership show that between 1788 and 1793 the church nearly doubled its official membership, drawing converts from the South Carolina side of the Savannah River as well as the city and the surrounding county.[43] It was generally perceived that to preach effectively, enslaved ministers should be freed from their bondage. The evangelical and missionary capabilities of black ministers were certainly enhanced by their free status and ability to travel, though many informal preachers on the plantations remained enslaved. The most prominent African American preachers in Savannah in 1800 could obtain their freedom through the agency of whites. Andrew Bryan purchased his own freedom cheaply from William Bryan, who had inherited him from Jonathan Bryan, and Henry Francis, the slave of Colonel Leroy Hammond, had his manumission purchased for him by "a few humane and benevolent citizens of Savannah."[44]

The separate black Baptist community in Savannah was, to some extent, tolerated by the white elite because of its publicly demonstrated decorum. Mrs. Smith, a Northern visitor to Savannah, was intrigued by the religious sentiment of African Americans, believing that "there was more appearance of devotion in them than in the whites."[45] According to her observations, fascinated white people gathered on the banks of the Savannah River to watch the baptism of new members of the African church such as that of Mary Jackson, a seventeen-year-old resident of Bull Island, South Carolina, who was immersed by Andrew Bryan.[46] Mrs. Smith was even more impressed when she attended a service of "great order and decorum" led by Bryan, whom she described as "quite the orator."[47] The sorrow displayed by local white Baptists at Bryan's death in 1812, lauding "his extensively useful, and amazingly luminous course," is a sign of the respect with which he was regarded in white society. At his funeral both white and black preachers offered eulogies.[48] Following his death, his mantle was taken up by Andrew Marshall, who, in accepting the appointment as minister to the First African Baptist Church, stipulated that he still intended to preach "one Sabbath in each month to the destitute people about Savannah."[49] Clearly the Baptist Association did not find it unusual that an African American preacher would minister to the poor in Savannah. On the rare instances when white people attended the services of the First African church, they were "shown to a seat reserved for strangers near the preacher"; by the mid-1840s, when Charles Lyell attended one such service, he was the only white person in the church. Andrew Marshall's sermon on this occasion, which emphasized the equality of "the poor and the rich, the black man and the white," demonstrates the obvious appeal his spiritual message held for bondspeople.[50]

Links between black and white Baptists existed on more than the personal level; local Baptist Associations, together with the white First Baptist Church in Savannah, often became involved in the regulation of the African churches in the environs of Savannah during the antebellum era.[51] The black churches seemed to have both expected and accepted the interference of white Baptists in their affairs. In 1803 leading white Baptists such as Henry Holcombe and John Goldwire assisted in the removal of Wilson Connor from the pastorship of the Great Ogechee African Church "for gross misconduct." [52] A year later, some members of the Great Ogechee church wrote seeking the help of the association and stating that Connor had "been restored by a majority of the members present." In a report in 1805, a new committee stated that Connor's restoration had been irregular and "he was still out of the church." [53] Clearly the spiritual independence offered to the African churches did not extend to temporal freedoms as well: in disputes between white and black churches the white churches rarely backed down. Yet the common biracial religious language and culture offered to African Americans in the lowcountry by Baptist churches did make racial boundaries less distinct in the immediate aftermath of the American Revolution and the Great Revival.

In 1812 the First African Baptist Church requested that the Savannah River Baptist Association appoint a committee "to assist them in regulating their affairs." [54] Which affairs needed regulating is unclear, but in August of that year Henry Holcombe, the pastor of the First Baptist Church, had assisted in the ordination of Jonas as a minister at the First African Baptist Church. [55] The following year's minutes of the Baptist Association stated that the ongoing war with Great Britain prevented resolution of the problem because of "the delicate situation of people of color, in such state of things." [56] In general, though, the minutes of the three Baptist Associations to which the First African church belonged between 1788 and 1865 document that the church's black representatives were accorded great respect. They had full voting rights with white members, though the fact that each church, despite differences in size, sent only two or three representatives to associational meetings meant that white churches with few members were proportionally overrepresented. [57] The situation did not change when in 1818 the Savannah River Baptist Association was divided into the principally white Savannah River Association for South Carolina churches and the decidedly black Sunbury Baptist Association in Georgia. [58] An overwhelming black majority among Baptist church members in Georgia did not prevent the dependence of the black churches on the two original white congregations in Savannah and Newington. When the First African Baptist Church was divided into several daughter congregations, the white elders of the association "invited the . . . officers of the first colored church, to set with us" in an advisory capacity.[59] Despite the framework of spiritual equality espoused by the Baptist Associations, some status differences between white and African American delegates remained.

In the early 1830s both the white First Baptist Church and the Sunbury Baptist Association became deeply involved in a theological controversy at the First African Baptist Church. Andrew Marshall, pastor at First African, was suspended "indefinitely" in 1832 and his church dissolved because he had promoted the heretical teaching of Alexander Campbell. For a while, all the remaining African churches in the city came under the auspices of the white First Baptist Church, including more than 150 breakaway members of First African who formed the Third African Baptist Church. The crisis was finally resolved in 1836, when Marshall was restored to his pulpit and the religious life of First African returned to normal. During the four years that First African was officially dissolved, meetings continued to take place, demonstrating both the attachment of the vast majority of African American members to their church and their rejection of absolute white control.[60] For the remainder of the antebellum period black Baptists numerically dominated the Sunbury Baptist Association, usually accounting for nine of every ten lowcountry Baptists.[61]

The status given to the African American delegates attending associational meetings was only one of the privileges membership of an evangelical church granted. Church membership in Savannah was generally, but not entirely, racially segregated. Even the white First Baptist Church had some black members in its earliest years. In 1802 the white church received a free black, Henry Cunningham, who had left the First African Baptist Church after being passed over for the position of preacher to the newly formed Second African Church.[62] Cunningham received far more respect in the church, which permitted him to serve with white people on committees investigating the conduct of members, than African Americans could expect in wider society.[63] The First Baptist Church clearly trusted Cunningham's beneficial influence over fellow African Americans enough to dismiss four of its black members in 1808 to attend his Second African Baptist Church.[64]

The special rights and privileges granted to African Americans at First Baptist even permitted them to give evidence in cases of discipline involving white people. When Thomas Williams charged his overseer and coreligionist Aaron Shave with killing one of his slaves, the church reluctantly agreed to admit the testimony of two other slaves, "members of a church in our fellowship," but only with Shave's explicit agreement. The two bondsmen stated that Shave had indeed struck the fatal blow, but they were unable to confirm his story that he had been provoked. Williams certainly preferred to believe the statements of his slaves above the protestations of Shave, whom he claimed "invented that story for the purpose of avoiding justice." Shave's "humble and meek" disposition before the church and his willingness "to submit without a murmur to the church's disciplinary rule of order" ensured that he was only suspended from the church rather than excommunicated.[65] Thus it appears that in evangelical churches the power dynamics between nonslaveholding whites and African Americans could be reversed. In this instance Shave was no longer in a position of authority over these bondsmen, and his public humiliation would have demonstrated that racial ties with the elite did not necessarily ensure special privileges.

Although black and white Baptist congregations generally met separately in Savannah, the Independent Presbyterian Church was home to both races throughout the antebellum period. The existence of a biracial congregation, however, did not necessarily entail anything more than theoretical spiritual equality. In 1808 the trustees of the church ordered that African Americans should not be allowed to hire the gallery pews in their church, where they had previously sat together with some white people.[66] To differentiate between white and black members, the trustees also resolved that "a partition be made in the gallery of the Presbyterian church between the white persons and persons of color."[67] This separation apparently did not arouse protests from white members concerned with the spiritual propriety of separating co-religionists. To them, the acknowledgment of spiritual equality did not necessitate equal treatment with whites: African Americans were still "inferior" despite their shared religious beliefs.

The partition in the gallery was perhaps erected partly in response to the concerns of some elite white people sitting there. While the 1806 Chatham County tax digest demonstrates that those who rented the large pews on the floor of the church generally paid more tax than those who rented the small pews, who in turn paid more tax than those renting pews in the gallery, the social differences between them would have been relatively small.[68] Of course, the poorest members of any church would not have been able to afford pew rents at all. Usually a few benches at the back of a church were reserved as free. But the meager social status of these worshipers would have been clear to all other members, and it is possible that some individuals preferred to absent themselves from church rather than sit in the free pews.[69]

While Baptists, Presbyterians, Anglicans, and Lutherans all flourished in the cosmopolitan atmosphere of Savannah, Methodists struggled to gain a foothold in the city. Their difficulties arose principally from the antislavery stance of the Methodist conference during the Revolutionary period. In 1780 the Methodist conference had declared "that slavery is contrary to the laws of God, man and nature, and . . . contrary to the dictates of conscience and pure religion."[70] In addition, a prominent Baptist, Stephen Cooke, noted that the Methodist policy of permitting slaves to join the congregation without the permission of owners had "not only prevented the increase of their church [in Savannah], but has raised them many enemies."[71] Thus it was elite opposition to Methodist theology which ensured that, despite a reasonably vigorous start in the city in the early 1790s, by 1800 there was no Methodist minister in Savannah, and many Methodists were being hounded out of lowcountry towns by "mob violence."[72] Even following the reestablishment of the Savannah congregation in 1807 membership grew slowly and in 1812 numbered only five.[73] A Rhode Islander visiting the Savannah Methodist church in 1820 reported that "the state of religion here is lamentable indeed," particularly citing the fact that on "evenings for prayer, the church is almost empty."[74] William Capers, who preached in Savannah in the same year, stated that his congregation was "but few," noting especially that African Americans preferred the "economy and doctrines" (and presumably the independence) of the African Baptist churches in Chatham County to those of the Methodist church.[75]

This situation changed gradually once Methodists, like other evangelical denominations, reached an accommodation with slavery. Between 1804 and 1808 the General Conference first exempted the Deep South states from some of its slavery statutes and ultimately permitted each state conference to determine its own policy regarding slavery.[76] By reinterpreting Christianity as offering slaves a vision of the afterlife that alleviated some of the mental stress of slavery without necessitating emancipation, Methodists accepted elite views regarding the propriety of bondage and consequently embarked afresh upon evangelism in the lowcountry.[77] Not all planters were convinced by this change of heart. The Charlestonian elite informed James Andrew that Methodism only taught bondspeople "insubordination and idleness," and the popularity of Methodism among African Americans in South Carolina seemed to confirm their worst fears.[78] The growth of Methodism in the lowcountry was undoubtedly biracial. A Savannah revival in 1822 among whites added more than a hundred "promising young men and women, from whom we have much reason to expect a permanent support to the cause of Christ in this place."[79] Despite the growth of lowcountry Methodism between 1810 and 1830 (there were more than two hundred black Methodists in Savannah by 1828), however, Methodist congregations were less than a fifth of the size of lowcountry Baptist churches.[80] Only with the establishment of Trinity Methodist Church in 1848, with more than three hundred members, did Savannah Methodists gain a formal base from which to evangelize the urban population. Many new converts to Methodism in the 1850s were African Americans attracted by a semi-autonomous church, named Andrew Chapel, with its own Sunday school and conveniently located in Oglethorpe ward.[81]

St. John's Catholic Church was smaller than the Baptist, Methodist, and Presbyterian churches. The membership of this body, the only Catholic church in lowcountry Georgia, seems to have been drawn entirely from Irish immigrants and black and white French-speaking refugees from the revolution in San Domingo.[82] The baptism, marriage, and burial records of this church demonstrate that Irish and French immigrants often acted as godparents and witnesses for free African Americans. Some of these white people may have had a personal acquaintance with the African Americans, especially the émigrés from San Domingo. For example, in 1804 at the wedding of Jean Fromentin and Marie Charlotte, both free mulattoes "born in St. Domingue," four white men signed the register as witnesses.[83] At one baptism of an African American child the priest recorded that the white sponsors had both been "planters of St. Domingo."[84] This religious respect was reciprocated: the priest noted that among those attending the burial of French-born Jeanne Suzanne were "some black people who knew not how to sign."[85] Moreover, Catholic priests were not above baptizing the illegitimate products of interracial unions and naming the white men involved.[86] Clearly shared religious beliefs led some white people to grant African Americans a degree of respect which their socioeconomic position normally prevented. This, of course, does not deny that racial differences in church existed, but rather that white people could behave in a manner that belied their normal racial ideology.

Manifestly white people and African Americans did interact in urban evangelical churches, even where worshipers were physically separated. Because most African Americans did not reside in Savannah, Darien, or St. Marys, however, their religious experiences were often confined to the plantation or the local white church. Emily Burke described one lowcountry rural church where "both the white people and the colored people are seated upon the floor, with only this difference, the white people sit nearest the pulpit."[87] In this instance, the absence of tangible barriers necessitated actual physical separation. Even at camp meetings, "love-feasts" could be held separately for blacks and whites, suggesting that ministers and preachers deemed it proper to discourage biracial interaction.[88] As a result, rural slaves usually preferred that meetings and services be held on their plantations, rather than attending official white meetings. Partly this was because plantation meetings gave African Americans greater liberty to engage in the singing, shouting, and dancing that became characteristic of African American lowcountry Christianity, but it also enabled them to hear itinerant black preachers.[89] Francis Asbury reported in 1789 that one of his meetings was sparsely attended, "occasioned . . . by a black man's preaching not far distant."[90] One visitor to the lowcountry overheard a black preacher on a plantation exhort his mainly female audience to "love one another . . . and he [God] will make us free."[91] Such messages led some planters to restrict the visits of black preachers to their plantations and to limit the times for religious observance both on and off the estate.[92] Fanny Kemble stated that the slaves on her plantation, "almost all of them Baptists," were permitted to attend services at the black Baptist church in Darien once a month while "on the intermediate Sundays, they assemble in the house of London, Mr Butler's head cooper." Certainly the experiences of attending the church in Darien, where bondspeople had to listen to white preachers following the expulsion of their free black pastor, and of hearing London "address them with extemporous exhortations" would have been startlingly different.[93] Religious observance evidently formed a regular part of the lives of a significant portion of lowcountry bondspeople. George Lewis was told by the black overseer on a Savannah River rice plantation that half the slaves "travelled every Sabbath to Savannah" to attend one of the African churches in the city and "that there were prayers every night at the plantation, conducted by one of the slaves."[94] Some bondspeople also no doubt attended religious services on Saturday night when they made their weekly trips to the Savannah market.[95]

Of course, it is possible that many African Americans resident on lowcountry plantations were not particularly devout or interested in religion. Many African Americans spent their Sundays in independent economic activity, bringing them into a different relationship with nonslaveholding whites, though these activities were not mutually exclusive.[96] Philadelphian Jonathan Evans observed that for slaves in Charleston, Sunday was "a time generally allotted for recreation and amusement" rather than religious observance, and lowcountry grand juries certainly believed that many African Americans were "disorderly" on the Sabbath.[97] The scattered nature of church records makes it impossible to determine how many African Americans in a specific region attended church, but we can estimate that around 1820 anywhere between a tenth and a third of resident African Americans in a particular county were baptized church members.[98] An unknown number of unbaptized African Americans may also have attended these services. When membership of the black Baptist churches in Chatham County peaked at more than sixty-five hundred in 1831 seemingly the entire adult slave population of the county were members. Because this is highly unlikely, especially when we consider that Chatham County slaves also attended the churches of other denominations, the obvious explanation is that the independent black churches in Savannah attracted considerable numbers of the thirteen thousand adult slaves in neighboring Beaufort District, South Carolina.[99] This relative popularity did not last. Between 1830 and 1840 the slave population of Chatham County doubled, and it doubled again between 1840 and 1860. In contrast, the membership of the black Baptist churches remained static, so that by 1860 only about a third of Chatham County slaves were regular attendees.[100] Religious sentiments among African Americans throughout the antebellum period were significantly stronger in Savannah than in the rest of the lowcountry, probably because of the independence offered by the African Baptist churches in Chatham County. In contrast, similar proportions of white people attended church both in Savannah and elsewhere in the lowcountry, but the proportional decline in membership seen in black Baptist churches also occurred in white churches.[101] Church membership, of course, was not uniform throughout the lowcountry: in 1830, at precisely the time that religiosity was peaking in Savannah, Mrs. Steele remarked that there was "no particular attention to religion" in St. Marys.[102]

Although in wider society the social status of African Americans, whether slave or free, was restricted by their color, in many biracial evangelical lowcountry churches slavery did not necessarily entail obvious discrimination against them. The minutes of some evangelical churches demonstrate that African American members were given far wider civil rights in church than they normally expected or received in secular society.[103] When Emily Dobson and an African American woman named Rose were jointly cited before the Independent Presbyterian Church for showing "an unchristian spirit towards each other," the church resolved to suspend them both until their dispute was settled.[104] But though whites could be held to the same moral code as African Americans, such spiritual equality clearly did not cross over into the temporal world. Whatever their theoretical position in biracial evangelical churches, African Americans remained under the supervision and control of whites.

The citing of individuals before evangelical churches was part of an attempt by ministers to control the behavior of members in wider society. The common belief that spirituality was "the grand prop of the government and the regulator of manners" inevitably led to the conclusion that irreligion was the cause of nearly all social ills, especially crime and intemperance.[105] In marked contrast to the perceptions of the colonial era, Christianity came to be viewed increasingly in the early national period as an effective method of social control. By stressing that decent public conduct was as important for salvation as spiritual piety, evangelical churches hoped to influence the behavior of both African Americans and nonelite whites. This quest for public morality was powerfully reinforced in the conduct of church discipline meetings. The fearsome nature of evangelical preaching, designed to bring the reality of sin and God's power to the mind of the sinner, was in many respects intended to control the antisocial behavior of nonelite members of church congregations.[106] Poor whites and African Americans do not always seem to have absorbed this aspect of the message. Rather, it was the promise of salvation for all, regardless of race, class, or gender, that attracted both poor white people and African Americans to evangelical denominations.[107]

Churches did not usually suspend or expel individuals solely on reports of improper behavior, whatever their color. Like their white coreligionists, African Americans were entitled to plead their case in front of the church, and white members often made strenuous efforts to cite offending black members properly and to hear their explanations. Thus when bondsman Prince was charged with "improper use of his master's goods," Mr. Baker was "appointed to see and converse with him on the subject." Mr. Baker's favorable report enabled Prince to avoid suspension.[108] The citing of African American members was to some extent gendered. When Jones's Creek Baptist Church sought to determine the case of "Fanny, a black woman," it appointed "a committee of five sisters to investigate" rather than delegate the responsibility to men.[109] In this case it was believed that only someone of the same gender could approach the subject with due propriety—reinforcing the conclusions of other scholars that antebellum evangelical churches existed within the gendered framework of wider society.[110]

All members of evangelical churches were granted a common identity through the title of "brother" or "sister," regardless of race or class.[111] Sometimes churches appointed an African American as an elder to oversee the black members of a church and to ensure that they lived up to Christian ideals.[112] African Americans also had the same rights of dismissal to other churches as white people, and their acceptance by their new church rested entirely on the letter of recommendation from their previous pastor.[113] In 1823 the elders of Little Ogechee Baptist Church received Prissy from the First African Baptist Church of Savannah together with the letter of dismissal written by its minister, Andrew Marshall.[114] Thus African Americans and white people were brought into the language and ideology of fraternity and togetherness, to form what John Boles has termed a common "religious culture" in the lowcountry.[115] By meeting each other in a forum where neither held formal sway, African Americans and whites perhaps began to understand and relate to each other in a manner that would have been frowned upon outside the Christian sphere. The church environment was the only one where the association of races was encouraged and where mutual toleration, within certain parameters, was perceived as entirely appropriate.

During the antebellum period the number of biracial churches in the lowcountry increased. In 1800, aside from those in Savannah, the Congregational church at Midway was the only biracial church in the lowcountry, and most white members of that church were elite slaveholders. By 1830, however, the establishment of several important new churches in the coastal counties had increased the opportunity for biracial gatherings. Presbyterians established churches in Darien and St. Marys, Methodists made their first inroads in Savannah with the foundation of the Wesley Chapel, and Baptists formed several churches in rural areas. By 1860 even more churches had been founded by all three evangelical denominations in both urban and rural areas. In the sixty years before the Civil War the lowcountry populace was given more and more opportunities to partake of a biracial religious experience.[116]

Although whites and blacks in rural lowcountry churches increasingly shared the same physical spaces, this did not necessarily entail cultural and racial intermingling. As Sylvia Frey has commented, though biracial religious meetings made racial barriers "fluid and imprecise," the separation of races and genders in the church "made it possible for each group to develop and maintain its own distinctive ritual forms."[117] James Silva recalled that at the Methodist church in St. Marys "the opposite sexes were not allowed to sit together," and, in addition, some evangelical churches chose to establish separate services for whites and blacks to prevent improper mingling of the races.[118] Many smaller churches, however, chose to seat African Americans at the back or in the gallery during normal services, symbolically maintaining their marginal social status.[119] Biracial religious meetings in the early national period even extended some African American influence to white people. The shouting, dancing, and singing common to African American religious practices were sometimes unconsciously adopted by white people to demonstrate the actions of the Holy Spirit. It was only in the 1820s that the appropriateness of this behavior began to be questioned by church elders and restraint of white people urged.[120] The impact of African American religion could even spread to their overseers. Leonard Venters, overseer at Gowrie on Argyle Island, lost his job because of "a strong . . . religious feeling" which involved "placing himself on a par with the negroes, by even joining them at their prayer meetings." Louis Manigault, Venters's employer, believed that this biracial religious sentiment had caused a "breaking down [of] long established discipline" on the plantation and could not be tolerated.[121]

Clearly lowcountry evangelical churches were places of human interaction regardless of class, race, or gender. That congregations consisted of "people of different professions and ranks" is attested to by the membership records of the First Baptist Church in Savannah, which demonstrate that up to half of white male members were nonslaveholders.[122] In rural areas, that proportion could be even greater; more than four-fifths of the white members of Jones's Creek Baptist Church, situated in the inland area of Liberty County, were nonslaveholders.[123] Some ministers especially encouraged a cosmopolitan church. Charles Colcock Jones believed that black and white should "meet in the same building, that they be incorporated in the same church, under the same pastor, having access to the same ordinances, baptism, and the Lord's Supper, and at the same time and place, and that they be subject to the same care and discipline; the two classes forming one pastoral charge, one church, one congregation."[124]

Although both men and women populated the pews of evangelical churches, in all congregations men were outnumbered by women by an average of two to one. In some churches four of every five members were women.[125] Donald Mathews has argued that as a result of this female majority, Southern evangelical churches were a focal point for female self-expression.[126] This is not to deny that evangelical churches remained dominated by white men, who held all the important church offices and who presided over the weekly discipline councils.[127] One lowcountry church had as its prime rule that the only members entitled to vote were white adult males who regularly attended worship, rented a pew, and "paid not less than five dollars to the support of the church."[128] Thus white women to some extent shared the same status as African Americans because neither had a formal role to play in church, even though they frequently formed a large majority of members. Yet the fact remains that pious women of both races enjoyed a higher status and role in church than in society as a whole.[129]

African American women could rise to prominence in lowcountry society because of their religious fervor. One bondswoman, Clarinda, was received "with respect and kindness by the first ladies of Beaufort as . . . one of the greatest prodigies in the Christian world," despite having lived a life that was "profane and dissolute" before her conversion experience. According to Henry Holcombe, then minister at Euhaw, Clarinda "was liberally supported on account of her piety" and eventually obtained her freedom.[130] Other bondswomen preached in biracial lowcountry camp meetings. John Melish describes one such female preacher who "had the art of playing upon the passions so effectually that she would sometimes trip half a dozen of her hearers."[131] The fact that evangelical churches permitted both male and female African Americans to hold such roles shows how their theology could subvert the usual pattern of race and gender interaction in the lowcountry.

Although African Americans and white women were granted a higher status in evangelical churches than in secular society, white men ensured that they retained the reins of power among lowcountry church members. The dominance of white men in church discipline councils publicly demonstrated the dependency of women and bondspeople.[132] Discipline meetings were public forums intended to ensure that members led "an orderly life." Those cited before the meetings were instructed "not to take it as offence when reproved by his brother or brethren [as] such reproofs be given in the spirit of meekness and fear."[133] Above all, members were encouraged to "obey them that have the rule over you and submit your-selves, 'for they watch for your souls.'"[134] Those whose sins were so grievous as to merit excommunication were publicly denounced "in a sol-emn and impressive manner" from the pulpit during a service so that "the world may know that the church is no longer responsible for the conduct of the party."[135] On occasion this formality was dispensed with when it was believed that no benefit would be gained from public exposure or that publicity might embarrass the church.[136] In 1823 the First Baptist Church in Savannah decided not to expel sister Fahm publicly because her total disregard for the authority of the church over a lengthy period would have reflected badly on its inability to control errant members.[137]

To some extent churches supplanted civil authority by claiming juris-diction over temporal matters. When Ann Lillibridge was cited for retail-ing on Sundays, she may have been forgiven for thinking that she was before the Mayor's Court instead of the First Baptist Church.[138] To some members, turning to the church for assistance would have seemed per-fectly natural because of its central role in their everyday lives: church discipline records even contain cases where members sued for debts due to them from other members.[139] Churches also assumed some responsi-bility for charitable provision. When the First Baptist Church became aware of the pecuniary circumstances of Jane Mulryne, which had neces-sitated her withdrawing her children from the Union Society to put them to work, the church "unanimously agreed that the wants of our said sister be relieved, as speedily as possible, at the discretion of our deacons." While the church was no doubt acting to alleviate the poverty of one of its members, it was also concerned with the impropriety of Jane's "con-duct with respect to her children."[140] Yet the fact remains that Jane Mul-ryne's church was far more relevant and helpful to her situation than any petition to the Inferior Court would have been.

While white men attempted to assert their masterdom by presiding over discipline meetings, as a group they were not immune from censure themselves, but cases involving white men often reflected a class bias. Men who held offices in church were often the richest and most powerful in their locality, and one method of asserting their social control was by regulating the private affairs of less privileged members. Among the elders of the Darien Presbyterian Church were local planter John Kell and Revolutionary War hero General Lachlan McIntosh.[141] Yet the white men brought before discipline councils were disproportionately nonslave-holders. At the First Baptist Church in Savannah, nonslaveholding white men were twice as likely as slaveholding men to be excommunicated by the church for indiscipline.[142] The abject and public apologies which the church demanded from offending members if they were to avoid suspension placed nonelite white men in a similar position of dependency upon the elite to that of African Americans and white women.[143] Thus elite white men had found a new and powerful way of controlling the behavior of their social inferiors and demonstrating their own superiority.

When elite white men themselves transgressed church rules, they were sometimes not prepared to countenance the imposition of discipline from their church, cognizant of the symbolism of submission that was required. When the First Baptist Church in Savannah queried the attendance of the merchant George A. Ash on a "maruning excursion," they were somewhat taken aback by his response. Although the church took no action against him, the mere fact that it had seen fit to investigate him resulted in a request for a letter of dismissal, even though "he has not at present any such notion [of using it]."[144] Others were prepared to go even further to defend their own interpretation of church discipline. John Morrow was expelled from Salem Baptist Church for expressing "his contempt of the church" after its investigation of his financial dealings. His co-religionist Brother Wilson was similarly expelled for refusing to make any acknowledgment of his offense of playing the fiddle: indeed, he declared to the church "that he did not think it any harm to play the fiddle and if the church thought fit to expel him she could do it."[145] To some white men, therefore, the maintenance of symbolic mastery, especially where the church itself was perceived and described as feminine, was more important than remaining a member of the church.

As a whole, white men were far more likely than women to be brought before church discipline councils even though they constituted less than a third of the membership of lowcountry evangelical churches.[146] The offenses for which white men were cited differed in several respects from those of white women and from African Americans of both sexes. More than half of all cases involving white men concerned accusations of intemperance. In contrast, white women were cited for intoxication in only about a fifth of cases and African Americans only rarely.[147] Slaves were officially denied access to alcohol, but the determined slave usually was able to obtain liquor. In the 1820s and 1830s, however, temperance societies became increasingly popular among African Americans. Andrew Marshall, the pastor at the First African Baptist Church, informed George Lewis that any member found drunk would "be suspended or cut off from the church."[148] By the early 1830s both the Sunbury and the Second African churches reported that they had flourishing temperance societies, drawing members both from the surrounding localities and from within the congregation.[149] In contrast, a white temperance society, under the direction of the First Baptist Church, was formed only in 1832.[150] Intemperance was generally believed to lead "the mind astray from God [by] a too free indulgence of the appetites and passions."[151] The common perception among evangelical churches that alcohol had "a tendency to produce a state of mind unfavorable to the worship and enjoyment of God" resulted in frequent strictures warning members against it.[152] Intemperance was the offense most frequently dealt with by church discipline councils and was given special weight when committed by white men because it incapacitated them from fulfilling their Christian role of leadership. Men who failed in their Christian duty could hardly be held up as an example to their dependents. The failings of white men, most often nonslaveholders, would therefore have been brought home clearly to African American members, and in this manner the biraciality of congregations challenged notions that white people were innately superior to African Americans.

African Americans were most frequently cited for sexual misdemeanors, usually adultery or illegitimacy.[153] An integral part of any evangelical church discipline was the view that "carnal gratifications and vain indulgences . . . are all contrary to the love of God."[154] Thus even though state law did not recognize the validity of slave marriages, evangelical churches expected African Americans to live up to the spirit of Christian marriage. For example, Little Ogechee Baptist Church made a statement to its African American members "as it regards their marrying and separation." The elders of the church pointed out that no Christian should marry another while the spouse lived, nor should a single person marry someone whose spouse was still alive. Even in cases where the actions of owners dictated the separation of a couple, churches counseled that bondspeople should seek the advice of white members on an appropriate course of action.[155] In 1849 the Savannah River Association made it clear that remarriage while a spouse lived was "of doubtful morality" and would lead to exclusion from the church.[156] These stipulations were intended to allow the church to act as mediator and to reinforce its centrality in the lives of African Americans. In this way white people from all social classes could have a direct impact on the private lives of African Americans with whom they perhaps had no other formal association. White people were generally less likely than bondspeople to be summoned to answer charges of a sexual nature, indicating either that they did not commit such offenses, or perhaps more plausibly, that such offenses were less likely to become public knowledge.

The social status of evangelical white women is extremely difficult to determine because there are few historical sources that comprehensively include women. Given that up to half of the male members of the First Baptist Church were nonslaveholders and that church membership was often familial, however, it is likely that a similar proportion of the white female members of this church were from nonslaveholding families.[157] White women were most frequently cited for "disorder" rather than intemperance or sexual offenses.[158] The precise nature of these offenses is often lost behind such phrases as "improper walks" and "unbecoming behaviour"; but the public deportment of white women was clearly as significant to church elders as that of white men. The First Baptist Church was forced to excommunicate Elizabeth Jones after she became so drunk that "she fell down once in the public street and again at her mother-in-law's door," thus humiliating not only herself but the whole church before the citizens of Savannah.[159] As Martha Blauvelt has shown, white women who did not live up to the religious ideals of evangelical churches were often labeled as "immoral."[160]

The discipline records of evangelical churches also reveal the wide disparity in treatment of certain status groups for the same offense. Intemperate white women were, for example, significantly more likely than white men to be excommunicated. African American offenders were generally more liable than whites to be suspended or expelled by the church.[161] Overall, nearly a third of white men cited were forgiven for their crimes, without even an admonishment, and several of the worst offenders were suspended many times before their church finally expelled them.[162] It is patently clear from the records of lowcountry evangelical churches that discipline councils operated under a gender as much as a racial bias, and as such they further strengthened the position of all white men in Southern society. Yet even though women and African Americans were generally treated with more severity by discipline councils, some offenses committed by men could not be overlooked. White women found that an appeal to their local church sometimes brought a swift and public condemnation of mistreatment by their husbands. In 1770 the Congregational church at Midway suspended three prominent and wealthy white men who failed to treat their wives in what was perceived as the appropriate manner.[163] Although these cases were comparatively rare in the discipline meetings of evangelical churches (and we have no idea of how many cases never came before the church), when they arose the public humiliation of the man in question was complete. In 1829 Little Ogechee Baptist Church went so far as to excommunicate Lucas Bob for leaving his wife and "taking up with another woman."[164] His actions were not tolerated by a community that expected husbands to live up to their responsibilities to their families and was prepared to challenge the power of men at home and to defend women, children, and even slaves from abuse.[165] In this sense, some churches were prepared to interfere in the paternal relations that were normally the sole prerogative of the owner. One slave owner, Harriet King, was excommunicated from her church following reports that she had "been cruel to her servants."[166]

The interest of churches in the private domestic arrangements of their members extended even to the bedroom. Women found to be living in adultery and who failed to live up to the standards of "passionlessness" set by the churches could expect censure either through suspension or excommunication.[167] Both Morning Shepherd and Mrs. Jenkinson were expelled from their religious communities for improper physical relations.[168] The Independent Presbyterian Church in Savannah gave Jennett Gale a chance to redeem herself while on suspension for having an illegitimate child, but when she became "more & more confirmed in her dissolute course," she was expelled.[169] Some evangelical churches declared that betrayed husbands were no longer bound by marriage vows to an unfaithful spouse. In such cases even in South Carolina, where divorce was not possible, "a subsequent marriage of the said innocent party shall not be a bar to communion in our church."[170] Yet it is important to remember that while sexual involvement with another man would probably result in excommunication for women of both races, separation from a violent husband would not necessarily involve long-term consequences.

Churches did not see it as their role to support husbands who forced "an affectionate wife and helpless children . . . to pay an unnatural tribute to support his folly."[171] Indeed, by demanding such high standards of morality from female members, churches felt bound to protect those women who met them but whose husbands did not. In 1810 the First Baptist Church in Savannah dealt with an awkward case that challenged, but ultimately affirmed, the propriety of ministerial interference in household relations. Hannah Jordan joined the church in 1809, evidently without her husband.[172] On her application for dismissal to Nevill's Creek Baptist Church several members objected, claiming that she had left her husband improperly. Hannah spoke up for herself at the meeting, stating that her husband had thrown her out, forbidding her to live in town and setting her at liberty to remarry. She was quick to point out that she had no intention of remarrying but that her husband intended to do so in a fortnight's time. She also placed her faith in the church to effect a reconciliation, in which case she would stay. Evidently the church agonized over the proper course of action. The male members probably believed that she should not have left her husband. But her eloquence in describing herself as the injured party was such that the church, in recognition of the righteousness of her argument, "unanimously agreed to dismiss her as an orderly member."[173]

Even though poorer white people and slaves constituted a majority of the congregations of lowcountry Baptist and Methodist churches, attracted by a theology that preached equality for all before God, elite perceptions of race and gender evidently remained dominant. Evangelical religion thus effected a dual and somewhat conflicting purpose of weakening the spiritual distinctions between blacks and whites, especially the poorest whites, while reinforcing established temporal social hierarchies.[174] Evangelical churches were certainly not seeking to undermine society. In 1807 the Savannah River Baptist Association wrote a circular letter to its member churches regarding domestic relations. While it emphasized that husbands had a duty of care and love toward their wives, it also stressed, above all, that women had a duty "to be obedient." This submission to the authority of husbands would "promote greater union, which will produce greater happiness."[175] The consolidation of established gender structures which the Baptist Association was advocating also applied to race and familial responsibility. Thus white males were held as the supreme temporal authority over their wives, their children, and their slaves.

Stephanie McCurry has argued that the ideology of evangelical Christianity united white men of all classes by distinguishing between them and their dependents, namely, white women and slaves.[176] This point was increasingly true as the Civil War approached, as the promotion of temporal hierarchy in lowcountry churches became more frequent in the later antebellum period and churches made a explicit distinction between spiritual equality and temporal obedience. In 1845 the constituents of the Sunbury Baptist Association were informed that the role of white men should be analogous to the ministry, that each should be a "priest of his own house." Moreover, it was their duty to inform those in their care, women, children and slaves, that God "will punish them if they are bad and bless them if they are good." [177] In 1852 the Piedmont Baptist Association went even further, exhorting "pious mothers" to educate their children in religious exercises and fathers, as head of families, to "assemble your children around the family circle, and there endeavor to instruct them in all the ways of piety." As for slaves, it was the duty of all slaveholders to filter the message of Christianity to take into account "their simple style of thinking" and instill the basic tenets of repentance and faith.[178] By adopting familial power structures, evangelical churches explicitly and deliberately reinforced the symbolic dominance of white male heads of households.

There was, however, no point in expounding on the duties of dependents unless they were actually hearing and absorbing the message. To this end, all evangelical denominations to some extent pursued a policy of missionary work to gain new converts, both black and white, in parts of the lowcountry that hitherto had lacked organized religion. In this effort the churches believed they were fulfilling the biblical command to diffuse "the knowledge of the Lord." [179] While some missionary work was attempted in the colonial and Revolutionary periods, the first significant Southern revival was the Great Revival of 1800–1805.[180] Starting in Kentucky, this revival pioneered the technique of the camp meeting (three-day multidenominational gatherings), which proved popular with blacks and whites alike. The impact of this revival on the lowcountry was patchy, however. The Baptist minister Richard Furman stated that despite reports of revival in backcountry areas of South Carolina, "in Charleston we remain much as we have been for a number of years." [181] Indeed, apart from several meetings in Liberty County organized by the Methodist missionary Jesse Lee, which produced "an uncommon prosperous time in religion," and a notable meeting near Beaufort in 1803, attended by over a thousand people, lowcountry churches generally did not report large additions to their membership during this period.[182] This was partly owing to the elite's dislike of the highly emotional nature of camp meetings, where some "could not abstain from crying out in the most public manner" and those affected "remained sobbing, weeping and often crying aloud until the service was over." Some less generous-spirited lowcountry residents also viewed conversions achieved at camp meetings as only temporary, with "too much stress on bodily exercises and substituting them in place of moral virtues or inward piety."[183]

While religious sentiments in Savannah and Charleston may have been only marginally affected by the Great Revival, more success was achieved in the surrounding rural areas, and some missionaries hoped that rural success would eventually lead to the same in urban areas.[184] Henry Holcombe reported that before the arrival of a young Baptist preacher, the inhabitants of Black Creek were "willing captives of Satan."[185] But the preaching of Mr. Peacock, despite being "without the advantages of a learned education . . . commanded very general attention, and powerful impressions were made." The thirteen converts he made came together to form the Black Creek Baptist Church.[186] The biracial rural churches founded in the early nineteenth century were often simple wooden-framed buildings, in stark contrast to the magnificent edifices constructed in Savannah, but they served their congregations adequately.[187] The races and genders mixed in these environments far more than they did in urban churches, which had galleries and partitions. Therefore, the new rural churches established through missionary work were often the sites of the greatest biracial interaction and identification, especially when the evangelical message of spiritual equality was fresh in the mind.

The main problem with revivalism was its temporary nature. Increases in church membership were rarely sustained over many years. In an attempt to boost both white and black church membership outside of Charleston and Savannah in the second decade of the nineteenth century, the Baptist Associations planned "a scheme of itinerant preaching or home missions."[188] Preachers were to be "of approved character" and to minister to "destitute churches" with the expressed aim of "the conversion of sinners and the regular formation of churches." Importantly, these missions were not aimed specifically at winning people to the Baptist faith; rather, they sought to evangelize the irreligious. Indeed, the missionary board ordered that its appointees should "avoid entering into contentions with Christians of other denominations, and giving offence."[189] The missions were funded by contributions from the member churches. Although the majority of the money came from the white Baptist churches, each of the African churches made a small but symbolically important contribution.[190]

Other denominations also began a concerted missionary effort in Georgia in the early nineteenth century, aimed primarily at the poorest members of white and black society. In 1811 Harmony Presbytery resolved to collect Bibles and religious tracts which could be "given away to children or poor persons."[191] In addition, each member was instructed to spend two weeks annually in missionary work to "the destitute parts contiguous to their residence."[192] The following year, the churches reported that not only had this effort produced many new converts but also that "the blacks are more attentive & serious than we have ever seen them."[193] In Savannah, however, missionary efforts to African Americans remained the preserve of Baptist and Methodist preachers.[194] In 1832 the Georgia Methodist Conference specifically sought African American converts by resolving to send "a missionary to the slaves and colored people [to] collect them into societies and divide them into classes wherever it is practicable."[195]

These missionary efforts did not meet with immediate or continuous success. In both 1819 and 1820, the Sunbury Baptist Association ruefully noted "the state of our churches" and "the declining state of religion among us."[196] By 1822, however, "a general religious excitement" had begun to occur "throughout the whole of this section of the country." The associations praised the "labors of our domestic missionaries," whose work had resulted in "most urgent solicitations that [local people] may still be allowed to share the benefit of their services."[197] These missions were evidently to both the white and black populations of rural localities, such as Harris' Neck near Darien.[198] In 1825 the Sunbury Baptist Association praised Brother Dunham for his missionary work "both among the blacks and the whites" in Liberty and McIntosh Counties.[199] The life of itinerant Baptist preachers was one of constant traveling and frequent services and exhortations. In the 1840s it was common for William P. Hill to travel up to five hundred miles a month on his missionary circuit in South Carolina.[200] His efforts, of course, encompassed both black and white residents, often involving the preaching of successive sermons to congregations of different races.[201] David Ramsay documented that the several itinerant Methodist preachers in South Carolina traveled six days a week, together preaching more than eight thousand sermons in a year. Significantly, Methodists found "most success in the woods, the swamps, the pine barrens, and all new and dispersed settlements," precisely those areas inhabited by the poorest white people.[202] Multidenominational camp meetings were still being organized in the lowcountry in the late antebellum period, attracting the local populace for many miles around to gather as much for socializing as for worship. At one such meeting, attended by Fredericka Bremer, African Americans "were considerably more numerous" than whites, even having their own preachers.[203]

As was true of many other spiritual activities, missionary work was to some extent gendered. Itinerant missionaries found that family visits regularly brought about conversions when they used "the retirement of the fireside to explain the doctrines & inculcate the precepts of our holy religion."[204] This brought them into direct contact with rural women, who in turn took the spiritual message of renewal to their husbands. Thus the family became one method of transmitting revivalism. Women, not content with constituting the majority of church members and being the driving force behind most benevolent work in the lowcountry, also became deeply involved in efforts to evangelize the unchurched black and white masses. In the 1820s a multidenominational group of elite women in Savannah formed the Domestic Female Missionary Society, which contributed between $100 and $120 per year toward the work of the American Home Missionary Society. This money, it was hoped, would be put to good use in Burke and Screven Counties, where "the people are hungry for preaching."[205] The Presbyterian missions found it difficult to progress rapidly in the lowcountry partly because the dominance of Baptist and Methodist churches made it hard to establish Presbyterian congregations but also because of internal divisions among the Presbyterian churches. As Edwin Holt informed the Home Missionary Society, "sectional jealousies" primarily prevented the small but wealthy number of Presbyterians in the lowcountry from financially assisting the upcountry churches.[206]

Between 1830 and the onset of the Civil War, missions to African Americans in the lowcountry intensified.[207] Led by noted the Presbyterian Charles Colcock Jones, the Association for the Religious Instruction of the Negroes in Liberty County, Georgia, started work in 1835. It aimed, by regular plantation visits and the establishment of Sabbath schools, to evangelize the enslaved population. To do this, missionaries had to follow guidelines dictated by slaveholders, including asking permission before visiting a plantation, ignoring any pleas for material help from slaves, and impressing on the slaves the need for "respect and obedience" toward those in authority.[208] There is considerable evidence, however, that African Americans on coastal plantations were not overly impressed with these white missionaries. Lowcountry slaves seem to have resented the interference of white people, partly because, left to their own devices on the plantation, slaves had formed their own methods of religious expression without white help.[209] For example, despite several complaints by the St. Marys town council, slaves continued to gather there without white supervision for religious purposes until their church was destroyed "by hot-headed young men of the town during the excitement that prevailed over a rumored insurrection of the negroes."[210] Slaves also took a dim view of the version of Christianity offered by white preachers. One missionary recorded his astonishment when slaves showed their dislike of his spiritual message by walking away:

> I was preaching to a large congregation on the Epistle of Philemon: and when I insisted upon fidelity and obedience as Christian virtues in servants and, upon the authority of Paul, condemned the practice of running away, one half of my audience deliberately rose up and walked off with themselves, and those that remained looked anything but satisfied, either with the preacher or his doctrine. After dismission there was no small stir among them: some solemnly declared "that there was no such an Epistle in the Bible" others "that it was not the gospel" others "that I preached to please the masters" others "that they did not care if they ever heard me preach again."[211]

In this case the missionary came up against slaves who were conversant in another interpretation of the Bible and preferred it to any other version. White missionaries were also unlikely to win the respect of slaves when they declared that observation of the Sabbath prohibited all activities "such as planting, attending to their crops, harvesting, repairing their fences or houses, trading, washing, grinding, and all pleasure, such as hunting and fishing and playing at games."[212]

The alternative vision of evangelicalism offered to, and preferred by, the slaves came from the black Baptist churches in and around Savannah. In 1845 and 1846 white Baptist missionaries complained to the annual association that their efforts on the plantations were in vain. According to one missionary, "this may be attributed to their proximity to the city, and in no small degree to the fact of their connection with city churches."[213] These "connections" were most likely informal, consisting of attendance at services when in Savannah to trade. Still, the urban black Baptist churches in Savannah had some influence on the surrounding lowcountry churches. In 1852 and again in 1853, white Baptist missionaries reported that they were unable to monitor the activities in rural African churches, having been refused access by the members. This spirit of independence toward the missionary was apparently caused by "influences, over which he has no control." Since local planters had requested the interference of the Baptist Association in the affairs of the two African churches concerned, it is likely that the counterinfluence was the First African Baptist Church in Savannah.[214] Following the onset of Civil War in 1861, Charles Colcock Jones stated that it was more important than ever to use the mission system to preach to African Americans, claiming that "the stability and welfare of both church and state depend largely upon it."[215] One former slave recalled that whites in Savannah "told us to pray for their cause," but in reality "we prayed against them."[216] The inability of white missionaries to impose their religious views on African Americans demonstrates that the independence of black churches was highly prized. Moreover, the willingness of slaves, by the end of antebellum era, to defend their religious autonomy is a clear sign that the biracial religious experience in the lowcountry was coming to an end.

More than seventy years elapsed between the ending of the American Revolution and the start of the Civil War. During that time large numbers of African Americans were brought into the orbit of evangelical denominations, but their status in those churches changed markedly. In the early years of evangelism, religious roles were flexible and ambiguous, allowing for much contact between blacks and whites in a sphere where hierarchy was still being mapped out. In these environments nonslaveholders and slaves came to know each other as fellow converts to religion. In no other social forum did they meet on terms of theoretical equality before God, and there is evidence that despite status differences between whites and blacks, they shared a common evangelical religious experience.[217] By the early national period, Christian nonslaveholding whites were hearing a spiritual message that fostered the acceptance of African Americans as religious equals. As the antebellum era progressed, however, that situation changed. Elite whites became converts to evangelicalism in increasing numbers, and as they did so they stamped their social hierarchy on the churches, with one where men still ruled over women and white ruled over black.[218] Nonelite white men especially acquired a privileged position in evangelical churches solely by virtue of their race and gender, even though they remained under the control of the elite. African Americans responded by retreating to their own African churches, which on the whole white people left alone, and by taking their own message of comfort from the Bible. Biracial churches in 1860 were very different than they had been in 1810. The social fluidity and the ready intermixing of black and white was almost entirely gone, and those blacks attending white churches were confined to galleries. One of the most dangerous environments for racial mixing had been neutralized, indeed it had been turned into a mechanism for disseminating the elite's own worldview. After secession, among the most vocal supporters of the war was the *Christian Index,* the newspaper of Georgia Baptists.[219] Religious encounters did not erode the status difference between black and white so far as to alienate the racial loyalties of nonslaveholders. Therefore, while evangelical Christianity in the lowcountry served to weaken spiritual distinctions that divided white from black and men from women, it simultaneously reinforced temporal distinctions and supported the established social order.

CONCLUSION

The Implications
of Biracial Interaction

NO SOCIAL GROUP in the antebellum Georgia lowcountry existed in complete isolation. Whites interacted with African Americans, rich encountered poor, and men and women coped alike with the vagaries of the opposite sex. The fundamental multiplicity of lowcountry social relations is the common theme of this book. Nonslaveholding men and women met and interacted with African Americans in formal and informal environments: in church and in the marketplace, in the local tavern and in the county jail, in bed and in the workplace. The reasons why white people chose to meet African Americans in social spheres and why African Americans did not reject these contacts are many and varied. It would be as misleading to stereotype the motives of white shopkeepers who traded with African Americans as solely profit-oriented as it would be to characterize assaults on African Americans by nonslaveholders as always motivated by racism. The encounters between nonslaveholding whites and African Americans in lowcountry Georgia were altogether more complex and ambiguous.

Nearly all nonslaveholders had some contact with African Americans. Nonelite whites who sat alongside African Americans in church or at the camp meeting were most likely not the same individuals who drank and gambled with bondspeople in lowcountry dramshops. In this sense, the stark reality of African American bondage permeated the world of every nonslaveholder just as much as it did that of slave owners. For some nonelite whites, most notably overseers and patrollers, contacts with African Americans were constructed largely on the same control dynamic as that of owners. For the majority of nonslaveholders, however, especially women, their principal encounters with African Americans did not entail control or supervision. Rather, they involved informal socialization and clandestine economic or criminal cooperation. The race barriers of late eighteenth-century and early nineteenth-century lowcountry society were, to some degree, perceived by nonslaveholders and African Americans alike as flexible and permeable. The encounters described here were facilitated by such interpretations.

What, therefore, is the overall relationship between race and motivation in the variety of encounters described in this book? On the one hand, many of points of contact, especially those concerning fugitive slaves or the purchase of stolen goods, were deliberate acts that not only contravened racial barriers but also threatened the security of white society by empowering African Americans. Nonslaveholding whites were able to form class alliances that crossed the race divide. Yet race in the lowcountry clearly remained an important social determinant. Indeed, some scholars have seen no other reason for the attachment of the majority of whites, both slaveholders and nonslaveholders, to the institution of slavery.[1] To all whites it was obvious that no matter how often slaves purchased alcohol from a white shopkeeper, or how often they went to the same lowcountry Baptist church, they remained enslaved. The interaction with nonslaveholding whites, with very few individual exceptions, did not engender freedom for African Americans. Yet bondspeople's provision of cash to shopkeepers and the reception of goods in return, or jointly planned and executed thefts, helped to mitigate the harshness of material life for both parties. Neither whites nor blacks had an interest in ending mutually beneficial relationships or shying away from advantageous social encounters. The only people in some way threatened by a thriving relationship between poor whites and slaves were the white elite.

I have tried to expose just how far the institution of slavery itself engendered and encouraged contact between nonslaveholders and African Americans. Not only did slavery as an economic system confine many nonslaveholding whites to socioeconomic marginalization, but it also enabled African Americans to engage in the lowcountry economy. The desires of owners for more valuable slaves led them to train their bondspeople in trades that allowed them to work side by side with nonslaveholding whites. Without the implicit cooperation of owners, bondspeople would not have been able to grow the range of crops or have the free time to hunt or make handicrafts, which they subsequently sold to white traders. Indeed, the willingness of some owners to permit slaves to hire their own time greatly facilitated bondspeople's social interaction with poorer white people. The wealth of slaveholders in Savannah and in other lowcountry towns provided employment for numerous enslaved and free black domestics in the city, who were able to interact with urban non-slaveholders. The self-congratulatory paternalist ideology of the elite also facilitated religious contacts between white and black. Owners who permitted their slaves a degree of religious freedom hoped to demonstrate their own humanity and piety. Above all, slavery, by subjecting and controlling the African American legally and socially, eliminated any lingering psychological concerns of the nonelite. Despite how we may now depict the power relationships exposed by nonslaveholders' interaction with African Americans, nonelite whites at the time would have been confident of their own superior social standing solely by virtue of their race. The fact that racial barriers existed and had the force of law behind them permitted nonslaveholders to circumvent them without actually threatening the social order of the lowcountry. In this sense, racial barriers were indeed "lines in the sand," lines that were impermanent, movable, and vulnerable but still existed. Without slavery to separate the races, much of the biracial interaction described here would not have happened. The relationship of slaves and nonslaveholders was inconsistent and, to some degree, pragmatic, but it is clear that the nonelite fashioned their own relationship with slaves without the help or controlling influence of the elite.

Some nonslaveholders failed to realize just how much their actions empowered African Americans, who eagerly grasped at every opportunity to improve their material and spiritual life. Interaction with white non-slaveholders was often the easiest avenue to achieve those material gains usually denied by owners. The fact that some nonslaveholders were unwitting accomplices in ameliorating the lives of bondspeople shows just how fluid the perceptions of racial propriety could be in the lowcountry. Altogether more subversive were those nonslaveholding whites who deliberately chose to ally with African Americans against the established order. By 1830 the loyalty of a significant portion of lowcountry shopkeepers, artisans, and farmers to the Southern regime was highly questionable, and consequently the contacts between nonslaveholders and African Americans provoked a confrontation with the white elite. Anything that undermined the centrality of owners in the lives of bondspeople met with fierce resistance from the elite. Slaveholders often encouraged an attitude of contempt for "poor white trash" among their slaves, while simultaneously subscribing to a definition of freedom and independence based primarily on race.² Planters in the late antebellum era began to appreciate the potential for poor white alienation and the threat to their own position that might result from a class alliance between nonelite whites and African Americans. This possibility forced the elite to develop several stratagems to limit class conflict in the years before secession.

Aware of their diminishing control over the prevalent Southern social ethic, members of the elite began to treat nonslaveholders more carefully in the thirty years before the Civil War to ensure their loyalty toward the slave system. More social distinctions were made between nonelite whites and African Americans, and the elite repeatedly stressed the ties of family, gender, and race and a concept of liberty based on personal freedom.³ It was this more than anything else that led nonslaveholders to support the Southern regime. In a further attempt to tie nonslaveholders firmly to the institution of slavery, many of the new jobs created by the industrial development of the 1850s were reserved by the elite for the poorer members of white society.⁴ Most of these new positions went to native-born whites, leaving the large urban immigrant Irish population in Savannah to compete with African Americans for the remaining work.⁵ In this way the elite attempted to avoid complaints such as that to the *Savannah Republican* of "Nothing Laid Up," who blamed "an abundance of Negroes" for the fact that "poor white men will stand no chance at all to make a support . . . and the poor would grow poorer while the rich grew richer."⁶ By bringing some white mechanics into the privileges of race, while engendering racial hatred in others because of black competition, the elite prevented a general combination of nonslaveholding whites against them.

Ultimately, the issue of white liberty and independence went to the very heart of why nonslaveholders overwhelmingly supported the Southern cause during the Civil War. In contrast to some backcountry areas, lowcountry nonslaveholders were vocal in their defense of the Southern cause in 1860–61.⁷ William Capers, overseer for Louis Manigault on Argyle Island, expressed his belief that "the Southern states have remained in the Union too long" in the face of Northern provocation.⁸ Following Abraham Lincoln's election in 1860, a meeting was held in Savannah to allow the mayor, Charles Colcock Jones Jr., to hear the views of the public on the sectional crisis. Among the most strident supporters of the Southern cause was an Irish priest, Father O'Neill, who declared that he was "a rapublican, and a sacessionist and a satizen of Georgia; and in case there should be war, he would be the first to lade them into battle, he would!" When a vote on the resolutions of the meeting was taken, not a single Savannahian voted against them.[9] By the time of the secession vote in 1861, there was little doubt that nonslaveholders would toe the established white line and support the continued enslavement of African Americans.[10]

By 1860 the lowcountry elite had avoided the "nightmare scenario" that would see them isolated in Southern society in the face of a biracial alliance of African Americans and nonslaveholders. Evangelicalism was probably the most important element in this web of control exerted so successfully by slaveholders. By placing more emphasis on the racial and gender status of nonslaveholding men, evangelical churches provided the ideal forum for the dissemination of a message reinforcing racial and gender hierarchies among the nonelite classes. Slavery and social hierarchy were increasingly portrayed as divinely ordained, and those who did not accept this ideology were perceived as rebelling not only against Southern society but also against God.[11] The elevation in status of nonelite whites was combined with the stricter enforcement of laws pertaining to biracial contacts. Those whites who failed to join the new racial solidarity of the 1850s, for example by continuing to trade illegally with slaves or helping runaways, were dealt with more severely by civic and local authorities than they had been previously.

The spheres of interaction between nonslaveholders and African Americans were therefore increasingly challenged as the Civil War approached. Indeed, the late antebellum period can be characterized generally as one of rising racial tension, with the white elite more aware than ever of the potential threat posed by biracial encounters. Tighter restrictions were placed on the free time activities of bondspeople, thus reducing their opportunities to alleviate their situation through contacts with poor whites.[12] The new attitude of the elite sent a clear message to the poorest members of white society that the threat biracial interaction posed to Southern society would no longer be tolerated. It is also apparent that nonslaveholders absorbed at best only part of the message. While evangelicalism and economic competition increasingly divided white from black, alliances of mutual convenience continued to be formed. Nonslaveholders continued to trade illegally and sleep with slaves as well as harboring those fleeing bondage, right up to the Civil War. Demonstrating that nonslaveholders became more aware of their racial and class position is not to claim that they consistently applied their new ideology. It is entirely possible that nonslaveholders were totally inconsistent in their relationships with African Americans: protesting about economic competition, while going home to a black lover or to a bar frequented by slaves.

Once the war was over and the slave population of the lowcountry freed, the old patterns of biracial interaction between nonelite whites and African Americans were not recreated. Indeed, the lack of slavery to form a clear legal distinction between white and black evidently necessitated the creation of a much more robust mental color barrier. As one scholar has put it, "With the demise of slavery, the total separation of blacks and whites was essential to whites if they were to retain legal and social authority."[13] The easiest way to distinguish and discriminate between whites and freedpeople was by color. Racism in the postwar years was more virulent and extreme than in the antebellum era. The greater threat which African Americans now posed to the social position of poor whites, especially through economic and social competition, ensured that racial barriers between them were reerected and fiercely defended. Thus the end of slavery also ended the nascent relationship that had become established in the lowcountry between poor and marginalized people of both races.

NOTES

ABBREVIATIONS

CCM   Savannah City Council Minutes, Georgia Historical Society, Savannah

Col. Recs. Allen D. Candler, ed. *The Colonial Records of the State of Georgia.* 32 vols. New York, 1970, Athens, 1988–95.

DU   Duke University, Durham, North Carolina

GDAH   Georgia Department of Archives and History, Atlanta

GHS   Georgia Historical Society, Savannah

MU   Mercer University, Macon, Georgia

RoD   *Register of Deaths in Savannah, Georgia, 1803–1847.* 6 vols. Savannah, 1989.

SBAM   Sunbury Baptist Association Minutes, Mercer University, Macon, Georgia

SCDAH   South Carolina Department of Archives and History, Columbia

SCHS   South Carolina Historical Society, Charleston

SHC   Southern Historical Collection, University of North Carolina, Chapel Hill

SRBAM   Savannah River Baptist Association Minutes, Mercer University, Macon, Georgia

UGa   University of Georgia, Athens

USC   University of South Carolina, Columbia

1. Hundley, *Social Relations in Our Southern States*, 10.

2. Helper, *Impending Crisis*, 41, 47–49.

3. Wolfe, *Helper's Impending Crisis Dissected*, 58, 61–62.

4. Hundley, *Social Relations*, 193–239.

5. Phillips, *American Negro Slavery*, 356.

6. Buck, "Poor Whites," 41–54; Craven, "Poor Whites and Negroes," 14–25; Hollander, "Tradition of Poor Whites."

7. Phillips, *Life and Labor in the Old South;* Mell, "Poor Whites of the South"; Mell, "Definitive Study of the Poor Whites of the South"; Brown, "Role of Poor Whites"; Bonner, "Profile of a Late Antebellum Community."

8. Owsley and Owsley, "Economic Basis of Society in the Late Antebellum South"; Owsley, *Plain Folk of the Old South.*

9. Linden, "Economic Democracy in the Slave South." Linden also criticized the tendency to extrapolate data from one specific region to cover larger areas without any regard for clear geographical differences.

10. Flynt, *Dixie's Forgotten People.*

11. Ibid., 11; Genovese, *Roll, Jordan, Roll*, 89–97.

12. Hahn, *Roots of Southern Populism*, 1–60; Hahn, "Yeomanry of the Non-Plantation South," 29–56.

13. Harris, *Plain Folk and Gentry*, 1–101, esp. 64–93.

14. Ford, *Origins of Southern Radicalism*, 66–122; Ford, "Popular Ideology of the South's Plain Folk: The Limits of Egalitarianism in a Slaveholding Society," in *Plain Folk of the South Revisited*, ed. Hyde, 205–27. In *Cracker Culture*, Grady McWhiney has posited that nonslaveholders shared a common Celtic heritage and culture that distinguished them from the primarily Anglo-Saxon elite.

15. Fronsman, *Common Whites*, 85, 159.

16. Bolton, *Poor Whites*, 118–22.

17. McCurry, *Masters of Small Worlds.* For the most recent scholarship, see Hyde, ed., *Plain Folk of the South Revisited.* Terms such as "redneck" and "white trash" are still in pejorative use today. See F. N. Boney, *Southerners All* (Macon, Ga., 1984), 31–67, and Matt Wray and Annalee Newitz, eds., *White Trash: Race and Class in America* (New York, 1997).

18. Phillips, "Central Theme of Southern History"; Kenzer, *Kinship and Neighborhood*, 29–41.

19. Brown, "Role of Poor Whites," 261.

20. Genovese, *Roll, Jordan, Roll*, 13, 89–97; Genovese, "'Rather Be a Nigger Than a Poor White Man.'" For an excellent study of a biracial world, see Morgan, *Slave Counterpoint*, 257–437.

21. The best criticisms of Genovese are found in Oakes, *Ruling Race.* See also Paul D. Escott, *Slavery Remembered: A Record of Twentieth-Century Slave Narratives* (Chapel Hill, 1979), 97–98; Fronsman, *Common Whites*, 68–94; Kaplanoff, "Making the South Solid," 66–73.

22. For notable exceptions, see McCurry, *Masters of Small Worlds*, 105–21; Bolton,

Poor Whites, 109–10; and Johnston, "Participation of White Men in Virginia Negro Insurrections."

23. Fields, "Ideology and Race in American History." See also Roediger, *Wages of Whiteness*, 3–17.

24. Avery Craven, A. Hollander, and U. B. Phillips all separate nonslaveholders into yeoman farmers and "white trash," yet they all fail to make a clear, or indeed a common, distinction between the two groups. See Craven, "Poor Whites and Negroes," 17; Hollander, "Tradition of Poor Whites," 403–31; Phillips, *Life and Labor in the Old South*, 339–46.

25. Fronsman, *Common Whites*, 1; Bolton, *Poor Whites*, 4; McCurry, *Masters of Small Worlds*, 48–49.

26. Gillespie, "Planters in the Making"; Gillespie, "Artisan Accommodation."

27. Both Brown and Bonner have argued that because landownership was easily available in the South, it is wrong to measure social status by economic criteria alone. See Brown, "Role of Poor Whites," 258–68; Bonner, "Profile of a Late Ante-Bellum Community," 663–80.

28. By 1790 slaves constituted three-quarters of the total lowcountry population in both Georgia and South Carolina. In 1790, 16,852 people resided in lowcountry Georgia, 12,511 (74.2%) of whom were slaves. A total population of 84,405 dwelled in Charleston and Beaufort districts in South Carolina, of whom 64,869 (76.8%) were enslaved. All census statistics were taken from http://fisher.lib.virginia.edu/census in 1999.

29. Mallard, *Plantation Life*, 155.

30. Gallay, "Jonathan Bryan's Plantation Empire," 256; Chesnutt, "South Carolina's Expansion into Colonial Georgia," iv; Wood, *Slavery in Colonial Georgia*, 91–93.

1. NONSLAVEHOLDERS IN THE GEORGIA LOWCOUNTRY

1. On planter hegemony, see the debate between Eugene Genovese and James Oakes: Genovese, *Political Economy of Slavery;* Genovese, *World the Slaveholders Made;* Genovese, *Roll, Jordan, Roll;* Oakes, *Ruling Race;* Oakes, *Slavery and Freedom.*

2. The most obvious status difference existed between those who paid for their own passage and those who did not. Before 1752, 2,122 charity settlers and 3,482 paying settlers immigrated into Georgia. The latter increased dramatically in number only after 1742. See Taylor, "Colonizing Georgia," 123–24.

3. In 1790 the four lowcountry counties of Georgia (Chatham, Liberty, Glynn, and Camden) were inhabited by 4,183 white people, 12,511 slaves, and 158 free people of color. By 1830 the population had grown to 9,692 white people, 28,352 slaves, and 573 free people of color. In 1860 the lowcountry was inhabited by 23,161 whites, 34,314 slaves, and 805 free blacks. All census statistics were taken from http://fisher.lib.virginia.edu/census in 1999.

4. In 1810, for example, the enslaved population of the six lowcountry counties of Chatham, Bryan, Liberty, McIntosh, Glynn, and Camden numbered 25,309, of whom 22,780 (90%) lived in rural districts.

5. In 1810 the federal census enumerated 7,879 white people in the lowcountry, 3,209

(37.8%) of whom lived in urban areas. By 1860 whites were the majority race in Chatham County, amounting to 52% of residents; the rest of the lowcountry remained 71% black. Of 728 free African Americans in the lowcountry in 1810, 570 (78.3%) resided in Savannah. By 1860, 725 (90%) of 805 lowcountry free blacks were living in the city.

6. McCurry, "Defense of Their World," 6, 31–47; McCurry, *Masters of Small Worlds,* 22–84. For an argument that tries to uphold the idea that lowcountry populations rarely included nonslaveholding whites, see Russel," Effects of Slavery upon Nonslaveholders," 148.

7. McCurry, *Masters of Small Worlds,* 38–42.

8. Ibid., 22–84.

9. Charter of the Colony of Georgia, June 9, 1732, *Col. Recs.,* 1:11.

10. *An act for rendering the colony of Georgia more defensible by prohibiting the importation and use of black slaves or Negroes into the same,* passed January 9, 1734/5, *Col. Recs.,* 1:50. This act took effect on June 24, 1735. See also Wood, *Slavery in Colonial Georgia,* 4–10.

11. Wood, *Slavery in Colonial Georgia,* 4–10. Wood notes that James Oglethorpe himself was a member of the Royal African Company, which shipped many thousands of slaves to British America in the eighteenth century and that slavery was not actually prohibited in Georgia until 1735, three years after the granting of its charter.

12. Betty Wood highlights the role of the Parliamentary Gaols Committee in the settlement of Georgia. Many of the Trustees were members of this committee, which was dedicated to penal reform and social philanthropy. Julia Floyd Smith argues that sixteenth- and seventeenth-century concepts of the natural rights of man also influenced the decision of the Trustees to bypass the normal capitalist approach to colonial settlement. See Wood, *Slavery in Colonial Georgia,* 3; Smith, *Slavery and Rice Culture,* 16–20.

13. Wood, *Slavery in Colonial Georgia,* 5–7, 12–15.

14. Oglethorpe to the Trustees, August 12, 1733, Egmont Manuscripts, Letters from Georgia, vol. 14200, pt. 1, 105–6, UGa.

15. See Wood, *Slavery in Colonial Georgia,* 16–23.

16. John Dobell to John Martin Bolzius, July 4, 1746, *Col. Recs.,* 25:78. For a full discussion of the slavery debate in Georgia before 1750, see Wood, "The One Thing Needful," and Wood, *Slavery in Colonial Georgia,* 1–87.

17. Oglethorpe to the Trustees, January 17, 1739, Egmont Manuscripts, vol. 14203, pt. 2, 376, UGa.; and Jones, ed., *Detailed Reports,* 6 (1739), 45. For more on the Salzburgers, see George Fenwick Jones, *The Georgia Dutch* (Athens, 1992); Jones, *The Salzburger Saga* (Athens, 1984).

18. Petition of the settlers and freeholders at Darien against the introducing of Negroes into Georgia, January 3, 1739, Egmont Manuscripts, vol. 14203, pt. 2, 363–68, UGa. Harvey Jackson argues that the Darien petition was, in part, motivated by offers of material support for the town from James Oglethorpe ("The Darien Anti-Slavery Petition of 1739 and the Georgia Plan," *William and Mary Quarterly,* 34 [1977]: 628–31). See also Anthony W. Parker, *Scottish Highlanders in Colonial Georgia: The Recruitment, Emigration and Settlement at Darien, 1735–1748* (Athens, 1997), 72–75.

19. Oglethorpe to the Trustees, January 16, 1739, Egmont Manuscripts, vol. 14203, pt. 2, 376, UGa.

20. The Earl of Egmont believed that leading malcontents had "spent their money extravagantly in Savannah, and lived on their servants, whose hire being expired, they were not able to engage new ones" (*Diary*, 202).

21. Character of the persons who signed the representation for Negroes, December 9, 1738, Egmont Manuscripts, vol. 14203, pt. 2, 338–58, UGa.

22. Oglethorpe to the Trustees, January 16, 1739, Egmont Manuscripts, vol. 14203, pt. 2, 376, UGa.

23. Representation to the Trustees of Thomas Christie as recorded by the Earl of Egmont, June 24, 1740, Egmont, *Diary*, 150. A South Carolina merchant, Mr. Crockat, later corroborated Christie's perception (ibid., 202).

24. Petition to the Honorable Trustees, December 9, 1738, Egmont Manuscripts, vol. 14203, pt. 2, 333, UGa. See also Trevor R. Reese, ed., *The Clamorous Malcontents: Criticisms and Defences of the Colony of Georgia, 1741–1743* (Savannah, 1973), 78.

25. See the representation to the Trustees of Thomas Christie as recorded by the Earl of Egmont, June 24, 1740, Egmont, *Diary*, 150. More than 5,500 people emigrated to Georgia between 1733 and 1752, but by late 1751 only 1,700 whites remained in the entire colony. One scholar has estimated that about 2,000 migrants would have died in the first twenty years from disease or natural causes; many of the other 1,800 people left for Carolina (Taylor, "Colonizing Georgia," 123–24; Trustees to the King, May 6, 1751, *Col. Recs.*, 33:507; Cates, "The Seasoning," 154).

26. Report of Trustee Meeting, June 26, 1740, Egmont, *Diary*, 152.

27. Jones, ed., *Detailed Reports*, 6 (1739), 226.

28. Egmont, *Diary*, 201.

29. *An act for repealing an act intitled (an act for rendering the colony of Georgia more defensible by prohibiting the importation and use of black slaves or Negroes into the same) and for permitting the importation and use of them in the colony under proper restrictions and regulation, and for other purposes therein mentioned,* passed August 8, 1750, *Col. Recs.*, 1:56–62. See also Benjamin Martyn to the President and Assistants, March 16, 1747, *Col. Recs.*, 31:56–67. The Trustees were concerned that Thomas Bosomworth was reported in August 1746 as employing six slaves from Carolina on his plantation.

30. Bolzius was the pastor at Ebenezer. His voluminous correspondence to the Trustees and other friends and the daily journal he kept make him one of the better-known figures of early Georgia. He is one of the best sources on the life of poor people in the colonial period.

31. John Martin Bolzius to Mr. Van Munch in Augsberg, May 6, 1747, *Col. Recs.*, 25:167–75. In his journal Bolzius recorded the case of Mr. Held, a German weaver, who left Ebenezer for Carolina but now faced unemployment because he was training two slaves in his trade, whom Bolzius believed would supersede him (Jones, ed., *Detailed Reports*, 11 (1747), 90, entry for July 25, 1747). See Chapter 3 for a more detailed discussion of the competition posed by slave artisans to whites both during and after the colonial era.

32. President and Assistants to Benjamin Martyn, May 4, 1748, *Col. Recs.*, 25:292.

33. Bolzius to John Dobell in Charleston, May 20, 1748, *Col. Recs.*, 25:283.

34. Jones, ed., *Detailed Reports*, 12 (1748), 101, entry for December 1, 1748.

35. This letter, written on August 26, 1748, does not appear to have survived. It is

mentioned in the letter of the President and Assistants to Benjamin Martyn, January 12, 1749, and in Martyn's reply, May 19, 1749, *Col. Recs.*, 25:351–52, and 31:134.

36. President and Assistants to Benjamin Martyn, January 10, 1749, *Col. Recs.*, 25: 347–51.

37. John Martin Bolzius to Benjamin Martyn, October 27, 1749, *Col. Recs.*, 25: 437–38.

38. *An act for repealing an act intitled (an act for rendering the colony of Georgia more defensible by prohibiting the importation and use of black slaves or Negroes into the same) and for permitting the importation and use of them in the colony under proper restrictions and regulation, and for other purposes therein mentioned,* passed August 8, 1750, *Col. Recs.*, 1:56–62. The President and Assistants originally requested that the ratio be one to five, but the Trustees overruled them, citing the "danger which must attend too great a disproportion of blacks to white men and the facility with which the Negroes may make their escape from Georgia to Augustine" (*Col. Recs.*, 25:348 and 31: 144–46).

39. These statistics were compiled from *Col. Recs.*, 7:102–302. Governor Henry Ellis acknowledged that laws "to oblige planters to augment their whites, in proportion to the increase of their Negroes . . . have not produced their effect" (Henry Ellis to the Board of Trade, April 24, 1759, CO 5/646, 244r, microfilm, GDAH).

40. *Col. Recs.*, 1:56–62; 25:348; 31:144–46.

41. Gallay, "Jonathan Bryan's Plantation Empire."

42. Jones, ed., *Detailed Reports,* 13 (1749), 44, entry for April 28, 1749.

43. Ibid., 14 (1750), 12, entry for January 27, 1750.

44. Glen, "Slavery in Georgia," 60–61. Glen studied the month of June 1755.

45. Alan Gallay argues that the influx of South Carolina planters into Georgia in the 1750s was owing to a static social structure for new migrants in South Carolina. They found that Georgia offered good lands, which were freely available, and a fluid social structure (Gallay, "Jonathan Bryan's Plantation Empire," 256).

46. There is general acceptance that many of the planters coming into Georgia in the 1750s were from South Carolina or the West Indian islands. In 1752 alone, more than one thousand slaves accompanied the Dorchester migrants from South Carolina to their new settlement at Midway. See Wood, *Slavery in Colonial Georgia,* 91–93; Gallay, "Jonathan Bryan's Plantation Empire." David Chesnutt argued that this migration was fostered by the lack of economic opportunity in South Carolina for middling planters ("South Carolina's Expansion into Colonial Georgia," iv, 204–6).

47. Petition of the inhabitants of Abercorn, July 13, 1750, CO 5/643 ff.4r, microfilm, GDAH.

48. There is evidence that their fears were well founded. Of the twelve individuals who signed this petition, only one subsequently received a substantial grant from the Crown. James Grant was granted five hundred acres on December 4, 1759, and a further sixty-five acres on February 8, 1760. See Marion R. Temperly, ed., *English Crown Grants in St. Matthew Parish in Georgia* (Atlanta, 1973).

49. Coulter and Saye, *List of the Early Settlers of Georgia,* 75.

50. Isaac Gibbs to the Trustees, October 3, 1738; John Pye to the Trustees, November 13, 1740; Minutes of the President and Assistants, September 29, 1742; Isaac

Gibbs and Isaac Gibbs Jr. to the Trustees, October 18, 1743, *Col. Recs.*, 22: pt. 1, 270–74; 22: pt. 2, 432–33; 6:46–47; 24:140–42.

51. Beckemeyer, *Abstracts*. In the 80 transactions in which artisans were vendors, planters/merchants were purchasers in 42 cases (52.5%). In the 125 transactions in which planters/merchants were vendors, artisans were purchasers in only 31 cases (24.8%).

52. *Col. Recs.*, 7:102–302; Beckemeyer, *Abstracts*.

53. President and Assistants to the Trustees, July 19, 1750, *Col. Recs.*, 26:17–28.

54. Bolzius and the Salzburgers were offered credit to purchase slaves by James Habersham and various merchants in South Carolina. See Jones, ed., *Detailed Reports,* 14 (1750), 18, entry for February 1, 1750.

55. Ibid., 121, entry for August 23, 1750.

56. Loewald, Staricka, and Taylor, eds., "Johann Martin Bolzius Answers a Questionnaire," pt. 1, 261.

57. Vorsey, ed., *De Brahm's Report,* 162–65.

58. Jones, ed., *Detailed Reports,* 14 (1750), 88, entry for July 8, 1750. Bolzius stated that some white people demanded 18d to 2/- for a day's work. Consequently, most employers had turned to slaves to meet their labor demands.

59. Of the seventy-three wills left by artisans between 1733 and 1777, fifty listed a Savannah residence. See Colonial Books A and AA, Wills, GDAH.

60. Such a ship was the *Chance* from Rhode Island, while docked in Savannah, sold sugar from Havana, rum from New England, and manufactures from England. The *Chance* was in Savannah for nearly two months, docking on April 13, 1765, and sailing back to Rhode Island on June 6, 1765 (*Georgia Gazette,* April 18, June 7, 1765).

61. Jones, ed., *Detailed Reports,* 17 (1759–60), 100, entry for August 15, 1759. See also Loewald, Staricka, and Taylor, eds., "Johann Martin Bolzius Answers a Questionnaire," pt. 2, 245, for the cost of living in Savannah in 1751.

62. Loewald, Staricka, and Taylor, eds., "Johann Martin Bolzius Answers a Questionnaire," pt. 1, 242.

63. Ibid. Jacob Holbrook appears in Colonial Book C-1, Conveyances, 32, 91, deeds dated March 14, 1748, and August 1753. George Peters appears in Colonial Books S, Conveyances, 461, and V, Conveyances, 510, deeds dated November 24, 1767, and March 28, 1771. Of 390 artisans listed in Colonial Books C-1, S, U, and V, Conveyances; Colonial Books J and O, Miscellaneous; and Colonial Books A and AA, Wills, all in GDAH, twenty-nine individuals listed more than one occupation.

64. Jones, ed., *Detailed Reports,* 14 (1750), 86, entry for July 7, 1750. The builder was a Scottish immigrant by the name of Brown. It was apparently standard practice for merchants and artisans to offer six months' credit in Savannah. See Loewald, Staricka, and Taylor, eds., "Johann Martin Bolzius Answers a Questionnaire," pt. 1, 251.

65. Jones, ed., *Detailed Reports,* 14 (1750), 142–3, entry for September 18, 1750.

66. Loewald, Staricka, and Taylor, eds., "Johann Martin Bolzius Answers a Questionnaire," pt. 1, 242.

67. Memorial of the Trustees to the King, May 6, 1751; De Brahm's Report to the Board of Trade ca. 1773. *Col. Recs.*, 33:507; 39:464.

68. Henry Laurens to John Polson, February 9, 1768, Laurens to Mark Noble,

November 21, 1768, and James Laurens to Henry Laurens, December 19, 1772, in Rogers, Chesnutt, Clark, et al., eds., *Papers of Henry Laurens,* 5:590, 6:173, 8:505.

69. Vice-President and Assistants to Benjamin Martyn, January 2, 1751; Proceedings of the Governor and Council for November 9, 1754, *Col. Recs.,* 26:120; 7:32.

70. Journal of the Commons House of Assembly, October 20, 1769–June 16, 1782, *Col. Recs.,* 15:386, entry for February 11, 1773.

71. It is difficult to estimate how many artisans were employed in any one trade because there is no surviving colonial census. Of 390 artisans listed in Colonial Books C-1 (1750–61), S (1766–69), U (1769), and V (1769–71), Conveyances; Colonial Books J (1755–62) and O (1762–65), Miscellaneous; and Colonial Books A (1754–72) and AA (1772–77), Wills, all in GDAH, 75 individuals (19.2%) listed themselves as involved in the construction trades.

72. *Col. Recs.,* 15:453, entry for July 7, 1773. See Davis, *Fledgling Province,* 101–2. In Colonial Books C-1 and J, 13.6% of artisans claimed their trade to be in the food industry. Victualler Mary Smith sold a slave on November 9, 1763 (Colonial Book O, 109).

73. Presentments of the Grand Jury, *Georgia Gazette,* June 21, 1775.

74. See Chapter 3 for more on the economic activities of slaves and their impact on white people.

75. Jones, ed., *Detailed Reports,* 14 (1750), 155, entry for October 4, 1750.

76. These licenses were listed in the *Georgia Gazette,* January 19, 1764.

77. Colonial Book J, 198, deed dated March 25, 1761.

78. See Lockley, "Spheres of Influence."

79. Of 390 artisans listed in Colonial Books C-1, S, U, and V, Conveyances; Colonial Books J and O, Miscellaneous; and Colonial Books A and AA, Wills, all in GDAH, 91 individuals (23.3%) listed themselves as involved in service trades.

80. Bolzius also noted that weavers could spend half their time farming and still meet their commitments to customers, thus reducing their living costs. See Loewald, Staricka, and Taylor, eds., "Johann Martin Bolzius Answers a Questionnaire," pt. 1, 250, pt. 2, 247.

81. James Wright to the Earl of Hillsborough, May 31, 1768, CO 5/659 ff. 42 r, microfilm, GDAH.

82. Jones, ed., *Detailed Reports,* 15 (1751–52), 259, entry for November 25, 1752.

83. Henry Laurens to Mark Noble, November 21, 1768; Laurens to James Habersham, October 1, 9, 1770; Laurens to William Godfrey, December 16, 1771; John Lewis Gervais to Henry Laurens, May 5–10, 1772, in Rogers, Chesnutt, Clark, et al., eds., *Papers of Henry Laurens,* 6:173, 7:376, 380; 8:100–101, 287–91.

84. Henry Laurens to Frederick Wiggins, March 19, 1766; Laurens to Lachlan McIntosh, March 13, 1773; Laurens to William Gambell, March 15, 1773, ibid., 5:91; 8:616–17, 621.

85. Colonial Book A, Wills, March 15, 1770, GDAH.

86. Of 390 artisans listed in Colonial Books C-1, S, U, and V, Conveyances; Colonial Books J and O, Miscellaneous; and Colonial Books A and AA, Wills, GDAH, 112 individuals (28.7%) listed themselves as either mariners or being involved in boat construction in some way. See also Davis, *Fledgling Province,* 44–46, 103–5.

87. Alan Gallay argued that the richest planters managed to secure all the best swamp-

land through the patronage of friends on the council. Small farmers were thus kept some distance away from the major rivers ("Jonathan Bryan's Plantation Empire," 259).

88. *An act for the better ordering and governing Negroes and other slaves in this province,* passed March 7, 1755, *Col. Recs.,* 18:102–44, esp. 128.

89. Henry Laurens to Alexander Tweed, October 11, 1765, in Rogers, Chesnutt, Clark, et al., eds., *Papers of Henry Laurens,* 5:23.

90. Of 390 artisans listed in Colonial Books C-1, S, U, and V Conveyances; Colonial Books J and O, Miscellaneous; and Colonial Books A and AA, Wills, GDAH, 8 individuals (2%) listed their occupation as luxury-good makers such as hatter, silversmith, and cabinetmaker.

91. Thomas Elfe Account Book, 1768–75, Charleston Library Society. Elfe details his wealth at the start of this volume. The rest of his wealth lay in property (£16,300), cash (£1,000), and outstanding debts (£12,280).

92. James Love died on June 6, 1768 (*Abstracts of Colonial Wills,* 80).

93. Wood, *Slavery in Colonial Georgia,* 5, 10. The bounty was set at two shillings per pound.

94. Jones, ed., *Detailed Reports,* 14 (1750), 28–29, entry for February 15, 1750. See also Davis, *Fledgling Province,* 158–63.

95. Jones, ed., *Detailed Reports,* 14 (1750), 38, entry for March 10, 1750; Davis, *Fledgling Province,* 161.

96. Jones, ed., *Detailed Reports,* 15 (1751–52), 4, entry for January 14, 1751.

97. Memorial of William Little to the Board of Trade, read April 12, 1758, *Col. Recs.,* 28: pt. 1, 126–27.

98. Henry Ellis to the Board of Trade, April 24, 1759, *Col. Recs.,* 28: pt. 1, 207.

99. William Knox to the Board of Trade, December 7, 1762, *Col. Recs.,* 28: pt. 1, 384. This meant that more than 3,000 people were engaged in silk culture in Georgia in the early 1760s as in 1761 James Wright had estimated the white population of Georgia at 6,100 (Wright to the Board of Trade, April 15, 1761, ibid., 308–9). Despite this high figure, no person listed a silk-related occupation in the Colonial Books. Perhaps these people were too poor to become involved with legal transactions, or perhaps they were listed under different occupations, with silk culture being a secondary activity.

100. James Wright to the Board of Trade, April 23, 1765, CO 5/649, ff. 85r. See also James Wright to the Board of Trade, October 21, 1766, CO 5/649, ff. 93–98. The bounty was being reduced from 2/- to 1/6 (microfilm, GDAH).

101. James Wright to the Board of Trade, October 21, 1766, CO 5/649, ff. 93–98, microfilm, GDAH.

102. Jones, ed., *Detailed Reports,* 14 (1750), 28–29, entry for February 15, 1750.

103. The arrival of these servants was discussed in a letter of John Martin Bolzius to James Vernon, October 17, 1749. Bolzius recorded that nineteen inhabitants of Ebenezer were supplied with servants (*Col. Recs.,* 25:425). Bolzius also recorded that twenty-one servants were kept in Savannah, but they were mainly craftsmen (Jones, ed., *Detailed Reports,* 13 [1749], 111, entry for October 10, 1749). For an excellent investigation into the lives of servants in Georgia, see Astrid M. O'Brien, "Female Servants Among the Salzburgers at Ebenezer, 1733–1750," Part II dissertation, University of Cambridge, 1999.

104. The Earl of Egmont noted in his diary that some servants in the late 1730s were unwilling to work, while others had fled to Carolina, "they meeting an asylum there" (Egmont, *Diary*, 14, 38).

105. Jones, ed., *Detailed Reports*, 13 (1749), 111, 113, entries for October 10, 12, 1749.

106. Ibid., 114, entry for October 16, 1749.

107. Ibid., 117, 120, entries for October 20, 30, 1749.

108. Ibid., 124, entry for November 5, 1749.

109. John Martin Bolzius to Governor Glen, November 9, 1749, *Col. Recs.*, 25:440.

110. Jones, ed., *Detailed Reports*, 13 (1749), 129, entry for November 20, 1749.

111. Minutes of the Board of President and Assistants, April 21, 1750, *Col. Recs.*, 6:316–17.

112. Bolzius to the Trustees, September 4, 1750, CO 5/643 ff. 48–50, in Great Britain, Public Record Office, Board of Trade, Correspondence with the Colony of Georgia, microfilm, GDAH.

113. The President and Assistants counted 349 working slaves in Georgia (202 men and 147 women—ignoring young children), a high figure considering that this was five months before the legalization of slavery in Georgia (President and Assistants to the Trustees, July 19, 1750, *Col. Recs.*, 26:17–28).

114. Bolzius to the Trustees, September 4, 1750, CO 5/643 ff. 48–50, microfilm, GDAH.

115. Jones, ed., *Detailed Reports*, 14 (1750), 142–43, entry for September 18, 1750. Bolzius recorded that "not only Englishmen, but also most of our own people are prejudiced against using white servants."

116. Gray and Wood, "Transformation from Indentured to Involuntary Servitude," 361–65.

117. John Martin Bolzius to Benjamin Martyn, January 5, 1751, *Col. Recs.*, 26: 131–32.

118. John Martin Bolzius to Benjamin Martyn, May 1, 1751, ibid., 198.

119. Ibid., 199–200.

120. Jones, ed., *Detailed Reports*, 15 (1751–52), 248, 250–51, entries for October 28, November 2, 1752.

121. Joseph Ottolenghe to the Board of Trade, June 13, 1754, CO 5/644, ff. 159–60, microfilm, GDAH.

122. Jones, ed., *Detailed Reports*, 16 (1753–54), 4–5, entry for January 3, 1753.

123. Betty Wood discusses the social mobility possible for James Habersham, Noble Jones, and Francis Harris, each of whom came from humble backgrounds to hold high office in Royal Georgia (*Slavery in Colonial Georgia*, 95–97).

124. Jones, ed., *Detailed Reports*, 16 (1753–54), 4–5, entry for January 3, 1753.

125. Ibid., 111, entry for July 1–7, 1753.

126. Richard Oswald to Benjamin Martyn, August 27, September 19, 1751, *Col. Recs.*, 26:243–44.

127. These figures have been taken from the Journal of the President and Assistants, *Col. Recs.*, 7:102–827. The last record of a white servant being brought into Georgia was

by Edmund Tannat on November 11, 1758. These figures list every time a planter claimed fifty acres for an indentured servant.

128. Journal of Commons House of Assembly, January 17, 1763–December 24, 1768, *Col. Recs.*, 14:181, entry for January 17, 1765.

129. Journal of Commons House of Assembly, October 30, 1769–June 16, 1782, *Col. Recs.*, 15:70–71, entry for December 12, 1769. The settlers at Queensborough received an additional £50 on January 21, 1771, but were refused further help on February 6, 1771 (ibid., 271). See also Green, "Queensborough Township."

130. Nearly 30% of all land claimants in 1755, many of whose petitions were refused, did not bring any slaves into Georgia (*Col. Recs.*, 7:102–302). In 1757, Henry Ellis doubted that there were more than ten men in Georgia worth more than £500 (Ellis to William Pitt, August 1, 1757, *Col. Recs.*, 28: pt. 1, 44).

131. Wood, *Slavery in Colonial Georgia*, 107.

132. Henry Ellis to William Pitt, August 1, 1757, *Col. Recs.*, 28: pt. 1, 44.

133. Report of James Edward Powell, Commissioner from the Province of Georgia to the Inhabitants of a certain settlement to the Southward of the River Altamaha, 1759, CO 5/646 ff. 219, microfilm, GDAH.

134. Henry Laurens to John Polson, February 9, 1768, and Laurens to Mark Noble, November 21, 1768, in Rogers, Chesnutt, and Clark, et al., eds., *Papers of Henry Laurens*, 5:590, 6:173.

135. *An act for the punishment of vagabonds and other idle and disorderly persons and for erecting prisons or places of security in the several parishes of this province and for preventing trespasses on the lands of the crown or lands reserved for the Indians and for the more effectual suppressing and punishing persons bartering with the Indians in the woods*, passed February 29, 1764, *Col. Recs.*, 18:588–98.

136. *An act for constituting and dividing the several districts and divisions of this province into parishes, and for the establishing of religious worship therein according to the rites and ceremonies of the church of England; and also for impowering the church wardens and vestrymen of the respective parishes to assess rates for the repair of churches, the relief of the poor, and other parochial services*, passed March 15, 1758, *Col. Recs.*, 18:258–72. For more on the Union Society and colonial charity, see Lockley, "Encounters Between Afro-Americans and Nonslaveholding Whites," 38–40.

137. Journal of Commons House of Assembly, January 17, 1763–December 24, 1768, *Col. Recs.*, 14:439, entry for February 18, 1767.

138. The importance of credit was discussed by James Wright in a letter to the Board of Trade, February 10, 1769, *Col. Recs.*, 28: pt. 2, 326. For social mobility, see Wood, *Slavery in Colonial Georgia*, 93–95.

139. Hewat, *Historical Account*, 2:148.

140. Alan Gallay makes the point that the council was run by a core of eleven men, who also acted as judges and board members of institutions ("Jonathan Bryan's Plantation Empire," 258–59).

141. Between 1750 and 1761, artisans were listed as the grantees in 32% of conveyances. But between 1766 and 1771 they were listed as grantees in only 17% of con-

veyances. This analysis is based on Colonial Books, C-1, S, U, and V, Conveyances, GDAH. In Book C-1, artisans transferred land to planters in 20.4% of cases, increasing to 25.6% between 1766 and 1771. Planters transferred land to artisans in 15.1% of cases in Book C-1 but only 9.1% in Books S, U, and V.

142. Of 489,031.5 acres granted to 1,086 people, 238,176 (48.7%) were given to just 238 (21.9%) individuals (Hemperly, ed., *English Crown Grants in Christ Church Parish;* Hemperly, ed., *English Crown Grants in St. John Parish;* Hemperly, ed., *English Crown Grants in St. Andrew Parish*).

143. The five were John Heinly (100 acres, November 27, 1761), Jacob Heinly (100 acres, April 13, 1761), Nicholas Helme (200 acres, June 7, 1774), and John and Ulrich Neidlinger (150 acres, December 4, 1759). See John Martin Bolzius to Benjamin Martyn, May 1, 1751, *Col. Recs.,* 26:198–200; Hemperly, ed., *English Crown Grants in St. Matthew Parish.* The Neidlinger brothers, partners in a tanning business, were the only two to take a full part in the capitalist economy, buying lots in Savannah and elsewhere between 1759 and 1771. See Colonial Books C-1, 313; S, 167; V, 550, Conveyances, GDAH.

144. Between 1755 and 1765 artisans constituted only 13% of the recipients of slave sales but 26% of the vendors. This analysis is based on Colonial Books J and O, Miscellaneous, GDAH. The difference between the 1750s and 1760s is clear when these books are viewed in isolation. Artisan vendors constituted only 18% of the total number in Book J but 36% in Book O.

145. Bonner, *History of Georgia Agriculture,* 8. The total white population was estimated at 16,000 in De Brahm's Report to the Board of Trade, ca. 1773, *Col. Recs.,* 39:464.

146. In 1790 a total of 4,173 white people resided in the lowcountry, 8% of the 52,000 white people in Georgia. At the same time, 12,511 bondspeople lived in the lowcountry, amounting to 42% of the 30,000 African Americans in the state.

147. Chatham County Tax Digest, 1793, GDAH. There were 370 slaveholding taxpayers, 70.7% of the total number of taxpayers.

148. In addition to the 523 taxpayers, 476 householders defaulted on their tax, giving a total number of 999 households. Some defaulters were undoubtedly slave owners, but arriving at an exact figure is not possible. In 1798, however, 21.5% of defaulters in Chatham County were slaveholders, and if this proportion is used, 374 of the 476 defaulters in 1793 were nonslaveholding. If the 374 nonslaveholding defaulters are included with the 153 nonslaveholding taxpayers, 52.7% of the 999 households in Chatham County were nonslaveholding. See Chatham County Tax Digest, 1793, GDAH; Chatham County, Inferior Court, Court of Ordinary, Defaulters, 1793, GDAH; Chatham County Defaulters, 1798, Telfair Papers, GHS.

149. Between 1800 and 1820 the population of Savannah increased by 45.6% from 5,166 to 7,523; by 1848 the population stood at 13,573 (Bancroft, *Census of the City of Savannah,* 1). For an excellent overview of urban and artisan life in colonial America, see Bridenbaugh, *Colonial Craftsman, Myths and Realities, Cities in Revolt,* and *Cities in the Wilderness.* The best studies of urban slavery remain Goldin, *Urban Slavery,* and Wade, *Slavery in the Cities.*

150. In Chatham County, 565 (14.1%) of the 4,569 white residents were employed

in manufacturing. In the lowcountry as a whole, only another 80 people (645 in total, 5.95% of the total population) were engaged in manufacturing (Federal Manuscript Census of Manufacturing, Chatham County, 1820, GHS).

151. Of 1,952 males over age 21, 760 (38.9%) were artisans or mechanics, 506 (25.9%) were professionals, and 303 (15.5%) were planters or merchants (Bancroft, *Census of the City of Savannah*, 8). In late eighteenth-century Charleston more than half of the inhabitants were manual workers. See abstracts of city directories for 1790 and 1794 in Hagy, *People and Professions of Charleston.*

152. Lockley, "Spheres of Influence." Records from Charleston confirm this gender division of work. Of 249 women with occupations in the 1802 city directory for Charleston, 96 (38.5%) operated some sort of retail business, with a further 83 (33.3%) undertaking a form of domestic work (Hagy, *People and Professions of Charleston).*

153. In 1830, 393 (68.5%) of the 573 free blacks in the lowcountry lived in Chatham County—most probably in Savannah.

154. For a discussion of slave self-hire, see Wade, *Slavery in the Cities,* 41–51; Schweniger, "Free-Slave Phenomenon," 293–307; Morgan, "Black Life in Eighteenth-Century Charleston," 190; Wood, *Women's Work, Men's Work,* 101–21; Mooney, "History of the Legal Regulation of Slave Hire"; and the discussion in Chapter 3.

155. The proportion of nonslaveholders varied from 51 to 61% among Savannah taxpayers. See Savannah Tax Digests, 1809–60.

156. Gillespie, "Artisan Accommodation"; Rousey, "From Whence They Came to Savannah," 332–34; Harris, *Plain Folk and Gentry,* 78–90.

157. The first sample of 95 nonslaveholders was taken from 1809 to 1813. Of these, 84 (88.4%) saw little or no change in their circumstances, 8 (8.4%) improved their lifestyle, and 3 (3.1%) saw it deteriorate. The second sample of 84 nonslaveholders was taken from 1826 to 1830. Of these, 70 (83.3%) remained static in the social scale, 9 (10.7%) saw an improvement, while 5 (5.9%) saw a decline (City of Savannah, Tax Digests, 1809–30, GDAH).

158. Liberty County Tax Digest, 1785, File Group II, Box 30, Folder, Liberty Taxes, GDAH.

159. Liberty County Tax Digest 1800–1801, Cate Collection, GHS.

160. Liberty County Tax Digest, 1861, GDAH; 46.4% of taxpayers were nonslaveholding.

161. In 1790, 4,025 (75.1%) of the 5,355 residents of Liberty County were enslaved. By 1830, 5,624 (71.4%) of 7,233 residents were bondspeople. Little had changed by the time of the Civil War, when 6,083 (72.7%) of 8,367 residents were enslaved. In 1785 slaveholders owned on average 11 slaves; by 1860 slaveholders averaged 20 slaves each.

162. Sixty-five individuals were listed in both the 1785 and 1800 tax digests. Thirty-one (47.6%) materially improved their status, twenty (30.7%) remained roughly the same, and only fourteen (21.5%) got poorer (Liberty County Tax Digest, 1785, UGa; Liberty County Tax Digest, 1800, GDAH).

163. In Glynn County in 1790 the richest 20% paid 76% of the total tax bill. Similar figures can be found from Chatham County in 1806 (75%) and Camden County in 1809 (73%) (all in GDAH).

164. For example, in Camden County in 1809, tidal swamp was taxed at the rate of 3.7 cents per acre, while pine woodland was taxed at only 0.6 cents per acre (Camden County Tax Digest, GDAH).

165. Glynn County Tax Digest, 1794, GDAH. Out of 2,306 acres of sea island land, 1,556 acres (67.4%) were owned by slaveholders. Out of 2,618.5 acres of corn land, 2,543 acres (97.2%) were owned by slaveholders. Only 35.9% of taxpayers were listed as slaveholders in this digest. For similar arguments regarding South Carolina, see McCurry, *Masters of Small Worlds,* 25–29.

166. Glynn County Tax Digest, 1794, GDAH, shows that 12 (23%) of 52 nonslaveholders owned only pine lands.

167. Camden County Tax Digest, 1794, GDAH, shows that 133 (78.7%) of 169 residents were nonslaveholders.

168. Camden County Tax Digest, 1809, GDAH, shows that of 119 nonslaveholding whites, 28 (23.5%) owned only pine land.

169. Only 36 taxpayers had been slaveholders in 1794, but by 1809 their numbers had grown to 131. Of the 95 new slaveholders, 89 (93.6%) were new residents (Camden County Tax Digests, 1794, 1809, GDAH).

170. For discussions of rice cultivation, see Bonner, *History of Georgia Agriculture;* Hilliard, "Antebellum Tidewater Rice Culture"; Chaplin, "Tidal Rice Cultivation"; Stewart, *"What Nature Suffers to Groe,"* 92–94, 98–116. In the immediate aftermath of the Revolution so sporadic was the settlement of coastal Georgia that John Smyth declared there was "a vast quantity of barren land" (Smyth, *Tour in the United States of America,* 2:50). Gradually, land unsuited to rice cultivation was used to grow long- or short-staple cotton.

171. McDonald and McWhiney, "Antebellum Southern Herdsman"; McWhiney, *Cracker Culture,* 51–52. Basil Hall in 1828 testified to the truth of the pastoral dominance: "We saw hundreds of cows, they were all let loose in the woods, and not tied up for domestic purposes" (Lane, ed., *Rambler in Georgia,* 76).

172. For support of this idea, see Buck, "Poor Whites"; Craven, "Poor Whites and Negroes"; Owsley and Owsley, "Economic Basis of Society in the Late Antebellum South."

173. Anthony Stokes, *A View of the Constitution of the British Colonies* (London, 1783), quoted in Commons et al., eds., *Documentary History of American Industrial Society,* 165.

174. Kemble, *Journal,* 92.

175. In contrast, the work of Bradley Bond suggests that most rural poor whites did produce something for market. See Bond, "Herders, Farmers and Markets on the Inner Frontier: The Mississippi Piney Wood, 1850–1860," in Hyde, ed., *Plain Folk of the South Revisited,* 73–99.

176. Mohl, ed., "Scotsman Visits Georgia in 1811," 264.

177. Ker, *Travels* (Elizabethtown, N.J., 1816), quoted in Commons et al., eds., *Documentary History of American Industrial Society,* 166–67.

178. The desire of people to eat clay has been explained by diseases such as malaria and hookworm and has also been assigned cultural significance. See Twyman, "The Clay Eater."

179. John Palmer to David Ramsay, December 3, 1808, in Commons et al., eds., *Documentary History of American Industrial Society,* 166.

180. *Constitutionalist,* October 18, 1831.

181. "Pine Woods," 306–7, 309.

182. Narrative of John Lambert in Lane, ed., *Rambler in Georgia,* 49–50. For a discussion of the definition of "cracker," see McWhiney, *Cracker Culture,* xiv–xv.

183. Ball, *Fifty Years in Chains,* 289–91.

184. Bremer, *Homes of the New World,* 361.

2. WORKING, DRINKING, AND SLEEPING TOGETHER

1. Frederickson, *Black Image in the White Mind,* 4, 49; Jordan, *White over Black,* 128–33; Fronsman, *Common Whites,* 73–74; McDonnell, "Work, Culture, and Society," 145; Phillips, *American Negro Slavery;* Phillips, "Central Theme of Southern History"; Buck, "Poor Whites," 52; Owsley, *Plain Folk of the Old South;* Griffen, "Poor White Laborers," 28; Hoetink, *Slavery and Race Relations,* 15; Flynt, *Dixie's Forgotten People,* 11; Roediger, *Wages of Whiteness,* 12.

2. See, for example, Morgan, *Slave Counterpoint,* 300–317; Hodes, *White Women, Black Men,* 1–122.

3. Buck, "Poor Whites," 48.

4. Kemble, *Journal,* 93.

5. Ball, *Life of a Negro Slave,* 117.

6. *Royal Georgia Gazette,* February 11, 1779. In 1784 an advertisement appeared for a white and two or three black apprentices to a cooper (*Georgia Gazette,* January 29, 1784). See also *Daily Georgian,* January 29, 1825.

7. *Savannah Republican,* January 8, 1819.

8. See advertisements for "a good cook, washer and ironer" and "a good pastry cook, also a washerwoman and a chambermaid," *Daily Georgian,* November 27, 1828, March 12, 1829.

9. Wood and Wood, eds., "Reuben King Journal," 61, 68, entries for February 13, July 8, 1803. Michele Gillespie cites further examples of African American and white artisans working together in Milledgeville and Athens in her "Artisans and Mechanics," 226–28.

10. Federal Manuscript Census of Manufacturing, Chatham County, 1820, GHS. Nine separate businesses were listed here, three of which certainly employed white and black workers. The race of the workers at four businesses cannot be determined. Two businesses employed only slaves. In 1848 many of the steam presses and mills in Savannah employed people of both races (Bancroft, *Census of the City of Savannah,* 34–36). For more on industrial slavery, see Ronald Lewis, *Coal, Iron and Slaves: Industrial Slavery in Maryland and Virginia, 1715–1865* (Westport, Conn., 1979); Stephen Whitman, "Industrial Slavery at the Margins: The Maryland Chemical Works," *Journal of Southern History* 59 (1993): 31–62; Charles B. Dew, *Bond of Iron: Masters and Slaves at Buffalo Forge* (New York, 1994); Charles B. Dew, "David Ross and the Oxford Iron Works: A Study of Industrial Slavery in the Early Nineteenth Century South," *William and Mary Quar-*

terly 31 (1974): 189–224; Robert O. Starobin, *Industrial Slavery in the Old South* (New York, 1970).

11. Census of Manufacturing, 1820. In contrast, the Darien Steam Mill employed slave workers under the supervision of white workers. See *Darien Gazette*, January 6, April 7, 1821.

12. Lauder, "Slave Labor in South Carolina Cotton Mills," 161; *Royal Georgia Gazette*, March 1, 1779. In 1828 Petit de Villiers advertised for "a sober, industrious and correct white man, to take charge of a rice-toll mill" (*Daily Georgian*, March 31, 1828).

13. *Georgia Gazette*, April 4, 1785.

14. Census of Manufacturing, 1820.

15. Accounts with W. C. Barton, Nicholas Dickson, and Orrin S. Perry, Anonymous Carpenters Book, 1853–54, GHS.

16. See, for example, the letter of William Williams, ironmonger, to the *Daily Georgian*, together with testimony from three of his white employees, *Daily Georgian*, June 7, 1826. For more information on working women, see Lockley, "Spheres of Influence." Richard Haunton argues that biracial workplaces mitigated against the formation of class-conscious working groups ("Savannah in the 1850s," 78–79).

17. *An ordinance regulating the hire of drays, carts and waggons; as also the hire of Negro and other slaves; and for the better ordering of free Negroes, mulattoes, or mestizoes; within the city of Savannah*, passed September 28, 1790, *Georgia Gazette*, October 7, 1790. In 1795 the fine was increased to £10, suggesting that the regulation was not widely observed. See *An ordinance to amend and repeal certain parts of an ordinance*, passed January 27, 1795, *Georgia Gazette*, February 5, 1795. For people fined, see CCM, May 18, 1801, April 30, November 19, 1804, November 1, 1819, March 3, 1825.

18. Account Book entry, May 23, 1829, Richard James Arnold Papers, Records of the Antebellum Southern Plantations, Series J, Part 4, Series 1.2, UGa.

19. Rules and Directions for my Thorn Island plantation, June 11, 1832, Rule 20, Box 5, Folder 51, Item 209, Telfair Family Papers, GHS.

20. Power, *Impressions of America*, 109. See *An act for the better ordering and governing Negroes and other slaves in this province*, passed March 7, 1755, *Col. Recs.*, 18: 102–44, esp. 128, which instructed that all boats had to have a white person on board; Henry Laurens to Alexander Tweed, October 11, 1765, in Rogers, Chesnutt, Clark, et al., eds., *Papers of Henry Laurens*, 5:23. For an interesting summary of the coastal trade in Georgia, see Charles E. Pearson, "Captain Charles Stevens and the Antebellum Georgia Coastal Trade," *Georgia Historical Quarterly* 75 (1991): 485–506.

21. W. C. Blott Account Book, entry for August 31, 1804, GDAH. African Americans received 75 cents per day, while whites received $1.50 per day.

22. Johnson and Sloan, eds., *South Carolina*, 238; Morgan, *Slave Counterpoint*, 326–34.

23. See advertisements in the *Georgia Gazette*, January 8, November 18, 1784, January 7, 1796; *Daily Georgian*, October 24, 1826, August 19, December 15, 1828. The City Council was willing to pay white men up to 3/6 per day to supervise slaves working on common ground in Savannah; see accounts presented by John McCullough and James McConkey, CCM, September 2, 1794, February 24, 1795.

24. Scarborough, *Overseer*, 196, 75.

25. "On Overseers; By a Subscriber," *Southern Agriculturalist* 3 (1829): 271–73.

26. Narrative of Alec Bostwick, in Rawick, ed., *American Slave,* 109. The standard of living for some overseers was little better than that of the slaves. See Otto and Burns, "Black Folks and Poor Buckras"; Moore, "Social and Economic Status on the Coastal Plantation," 141–60; Thomas, *Memoirs of a Southerner,* 17; Bremer, *Homes of the New World,* 304.

27. Burke, *Pleasure and Pain,* 80.

28. Genovese, "'Rather Be a Nigger Than a Poor White Man,'" 82.

29. One historian disagrees, arguing that the well-being of slaves was far less important to owners than the size of the crop produced (Dusinberre, *Them Dark Days,* 65–67, 309–11).

30. Henry Laurens to William Gambell, March 15, 1773, in Rogers, Chesnutt, Clark, et al., eds., *Papers of Henry Laurens,* 8:621.

31. Joseph W. Allston to Robert F. W. Allston, September 25, 1823, in Easterby, ed., *South Carolina Rice Plantation,* 63.

32. Chatham County, Inferior Court, Trial Docket, 1813–27, GDAH. Harry was first given a mistrial, then found guilty on March 4, 1827. He was executed, according to the docket on June 1, 1827. See also the reports in the *Daily Georgian,* April 4, May 1, June 2, 1827. See also Minutes of the Board of Police, February 17–19, 1779, Telfair Papers, GHS.

33. Narrative of John Melish in Lane, ed., *Rambler in Georgia,* 19.

34. Buckingham, *Slave States of America,* 87.

35. *Georgia Gazette,* December 7, 1774. Two slaves were burned alive for this crime. For reports of similar attacks, see *Georgia Gazette,* April 7, 1763, January 30, 1794; *Daily Georgian,* January 13, 1823, June 26, 1829. Between 1789 and 1796 the Savannah newspapers reported six separate incidents of owners being murdered by their slaves (*Georgia Gazette,* January 3, February 2, 1789, May 13, 1790, April 28, 1791, April 12, 1792; *Columbian Museum and Savannah Advertiser,* February 24, 1796).

36. Allard Belin dismissed two overseers within three and a half months, the first for "disobedience" and the second for "idleness and inattention" (Allard Belin Plantation Journal, June 18, September 22, 1792, SCHS). See also Charles Manigault to James Haynes, November 1, 1846, in Clifton, *Life and Labor on Argyle Island,* 41.

37. J. B. Grimball Diary, October 17, 20, 1832, Charleston Library Society, Charleston, South Carolina.

38. Journal entry for April 28, 1838, Kollock Papers, SHC. This attitude was apparently common. Henry Laurens knew that every time he disciplined his overseers they were likely to say, "Mr Laurens means to deprive me of all command over his Negroes, how can it be expected that I should make a crop?" (Henry Laurens to William Gambell, March 15, 1773, in Rogers, Chesnutt, Clark, et al., eds., *Papers of Henry Laurens,* 8:621).

39. Journal entry for June 12, 1838, Kollock Papers, SHC.

40. A "young and healthy" wet-nurse was advertised for in the *Georgia Gazette,* March 21, 1765. One woman described herself as "housekeeper, can work well at needle, and is a clear starcher" (*Columbian Museum and Savannah Advertiser,* July 26, 1796). One employer required "a middling aged woman as a cook, washer and ironer" (*Daily Georgian,* April 20, 1827). See also *Daily Georgian,* November 28, 1827, November 29, 1828, March 12, June 1, 2, 1829.

41. See advertisements in *Savannah Republican,* January 8, September 4, 1819, April 19, 26, 1820, January 17, 1821; *Daily Georgian,* January 28, 1820, April 21, 1821, June 2, 1829; *Darien Gazette,* August 28, 1823.

42. Mrs E. H. Steele Paper, April 1, 1830, GHS. Similarly, Mary Jones dismissed her black nurse and employed "a very clever white one" in her place (Mary Jones to Rev. C. C. Jones, November 25, 1859, in Myers, ed., *Children of Pride,* 542).

43. Murray, *Letters from the United States, Cuba and Canada,* 212, letter XVIII, Savannah, February 4, 1855.

44. Lockley, "Spheres of Influence."

45. Narrative of John Melish in Lane, ed., *Rambler in Georgia,* 20.

46. Griffen, "Poor White Laborers," 32.

47. Record of the Baron de Montlezun, published as Lucius Gaston Moffatt and Joseph Carrière, eds., "A Frenchman Visits Charleston, 1817," *South Carolina Historical and Genealogical Magazine* 49 (1948): 150. Some of these white people evidently had no objection to working alongside African Americans, sharing meals and refreshments with them. See Genovese, "'Rather Be a Nigger Than a Poor White Man,'" 87; Wood, "'Never on a Sunday?'" See also the discussion of slave hire in Chapter 3.

48. Narrative of Basil Hall in Lane, ed., *Rambler in Georgia,* 80.

49. Burke, *Pleasure and Pain,* 77.

50. McCurry, *Masters of Small Worlds,* 59–83.

51. Bolton, *Poor Whites,* 105.

52. This was the usual way of recruiting Irish laborers for work in the South. See Sean Mooney, "How the Irish Became Southern: Race and Class in Lowcountry Georgia, 1825–1865," paper presented at the Coastal Societies in North America Conference, University of Warwick, December 1997; Shoemaker, "Strangers and Citizens," 31–43, 73–86.

53. *Daily Georgian,* April 20, June 26, November 17, 1827; CCM, August, 30, 1827.

54. *Brunswick Advocate,* March 8, 1838, January 26, 1839.

55. Kemble, *Journal,* 84.

56. Ibid., 84–85. In February 1839 reports of fighting among Irishmen on the canal included references to the use of firearms and other deadly weapons (*Brunswick Advocate,* February 2, 1839).

57. *Brunswick Advocate,* February 2, 1839.

58. Immigrants also constituted 72% of Charleston's unskilled white labor force. See Berlin and Gutman, "Natives and Immigrants," 1183.

59. *RoD.* Of those dying in the city, 26% had been born in Georgia, 25% in the United Kingdom, 33% from elsewhere in the United States, and 16% in Europe and the West Indies. By the 1820s 20% of entries in the death records were for those born in Ireland.

60. The precise figure was 31.8%. See Rousey, "From Whence They Came to Savannah," 312; Clark, *Hibernia America,* 95; Diner, *Erin's Daughters in America,* 31; *RoD;* O'Hara, *Hibernian Society,* 5–7; Shoemaker, "Strangers and Citizens," 43. In 1848 less than a quarter of the adult male population of Savannah was native born, whereas more than a third were immigrants (Bancroft, *Census of the City of Savannah,* 14).

61. For example, "A young man lately from New York" sought "a situation, either in a counting house, or grocery store" (*Columbian Museum and Savannah Advertiser,* February 4, 1804). See also *Daily Georgian,* April 29, 1828, and the advertisements from

"a young man, a native of France" and "a young man from Europe," *Daily Georgian,*
June 1, November 3, 1829.

62. *An act for the better security of this state by obliging and making liable Negro*
slaves to work on the several forts, batteries or other public works within the same,
passed September 16, 1777, *Col. Recs.,* 19: pt. 1, 80–86; Petition of Ann and Elizabeth
Parker, Box 38E, Folder 12, Governor James Wright Papers, 1779–82, Cuyler Collection, UGa; CCM, November 25, 1814. See also Byrne, "The Burden and the Heat of the
Day," 84–85.

63. CCM, February 13, 1815.

64. *An act to impower the several surveyors hereafter named to lay out public roads*
in the province of Georgia, passed March 7, 1755, and *An act to impower the several*
commissioners, passed March 6, 1766, Minutes of the Governor in Council, July 26,
1779; James Wright to Lord George Germain, December 1, 1780, *Col. Recs,* 28:87–101,
717–42; 38: pt. 2, 191, 446.

65. *An act to impower the several commissioners,* passed March 26, 1767, *Col. Recs.,*
18:794–96. The night watch in Savannah was originally manned by residents in rotation,
but eventually this too was replaced by a levy. The road duty exemption apparently did
not apply to free African Americans who were required "to perform twenty days service
annually on the streets" (CCM, September 30, 1824).

66. By 1818 this was expressly widened to include all free African Americans. See *An*
act supplementary to, and more effectually to enforce an act, passed December 19, 1818,
Prince, ed., *Digest,* 797.

67. *An act to discharge females from the performance of road duty,* passed December 24, 1824, Prince, ed., *Digest,* 800.

68. Wood and Wood, eds., "Reuben King Journal," 106, entry for July 29, 1805.

69. Letter of Isaac Crews, Commissioner of the Roads for Camden County, to David
Lang, August 15, 1807, Camden County, Inferior and Superior Court, Miscellaneous
Records, 1790–1924, pt. 1, GDAH. See also similar summons of Chatham County Road
Commissioners, *Gazette of the State of Georgia,* August 10, 1786; *Georgia Gazette,*
July 30, October 10, 1789, August 7, 1800. Reuben King's brother went to work on the
Darien roads with "about 50 Negroes" (Wood and Wood, eds., "Reuben King Journal,"
30, entry for August 17, 1801). For more detailed records concerning road duty, see Rec-
ords of the Commissioners of the Roads, St. Paul's Parish, South Carolina, SCDAH.

70. Twenty of the twenty-two identifiable "gang-leaders" in 1804 were slaveholders.
Two-thirds of slaveholders who arrived for road duty were employed in this manner. See
Camden County, Road Duty Records, 1804–5, GDAH; Camden County Tax Digest,
1809, GDAH. See also Isaac Germond Papers, Journal, July 11, 1856, GHS.

71. Only two nonslaveholding whites were "gang-leaders," while 80 percent of the
nonslaveholding whites summoned were employed in manual labor (Camden County,
Road Duty Records, 1804–5, GDAH). These returns were cross-referenced with the Camden County Tax Digest, 1809, GDAH.

72. *An act to impower the several surveyors hereafter named to lay out public roads*
in the province of Georgia, passed March 7, 1755; *An act to impower the several commis-*
sioners, passed September 29, 1773, *Col. Recs.,* 18:87–101, 19: pt. 1, 253–88.

73. *An act to impower the several surveyors hereafter named to lay out public roads*

in the province of Georgia, passed March 7, 1755, *Col. Recs.,* 18:87–101. In St. Paul's Parish, South Carolina, no road duty was undertaken between 1803 and 1806 because of the indifference of the elite commissioners. See Records of the Commissioners of the Roads, St. Paul's Parish, South Carolina, August 1, 1803–April 7, 1806, SCDAH.

74. Wood and Wood, eds., "Reuben King Journal," 47, entry for August 9, 1802. In 1805 Solomon Mews was recorded in the Camden Road Duty Records as being replaced "by substitute" and William Niblack avoided service altogether because the road commissioners had omitted his name by accident from the register (Camden County, Road Duty Records, 1804–5, GDAH).

75. Census figures were taken from http://fisher.lib.virginia.edu/census in 1999.

76. Camden County, Superior Court, Minutes, October Term 1824, GDAH.

77. CCM, February 7, 1833.

78. Fronsman, *Common Whites,* 35.

79. In 1825 S. B. Parkman and R. R. Cuyler were permitted to form the Savannah Fire Company (CCM, March 11, 1825; Johnson, *Black Savannah,* 137).

80. Byrne, "The Burden and the Heat of the Day," 194–97; CCM, January 21, 1833; Harden, *Recollections,* 19–20. In 1825 the Savannah City Council paid the funeral expenses of one free black and the medical costs of another who were injured while fighting a blaze in the city (CCM, January 10, 1825). In 1824 the council granted rare permission for the African American firemen to hold an official evening dinner (CCM, June 24, 1824). A year later the suggestion was mooted, but rejected, that all the African Americans who assisted at the fire of October 29, 1826, should receive 50 cents from the city treasury (CCM, November 23, 1826).

81. *Daily Georgian,* March 28, 1826; Shoemaker, "Strangers and Citizens," 197–200.

82. *An act for establishing and regulating patrols,* passed July 28, 1757, *Col. Recs.,* 18:225–35. As early as 1740 John Martin Bolzius recorded that patrols in South Carolina were principally undertaken by poor men (Jones, ed., *Detailed Reports,* 7 [1740], entry for August 29, 1740). For the best work on patrolling, see Sally Hadden, "Law Enforcement in a New Nation: Slave Patrols and Public Authority in the Old South, 1700–1865" (Ph.D. dissertation, Harvard University, 1993), and her forthcoming *Slave Patrols: Law Enforcement and Public Order in Virginia and the Carolinas, 1700–1865* (Cambridge, Mass.).

83. Charleston Grand Jury Presentments, January 20, 1794, General Assembly Papers, 0010 0015 1794 00007, SCDAH.

84. Chatham County, Superior Court, Minutes, December Term 1800, vol. 5, 1799–1804, GDAH.

85. C. W. Jones to Louis Manigault, December 17, 1855; Louis Manigault to C. W. Jones, December 17, 1855; Charles Manigault to Louis Manigault, December 27, 1855, January 4, 10, 1856, in Clifton, *Life and Labor on Argyle Island,* 202–6.

86. Chatham County, Superior Court, Minutes, January Term 1808, vol. 7, 1804–8, GDAH. Charles C. Jones believed patrollers to be "notorious rascals" who exaggerated their achievements in order to claim runaway rewards from planters (Myers, ed., *Children of Pride,* 242).

87. For examples of complaints, see *Georgia Gazette,* June 27, 1770 (CO 5/660,

fol. 123 r); Presentments of the Chatham County Grand Jury, March 2–5, 1784, Record Group 1–1–5 Box 1A, Executive Department, Incoming Correspondence, 1781–1802, GDAH; *Gazette of the State of Georgia,* August 10, 1786; Chatham County, Superior Court, Minutes, January Term 1794, Book G, 1793–96, GDAH; *Savannah Republican,* January 17, 1818; *Daily Georgian,* January 8, 1828.

88. The regulations of the night watch in Savannah permitted individuals to find substitutes if they were indisposed to serve. See *An ordinance for establishing the night watch in the city of Savannah, and hamlets thereof,* passed June 18, 1793, *Georgia Gazette,* June 20, 1793.

89. *Columbian Museum and Savannah Advertiser,* February 2, 1801.

90. Ibid., February 10, 1801.

91. *An ordinance for establishing the night watch in the city of Savannah, and hamlets thereof,* passed June 18, 1793, *Georgia Gazette,* June 20, 1793.

92. Savannah City Watch Payroll, November 1819, Box 22, Folder 2, Read Collection, UGa; Mooney, "History of the Legal Regulation of Slave Hire," 47. The pay of the watch was a constant thorn in the side of successive city councils. Several petitions to increase the rate of pay were rejected. Indeed, wages actually fell from $30 a month in 1819 to $25 in 1833 and touched as low as $22 before returning to $30 a month in 1843. The increase was given only because watchmen successfully argued that policing all night left them unfit for other employment. See CCM, February 20, 1823, September 5, 1833, March 14, October 14, 1836, March 14, October 19, 1843.

93. See the accepted petition of J. C. Hodges for payment of partial wages for serving in the watch after his father's death forced him to leave before completing the term of his contract. Those wanting to be members of the watch had to apply to the council with two references stating that "the applicant is an honest and sober man" (CCM, June 4, 1829, April 2, 1810).

94. Savannah City Watch Payroll, November 1819, City of Savannah, Tax Digest 1819, GDAH.

95. Genovese, "'Rather Be a Nigger Than a Poor White Man,'" 79.

96. *An act for establishing a watch in the town of Savannah,* passed July 19, 1757; *An act for regulating the watch in the town of Savannah,* passed March 27, 1759, *Col. Recs.,* 18:212–17, 290–95. The postrevolutionary Savannah watch was ordered to take up any African American after 10 P.M. and any other person acting disorderly or suspiciously and to investigate disorderly houses (*An ordinance for establishing the night watch in the city of Savannah, and hamlets thereof,* passed June 18, 1793, *Georgia Gazette,* June 20, 1793).

97. Charleston District, Court of General Sessions, Bills of Indictment, Box 1, Folder 6, 1806–18A-1, SCDAH.

98. CCM, December 10, 1846; Police and Watch Ordinance, June 22, 1854, in Wilson, *Digest,* 324.

99. Communication of Levi D'Lyon, CCM, February 15, 1827. The watch's interpretation was of the ordinance as originally notified in the *Daily Georgian,* September 15, 1825.

100. CCM, July 3, 1828. The slave owners' interpretation was based on a revised ordinance published in the *Daily Georgian,* November 1, 1825.

101. CCM, February 3, 1835.

102. Narrative of William Craft in Bontemps, ed., *Great Slave Narratives*, 290.

103. See Chapter 4 for further details on assaults by nonelite whites on African Americans.

104. CCM, July 19, 1826. The costs were $10.

105. CCM, August 26, 1830. In 1843 bondsman Paul received twenty lashes for a similar offense (CCM, March 14, 1843).

106. CCM, August 13, 1840.

107. Ball, *Fifty Years in Chains*, 288. For similar views regarding North Carolina, see Bolton, *Poor Whites*, 45–46.

108. Susie King Taylor, *Reminiscences of My Life in Camp* (Boston, 1902), 7. See also Adams, *South Side View of Slavery*, 17.

109. Harn, "Old Canoochee-Ogeechee Chronicles," 149. See also Harden, *Recollections*, 18. Both authors claim that as children they wrote unofficial passes for slaves.

110. Chatham County Superior Court, Minutes, May Term 1851, vol. 20, 1850–53, GDAH.

111. Many masters seeking fugitive slaves knew that they were often "well-known in Savannah." See Chapter 4.

112. Narrative of William Grimes in Bontemps, ed., *Five Black Lives*, 95.

113. See Chapter 3 for a more detailed discussion of those prosecuted for "entertaining Negroes."

114. Camden County, Superior Court, Minutes, March Term 1811, GDAH. For an excellent study of nineteenth-century seamen, see Bolster, *Black Jacks,* 1–5, 190–219.

115. Presentments of the Grand Jury of South Carolina, January 19, 1770, Charleston District, Court of General Sessions, Session Journals, 1769–76, SCDAH.

116. John Fleetwood was a twenty-nine-year-old mariner from Virginia (*RoD,* 3:17, January 28, 1812). Ten months before his death, Fleetwood was remanded by the council to appear before the Superior Court on a charge of "keeping a riotous and disorderly house" (CCM, March 15, 1811). Apparently seamen regularly became "intoxicated in those (disorderly) houses, (and) sally forth in riotous mobs" (Chatham County, Superior Court, Minutes, January Term 1802, vol. 5, 1799–1804, GDAH).

117. W. B. Bulloch to the Governor of Georgia, December 24, 1811, Folder 1, Bulloch Family Papers, SHC; Savannah Police Department, Jail Register, 1809–15, GHS. Of 123 people arrested on November 15 and 16, 1811, most were released within a week. In 1808 the City Council had warned disorderly sailors that they would "be punished according to law" (CCM, February 8, 1808).

118. Anonymous Diary, Savannah, Georgia, 1820, DU. Apparently free black sailors as well as whites frequented these establishments and associated with slaves (*Daily Georgian,* July 8, 1826). It was partly to stop these activities that elite Savannahians formed the Savannah Port Society in 1843 to minister to visiting seamen. Despite their best efforts, in 1852 the society acknowledged "that the large portion of all seamen who frequent this port do not attend worship at all" (Savannah Port Society Minutes, Annual Report, January 12, 1852, GHS). See also *Sixth Annual Report of the Board of Managers of the Savannah Port Society* (Savannah, 1849); Bolster, *Black Jacks,* 190–91.

119. Harden, *Recollections*, 36.

120. Narrative of William Grimes in Bontemps, ed., *Five Black Lives*, 89. On the easy

availability of alcohol, see Genovese, "'Rather Be a Nigger Than a Poor White Man,'" 89, and Harris, *Plain Folk and Gentry,* 69–70.

121. State v. T. F. Hall, Chatham County, Superior Court, Criminal Evidence, 1824–26, January Term 1824, Testimony of Mrs. Ann Catherine Harris, GDAH.

122. Chatham County, Superior Court, Minutes, May Term 1819, vol. 10, 1818–22, GDAH.

123. Chatham County, Superior Court, Minutes, January Term 1817, vol. 9, 1812–18, GDAH. In 1764 the colonial authorities in Savannah had passed a law to "prevent excessive and deceitful gaming," but the hope of Governor James Wright that this would "nip it in the bud" was clearly overly optimistic. See James Wright to the Board of Trade, May 26, 1764, *Col. Recs.,* 28: pt. 2, 28.

124. Chatham County Superior Court, Minutes, January Term 1855, vol. 21, GDAH.

125. Narrative of Adam Hodgson in Lane, ed., *Rambler in Georgia,* 52.

126. Chatham County, Superior Court, Minutes, May Term 1818, vol. 10, 1818–22, GDAH; Wood, *Women's Work, Men's Work,* 135. In 1830 the Chatham County Grand Jury presented the "races recently run on the Augusta road" (*Daily Georgian,* May 29, 1830). For more on the popular recreations of Southerners, see Dale A. Somers, *The Rise of Sports in New Orleans, 1850–1900* (Baton Rouge, 1972), vi–38; Nancy L. Struna, "Sport and Society in Early America," *International Journal of the History of Sport* 5 (1988): 292–311; Scott C. Martin, "Don Quixote and Leatherstocking: Hunting, Class and Masculinity in the American South, 1800–1840," *International Journal of the History of Sport* 12 (1995): 61–79.

127. CCM, January 7, 1828. The *Daily Georgian,* November 29, December 25, 1828, stated that La Fayette's circus was "well-attended" in the town.

128. Savannah Police Department, Jail Register, 1809–15, GHS. Eleven slaves were confined for gambling on three separate occasions, January 22, 1813, May 19, 1814, and October 17, 1814. Two slaves were confined for drunkenness, October 6, 1809, and December 28, 1811.

129. Savannah Police Department, Jail Register, April 15, 1855, June 9, September 16, 1856, GHS.

130. See cases of Lawrence Leidburger, July 16, 1804; George Campbell, January 8, 1810; Richard Whitaker, January 8, 1810; James Blois, October 19, 1818; Robert Pooler, October 19, 1818; William Black, November 16, 1818; Adam Cope, November 16, 1818; D. Lebross, November 16, 1818; William Richardson, November 16, 1818; Edward Warren, November 16, 1818; Mary Garnet, November 13, 1823; Mrs Boddell, September 29, 1825. All dates refer to CCM. In 1827 John E. Thomas was sentenced to four months imprisonment for letting slaves gamble (*Daily Georgian,* April 27, 1827, see also June 2, 1829).

131. *Daily Georgian,* May 29, 1830.

132. *Georgia Gazette,* July 6, 1768, January 5, 1774, January 18, 1781. See also the presentments of 1771, *Col. Recs.,* 12:214. In 1771 Samuel Frink stated that forty slaves "live by themselves, and allow their masters a certain sum per week" (Correspondence of the Society for the Propagation of the Gospel, Christ Church Records, Box 5, Folder 110, Journal XIX, 1771–73, Minutes, October 18, 1771, GHS).

133. In 1798 173 African Americans lived in Oglethorpe ward (16% of the black

population); this population increased to 548 by 1825 (still 16%), 1,032 in 1835 (25%), and 1,327 by 1848 (21%). See People of Color Census, Savannah, May 28, 1798, File Group II, Ser. 4-2-46, Box 7, Folder, Archives, GDAH; City of Savannah, Board of Health Minutes, September 21, 1825, August 1835, GHS; Bancroft, *Census of the City of Savannah*, 9.

134. Of 391 free African Americans who listed their residence in 1817, 123 (31.7%) lived in Yamacraw and neighboring western suburbs (City of Savannah, Free People of Color Register, 1817, GHS).

135. *Royal Georgia Gazette,* January 18, 1781. White people letting property to slaves were liable to a £20 fine under the 1770 slave code. See *An act for Ordering and Governing slaves within this Province, and for establishing a jurisdiction for the trial of offenses committed by such slaves, and other persons therein mentioned, and to prevent the inveighling and carrying away slaves from their masters, owners or employers,* passed May 10, 1770, Sec. XXXVII, Prince, ed., *Digest,* 785.

136. Chatham County, Superior Court, Minutes, October Term 1796 and October Term 1798, vol. 4, 1796–99; *An ordinance for preventing slaves hiring houses and for other purposes herein mentioned,* passed June 30, 1800, published in the *Savannah Republican and State Intelligencer,* November 2, 1804.

137. Minutes of the Board, May 7, June 5, December 4, 1811, Savannah Home for Girls Records, 1810–43, GHS.

138. Chatham County, Mayor's Court of Common Pleas, November 25, 1806, GDAH. Williamson was a wealthy man in 1806, paying $51.95 in tax, which placed him among the fifty richest men in Savannah at the time. He was a planter, originally from South Carolina, and died at age fifty-seven in 1814 (Chatham County Tax Digest, 1806, GDAH; *RoD,* 3:79).

139. Rogers, "Free Negro Legislation," 32.

140. St. Marys Town Council Minutes, May 4, 1848, GDAH.

141. Charles C. Jones to Rev. C. C. Jones, October 1, 1856, Myers, ed., *Children of Pride,* 241.

142. Savannah Recorder's Court, Mayor's Court, December 3, 1856, GHS.

143. State v. Jehmael Hover, Chatham County, Superior Court, Criminal Testimony, January Term 1858, GHS.

144. Of 296 nonslaveholders who gave their residence in the tax digest for 1826, 40 (13.3%) lived in Yamacraw. A further 7 nonslaveholders were listed as residing in the adjacent areas of Ewensburgh or New Leeds, and 19 lived in Oglethorpe ward. These 66 people constituted 22.3% of the nonslaveholding people who listed a residence (City of Savannah, Tax Digest, 1826, GDAH). There is no extant digest for 1825.

145. Out of a total of 894 nonslaveholders enumerated in 1826, 598 (66.9%) gave no place of residence.

146. Of eighty-two resident artisans who died in Savannah in 1825 and 1826, forty-two (51.2%) resided in Oglethorpe and Franklin wards (*RoD,* 4:169–93). Mariners from out of state were not included in this sample. In 1830 the council decided to demolish a house inhabited in part by a carpenter, "the other part of it is occupied by Negroes" (CCM, November 25, 1830).

147. Burke, *Pleasure and Pain,* 17. For a good description of Factor's Walk and its population, see Harden, *Recollections,* 65, and Myers, ed., *Children of Pride,* 375.

148. In 1825 North Oglethorpe ward (the one nearest Yamacraw) was 62% black; by 1835 it was 66% black (Savannah Board of Health Minutes, September 21, 1825, August 1835, GHS; Shoemaker, "Strangers and Citizens," 113–18).

149. Report on the 1838 State Census, Bancroft, *Census of the City of Savannah,* Appendix.

150. Parsons, *Inside View of Slavery,* 9.

151. Weaver, "Foreigners in Ante-Bellum Towns," 62; and Weaver, "Foreigners in Ante-Bellum Savannah."

152. Burke, *Pleasure and Pain,* 89–90.

153. *Columbian Museum and Savannah Advertiser,* February 7, 1801.

154. Ibid., February 10, 1801.

155. *Georgia Gazette,* February 19, 1801.

156. Chatham County, Superior Court, Minutes, June Term 1801, vol. 5, 1799–1804, GDAH.

157. Boucher arrived in Savannah from New York in 1797 as a builder. See Box 68, Folder 1248, Hartridge Collection, GHS. In the 1798 tax digest for Chatham County he calls himself a bricklayer. His wife, Janet, died in 1804, when he was described as a carpenter (*RoD,* 1:13, entry for September 16, 1804). Nothing more is known about Boucher except that one of his children was placed on the lists of the Union Society, April 23, 1805. See *Minutes of the Union Society: Being an Abstract of Existing Records from 1750 to 1858* (Savannah, 1860), Child No. 57.

158. *Columbian Museum and Savannah Advertiser,* February 7, 1801.

159. In the 1798 tax digest Boucher is recorded as a defaulter owing $3, but no slaves are listed. He is listed in neither the 1793 nor the 1806 tax digests for Chatham County.

160. CCM, March 16, 1807; City of Savannah, Tax Digest, 1809, GDAH. See also the case of John Fleury, CCM, November 1, 1819.

161. CCM, February 20, 1809.

162. Nienhaus's five-month-old son died in Savannah on November 17, 1808. In the death record he is listed as "professing himself a doctor" (*RoD,* 2:53).

163. Loulie Brown to Nathan Brown, Thorn Hall (Camden Co.) December 28, 1861, Brown Papers, UGa; Morgan, *Slave Counterpoint,* 408.

164. Affidavit of Peter S. Ryan of Charleston, November 7, 1795, Governor's Messages, Roll IV, 1792–95, General Assembly Papers, 0010 006 0650 00000, SCDAH. William Cunnington owned fourteen slaves in 1790 (Federal Manuscript Census, 1790, Charleston District, St. Phillip's and St. Michael's Parishes, SCDAH).

165. James McBride may have known about the dance because his own slave was attending it. He owned one slave in 1790 (Federal Manuscript Census, 1790).

166. Affidavits of William Johnson and James Allison, November 7, 1795, Governor's Messages, Roll IV, 1792–95, General Assembly Papers, 0010 006 0650 00000, SCDAH.

167. Affidavit of William Ellison, November 7, 1795, ibid.

168. Affidavit of Peter S. Ryan of Charleston, November 7, 1795, ibid.

169. For discussions of the sexual exploitation of black and white Southern women,

see Alexander, *Ambiguous Lives,* 20–35; Clinton, "'Southern Dishonor'"; Harris, *Plain Folk of the Old South,* 56; Scarborough, *Overseer,* 75–78; Dusinberre, *Them Dark Days,* 111–14; Morgan, *Slave Counterpoint,* 399–412; Wyatt-Brown, *Southern Honor,* 296–98, 307–15; Wood, *Black Majority,* 97–98. For a history of mulattoes in the South, see Joel Williamson, *New People: Miscegenation and Mulattoes in the United States* (Baton Rouge, 1995), 5–60.

170. Genovese, *Roll, Jordan, Roll,* 421–61; Jordan, *White over Black,* 150; Wood, *Black Majority,* 236–38; Wyatt-Brown, *Southern Honor,* 315–18. Moreover, children resulting from these liaisons would be free. See Hodes, "Sex Across the Color Line," 39–40, 60; Hodes, *White Women, Black Men,* 28.

171. Indictments 1811–48A-2, 1811–48A-4, Box 3, Folder 5, Charleston District, Court of General Sessions, Bills of Indictment, SCDAH.

172. Fronsman, *Common Whites,* 91; Clinton, "Southern Dishonor," 58; Hodes, "Sex Across the Color Line," 84, 106–21.

173. Johnson and Roark, *Black Masters,* 54; McMillen, *Southern Women,* 22.

174. Loewald, Staricka, and Taylor, eds., "Johann Martin Bolzius Answers a Questionnaire," 235.

175. Sommerville, "Rape Myth." Martha Hodes argues that "the sexual conduct of a slave man mattered much less to the white community than that of a white woman" ("Sex Across the Color Line," 79, 41–63). See also Hodes, *White Women, Black Men,* 1–122; Wood, *Black Majority,* 99; Fronsman, *Common Whites,* 91.

176. Chatham County, Inferior Court, Issue Docket, 1813–27, GDAH. Flyming was convicted on May 31, 1820, and falsely recorded as executed on July 6, 1820.

177. Box 19, Folder 31—Negro Justice, October 25, 1820, Read Collection, UGa. Petitioners included the mayor, several aldermen, magistrates, lawyers, and merchants.

178. Sommerville, "Rape Myth," 512–13; Hodes, *White Women, Black Men,* 21–67. Philip Morgan has discovered that half of all similar cases in eighteenth-century Virginia engendered petitions for clemency (*Slave Counterpoint,* 405).

179. Bynum, *Unruly Women,* 109–10.

180. *Daily Georgian,* November 21, 1820. The paper reported only that a message from the governor had been received regarding Flyming, "whose execution has been suspended." See Lockley, "Sex and Race in the Early South: The Case of George Flyming," paper presented at the Early American Symposium in Honor of Professor Sylvia Frey, Cambridge University, April 27–28, 1998.

181. Chatham County Superior Court, Minutes, May Term, 1862, May 17, 21, 23, 29, 30, June 4, 1862, vol. 24, 1859–62, GDAH.

182. Chatham County Superior Court, Minutes, January Term 1863, May Term 1864, vol. 25, 1862–67, GDAH.

183. John A. Middlebrook v. Abel Nelson, argued before the Supreme Court of Georgia, August, 5, 1866, Supreme Court Records, File 34 Ga 506, GDAH.

184. Loewald, Staricka, and Taylor, eds., "Johann Martin Bolzius Answers a Questionnaire," 235.

185. Lyell, *Second Visit,* 1:366.

186. Narrative of William Craft in Bontemps, ed., *Great Slave Narratives,* 279.

187. Lockley, "Crossing the Race Divide," 161–62; Dusinberre, *Them Dark Days,* 111–14, 235–84.

188. *RoD,* 3:129, September 17, 1815.

189. *RoD,* 2:15, September 18, 1807.

190. CCM, June 28, 1791. The census of people of color aged over fifteen was taken in Savannah May 28, 1798. It revealed that 16.3% of the total adult African American population in the city resided in Oglethorpe ward. Oglethorpe ward was home to 29.1% of free African Americans (Box 7, Folder, Archives File Group II, ser. 4-2-46, GDAH).

191. See death records of William Dick (forty-eight-year-old mariner from the "US"), John Pierre (thirty-year-old seaman from Portugal), and Samuel Johnson (thirty-three-year-old mariner from Connecticut), *RoD,* 1:11, 29, 51, September 5, 1804, September 15, 1805, September 26, 1806. All three succumbed to the fever prevalent in the city in the late summer. A letter to the *Daily Georgian,* October 8, 1829, complained of vagabonds who "intrude upon the hospitality of the free Negroes," though it is not stated what manner this intrusion took. See also Morgan, *Slave Counterpoint,* 407.

192. *Savannah Daily Journal Courier,* March 24, 1855; Lockley, "Crossing the Race Divide," 169. By 1858 there was apparently one prostitute for every thirty-nine men in Savannah (Wyatt-Brown, *Southern Honor,* 293).

193. Chatham County, Superior Court, Minutes, March Term 1789, vol. 1, 1782–89; Chatham County, Superior Court, Minutes, January Term 1805, vol. 7, 1804–8, GDAH. McBride was officially jailed for two months, but her release was ordered by the City Council over a year later. She had probably remained confined for failing to pay jail fees. See CCM, April 7, 1806.

194. Edward Lauder received a $1 fine and a thirty-day jail term (Chatham County, Superior Court Minutes, vol. 7, 1804–8, GDAH).

195. Chatham County, Superior Court, Minutes, April Term 1805, vol. 7, 1804–8, GDAH.

196. Ibid., January Term 1808; Chatham County, Superior Court, Minutes, January Term 1809, vol. 8, 1808–12; see also Chatham County, Superior Court, Minutes, January Term 1814, vol. 9, 1812–18, GDAH.

197. *Daily Georgian,* June 13, 1829.

198. Presentment of Liberty County Grand Jury, *Gazette of the State of Georgia,* April 21, 1785.

199. CCM, March 15, 1811 (John Fleetwood).

200. Adeline Harris and Priscilla Johnson, CCM, March 10, 1819; Chatham County, Superior Court, Minutes, January Term 1830, vols. 12–13, 1826–36, GDAH. Margaret Carlton and Margaret O'Meara were presented by the Grand Jury for "indecent and disorderly conduct" (Chatham County, Superior Court, Minutes, May Term 1824, vol. 11, 1822–26, GDAH).

201. CCM, July 24, 1820. The three women were Rebecca Woodworth, Elizabeth Hart, and Adeline Harris. The governor granted them pardons a week later. See John Clark to Thomas U. P. Charlton, Mayor of Savannah, August 2, 1820, Governor's Letterbooks, RG 1-1-1, Box 11, 1814–21, GDAH.

202. Cott, "Passionlessness."

203. Clinton, "Southern Dishonor," 59; Bynum, *Unruly Women,* 41–57, 91–110.

204. Miller, "Enemy Within"; Painter, "Of Lily, Linda Brent and Freud," 258–59; Lockley, "Crossing the Race Divide," 167.

205. Lockley, "Crossing the Race Divide," 162–64, 169–70.

3. COMPETITION AND TRADE

1. Mintz and Hall, *Origins of the Jamaican Internal Marketing System,* 5–18. Hall, "Slaves' Use of Their 'Free Time,'" 22–43.

2. Morgan, "Work and Culture," 566; Morgan, "Ownership of Property," 411; Morgan, "Black Life in Eighteenth-Century Charleston," 190–222; McDonnell, "Money Knows No Master," 31–35; Wood, *Women's Work, Men's Work,* 12–30; Hall, "Slaves' Use of Their 'Free Time'"; Schweniger, "Slave Independence," 104–14; Campbell, "As 'a Kind of Freeman'?" 131–69; Reidy, "Obligation and Right," 140–41. See also McDonald, *Economy and Material Culture of Slaves,* 18, 51–57.

3. The Duc De La Rochefoucald-Laincourt believed that nearly all residents of Georgia were in debt to somebody. Personal trust would be needed to recover such debts. See Narrative of the Duc De La Rochefoucald-Laincourt in Lane, ed., *Rambler in Georgia,* 8.

4. Kemble, *Journal,* 299.

5. *Daily Georgian,* June 9, 1828.

6. For a discussion of the task system, see Morgan, "Work and Culture," 563–99.

7. Murdoch, "Letters and Papers of Dr. Daniel Turner," 102, entry for August 12, 1806.

8. Hall, *Travels,* 191.

9. Ibid., 223.

10. Beveridge and McLaughlin, eds., *Papers of Frederick Law Olmsted,* 185.

11. Hodgson, *Letters from North America,* 46; Kemble, *Journal,* 326. Jeremiah Evarts was informed by a Mr. Eddy that "the negroes on the islands are generally through their tasks by 2 o'clock" (Evarts Diary, 20, entry for March 23, 1822, GHS). Daniel Turner even saw slaves finish their tasks at noon (Murdoch, "Letters and Papers of Dr. Daniel Turner," 102).

12. Boney, ed., *Slave Life in Georgia,* 160; Blassingame, ed., *Slave Testimony,* 380.

13. *An Act for Repealing an Act Intitled an Act for Rendering the Colony of Georgia More Defensible by Prohibiting the Importation and Use of Black Slaves or Negroes,* passed August 8, 1750; *An Act for the Better Ordering and Governing Negroes and Other Slaves in This Province,* passed March 7, 1755; *An Act for the Better Ordering and Governing Negroes,* passed March 3, 1765, *Col. Recs.,* 1:56–62, 18:117, 667; *Act for Ordering and Governing Slaves,* passed May, 10, 1770, Prince, ed., *Digest,* 776. Both Adam Hodgson and Basil Hall noted that slaves were allowed three days' holiday at Christmas (Hodgson, *Letters from North America,* 46; Narrative of Basil Hall in Lane, ed., *Rambler in Georgia,* 66).

14. For example, Allard Belin gave his slaves free days in 1797 and 1798 to complete the planting of their own crops (Belin Plantation Journal, entries for June 1, 2, 1797, May 31, 1798, SCHS).

15. Wood, *Women's Work, Men's Work,* 19; Stewart, *"What Nature Suffers to Groe,"* 177.

16. Belin Plantation Journal, entry for January 15, 1798, SCHS.

17. Wood, *Women's Work, Men's Work,* 31–52. Emily Burke saw a wide variety of activities on a typical Sunday on a plantation, including games, dancing, and hunting (*Pleasure and Pain,* 49–50).

18. Bodichon, *American Diary,* 120.

19. Ball, *Life of a Negro Slave,* 74.

20. *Southern Agriculturalist* 1 (1828): 525.

21. Mintz and Hall, *Origins of the Jamaican Internal Marketing System,* 4–5; Schweniger, "Slave Independence," 104–5; Berlin and Morgan, eds., *Slaves' Economy,* 4; Reidy, "Obligation and Right," 140–41; Marshall, "Provision Ground and Plantation Labor," 204–5.

22. Olwell, "Reckoning of Accounts," 38; Wood, *Women's Work, Men's Work,* 12–30.

23. Evarts Diary, 16–18, entry for April 5, 1822, GHS; Conrad, *Reminiscences,* 7; Clifton, *Life and Labor on Argyle Island,* 49; R. Q. Mallard stated that slaves he knew ate "chickens and bacon of their own raising and curing, and fish of their own catching" (*Plantation Life Before Emancipation,* 31–32). See also Bartram, *Travels,* 467; Silva, *Early Reminiscences,* Paper No. 2. See also N. S. Tyler Paper, April 27, 1847, GHS; Ball, *Life of a Negro Slave,* 118–20; Padgett, ed., "Journal of Daniel Walker Lord," 188.

24. Hall, *Travels,* 188; Kemble, *Journal,* 26.

25. Michele Gillespie, in her study of Savannah mechanics, has argued that planters employed white artisans only on the most important and conspicuous commissions, preferring to use their own slaves for more mundane work ("Artisans and Mechanics," 172–74; Gillespie, "Artisan Accommodation," 266, 276–80). Reuben King built several "Negro houses" while working for Mr. Dunham near Darien (Wood and Wood, eds., "Reuben King Journal," 95–96, December 27, 1804–January 16, 1805).

26. Craft, *Running a Thousand Miles,* 10. James Habersham made precisely the same point in 1770: Habersham to Rev. Thomas Broughton, December 1, 1770, Habersham, "Letters," 100–101.

27. *Gazette of the State of Georgia,* August 31, 1786; *Georgia Gazette,* July 20, 1768; *Columbian Museum and Savannah Advertiser,* August 30, 1799; *Savannah Republican,* January 5, 1818. See also Wood, *Women's Work, Men's Work,* 101–21; Hall, *Travels,* 218; White Hall, List of Workers 1840, Records of the Antebellum Southern Plantations, Ser. J, pt. 4, ser. 1.2, Richard James Arnold Papers, UGa.

28. Wood, *Women's Work, Men's Work,* 62–70. Laurens purchased rice from his slaves and expressed concerns that articles he provided in exchange would be acceptable to them. See Henry Laurens to Abraham Schad, April 30, 1765, in Rogers, Chesnutt, Clark, et al., eds., *Papers of Henry Laurens,* 4:616. See also Olwell, "Reckoning of Accounts," 33–52.

29. Conrad, *Reminiscences,* 7.

30. Beveridge and McLaughlin, eds., *Papers of Frederick Law Olmsted,* 186. Fredericka Bremer understood that some planters even paid interest on this credit (*Homes of the New World,* 304).

31. Narrative of John Lambert in Lane, ed., *Rambler in Georgia*, 49. Fanny Kemble recorded the case of one slave who, by working in his free time over the years, had earned $1,700, $1,000 of which was used to purchase his own freedom (*Journal,* 195). In 1813 Roswell King, overseer on the Butler plantations, reported that value of slaves' crops destroyed in a hurricane collectively amounted to $1,000 (Stewart, *"What Nature Suffers to Groe,"* 138).

32. Account Book of Anna M. King, 1839–40, entries for December 27, 1839, February 17, 1840, June 19, and 20, 1840, ser. 6, vol. 1, King Papers, SHC.

33. Narrative of Basil Hall in Lane, ed., *Rambler in Georgia*, 67. In 1786 William Gibbons recorded that he had "Bought corn of Mr Zouberbuhler's negroes 31 bushels" (Ser. F, pt. II, reel 1: South Carolina and Georgia, William Gibbons Papers, Miscellaneous Receipts, Records of Ante-Bellum Southern Plantations from the Revolution through the Civil War, UGa).

34. Beveridge and McLaughlin, eds., *Papers of Frederick Law Olmsted*, 186.

35. Kemble, *Journal,* 40; Bodichon, *American Diary,* 120.

36. Wood, *Women's Work, Men's Work,* 70–79.

37. Hudson, " 'All That Cash,' " 81.

38. Ball, *Life of a Negro Slave,* 110. According to William Gibbons, bondswomen preferred to be given large pieces of cloth to fashion how they pleased. See William Channing to William Gibbons, June 26, 1770, Gibbons Papers, DU. In 1999 this document was available online at http://scriptorium.lib.duke.edu/slavery/plantation.html.

39. Kemble, *Journal,* 337.

40. Bodichon, *American Diary,* 125.

41. Wood, *Women's Work, Men's Work,* 91–92, 105–18. See also the protest of the Chatham County Grand Jury concerning the insults given by "certain persons" to "females and others" arriving to sell at the Sunday market in Savannah (Chatham County Superior Court, Minutes, November Term 1826, vols. 12–13, 1826–36, GDAH). For a comparison with Charleston, see Olwell, "Loose, Idle and Disorderly," 97–110.

42. Burke, *Pleasure and Pain,* 9. Furgus Wilson, a Camden County slave on hire in Savannah, contracted with slave women to sell the produce he grew in the weekly market (Southern Claims Commission, Settled Claim, RG 217, Camden County, Georgia, Case No 15215, GHS). See also Lockley, "Spheres of Influence."

43. CCM, January 26, February 9, 1801.

44. CCM, July 24, 1820.

45. CCM, July 2, 1829.

46. Such activities were one reason for the new ordinance of October 20, 1817 (CCM, August 25, 1817, July 2, 1829).

47. *Columbian Museum and Savannah Advertiser,* January 13, 1814.

48. *Daily Savannah Republican,* January 17, 1818. See also *Daily Georgian,* April 26, October 31, 1826.

49. See the descriptions in Beveridge and McLaughlin, eds., *Papers of Frederick Law Olmsted,* 157, and Harn, "Old Canoochee-Ogeechee Chronicles," 48. Emily Burke stated that she had "known women to come one hundred miles to sell the products of their own industry" (*Pleasure and Pain,* 10).

50. Entries for April 14–May 5, 1786. The goods Bristol took to Savannah were val-

ued at £11.9.8 (James Martin Gibbons Receipt Book, Ser. F, pt 2, Reel 1: South Carolina and Georgia, William Gibbons Papers, Records of Ante-Bellum Southern Plantations from the Revolution through the Civil War, UGa). Part of this document was available online in 1999 at http://scriptorium.lib.duke.edu/slavery/plantation.html. See also Miscellaneous Receipts for rice transported by bondsman Tom to town dated March 30 and April 5, 1786, ibid. One slave encountered by John Lambert walked one hundred miles per week to and from Charleston for similar reasons (Narrative of John Lambert in Lane, ed., *Rambler in Georgia*, 38).

51. See the description of Mrs. Smith from Massachusetts, who noted that "the Negroes carry everything upon their heads" up the bluff (Diary of Mrs. Smith, entry for March 7, 1793, DU).

52. CCM, May 18, 1801, January 10, 1803, January 14, 1792, November 19, 1804. See also the evaluation of South Carolina governor James Glen in 1751 in Merrens, *Colonial South Carolina Scene*, 183, and Fanny Kemble's description of slave artisans in *Journal*, 26.

53. CCM, July 24, 1809.

54. More than one hundred of these bondsmen were simply classed as "mechanics"; the rest were butchers, barbers, and engineers/pilots (Bancroft, *Census of the City of Savannah*. 16). In Richmond, Virginia, a quarter of male slaves worked as artisans (Sidbury, "Slave Artisans," 51).

55. CCM, July 25, 1822.

56. There is little published work on slave hire in the Georgia lowcountry, though there is now work in progress. See Mooney, "History of the Legal Regulation of Slave-Hire." For examinations of slave hire in other parts of the South, see Charles Dew, *Bond of Iron: Masters and Slaves at Buffalo Forge* (New York, 1995), 171–219; Schweniger, "Underside of Slavery"; James Walvin, "Slaves, Free Time and the Question of Leisure," *Slavery and Abolition* 16 (1995): 1–13; Sarah S. Hughes, "Slaves for Hire: The Allocation of Black Labor in Elizabeth County, Virginia, 1782–1810," *William and Mary Quarterly* 35 (1978): 260–86; Loren Schweniger, "John H. Rapier Sr.: A Slave and Freedman in the Antebellum South," *Civil War History* 20 (1974): 23–34; Clement Eaton, "Slave Hiring in the Upper South: A Step Toward Freedom," *Mississippi Valley Historical Review* 46 (1959–60): 603–78; Wood, *Black Majority*, 205–11.

57. *An Act to Empower Certain Commissioners Herein Appointed to Regulate the Hire of Porters and Labor of Slaves in the Town of Savannah*, passed March 12, 1774, *Col. Recs.*, 19: pt. 2, 23–30.

58. *An Ordinance Regulating the Hire of Drays; Carts, and Waggons; As Also the Hire of Negro and Other Slaves; Negroes, Mulattoes, or Mestizoes; Within the City of Savannah*, passed September 28, 1790, *Georgia Gazette*, October 7, 1790.

59. *An ordinance for consolidating the various ordinances of the city in relation to the regulation of slaves and negroes, and for the better ordering of free negroes, mulattoes and mestizoes within the city of Savannah, and for other purposes connected therewith*, passed December 10, 1857, Wilson, comp., *Digest*, 417–21. Skilled slaves were cabinetmakers, blacksmiths, and butchers; semiskilled slaves were pilots, boatmen, and hucksters; unskilled slaves were porters and laborers.

60. *An Ordinance for Regulating the Hire of Porters and Daily Labor of Slaves and*

Drays, Carts and Waggons in the Town of Savannah, passed by the Board of Wardens, June 26, 1787, *Gazette of the State of Georgia,* July 5, 1787; *An Ordinance Regulating the Hire of Drays; Carts, and Waggons; As Also the Hire of Negro and Other Slaves; Negroes, Mulattoes, or Mestizoes; Within the City of Savannah,* passed September 28, 1790, *Georgia Gazette,* October 7, 1790; *Extract of an Ordinance Entitled An Ordinance for Regulating the Hire of Drays, Carts and Waggons as Also the Hire of Negro and Other Slaves, and for the Better Ordering of Negroes, Mulattoes or Mestizoes, Within the City of Savannah,* Passed October 15, 1792, *Georgia Gazette,* January 3, 1793; *An ordinance for consolidating the various ordinances of the city in relation to the regulation of slaves and negroes, and for the better ordering of free negroes, mulattoes and mestizoes within the city of Savannah, and for other purposes connected therewith,* passed December 10, 1857, Wilson, comp., *Digest,* 417–21.

61. *An Act for the Better Ordering and Governing Negroes and Other Slaves in This Province,* passed March 7, 1755, *Col. Recs.,* 18:126–28. In 1771 Samuel Frink stated that forty slaves in Savannah "live by themselves and allow their masters a certain sum per week" (Box 5, Folder 110, Minutes, October 18, 1771, Correspondence of the Society for the Propagation of the Gospel, Christ Church Savannah Records, GHS).

62. Buckingham, *Slave States of America,* 122.

63. Wood, *Women's Work, Men's Work,* 101–21, esp. 119–20. Ball stated that he could earn up to $1.50 on a Sunday alone (*Life of a Negro Slave,* 145). In 1840 the trustees of the Georgia Infirmary hired a slave named Jerry as a caretaker for a wage of $150 per year (Minutes, March 23, 1840, Georgia Infirmary Papers, GHS). Similarly, a bondsman named Sam was paid $15 per month to clean Trinity Methodist Church (Book 9, Item 42, Account Book, 1837–87, January 31, April 25, May 9, 1838, Trinity Methodist Church Records, GHS). Not all slaves were so well paid; one observer recorded that slave seamstresses earned 37 cents per day (Adams, *South Side View of Slavery,* 39).

64. See, for example, the claims of William Anderson (Case 18215), Alfred Barnard (20092), Rachel Brownfield (13361), Samuel McIver (6609), Larry Williams (14157), Anthony Owens (18095), Southern Claims Commission, Settled Claims, Record Group 217, Chatham County, Georgia, GHS. For a more detailed exploration of the work of the Southern Claims Commission, see Morgan, "Ownership of Property."

65. Narrative of Adam Hodgson in Lane, ed., *Rambler in Georgia,* 56.

66. Blassingame, ed., *Slave Testimony,* 330.

67. Between January 10, 1803, and August 7, 1809, the CCM recorded only fifteen days when people were prosecuted for letting slaves work without badges. This suggests that there were periodic crackdowns by the city authorities against slave hire but no sustained campaign. For example, between September 19, 1808, and October 3, 1808, thirty-nine people were fined for letting their slaves work out without a badge.

68. Such was this sense of independence that one of William Gibbons's slaves promised to return from Connecticut, where he had fled seven years previously, only if Gibbons allowed him to hire his own time. See D. Mitchell to William Gibbons, August 11, 1801, Gibbons Papers, DU. In 1999 this document was available at http://scriptorium.lib.duke.edu/slavery/caesar.html.

69. Ball, *Life of a Negro Slave,* 155.

70. *South Carolina Gazette*, August 6, 1772.

71. For just a few examples of fugitives who were believed to be working in Savannah at a variety of trades, see *Daily Georgian*, January 24, 1823 (Lucy, retailer); July 19, 1823 (Ben, carriage driver); December 3, 1824 (Tom, cooper); January 8, 1825 (Celia, seamstress); July 25, 1826 (Quash, carpenter), and February 28, 1828 (Jack, boathand).

72. Boney, ed., *Slave Life in Georgia*, 48–50. Betty Wood makes the point that those hiring rural slaves would most likely have been known to masters, while those hiring in towns often were not ("Never on a Sunday?," 79–82).

73. Ball, *Life of a Negro Slave*, 73.

74. Reuben King also regularly hired other African Americans to work for him. See Wood and Wood, eds., "Reuben King Journal," 50, 48, 68, 75, 80–91. See also Quincy, "Journal," 455.

75. Chatham County, Superior Court, Minutes for Equity Purposes, Case No 1739: Accounts of the Brampton Plantation, vol. 15, 1841–46, GDAH. Total income for 1843–44 was $1,112.63 of which $158.98 came from the hire of three slaves.

76. Diary of Michael Gaffney, 1797–1853, 9, Gaffney Papers, SHC. See also Burke, *Pleasure and Pain*, 80–81.

77. This register was published by the *Daily Georgian*, March 10, 1828. Those not given an occupation were either children or the elderly. See also Wood, *Women's Work, Men's Work*, 80–100.

78. Of 116 free black women assigned an occupation, all but 19 recorded domestic/cook, seamstress, or washerwoman as their job. Of 72 free black men assigned an occupation, 41 were in an artisan trade, while another 14 were classified as laborers.

79. The 179 free black men with an occupation in Chatham County in 1860 were spread among forty-three different trades with mariner, carpenter, and bricklayer being the most popular. The 353 free black women, however, were spread among only fifteen occupations with servants and seamstresses accounting for more than two-thirds (Johnson, *Black Savannah*, 186–87). William Harden recalled one free black woman named Aspasia Mirault who ran a bakery and confectionery store and was famed for her ice cream (*Recollections*, 48–49).

80. In the 1830 census Chatham County was home to 393 free blacks, 239 women and 154 men (this figure is significantly more than the 246 registered in 1828, suggesting that up to a third of free blacks avoided registration). Bryan and Camden Counties possessed a male free black majority, while sex ratios were equal in other lowcountry counties.

81. Register of Free People of Color, 1817, GHS.

82. Johnson, *Black Savannah*, 187.

83. Camden County, Register of Free Persons of Color 1819, GDAH, shows that thirteen of twenty-two free black women were working: five (38.4%) were laborers, and three (23%) were house servants; fourteen of eighteen free black men were working: five (35.7%) were mariners, three (21.4%) were artisans, and Remie Brunett "from Charleston" was a merchant. Of five free African Americans listed in Liberty County in 1823, four were female (seamstress, washer, farmer, waiting girl) and one male (carpenter). The only two free blacks listed in Bryan County were a farmer, James Dolly, and his daughter, Jane (*Daily Georgian*, July 22, 1823, April 18, 1828). On the popularity of maritime profes-

sions among free blacks, see Bolster, *Black Jacks,* 23. The opportunities offered by the port at St. Marys probably accounts for the relatively high number of free blacks (fifty-four) resident in Camden County in 1860.

84. See Chapter 1 and Wood, *Slavery in Colonial Georgia,* 111–30.

85. *An Act for the Better Ordering and Governing Negroes and Other Slaves in This Province,* passed March 7, 1755, *Col. Recs.,* 18:102–44.

86. Loewald, Staricka, and Taylor, eds., "Johann Martin Bolzius Answers a Questionnaire," 244.

87. Journal of the Commons House of Assembly, January 28, 1758, *Col. Recs.,* 13:262. None of the committee appointed to bring in a bill were artisans. They were a minister, Joseph Ottolenghe, a merchant, Thomas Rasberry, a planter, Henry Yonge, and the gentleman William Francis.

88. Ibid., February 8, 10, 1758, *Col. Recs.,* 13:273–74, 276.

89. Journal of the Upper House, February 11, 1758, *Col. Recs.,* 16:268.

90. Johnson and Wylly were partners in a firm of merchants. Tannat described himself as a gentleman (Colonial Book J, Miscellaneous, 1755–62, 148, June 29, 1759, and 229, August 27, 1761). The two other named signatories of this petition were John Graham and William Handley, both merchants (Colonial Book S, Conveyances, 1766–69, 219, October 25, 1762, and Colonial Book J, Miscellaneous, 1755–62, 167, December 11, 1759, all in GDAH).

91. Journal of the Upper House of Assembly, February 13, 1758, *Col. Recs.,* 16:269–70. See also Davis, *Fledgling Province,* 96–98.

92. *Col. Recs.,* 16:269–70, February 14, 1758.

93. Ibid., 274–75, February 16, 1758.

94. Ibid., 282, February 23, 1758.

95. Ibid., 290–91, February 28, 1758.

96. Ibid., 292–93, *Col. Recs.,* 13:301–3; Henry Ellis to the Board of Trade, February 18, 1758, *Col. Recs.,* 28: pt. 1, 124.

97. *An Act to encourage White Tradesmen to settle in the several towns within this province of Georgia by preventing the employing of Negroes and other Slaves being Handicraft Tradesmen in said towns,* passed March, 15, 1758, *Col. Recs.,* 18:277–82.

98. *An Act for Better Ordering and Governing Negroes and Other Slaves in This Province and to Prevent the Inveigling or Carrying Away Slaves from Their Masters or Employers,* passed March 25, 1765, *Col. Recs.,* 18:649–88. See esp. p. 659.

99. Ibid. These rights did not extend to the franchise.

100. James Habersham to Rev. Thomas Broughton, December 1, 1770, Habersham, "Letters," 100–101.

101. Between 1791 and 1800 twenty-eight people were fined by the City Council for letting a slave work out without a badge. Between 1800 and 1810 one hundred people were fined (CCM, January 6, 1791, May 28, 1810).

102. In 1790 the lowcountry population consisted of 16,842 slaves, 4,173 whites, and 158 free blacks. In 1860 the population was 34,314 slaves, 23,966 whites. and 805 free blacks. Census statistics were taken from http://fisher.lib.virginia.edu/census in 1999.

103. Petition of the Inhabitants of St. Helena Parish, General Assembly Papers, 0010 003 ND 2815, SCDAH.

104. Powers, *Black Charlestonians*, 42. This was certainly believed by Louis Manigault, who employed a free black decorator from Charleston in preference to white artisans from Savannah (Louis Manigault to Charles Manigault, March 7, 1852, in Clifton, *Life and Labor on Argyle Island*, 94).

105. Petition of Mechanics, Artisans and Others of the City of Charleston, General Assembly Papers, 0010 003 ND 04330, SCDAH. For more on the high level of competition between white and black artisans in the lowcountry and the contrast of little competition in the upcountry, see Morgan, *Slave Counterpoint*, 311–15, and Lewis, *Artisans in the North Carolina Backcountry*, 46–47.

106. James Habersham also made this point in the 1770s, remarking that the existence of "ingenious" slave artisans proved that no one should doubt that bondspeople had the capacity for mastering complicated subjects (Habersham to Rev. Thomas Broughton, December 1, 1770, Habersham, "Letters," 100–101).

107. Of course, some slaves operated in an informal medical capacity on their own plantations. One of Alexander Telfair's bondswomen, Elsey, acted as midwife to the whole neighborhood, "black and white," near her own Thorn Island plantation ("Rules and directions for my Thorn Island plantation by which my overseers are to govern themselves in the management of it," Rule No. 14, June 11, 1832, Box 5, Folder 51, Item 209, Telfair Papers, GHS).

108. Petition of Mechanics, Artisans and Others of the City of Charleston, General Assembly Papers, 0010 003 ND 04330, SCDAH.

109. Petition of Sundry Mechanics of the City of Charleston, General Assembly Papers, 0010 003 1811 0048, SCDAH.

110. Petition of the House Carpenters and Bricklayers of Charleston, February 19, 1783, General Assembly Papers, 0010 003 1783 00258, SCDAH. See also Petition of the Subscribers of the City of Charleston Master Coopers, December 3, 1793, General Assembly Papers, 0010 003 1793 0063, SCDAH.

111. Charleston Grand Jury Presentments, September 21, 1795, General Assembly Papers, 0010 015 1795 00003, SCDAH.

112. Petition of Sundry Mechanics of the City of Charleston, General Assembly Papers, 0010 003 1811 00048, SCDAH.

113. The Petition of the Undersigned Citizens of Charleston, General Assembly Papers, 0010 003 ND 0281, SCDAH.

114. CCM, July 25, August 8, 1822. Debate was supposedly postponed until February 31, 1823 (*sic*) on a vote of aldermen of 8 to 2. It is unknown what Sections III and IV of the ordinance referred to. Alderman William Davis later became a judge of the Superior Court of Chatham County (*RoD*, 228, May 1, 1829).

115. *Savannah Republican*, April 20, 1820.

116. CCM, December 22, 1825, June 22, July 2, 1829, March 24, May 19, June 2, 1842, December 5, 19, 1860. In 1848 Joseph Bancroft counted seven black butchers working in Savannah (*Census of the City of Savannah*, 16).

117. *Daily Morning News*, December 5, 1856.

118. For the replacement of white lumbermen by slaves, see Thayer, ed., "Nathaniel Pendleton's 'Short Account of the Sea Coast of Georgia in Respect to Agriculture, Ship-Building, Navigation, and the Timber Trade,'" 74.

119. *Daily Morning News,* June 30, 1851. For the resolutions against "negro mechanics" passed at the convention, see *National Anti-Slavery Standard,* July 31, 1851; Shoemaker, "Strangers and Citizens," 185–86, 279–86. One historian argues that interracial competition in Savannah peaked in the 1840s and declined in the 1850s as bondspeople were taken to the western states. The evidence presented here suggests that if any decline took place, its effect was minimal. See Siegel, "Artisans and Immigrants," 223–25.

120. Kemble, *Journal,* 178.

121. Savannah Cash Book, 1806–10, entry for November 29, 1806, UGa.

122. Charles Caleb Cotton to His Parents, October 24, 1799, Cotton Letters, SCHS.

123. Lockley, "Spheres of Influence."

124. *An Act for the Better Ordering and Governing Negroes and Other Slaves in This Province,* passed March 7, 1755, *Col. Recs.,* 18:125–26, 128–29. For similar restrictions in South Carolina, see Wood, *Black Majority,* 212–17.

125. Details of the offenders and the offenses they committed, together with the fine they paid, are included in CCM, March 8, 1790–March 17, 1848. People were also fined between 1782 and 1790, when the town of Savannah was governed by a Board of Wardens, and after 1848, but no record of these fines survives.

126. Early city ordinances from Savannah have not survived unless they were reprinted in the city press. Illegal traders were mainly convicted of violating the market and shop ordinances. For examples of these ordinances, see *An ordinance for regulating the market in the town of Savannah,* passed April 8, 1788, *Gazette of the State of Georgia,* April 17, 1788; *An ordinance regulating shops, stores, and barrooms, and for granting licenses for retailing spirituous liquors, or for vending goods, wares and merchandise in the streets, lanes, alleys, and squares, within the City of Savannah and its extended limits,* passed October 12, 1826, Henry, comp., *Digest,* 298–304.

127. Craft, *Running a Thousand Miles,* 30.

128. Beveridge and McLaughlin, eds., *Papers of Frederick Law Olmsted,* 186.

129. Grand Jury Presentment published in the *Georgia Gazette,* June 21, 1775; Wood, *Black Majority,* 210–11.

130. *An Act for Preventing and Punishing Vice, Profaneness, and Immorality, and for Keeping Holy the Lord's Day, Commonly Called Sunday,* passed March 4, 1762, Prince, ed., *Digest,* 886–89. secs. II, VI, and VII.

131. *Georgia Gazette,* December 24, 1766; quote from *Gazette of the State of Georgia,* October 6, 1785. When reviewing the market ordinance in 1827, the City Council acknowledged that the 1762 law had been widely disregarded for decades (CCM, May 24, 1827).

132. See, for example, *Georgia Gazette,* October 19, 1786, February 20, 1794; *Columbian Museum and Savannah Advertiser,* January 14, 1814; *Daily Georgian,* June 4, 1823; Chatham County Superior Court, Minutes, January Term 1802, vol. 5, 1799–1804; January Term 1805, January Term 1807, January Term 1808, and April Term 1808, vol. 7, 1804–8; May Term 1820, vol. 10, 1818–22; January Term 1823, May Term 1824, January Term 1826, vol. 11, 1822–26, all in GDAH.

133. Wood and Wood, eds., "Reuben King Journal," 118.

134. In 1825 the Liberty County Grand Jury complained about the retailing of liquor to slaves. Cross-referencing with the 1830 Tax Digest (the nearest extant digest) for Lib-

erty County showed that every jury member who could be located in the records owned slaves. See Liberty County Superior Court, Minutes, 1822–59; Liberty County Tax Digest, 1830, GDAH.

135. *An Act to Regulate Taverns and to Suppress Vice and Immorality,* passed August 14, 1786, *Col. Recs.,* 19: pt. 2, 556–60; *An Act for the Better Regulating of Taverns,* passed February 1, 1788, Statutes of Georgia, 1778–89, Microfilm Records of the States of the United States, University of Cambridge Library.

136. *An Act to Alter and Amend an Act to Prohibit Slaves from Selling Certain Commodities Therein Mentioned,* passed December 19, 1818, Prince, ed., *Digest,* 794.

137. Chatham County, Superior Court, Minutes, April Term 1826, vols. 12–13, 1826–36, GDAH; *Daily Georgian,* May 12, 1826.

138. See Atherton, *Southern Country Store,* 94; McCurry, *Masters of Small Worlds,* 96–100; Fronsman, *Common Whites,* 94.

139. See, for example, the overseer's contracts with A. M. Sandford (1829) and John B. Cross (November 1, 1843), which stated that the overseer should "do all in his power to keep the negroes from trading at the grog shops and as far as in his power to keep them at home" (Ser. J, pt. 4, ser. 1.2, Richard James Arnold Papers, Records of the Antebellum Southern Plantations, UGa).

140. Ball, *Life of a Negro Slave,* 120–21.

141. Ibid., 77.

142. Murdoch, "Letters and Papers of Dr. Daniel Turner," 481.

143. For further discussion of the role of country stores in the South, see Atherton, *Southern Country Store.*

144. Wood and Wood, eds., "Reuben King Journal," 77.

145. Lyell, *Second Visit,* 2:2.

146. Bremer, *Homes of the New World,* 304.

147. Evarts Diary, 20, GHS. Sabbatarians who succeeded in closing the city market on Sunday in 1829 claimed that "more than one half of their (i.e., bondspeople's) money is expended on ardent spirits" (CCM, July 2, 1829).

148. Wood, *Women's Work, Men's Work,* 131–32.

149. Ball, *Life of a Negro Slave,* 123–25.

150. Liberty County, Superior Court, Minutes, December Term 1838, December Term, 1847, GDAH.

151. *Preamble and Regulations of the Savannah River Anti–Slave Traffick Association* (N.p. 1846); Harris, *Plain Folk and Gentry,* 60–61. Similar organizations to control the liquor trade with slaves were established by planters in McIntosh County in Darien in 1808; in Pinesville, South Carolina, in 1822; and in Effingham County, Georgia, in 1859. See Roswell King to Major Pierce Butler, September 23, 1808, Box 2, Folder 17–Plantation Manager's Correspondence, 1786–1814, Butler Plantation Papers, microfilm, University of Warwick Library; Stewart, *"What Nature Suffers to Groe,"* 132–33; McCurry, *Masters of Small Worlds,* 117; Mohr, *On the Threshold of Freedom,* 6. When considering the merits of several new slaves, Roswell King thought those who "know nothing of trade" were the least troublesome (King to Major Pierce Butler, May 25, 1811, Butler Plantation Papers, University of Warwick Library).

152. Beveridge and McLaughlin, eds., *Papers of Frederick Law Olmsted,* 185.

153. McCurry, *Masters of Small Worlds*, 118. The apparent contradiction between the protests of grand juries relating to biracial trading and the unwillingness of juries to convict those indicted is resolved by the fact that grand jury presentments did not necessarily have to be unanimous, allowing the elite social ethic to come through. Criminal juries, on the other hand, did require unanimity for conviction.

154. Peter Horry's Justice Book, 1783, entry for July 26, 1784, SCDAH.

155. Ibid., August 25, 1784.

156. Eiffort Papers, dated 1815, USC.

157. *An Act for the Better Ordering and Governing Negroes and Other Slaves in This Province*, passed March 7, 1755, *Col. Recs.*, 18:126; Harris, *Plain Folk and Gentry*, 69–70.

158. *An Act for Regulating Tavern and Punch Houses and Retailers of Spirituous Liquors*, passed July 23, 1757, *Col. Recs.*, 18:218.

159. *Georgia Gazette*, January 19, 1764; *An Act to Amend and Continue an Act for the Establishing and Regulating Patrols and for Preventing Any Person from Purchasing Provisions or Any Other Commodities from or Selling Such, to Any Slave Unless Such Slave Shall Produce a Ticket from His or Her Owner, Manager or Employer*, passed December 24, 1768, *Col. Recs.*, 19: pt. 1, 75–82. See also Grand Jury Presentments, June 14, 1771, *Col. Recs.*, 22:78; *An Act to Regulate Taverns and to Suppress Vice and Immorality*, passed August 4, 1786, *Col. Recs.*, 19: pt. 2, 559–60; *An Act for the Better Regulation of Tavern and Shopkeepers, and More Effectively to Prevent Their Trading with Slaves*, passed December 22, 1808, *Acts of the General Assembly* (1809), 33–35.

160. Entries for April 23, November 7, 12, 1804, Peter Gaillard Planting Book, 1803–6, SCHS.

161. CCM, September 12, 1796.

162. Letters of "Don't Give Up the Ship," "Fides," "Lex Nature," "Reform," "Rachel," and "Carolus," *McIntosh County Herald*, September 3, 10, 17, 24, October 1, 8, 1839.

163. Chatham County Superior Court, Minutes, May Term 1841, vol. 16, 1841–43, GDAH.

164. Extracted from CCM, 1790–1848. Fines averaged $15.58 for retailing liquor without a license and $14.88 for entertaining Negroes.

165. Between 1830 and 1848 fines for entertaining Negroes averaged only $10.18.

166. Wood, *Women's Work, Men's Work*, 155.

167. *Gazette of the State of Georgia*, October 16, 1783.

168. *Georgia Gazette*, October 23, 1788.

169. Ibid., February 20, 1794. All the members of this Grand Jury owned slaves (Chatham County Tax Digest, 1793, GDAH).

170. See Chapter 4 for further discussion of the trade in stolen goods.

171. *Columbian Museum and Savannah Advertiser*, October 24, 1797.

172. These figures are taken from the CCM, 1790–1820. Out of 508 liquor licenses granted, 93 licensees were also fined. After 1820 liquor licensees were no longer recorded in the CCM.

173. Ibid. Out of a total of 472 people prosecuted, both with and without liquor licenses, 87 were fined more than once.

174. Report of the Chief of Police, March 20, 1855, *Savannah Daily Journal Courier,* March 24, 1855; CCM, May 21, 1793. Only about one hundred licenses were given out in 1851, suggesting that as many as half the liquor shops had no license (Savannah Clerk of Council, Liquor License Book 1850–51, GHS).

175. CCM, April 1, 1814. Total expenditure in 1814 was $26,000.

176. *Mayor's Annual Report, 1860* (Savannah, 1860), 26.

177. Chatham County, Superior Court, Minutes, April Term 1807, vol. 7, 1804–8, GDAH.

178. To be exact, 304 (34.5%) of the 879 offenders appeared in the tax records (City of Savannah, Tax Digests, 1809–48, GDAH).

179. Indeed, there is a marked gender difference in the numbers located: 35.4% of male offenders but only 26.2% of females were listed in the city tax records.

180. Exact figures were 73.7% nonslaveholding, 26.3% slaveholding. Elite status here is suggested by owning more than three slaves, which might start to produce a notable improvement in the standard of living of the owner.

181. Among women, 57.2% owned slaves; among men only 23.7% owned slaves.

182. For more on the working lives of black and white women in Savannah, see Lockley, "Spheres of Influence" and Wood, *Women's Work, Men's Work,* 1–121.

183. Of 80 female offenders, 36 had been, or were, married. It is impossible to tell how many were widowed at the time of their offense.

184. CCM, February 8, November 14, 1844, April 28, 1836, December 19, 1839. The Gilligans were married on May 9, 1842, the Prendergasts on November 4, 1836 (*Marriages of Chatham County,* 1:136, 173). Bridget Gilligan ran the store after Dominic's death from fever on June 30, 1844 (*RoD,* 5:207).

185. Chatham County, Superior Court, Minutes, January Term 1804, vol. 7, 1804–8, GDAH.

186. Ibid., April Term 1805.

187. Clifton, *Life and Labor on Argyle Island,* 22. John Brown declared that his master, Thomas Stephens, had previously been a "poor jobbing carpenter" who had made all his money from selling whiskey to slaves, allowing him sufficient profits to buy his own plantation (Boney, ed., *Slave Life in Georgia,* 22).

188. Mary Garnett was originally married to a shoemaker named John Manley from Bryan County. She was a nonslaveholder before 1810, but on John's death in 1813, she inherited one slave. In 1815 she married sixty-five-year-old Joseph Garnett, who died five months later. She then disappears from the records until 1824, when she began to appear before council as the owner of three slaves. She owned six slaves in 1826, eight in 1828, and eleven in 1830. In 1828 she married for a third time, a thirty-four-year old Irish immigrant named Thomas Sullivan, who had himself been fined for retailing without a license in 1822. There is no record of her death in Savannah. See City of Savannah, Tax Digests, 1809–30, GDAH; *Marriages of Chatham County,* 1:76, 133, 184; *RoD,* 3:57, 138, 4:273; Alien Declarations, Chatham County, 1825, CCM, 1823–27.

189. Shadrack Winkler was fined $53 for seven offenses of "Entertaining Negroes"

between May 18, 1818, and June 22, 1826. He owned no slaves in 1819, but by 1834 he possessed twenty-six slaves and eleven town lots. On his death in 1842 he was brought from his county estate for burial in Savannah (CCM, 1818–26; City of Savannah Tax Digest 1819, GDAH; Chatham County Tax Digest, 1834, GDAH; *RoD*, 5:184).

190. Communion Roll, 1830, Independent Presbyterian Church Records, GHS.

191. In 1819 Irish shopkeeper McGran owned no property, but by 1821 he paid tax on $200 worth of merchandise. He died on September 8, 1821 (City of Savannah Tax Digests, 1819–21, GDAH; *RoD*, 4:115).

192. Carre had $500 worth of stock in trade in both the 1809 and 1811 Tax Digests. He is not listed after 1811, and he is not recorded as dying in the city (City of Savannah Tax Digests, 1809–11, GDAH).

193. CCM, 1824–45; City of Savannah Tax Digests, 1826–32; *RoD*, 6:43, December 15, 1849.

194. See the death records of John Dillon, John Doon, Bernard McGran, Pierce Howard, and Lawrence Durphrey and the marriage record of Constantine Connoly, *RoD*, 5:106, 3:73, 4:115, 6:43, 5:25; *Marriages of Chatham County*, 1:90; Shoemaker, "Strangers and Citizens," 216, 264–65.

195. See Timothy Lockley, "Blurring the Boundaries of Race: Interaction between African Americans and Irish Immigrants in Antebellum Savannah," paper presented at the Organization of American Historians Annual Conference, Indianapolis, April 1998, and Lockley, "The Irish in the Social Milieu of Antebellum Savannah," paper presented at the annual Conference of the Georgia Association of Historians, Savannah, April 1999.

196. Chatham County, Superior Court, Minutes, January Term 1808, vol. 7, 1804–8, GDAH.

197. Ibid., January Term 1805, vol. 6, 1804.

198. Ibid., January Term 1808, vol. 7, 1804–8.

199. See the notice in *Georgia Gazette*, October 21, 1801.

200. Chatham County, Superior Court, Minutes, April Term 1808, vol. 7, 1804–8, GDAH.

201. Camden County, Superior Court, Minutes, March Term 1811, GDAH. See also Presentments for March Term 1797 and October Term 1811 in Camden County, Grand Jury Presentments, 1797–1859, GDAH.

202. Liberty County, Superior Court, Minutes, January Term 1830, GDAH. See also December Term 1825.

203. Liberty County, Superior Court, Minutes, December Term 1841, GDAH.

204. Presentment of the Charleston Grand Jury, 1859, in Powers, *Black Charlestonians*, 24.

205. Chatham County, Superior Court, Minutes, January Term 1812, vol. 9, GDAH. In January 1814 one of these houses was recorded as owned by Jacob Vaver, a publican, most likely an immigrant from San Domingo. See *RoD*, 3:74, entry for January 19, 1814. Those granted licenses in 1763 located their shops either in the towns or on the main roads between them (*Georgia Gazette*, January 19, 1764).

206. Register of Free People of Color, Savannah, 1817, GHS. This number represented about 6% of the total number of free African Americans in Savannah who listed a place of residence in this register.

207. *Georgia Gazette,* January 19, 1798.

208. CCM, May 4, 1818. Mrs. Falligrant still managed to trade with African Americans, as is shown by her prosecution for "entertaining negroes" in 1826 (CCM, December 7, 1826).

209. Chatham County, Superior Court, Minutes, January Term 1823, vol. 11, 1822–26, GDAH.

210. Between 1790 and 1819 only 127 cases of entertaining Negroes came before the City Council. Between 1820 and 1829 the City Council dealt with 202 similar cases (CCM 1790–1829).

211. Chatham County, Superior Court, Minutes, May Term 1824, vol. 11, 1822–26, GDAH.

212. Ibid., January Term 1826.

213. CCM, December 2, 28, 1824; *Daily Georgian,* December 29, 1824.

214. Letter of "Philo-Honestus," *Daily Georgian,* December 4, 1820. "Philo-Honestus" claimed that nothing was "done to prevent . . . negroes trading at the shops with or without a ticket." This was a response to a letter to the *Savannah Republican,* November 29, 1820, by "Humanitas," a city alderman, who defended the trade with slaves because prohibition would be ineffective, encouraging "unprincipled men" to conduct "a species of traffic calculated to corrupt the interests of their masters." "Humanitas" also stated that the criticism of "Honestus" was hypocritical because almost every resident of Savannah either purchased something at the Sunday market or sent slaves on errands on that day. This letter was in response to opening salvos from "Honestus," *Daily Georgian,* November 21, 22, 25, 1820. See also the letter of "Benevolens," *Savannah Republican,* December 3, 13, 1820.

215. Chatham County, Superior Court Minutes, April Term 1826, vols. 12–13, 1826–36, GDAH.

216. This struggle is discussed in detail by Betty Wood in *Women's Work, Men's Work,* 140–59. For the public nature of these divisions, see the letters of "Justice and Co.," "Grocers and Co.," "One of the People," and "A Citizen" to the *Daily Georgian,* August 24, 29, 31, September 9, 1826. In the election, all but one of the "Grocers Ticket" were elected (ibid., September 9, 1826).

217. *Daily Georgian,* August 29, 1826.

218. CCM, May 24, 1827, August 14, 1828. According to article two of the Sabbath Union constitution, "this society shall consist indiscriminately of friends of morality, and religion, of all denominations." Although officially invited, Savannah Catholics felt excluded from this predominantly evangelical protestant organization. See *Daily Georgian,* July 24, August 6, 1828. On the Sabbath-breaking culture of the South, see McWhiney, *Cracker Culture,* 179–92.

219. Report of the Petition of the Sabbath Union, *Daily Georgian,* August 2, 1828.

220. *Argus,* May 30, 1828.

221. Wood, *Women's Work, Men's Work,* 140–59.

222. *Daily Georgian,* July 31, August 16, 1828.

223. Letter from "A Member," *Daily Georgian,* December 5, 1828. According to one correspondent to the *Argus,* the Sabbath Union was dominated by Baptists. See letter

of "Philo-Reipublicae," *Argus*, August 28, 1829; Wood, *Women's Work, Men's Work,* 157–58.

224. *Daily Georgian*, May 20, 21, 1829. This ruling was based on the fifth section of the ninth division of the penal code. Mr. Whiting did not receive a punishment because prosecutors accepted that he "retailed under a belief that he had infringed no law." J. C. Whiting was a nonslaveholder in 1827 and had been fined $3 for retailing liquor without a license in 1828 (City of Savannah Tax Digest 1827, GDAH; CCM, July 3, 1828).

225. Letter of "Vox Populi," *Argus*, July 23, 1829.

226. CCM, June 22, July 2, 1829.

227. *Daily Georgian*, June 13, 1829. For the postponements, see CCM, July 16, September 24, 1829.

228. Letter of "Philo-Reipublicae," *Argus*, August 28, 1829.

229. Of 25 men standing for election, 4 did not own slaves; 1 was a doctor, and the other 3 were merchants/storekeepers (City of Savannah Tax Digest, 1829, GDAH).

230. CCM, November 19, 1829, *Argus*, August 27, September 3, 1829.

231. CCM, November 15, 1819, May 24, 1827, July 16, 1829; *Argus*, May 30, 1828.

232. Wood, *Women's Work, Men's Work,* 157–58.

233. Bryan County, Superior Court, Minutes, December Term 1831, December Term 1832, GDAH; *An ordinance entitled an ordinance forbidding trading on the Sabbath in the city of Darien, Darien Telegraph,* February 5, 1835; *An ordinance to prevent vice and immorality on the Sabbath [passed by the] Mayor and council of the city of Brunswick, Brunswick Advocate,* July 12, 1838; *An ordinance for the better regulation of slaves and free persons of color in the town of St. Mary's,* St. Marys Town Council, Minutes, May 4, 1848, GDAH.

234. Chatham County, Superior Court, Minutes, January Term 1830, vols. 12–13, 1826–36, GDAH.

235. Letter of "Philo-Reipublicae," *Argus*, August 28, 1829. See also the letters of "A friend to liberal principles, morality and religion, in their proper place" and "Observer," *Argus*, September 3, 1829, and letters of "Sincerity" and "Senex," *Argus*, September 10, 1829. The new ordinance was read a first time on November 5, 1829, and passed on a vote of 7–4 on November 19, 1829 (CCM). The ordinance was published in the *Daily Georgian*, November 6, 1829. See Wood, *Women's Work, Men's Work,* 158–59; Wood, "Never on a Sunday?," 88.

236. CCM, October 17, 1833.

237. CCM, 1830–39.

238. CCM, May 12, 1836.

239. Chatham County, Superior Court, Minutes, January Term 1830, vols. 12–13, GDAH. Only five of the twenty jurors were nonslaveholders (City of Savannah Tax Digest, 1830, GDAH; CCM, June 3, December 12, 1830, October 17, 1833, December 3, 1835, May 12, 26, 1836).

240. CCM, May 26, 1836; *Daily Georgian*, May 31, 1836.

241. *Daily Georgian*, May 31, June 28, July 12, 1836.

242. Between 1830 and 1835 a total of 180 people were fined for violation of Sabbath ordinances; average fines were $6.63. Between 1836 and 1841, 168 people were fined an average of $14.38.

243. CCM, July 5, 19, 1838; *An Ordinance for Enforcing the Observance of the Sabbath or Lord's Day,* passed April 11, 1839; *An Ordinance for Regulating the Public Market in the City of Savannah,* passed July 22, 1839, Wilson, *Digest,* 263–67, 391–93.

244. Pro-shopkeeper councils were elected in 1841, 1843, 1844, 1848, 1849, 1850, 1852, 1857, and 1858. Anti-shopkeeper councils were elected in 1842, 1851, 1859, and 1860 (CCM, 1840–60).

245. Chatham County, Superior Court, Minutes, May Term 1841, vol. 16, 1841–43, GDAH.

246. Richard Arnold to Mrs. Louisa McAllister, December 6, 1850, and Arnold to Col. John W. Forney, December 18, 1850, in Shryock, ed., *Letters of Richard D. Arnold M.D.,* 39, 46. Arnold was elected mayor of Savannah in 1842, 1851, and 1859. See Siegel, "Artisans and Immigrants," 226–27; Rousey, "From Whence They Came to Savannah," 327; Shoemaker, "Strangers and Citizens," 343–65.

247. Chatham County Superior Court, Minutes, January Term 1852, vol. 20, 1850–53, GDAH.

248. Ibid., May Term 1852.

249. *Daily Georgian,* January 14, 1854; Wilson, *Digest,* 394.

250. *Savannah Morning News,* May 9, 1854.

251. It was for this reason that the South Carolina General Assembly refused to pass new laws relating to trading as "the evil complained of is already provided for by the act of 1834 which makes it unlawful for any owner of slaves to give their slaves a permit to sell any cotton, corn, rice or other produce" (Report of the Committee on grievances to whom were referred the presentments of the Grand Jury for Beaufort District Fall Term 1849, General Assembly Papers, 0010 004 1849 00018 00, SCDAH).

252. *Daily Morning News,* July 14, 1854.

253. Savannah Board of Health Minutes, 1850–55, September 11, October 11, 18, 1854, GHS.

254. *Savannah Morning News,* January 24, 1855.

255. *Savannah Daily Journal and Courier,* May 21, 1855.

256. Letter of "Yamacraw," *Savannah Republican,* September 28, 1857. For Wayne's election see ibid., October 13, 1857. This was Wayne's sixth and final election as mayor (the others were in 1844, 1848, 1849, 1850, and 1852). He died in office on June 27, 1858, aged fifty-four. He was succeeded by Philadelphia-born apothecary Thomas Turner, who continued the pro-shopkeeper policy of Wayne. See *Laurel Grove Cemetery Records,* 144.

257. *Savannah Republican,* October 9, 1857, October 10, 1859. Between 1844 and 1857 the election was held in December.

258. *Savannah Republican,* October 10, 1859; Mohr, *On the Threshold of Freedom,* 45.

259. Charles C. Jones to Rev. C. C. Jones, October 6, 11, 1859, in Myers, ed., *Children of Pride,* 523–25.

260. *Savannah Republican,* October 11, 1859, January 9, March 7, 1860.

261. Hon. Charles C. Jones to Mrs. Mary Jones, October 27, 1860, in Myers, ed., *Children of Pride,* 623–24.

262. Chatham County, Superior Court, Minutes, January Term 1860, vol. 24, 1859–62, GDAH.

1. State of Georgia, Board of Corrections, Inmate Administration Division, Central Register of Convicts, vol. 1, 1817–68, GDAH. Of 222 inmates from the lowcountry, only 2 were termed planters and 6 were termed merchants. By contrast, more than half of all lowcountry inmates were artisans, a further 50 were farmers, and 24 had no occupation.

2. Of the 222 inmates, 65 were from Europe and 50 from Northern states. Fewer than half were from Southern states.

3. See Bolton and Culclasure, eds., *Confessions of Edward Isham*, especially the two articles by Culclasure. For more on the culture of honor, see Ayers, *Vengeance and Justice*, 9–14; Wyatt-Brown, *Southern Honor*, 165–66, 355–57, 369–71; Dickson D. Bruce Jr., *Violence and Culture in the Antebellum South* (Austin, Tex., 1979), esp. 89–103; Greenberg, *Honor and Slavery*, 3–23, 51–86.

4. Savannah Police Department, Jail Register, 1809–15, GHS. Of 459 white offenders, 321 (69.9%) were jailed for violent crimes, whereas only 69 (15%) were jailed for property crimes.

5. Ibid. Josh Gonzales and Joseph Perez, most likely visiting sailors, were confined for pickpocketing between June 15 and October 20, 1811.

6. Ibid. The longest terms spent in jail for assault were sixty-eight days for Lewis Caton, Helena Garson, Anthony Josquin, and Jean Palace between November 15, 1811, and January 22, 1812.

7. Central Register of Convicts, GDAH. Of 222 lowcountry criminals imprisoned before 1865, 132 (59.5%) committed property crimes and only 40 (18%) violent crimes.

8. Maximum possible sentences in 1833 were four years for violent crimes and seven years for property crimes, though horse stealing could earn up to fourteen years in jail. See Prince, ed., *Digest*, 623–30; Penal Code 1833, secs. 55–58, 89–92, 112–25, 136. A similar story is told by records from colonial Charleston, where a conviction for larceny earned anything from thirty-nine lashes to the loss of an ear or imprisonment. The maximum sentence handed down for assault was a £10 fine. See Charleston District, Court of General Sessions, Session Journal, 1769, SCDAH.

9. In 1826, Thomas Hearn was acquitted of the murder of John Smith in Bryan County, though he was proved to have delivered the fatal blow (*Daily Georgian*, December 9, 1826).

10. Petition for remittance of fines, January 23, 1804, Box 45, Folder: Georgia Governors, Milledge, John, 1804, Cuyler Collection, UGa. Arnold's death record described him as a merchant (*RoD*, 2:41). Howard was described as a merchant in his daughter's death record (*RoD*, 3:89). Howard's wealth was such that he paid $170 tax in 1806, one of the largest amounts paid by an individual in that year (Chatham County, Tax Digest, 1806, GDAH). We have no information on Emmanuel Coryell, who neither died in Savannah nor was recorded as paying tax in the 1798 or the 1806 Tax Digests.

11. For an in-depth discussion of this topic relating to Louisiana, see Judith Kelleher Schafer, *Slavery, the Civil Law, and the Supreme Court of Louisiana* (Baton Rouge, 1995), 28–56. For a more general discussion, see Morris, *Southern Slavery and the Law*, 161–208.

12. Case of William Moore, Chatham County, Superior Court, Minutes, January Term 1806, vol. 7, 1804–8; *RoD*, 5:71, September 13, 1837.

13. Case of William Moore, Chatham County, Superior Court, Minutes, January Term 1806, vol. 7, 1804–8. Under the constitution of Georgia, white persons convicted of murdering slaves received the same punishment, namely death, as if the deceased had been a white person. The only exceptions were for slaves who died under "moderate correction" or for slaves in open revolt. See *An act to carry into effect the 12th section of the 4th article of the constitution,* passed December 2, 1799, Prince, ed., *Digest,* 786.

14. See, for example, Savannah Police Department, Jail Register, 1809–15, GHS; those imprisoned for assault averaged only ten days in jail.

15. Chatham County, Tax Digest, 1806, GDAH.

16. The petition of sundry citizens and inhabitants of Chatham County, February 1806, Box 45, Folder: Georgia Governors' Papers, Milledge, John, 1805, UGa. The fourteen signatories were Ed White, Wm Sponer, Josiah Goteax, T. Robertson, John Johnston, Haney Fisher, Daniel Johnston, William Pinder, Th. Miller, James Biggs, John Miller, M. Whitely, R. M. Limon, and John Hellon.

17. Chatham County, Tax Digest, 1806, GDAH. T. Robertson paid 31.5 cents, Henry Fisher paid 85 cents, and John Miller paid $1.12.5. This digest does not list the number of slaves owned.

18. *RoD,* 1:48, August 27, 1806.

19. Ed. White was a mate on the *Alfred;* Josiah Goteax was a clerk at a store with "no relations or property in America"; Hendrick Fisher was a mariner living in Yamacraw; Daniel Johnston was a cigar maker living in Oglethorpe ward; James Beggs was a shopkeeper (*RoD,* 2:38, 5, 55, 4:71, 79).

20. Josiah Goteax, *RoD,* 2:5, April 8, 1808.

21. For detailed work on the various workers associations, see Gillespie, "Artisans and Mechanics."

22. Between 1795 and 1865, thirty-nine white people were prosecuted, of whom nineteen were convicted and either jailed or fined, whereas between 1813 and 1827 (the only dates for which evidence survives), only three African Americans were prosecuted. The prosecutions of whites were listed in Chatham County, Superior Court, Minutes, 1795–1865, GDAH, and the Savannah Police Department, Jail Register, 1809–15, 1855–60, GHS; Savannah Mayor's Recorders Court, 1858–60, GHS. Trials of African Americans were listed in Chatham County, Inferior Court, Trial Docket, 1813–27, GDAH.

23. Under the 1770 slave code bondspeople could be executed for any serious physical assault on a white person. See *An act for ordering and governing slaves within this province, and for establishing a jurisdiction for the trial of offenses committed by such slaves, and other persons therein mentioned, and to prevent the inveighing and carrying away slaves from their masters, owners, or employers,* passed May 10, 1770, sec. XXXIII, Prince, ed., *Digest,* 781. See also Wood, "'Until He Shall Be Dead, Dead, Dead.'"

24. Case of Samuel Patterson, Chatham County Superior Court, Minutes, January Term 1821, vol. 10, 1818–22, Testimony of Joel Chilterden, GDAH.

25. Ibid., Testimony of Daniel Coyle.

26. Ibid., Testimony of Joel Chilterden.

27. Ibid., Testimony of Justice Russel.

28. On Southern honor, see, for example, Ayers, *Vengeance and Justice,* 9–14; Wyatt-Brown, *Southern Honor,* 165–66, 234–47, 272–99.

29. Central Register of Convicts, GDAH. Patterson was admitted on January 26, 1821, and released January 26, 1822.

30. Daniel Coyle died at the age of thirty-two on October 7, 1822. His death record listed his occupation as a shopkeeper and his nativity as Ireland (*RoD,* 4:137). Owen O'Rourke, another Irish immigrant, escaped with a $10 fine after conviction for "assault and battery upon a Negro," but his "indecorous conduct" in court led the judge to double the fine (*Daily Georgian,* February 9, 1826). O'Rourke was from Sligo in Ireland, having arrived in New York at the age of fourteen in 1820 (Chatham County, Aliens' Declarations, 1824, GDAH).

31. The Chatham County Grand Jury believed that "the frequent infractions of the public peace" were often caused by "persons who have sought and received an asylum in this county from the tyrannick government of their own" (Chatham County, Superior Court, Minutes, April Term 1808, vol. 7, 1804–8, GDAH).

32. Box 3, Folder 2, 1811–15A-1, Charleston District, Court of General Sessions, Bills of Indictment, SCDAH.

33. William Clements was convicted of murder in 1795 and died in 1809 (Chatham County, Superior Court, Minutes, August Term 1795, vol. 3, 1793–96; *RoD,* 2:71, October 24, 1809). John Gabriel was convicted of assault in 1830 and died in 1845 (Chatham County, Superior Court, Minutes, January Term 1830, vol. 12, 1826–36, GDAH; *RoD,* 5:230, October 29, 1845).

34. Chatham County, Superior Court, Minutes, August Term 1795, vol. 3, 1793–96, GDAH. A similar sentence was inflicted on Henry Johnston, convicted of murdering a slave in 1792 (Liberty County, Superior Court, Minutes, July 21, 1792, GDAH).

35. Entries for November 6, 1814, December 16, 1809, Savannah Police Department, Jail Register, 1809–15, GHS. Stilwell died in 1818 and was described as a carpenter. Ventres's child died in 1805, when he was overseer to George Millen (*RoD,* 3:211, 1:30). John Sykes was dismissed from his position as overseer on the public roads after killing one of the slaves in his care (CCM, June 2, 16, 22, 1831).

36. Chatham County, Superior Court, Minutes, April Term 1806, vol. 7, 1804–8, GDAH; *RoD,* 1:44, March 29, 1806.

37. See Penal Code, 1833, sec. 298, Prince, ed., *Digest,* 656–57.

38. Morris, *Southern Slavery,* 161–81. One visitor to the lowcountry was told that this had actually happened, but no evidence remains to substantiate the claim (Adams, *South Side View of Slavery,* 17).

39. State v. T. F. Hall, Chatham County, Criminal Testimony, January Term 1824, Testimony of Philip Ashton, GDAH.

40. Ibid., Testimony of Mrs. Ann Catherine Harris.

41. Report in the *Savannah Republican,* February 7, 1825. Hall did not escape punishment altogether. Only a few days after being released from jail, Hall, together with an accomplice, Samuel Ellsworth, was arrested for theft. At Hall's second trial during the same session of Chatham County Superior Court, both he and Ellsworth received lengthy prison sentences (Central Register of Convicts, GDAH). Hall was sentenced to eighteen

years in jail on July 3, 1825. He was released early on July 3, 1835. Ellsworth received a sentence of sixteen years and was released in 1834.

42. Chatham County, Superior Court, Minutes, May Term 1853, vol. 21, 1853–55, GDAH; Chatham County, Criminal Testimony, 1851–61, GDAH. Wilson arrived at the penitentiary on February 12, 1854, and was released on July 19, 1857 (Central Register of Convicts, GDAH; City of Savannah, Tax Digest, 1849–53, GDAH).

43. Wyatt-Brown, *Southern Honor*, 165–66, 234–47, 272–99.

44. Case of Levi Cobb, Chatham County, Criminal Testimony, November Term 1826, GDAH; Central Register of Convicts, GDAH. Cobb was sentenced to four years' imprisonment on December 8, 1826. He escaped on August 8, 1828, and was not recaptured although a $50 reward was offered (*Daily Georgian*, August 16, 1828).

45. Case of Levi Cobb, Chatham County, Criminal Testimony, November Term 1826, Testimony of William C. Barton, GDAH.

46. For a full account of paternalism, see Genovese, *Roll, Jordan, Roll*, 1–89.

47. For more on the application of criminal law on African Americans, see Wood, "'Until He Shall Be Dead, Dead, Dead'"; Hindus, "Black Justice Under White Law"; Schafer, *Slavery, the Civil Law, and the Supreme Court of Louisiana*, 58–89; Morris, *Southern Slavery*.

48. Entry for December 16, 1814, Savannah Police Department, Jail Register, 1809–15, GHS; Chatham County, Inferior Court, Trial Docket, December 16, 1814, GDAH.

49. *RoD*, 3:111, December 26, 1814.

50. Entries for December 8, 1814, May 10, 1815, Savannah Police Department, Jail Register, 1809–15, GHS.

51. Liberty County, Superior Court, Minutes, December Term 1851, April and November Terms 1852, GDAH.

52. *Daily Morning News*, March 4, 7, 9, 1861. Brady's age (forty-one), occupation, and nativity are given in *1860 Census of Chatham County*, 32.

53. Entry for February 25, 1824, Chatham County, Inferior Court, Trial Docket, 1813–27, GDAH.

54. Box 4, Folder 5, 1815–21A-1, Charleston District, Court of General Sessions, Bills of Indictment, SCDAH.

55. Penal Code, 1833, sec. XI. Prince, ed., *Digest*, 620–21. Thomas Morris makes the point that throughout the South the judicial treatment of slaves accused of harming white people varied according to the circumstances of each case (*Southern Slavery*, 289–99).

56. Lewis's Trial, Box 71, Folder—Georgia Slavery Trials, Cuyler Collection, UGa.

57. James McCabe was born in Ireland and died in Savannah at the age of sixty-three on March 15, 1807, still employed as customs house officer. He left "no property in Savannah" (*RoD*, 2:4).

58. Lewis's Trial, Testimony of John Habersham Esq., October 2, 1795, Cuyler Collection, UGa; Bolster, *Black Jacks*, 45–67.

59. Box 43, Folder—Georgia Governors' Papers, Mathews, George, June 1, 1795–December 29, 1795, October 10, 1795, Cuyler Collection, UGa.

60. William Wallace to George Mathews, October 10, 1795, ibid.

61. Thomas Cumming to George Mathews, October 14, 1795, ibid.

62. George Woodruff to George Mathews, October 10, 1795, ibid.

63. In 1827 the solicitor general of Chatham County complained that he found it difficult to collect his usual fees from defendants "as most of the criminals for trial in the Superior Court are paupers" (*Daily Georgian,* January 8, 1828). See also Spindel, *Crime and Society in North Carolina,* esp. chaps. 3 and 6, and Spindel, "Administration of Criminal Justice in North Carolina"; Morgan, *Slave Counterpoint,* 302–4; Genovese, "'Rather Be a Nigger Than a Poor White Man,'" 89.

64. In 1817 only 26 (6%) of the 410 free blacks enumerated in the Savannah Register of Free People of Color owned more than one house or owned slaves. Forty-two (10%) owned their own house or lot, and the other 344 (84%) possessed no real property (Register of Free People of Color 1817, GHS). There were obvious exceptions to this generalization; for example, William Ellison, a free black in South Carolina, owned more than seventy slaves (Koger, *Black Slaveowners,* 1–18).

65. Lichtenstein, "That Disposition to Theft," 417–28. Some historians believe that nonelite whites shared this moral economy (Fronsman, *Common Whites,* 74–75; Bolton, *Poor Whites,* 60).

66. Murray, *Letters from the United States,* 225, Letter XIX, Hopeton, Altamaha, February 14, 1855. See also Harden, *Recollections,* 45–46.

67. The State v. Henry E. Forsyth, Chatham County, Superior Court, Criminal Testimony, 1837–40, GDAH. Isaac Morell was a cabinetmaker in Savannah. See also Lockley, "Partners in Crime," 57–58, 61–63.

68. Chatham County, Superior Court, Minutes, May 14, 25, 1838, June 15, 1838, v. 14, 1836–39, GDAH; Central Register of Convicts, GDAH. Forsyth was prisoner No. 690. The criminal code of 1833 stated that the theft of money from the house of another was punishable by a sentence of one to four years in prison (Penal Code, 1833, sec. 131. Prince, ed., *Digest,* 631).

69. The State v. Henry E. Forsyth, Chatham County, Superior Court, Criminal Testimony, 1837–40, Testimonies of Thomas J. Walsh and Henry H. Bogardus, GDAH; Central Register of Convicts, GDAH. On his release from prison in 1841, Forsyth returned to Savannah, where he married Mary Ann Green in 1842. Significantly, though, he never paid tax in Savannah despite still being resident in Chatham County at the time of his second marriage to seventeen-year-old Margaret Fennel in 1855. In 1856 he spent four days in the Chatham County jail for jumping bail. Forsyth was not listed in either the 1837 or 1844 Tax Digests (City of Savannah, Tax Digest, 1837, 1844 [there are no extant tax digests for Savannah or Chatham County between 1837 and 1842], GDAH; *Marriages in Chatham County,* 1:130, April 19, 1842, 2:23, dated July 10, 1855). Margaret Forsyth died at the age of fifty on November 28, 1889 (*General Index to the Keeper's Record Books at Laurel Grove Cemetery;* Entry for June 26, 1856, Savannah Police Department, Jail Register, 1855–60, GHS).

70. City of Savannah, Tax Digest, 1837, GDAH.

71. The State v. Henry E. Forsyth, Chatham County, Superior Court, Criminal Testimony, 1837–40, Testimony of Isaac W. Morell and of Thomas J. Walsh, GDAH.

72. *Savannah Republican,* January 26, 1819; Morgan, *Slave Counterpoint,* 302–4.

73. Case 1811–22A-3, Box 3, Folder 1, Charleston District, Court of General Sessions, Bills of Indictment, SCDAH.

74. Chatham County, Criminal Testimony, January Term 1858, GDAH.

75. *Daily Georgian,* September 7, 1822.

76. *An act to amend the law prohibiting slaves from selling certain articles without license,* passed December 20, 1824, *Records of the States of the United States,* Georgia Laws 1813–25, microfilm, University of Cambridge Library.

77. Martin, ed., "New Englander's Impressions of Georgia," 260.

78. Rules and Directions for my Thorn Island Plantation #31, June 11, 1832, Box 5, Folder 51, Item 209, Telfair Papers, GHS.

79. K. Washington Skinner to Charles Manigault, June 6, 1852, in Clifton, *Life and Labor on Argyle Island,* 99.

80. Chatham County, Superior Court Minutes, April Term 1826, vols. 12–13, 1826–36, GDAH.

81. *Daily Georgian,* June 7, 1826. Williams had been fined $5 for "entertaining Negroes" in 1820 (CCM, December 18, 1820).

82. *Daily Georgian,* June 7, 1826, statements of John M. Gugel, John D. McLean, and Richard Gorham.

83. Statements of James Morrison, John Haupt, William Davis, and William Adams, ibid.

84. William Williams was originally acquitted of charges "for buying or receiving from a Negro slave or slaves to the jurors unknown the property of the company of Georgia without a ticket." The charge was then changed to "buying or receiving stolen goods knowing the same to be stolen as and for a misdemeanour." This indictment was quashed, but he was reindicted "for buying or receiving stolen goods knowing the same to have been stolen of and from certain evil disposed person or persons to the jurors unknown." The jury eventually found him not guilty (Chatham County, Superior Court, Minutes, November Term 1826, vols. 12–13, 1826–36, GDAH).

85. Grimes, "Life," 75.

86. Chatham County, Superior Court Minutes, 1782–1865, GDAH. Convictions were obtained against George Jennings (January Term 1824), Elizabeth Dobson (April Term 1826), James A. King (December Term 1827), and Hiram Withington (January Term 1846).

87. For example, the case of Catherine Ann Harris involved Thomas Hall and Samuel Ellsworth, two white men, whose case was reported in the *Savannah Republican,* February 7, 1825. Further evidence was given in Chatham County, Superior Court, Criminal Testimony, January Term 1825, GDAH. Harris was eventually acquitted.

88. Chatham County, Superior Court, Minutes, October Term 1796, vol. 4, 1796–99, GDAH; CCM, December 8, 1795, January 19, 1796. See also the cases of Elias Roberts indicted for receiving stolen goods, January Term 1805, who was fined $40 for retailing liquors without license (CCM, February 11, 1805); Edward Quinn indicted for receiving stolen goods, April Term 1806, who was fined $2 for retailing liquors without license (CCM, January 30, 1806); William Williams, indicted for receiving stolen goods, November Term 1826, who was fined $5 for entertaining Negroes on Sunday (CCM, December 18, 1820).

89. Chatham County Superior Court, Minutes, May Term 1842, vol. 16, 1841–43, GDAH; CCM, June 25, 1835–September 19, 1844.

90. Central Register of Convicts, GDAH. King was admitted on February 2, 1828,

and released on February 2, 1832. Four other individuals have been identified in the Savannah Tax Digests, Elias Roberts, Edward Quinn, Ebenezer Parker, and William Williams. Only William Williams owned slaves, and he was acquitted.

91. Chatham County, Superior Court, Minutes, April Term 1826, vols. 12–13, 1826–36, GDAH. The governor later remitted her fine (*Daily Georgian*, May 12, 1826).

92. For a more thorough account of the gender relations between poorer white men and women, see McCurry, *Masters of Small Worlds*, 7–19, 72–88, 117–25, 130–34, 181–98, 218–33.

93. Wood and Wood, eds., "Reuben King Journal," 49, Entry for September 8, 1802; Wood, *Black Majority*, 212–17.

94. Box 71, Folder—Georgia Slavery Trials and Box 43, Folder—Georgia Governors' Papers, Irwin, Jared Petitions: January 21, 1797–May 31, 1797, Cuyler Collection, UGa. In 1794 William Moubray paid tax on buildings worth £200 and on stock in trade worth £100. At that time he owned no slaves, though during the trial he testified that his own slaves had helped him recover some of the items taken during the theft (Camden County, Tax Digest, 1794, GDAH).

95. Box 42, Folder—Georgia Governor's Papers, Telfair, Edward, Petitions, January 1, 1792–June 30, 1792, Cuyler Collection, UGa.

96. Ibid.; Chatham County Tax Digest, 1793, GDAH. Sir George Houstoun owned 60 slaves, James Mossman 127 slaves, and Francis Courvoisie 32 slaves.

97. Memorial of sundry wharf owners and residents of the city of Charleston, General Assembly Papers, 0010 003 ND 01895, SCDAH.

98. *Daily Georgian*, June 8, 1825. See also the letter of "Honestus," ibid., December 23, 1820.

99. Chatham County, Superior Court, Minutes, May Term 1841, vol. 16, 1841–43; May Term 1851, vol. 20, 1850–53, GDAH.

100. *Rules and Regulations of the Savannah River Anti–Slave Traffick Association* (N.p., 1846).

101. Chatham County, Superior Court, Minutes, May Term 1845, vol. 18, 1845–47, GDAH.

102. Liberty County, Superior Court, Minutes, December Term 1841, 1822–59, GDAH.

103. Ball, *Fifty Years in Chains*, 308–13. Some planters trapped shopkeepers by giving their slaves cotton to sell and then prosecuting those who purchased it. See Catterall ed., *Judicial Cases Concerning American Slavery*, 40; McCurry, *Masters of Small Worlds*, 118.

104. *An act for the better regulation of boats and boats' crews*, passed December 4, 1815, Prince, ed., *Digest*, 142; Bolster, *Black Jacks*, 17.

105. *An act to prevent boat-owners or patroons from permitting boat-hands, or other Negroes, from trafficking in corn, or other produce, or from carrying the same to market, on board of the boats accustomed to navigate the river Savannah, between Augusta and Savannah,* passed December 13, 1816, ibid., 142–43.

106. Presentment of Georgetown District Grand Jury, November 2, 1818, General Assembly Papers, 0010 015 1818 00007, SCDAH.

107. Kemble, *Journal*, 25; Bolster, *Black Jacks*, 7–43.

108. Kemble, *Journal*, 64.

109. Presentment of Georgetown District Grand Jury, Fall 1823, General Assembly Papers, 0010 015 1823 00014, SCDAH.

110. Presentment of Georgetown District Grand Jury, Spring 1823, General Assembly Papers, 0010 015 1823 00012, SCDAH.

111. Chatham County, Superior Court, Minutes, May Term 1851, vol. 20, 1850–53, GDAH. This presentment was made after the Chamber of Commerce made a formal complaint to the Savannah City Council about the "serious deficiency" of the contents of cotton bags left on the city wharves (CCM, April 24, 1851).

112. Chatham County, Superior Court, Minutes, May Term 1845, vol. 18, 1845–47, GDAH. Bryan County officials found it difficult to muster enough white men to carry out patrol duty. See Bryan County, Superior Court, Minutes, April Term 1838, GDAH.

113. Chatham County, Superior Court, Minutes, May Term 1851, vol. 20, 1850–53, GDAH.

114. Ibid., 1855, vol. 21, 1853–55, GDAH.

115. Ibid., January Term 1860, vol. 22, 1859–62, GDAH.

116. Chatham County, Superior Court, Criminal Testimony, 1824–26, GDAH.

117. Testimony of John Gardner, ibid.

118. Testimony of Mrs. Bailly, ibid.

119. Central Register of Convicts, GDAH.

120. *An act for establishing and regulating patrols,* passed July 28, 1757, *Col. Recs.,* 18:225–35, esp. 232–33; *An act for ordering and governing slaves with this province, and for establishing a jurisdiction for the trial of offenses committed by such slaves, and other persons therein mentioned, and to prevent the inveigling and carrying away slaves from the masters, owners or employers,* passed May 10, 1770, sec. XXIX, Prince, ed., *Digest,* 783.

121. Of 292 runaways, 64 (22%) were believed to be harbored (*Georgia Gazette,* 1763–70, abstracted by Windley, *Runaway Slave Advertisements).* For a comprehensive discussion of black runaways in the colonial period, see Wood, *Slavery in Colonial Georgia,* 169–87.

122. *Georgia Gazette,* July 12, 1764. See also advertisement of George Hipp, who believed that his slave Frank had been taken by "three white men" (ibid., April 18, 1765).

123. Ibid., July 20, 1768; Bolster, *Black Jacks,* 191.

124. *Georgia Gazette,* July 13, 1774.

125. Mrs. Deveaux believed that Flora was taken off "in Capt. Lewelling's vessel or concealed in the Georgia Packet." The *Hannibal,* Captain Josiah Lewelling, left Savannah for Jamaica on April 24; the *Georgia Packet,* Captain George Anderson, was bound for London (ibid., April 26, May 24, 1775).

126. Sixty-five (46.1%) of 141 runaways were believed to be harbored.

127. Wood, *Slavery in Colonial Georgia,* 178–81. Some fugitives did survive in the more remote parts of the lowcountry. In the 1780s a band of fugitive slaves living in swamps in the Savannah River necessitated joint action by the militias of Georgia and South Carolina. See Proclamation of Edward Telfair December 1, 1786, Proclamation Book AAA 1782–1823, GDAH; Thomas Pinckney to President and Members of Senate,

March 19, 1787, Joakim Hartstone to Senate, Purrysburgh, March 15, 1787, Governor's Messages, Roll 2, 1786–88, 0010 006 0423 00000, Report of the Joint Committee of Both Houses, March 19, 1787, 0010 004 1787 00020, SCDAH; Governor of South Carolina (Thomas Pinckney) to the Governor of Georgia (George Mathews), April 2, 1787, James Gunn to General (James) Jackson, May 6, 1787, (James) Jackson to his Excellency the Governor of South Carolina, 1787, James Jackson to his Honor the Governor of Georgia 1787, Folder 10, Items 83–87, Bevan Papers, GHS; "The trial of a negro man slave named Lewis the property of Oliver Brown esqr for the murder of John Casper Herman, robbing Philip Ilmer, John Lowerman of Georgia and Col Bouquin of South Carolina this 21st May 1787," Box 71, Folder—Georgia Slavery Trials, Cuyler Collection, UGa. Similarly, in 1829 the sheriff of Chatham County captured seven fugitive slaves in a camp "a few miles from town" (*Daily Georgian*, April 18, 1829). See also Wood, "'Until He Shall Be Dead, Dead, Dead.'" For more on maroon communities, see Richard Price, ed., *Maroon Societies: Rebel Slave Communities in the Americas* (New York, 1973), and Gad Heuman, ed., *Out of the House of Bondage: Runaways, Resistance and Marronage in Africa and the New World* (London, 1986).

128. See advertisements for Celia, "harbored by some of her mulatto acquaintances"; for Sally, harbored by her mother in Yamacraw; and for Bella, gone to her husband on the White Bluff road, *Daily Georgian*, January 8, February 22, 1825, August 22, 1826.

129. Ibid., June 25, 1825; see also June 25, 1826.

130. Ibid., March 13, 1827; see also May 11, 1827.

131. Only 5 (14.2%) female fugitives were listed with an occupation, compared to 26 (24.5%) males.

132. For female fugitives working out, see *Daily Georgian*, January 24, 1823, January 8, 1825, August 31, 1826, March 13, 1827, August 14, 1828. Jane, a slave from Liberty County, managed to convince a white Savannah woman to employ her as a chambermaid by claiming that her master permitted her to hire her own time in the city. No prosecution followed her recapture because her owner acknowledged that it was common for Savannahians to hire slaves without proper documentation. Jane was later sold (Charles C. Jones to Rev. C. C. Jones, October 1, 1856, and Rev. C. C. Jones to Mrs. Mary Jones, December 10, 1856, in Myers, ed., *Children of Pride*, 240–42, 270).

133. Nine (34.6%) of 26 male fugitives with occupations named were involved in boat making. See also Haunton, "Law and Order in Savannah," 9; Wood, *Women's Work, Men's Work*, 101–21.

134. Boney, ed., *Slave Life in Georgia*, 85–86.

135. Savannah Police Department, Jail Register, August 19, 20, 1856, GHS. David Bunker believed that his slave John Francis was harbored by other slaves on the bluff (*Daily Georgian*, December 23, 1825).

136. These holes can still be seen today in the basement of the church.

137. Box 44, Folder—Georgia Governor's Papers, Jackson, James, January 1, 1799–June 29, 1799, Cuyler Collection, UGa.

138. Testimony of Asa Hartford and Testimony of Phillis, ibid.

139. *Daily Georgian*, January 11, February 26, 1822.

140. Ibid.; Central Register of Convicts, GDAH. Champlain was released on February 26, 1824. See also Bolster, *Black Jacks*, 190–219.

141. For a similar argument relating to Virginia, see Schwarz, *Slave Laws in Virginia,* 135–45.

142. *Columbian Museum and Savannah Advertiser,* September 1, 1814. On sympathy, see Harris, *Plain Folk and Gentry,* 90–93.

143. *McIntosh County Herald, and Darien Commercial Register,* April 30, 1839. The sheriff also noted that Green was a notorious cattle thief.

144. Out of 141 fugitives, 20 (14.1%) were believed to have passes, 18 men and 2 women. Fugitives Frederick, Charles, and Pleasant were known to have written their own passes (*Daily Georgian,* October 6, 1825, February 26, April 15, 1829). Bondsman Wallace was given thirty lashes for giving a ticket to a slave illegally (CCM, September 20, 1847).

145. *Columbian Museum and Savannah Advertiser,* February 3, 1797.

146. Ibid., February 10, 1797.

147. *Georgia Gazette,* January 1, 1789; see also the advertisement for Jacob and Tim, who were "helped off by a waggoner," *Daily Georgian,* February 25, 1829.

148. Boney, ed., *Slave Life in Georgia,* 64.

149. *Columbian Museum and Savannah Advertiser,* Tuesday, September (illeg.) 1807.

150. Both crimes were punishable by four to ten years in prison (Prince, ed., *Digest,* 630, Penal Code, 1833, secs. 134 and 135).

151. Craft, *Running a Thousand Miles for Freedom,* 31.

152. Roper, *Narrative,* 71–72.

153. These figures were taken from Chatham County, Superior Court, Minutes, 1782–1860. Twenty-three of the forty cases were heard before 1810. Of the forty cases, only five resulted in a conviction.

154. Savannah Police Department, Jail Register, 1809–15, 1855–60, GHS.

155. Central Register of Convicts, GDAH. Allen Davis stole several slaves who were working out on hire making turpentine boxes in Wayne County. After bringing them to Savannah, Davis told several people they were his slaves and that he was fleeing a "false execution" against him. Davis was arrested and charged only after one of the slaves informed the city jailer that they had been stolen (Chatham County, Criminal Testimony, January Term 1860, GDAH).

156. Chatham County, Superior Court, Minutes, September 11, 1793, vol. 3, 1793–96, GDAH.

157. McCurry, *Masters of Small Worlds,* 121–22.

158. Camden County, Tax Digest, 1819, GDAH. Tapley Tullis owned 140 acres of pine land and one slave, paying 73 cents in tax. Cotton Ralls (*sic*) owned no land but eight slaves paying a total of $2.81¼ in tax. They lived in the same tax district of Camden County.

159. *An Act for ordering and governing slaves within this province, and for establishing a jurisdiction for the trial of offenses committed by such slaves, and other persons therein mentioned, and to prevent the inveigling and carrying away slaves from the masters, owners or employers,* passed May 10, 1770, Prince, ed., *Digest,* 782, sec. XXIV.

160. Camden County, Superior Court, Minutes, October Term 1821, GDAH; Central Register of Convicts, GDAH. Tullis served from November 12, 1821, to November 13, 1825.

161. Camden County, Tax Digest, 1819, GDAH; Federal Manuscript Census, Camden County, 1820. The census listed Tullis's household as consisting of a boy under age ten, a girl between ten and sixteen (presumably his children), a man in his twenties (presumably Tullis), a slightly older women (presumably his wife), and another woman over forty-five years old (perhaps his or his wife's mother).

162. In the Federal Manuscript Census of 1820 John Rawls (*sic*) was listed as having three children (two boys and a girl) but no wife. He himself was over forty-five. In 1820 he owned four slaves, a young boy under ten, an adolescent boy, an older man (perhaps Mingo), and a young girl. In 1819 he had paid tax on eight slaves.

163. Richard Francis Paper, USC.

164. See also the case mentioned in the *Darien Gazette,* November 11, 1820, when one white person caught in the "act of kidnapping" confessed that there was "a company of gentlemen in the same profession in the adjoining counties."

165. Camden County, Superior Court, Minutes, 1797–1809, March 10, 1797, GDAH. The three were William Talley, Francis Sterling, and David Mizell. Mizell owned 102 acres of pine barren in 1809 (Camden County, Tax Digests, 1794, 1809, GDAH). Talley and Sterling were listed in the 1794 digest, Mizell in the 1809 digest. There are no other digests for Camden County extant for this period.

166. The State v. John D. Roche, Chatham County, Superior Court, Criminal Testimony, 1837–40, GDAH.

167. Central Register of Convicts, GDAH. Roche was prisoner No. 754. Roche was released eight months early on October 20, 1843. Section 134 of the 1833 Penal Code stipulated a sentence of four to ten years for this crime. It is certainly possible that Roche's comparatively light sentence and early release were owing to the weakness of the case against him. See Prince, ed., *Digest,* 630. John Roche was born in Ireland, professed his trade as a rum seller, and was aged twenty-six at the time of his confinement. It was not the first time that he had been in trouble. As a young boy, Roche had twice been fined $5 by the City Council of Savannah for retailing liquor without a license, most likely to bondspeople visiting the Sunday market in Savannah. His youthful experience with the law evidently did not dissuade him from partaking in further criminal activity with African Americans. See CCM, September 19, 1822, September 18, 1823.

168. Penal Code of 1833, Sixth Division, secs. XX and XXI, Prince, ed., *Digest,* 630.

169. Central Register of Convicts, GDAH. The average term for stealing a Negro was 1,760 days. The longest sentence was that of twelve years given to John Fitzgerald on February 2, 1828, but he was also convicted of rape of an eighteen-year-old woman. He escaped from the penitentiary in 1831 (*Daily Georgian,* November 30, December 12, 1827, January 15, 1828). More common was the sentence of four years given to Mr. Grady for inducing slaves to escape with him to Boston (Grady v. State, February 1852, Catterall, ed., *Judicial Cases Concerning American Slavery,* 31).

170. Governor's Messages, 1783–85, November 12, 1783, 0010 005 0332 00021, SCDAH. Eleven years later the *Georgia Gazette,* October 17, 1793, reported that "on the 4th instant as hanged at Charleston,—Powell for stealing a Negro."

171. See, for example, the removal of slaves from Noble Wimberly Jones's plantation, Minutes of the Board of Police, January 28, 1779, Telfair Papers, GHS.

172. Sixty-eight advertisements for runaways appear in the *Royal Georgia Gazette* in 1781, listing 235 runaways. This represents 11% of ads and 20% of fugitives between 1763 and 1790 (Windley, *Runaway Slave Advertisements*). See also protests of the Royal Grand Jury, *Royal Georgia Gazette*, January 18, 1781.

173. File Group II 4-2-46: Box 7, Chatham: Folder, Grand Jury, October 3, 1782, GDAH.

174. Johnston, "Participation of White Men in Virginia Negro Insurrections," 160; *Savannah Journal and Courier*, June 20, 1855.

175. For example, $8.37½ was paid in jail fees for imprisoning Binah for fifty-nine days, dated October 9, 1812, Box 2, Folder 23: R. M. Stites Personal Accounts, Negro Records, 1805–13, Item 11, Anderson Papers, GHS.

176. Grand Jury Presentments in *Daily Georgian,* June 8, 1825. The Grand Jury advocated the establishment of a treadmill to make the slaves work harder, but such a treadmill was not constructed until 1847 (CCM, June 24, 1847).

177. *An act for regulating a work-house, for the custody and punishment of Negroes,* passed April 7, 1763, *Col. Recs.*, 18:558–66. There were an average of fifteen advertisements per year for captured slaves in the *Georgia Gazette* between 1763 and 1776. See Wood, "Prisons, Workhouses, and the Control of Slave Labor," 253.

178. *An act for regulating a work-house, for the custody and punishment of Negroes,* passed April 7, 1763, *Col. Recs.*, 18:565.

179. Burke, *Pleasure and Pain,* 13.

180. Wood, "Prisons, Workhouses, and the Control of Slave Labor," 249, 261–62. Roughly two-thirds of African American inmates stayed less than a week in the Savannah jail between 1809 and 1815 (Savannah Police Department, Jail Register, 1809–15, GHS).

181. Bibb, *Narrative*, 94–95.

182. *Darien Gazette*, October 3, 1822.

183. *Georgia Gazette,* July 26, 1769; see also ibid., January 5, 1774. For details of white jailbreaks, see *Georgia Gazette*, November 9, 1768, January 17, 1799; *Darien Gazette*, June 28, 1819, June 16, October 20, 1821.

184. Chatham County, Superior Court, Minutes, October Term 1787, vol. 1, 1782–89, GDAH; *Georgia Gazette*, October 18, 1787.

185. Box 24, Folder: Chatham County 1, February 15, 1790, Cuyler Collection, UGa. The five men involved were Justus Hartman Scheuber, William Lewden, Peter Karr, Frederick Fahm, and John Shick. See also Grand Jury presentments in the *Georgia Gazette,* August 4, 1791, and *Columbian Museum and Savannah Advertiser,* October 21, 1796, April 23, 1799.

186. See the escapes of "Bush, Blankinsop and one other," CCM, March 10, 1817. See also CCM, August 18, 1836, August 20, 1838.

187. Chatham County, Superior Court, Minutes, April Term 1826, vols. 12–13, 1826–36, GDAH. That this was true is shown by the escape of nine slaves from the jail in 1828 (*Daily Georgian,* February 28, 1828). Other lowcountry jails were equally insecure. Bryan County jail was described as being "insufficient to hold a New England rogue" (Herman Stebbins to Eliza Diggins, October 23, 1815, Stebbins Papers, DU).

188. Liberty County, Superior Court, Minutes, December Term 1831, GDAH.

189. In 1796 the City Council resolved to repair the "white jail," but work was not started on the new jail until 1801 and completed a year later (CCM, January 19, 1796; August 29, 1801, June 30, 1802).

190. Presentments of the Georgia Grand Jury, Journal of the Commons House of Assembly, January 26, 1763, *Col. Recs.*, 14:8.

191. Savannah Police Department, Jail Register, 1809–15, GHS. Of 459 white inmates in this period, only 11 (2.3%) were women. Of 3,050 African American inmates, 682 (22.3%) were women (Wood, "Prisons, Workhouses, and the Control of Slave Labor," 261–62). In the 1830s and 1840s black prisoners continued to outnumber whites. See CCM, March 8, 1832, August 6, September 9, October 1, 1835, August 18, September 1, December 8, 1836, January 5, May 11, 1837, October 11, 1838, July 8, 1839, July 2, 1840, April 7, 1842.

192. Narrative of Adam Hodgson in Lane, ed., *Rambler in Georgia*, 56.

193. See, for example, CCM, January 5, October 11, 1837. Jeffrey Bolster has shown that restrictions on free blacks in Georgia were imposed in 1830 following the publication of David Walker's *Appeal to the Colored Citizens of the World*. As a result, the proportion of free blacks serving on ships docking in Savannah fell from 15% in 1830 to 2% in 1836 (*Black Jacks*, 194–213). For a good discussion of the importance of David Walker, see Peter P. Hinks, *To Awaken My Afflicted Brethren: David Walker and the Problem of Antebellum Slave Resistance* (University Park, Pa., 1997).

194. CCM, May 5, 1835. The committee recommended that many prisoners should be held until they sobered up and then released. For another description of the jail, see Olmstead, "Savannah in the '40s," 244.

195. CCM, November 27, 1856.

196. Chatham County, Superior Court, Minutes, January Term 1855, vol. 21, 1853–55, GDAH. This was in violation of the jail rules, which stated that the sexes should be segregated (CCM, September 27, 1838).

197. CCM, November 27, 1856. How long this situation continued is debatable. In 1858 the mayor reported that 549 prisoners had been jailed in the previous twelve months: 286 whites and 263 blacks. In 1860 comparable figures were 483 whites and 257 blacks, for a total of 740 (*Report of Thomas M. Turner*, 28. *Report of R. D. Arnold*, 34).

198. Johnston, "Participation of White Men," 161.

199. See, for example, Maurice A. Crouse, "Papers of Gabriel Manigault, 1771–1784," *South Carolina Historical Magazine* 64 (1963): 2, and Harris, *Plain Folk and Gentry*, 56. In 1860 a nonslaveholder was arrested in McIntosh County on suspicion of inciting a slave revolt (Mohr, *On the Threshold of Freedom*, 33).

200. Council Records, February 2, 1748/9, in Merrens, *Colonial South Carolina Scene*, 166. On this particular occasion the application for freedom was refused, pending further inquiries.

201. Burke, *Pleasure and Pain*, 53.

202. Chatham County, Superior Court, Minutes, January Term 1857, vol. 22, 1855–57, GDAH.

203. M. Richardson to James Proctor Screven, Ser. 2.1.2, Folder 34, Arnold-Screven Papers, SHC.

204. Confession of John the slave of Mr. Enslow the Cooper, 1822, Ravenel Papers, 1807–23, SCHS.

205. Report in *Daily Georgian*, November 27, 1822. For an excellent work on the Vesey plot, including many original sources, see Edward A. Pearson, *Designs Against Charleston: The Trial Records of the Denmark Vesey Slave Conspiracy of 1822* (Chapel Hill, 1999).

206. *Savannah Republican*, December 25, 1856.

207. CCM, December 5, 1859. This was the main thrust of Daniel Hundley's perception of shopkeepers in *Social Relations in Our Southern States*, 193–239.

5. PRAYING TOGETHER

1. The best explorations of biraciality are Boles, "Slaves in Biracial Protestant Churches"; Frey, "Shaking the Dry Bones"; Owen, *Sacred Flame*, 19–22, 82–88; Frey and Wood, *Come Shouting to Zion*, 118–41, 176–92.

2. Bartholomew Zouberbuhler to Benjamin Martyn, December 20, 1750, CO 5/643, 98, microfilm, GDAH. See also Henry Thompson Malone, *The Episcopal Church in Georgia* (Atlanta, 1960), 26; and Hoskins, *Black Episcopalians in Savannah*, 9. The first baptized African American communicant in Savannah was a "Negroe woman" (Bartholomew Zouberbuhler to the Society for the Propagation of the Gospel, December 20, 1750, Box 5, Folder 108, Correspondence, Christ Church Savannah Records, GHS).

3. Only one list of the members of Christ Church exists from the colonial period, in the form of a record of pew holders between 1763 and 1767. Of 60 individuals renting pews, 25 (41.6%) professed an artisan occupation, 32 (53.3%) described themselves as merchants or esquires, and 3 (5%) were widows. According to wills left by these members, 12 (20%) were nonslaveholders, and 9 (15%) were slaveholders. The list is located in Colonial Book S, Conveyances, 1766–69, 38–47. Those identified as slaveholders or non-slaveholders were found in Colonial Books A and AA, Wills, GDAH. See also Corbin, "First List of Pew-Holders of Christ-Church."

4. Wood, *Slavery in Colonial Georgia*, 114–15, 161–65; Raboteau, *Slave Religion*, 98–103; Pierre, "Work of the Society for the Propagation of the Gospel in Foreign Parts"; Vibert, "Society for the Propagation of the Gospel in Foreign Parts," 186.

5. Ottolenghe to the SPG, October 4, 1759, Box 5, Folder 109, Christ Church Savannah Records, GHS; Ottolenghe to John Waring, November 19, 1753, in Van Horne, ed., *Religious Philanthropy*, 111; Wood, *Black Majority*, 133–42.

6. Minutes of the SPG, vol. 14, August 15, 1760, and Ottolenghe to the SPG, October 4, 1759, Box 5, Folder 109, Christ Church Savannah Records, GHS;. Wood, *Slavery in Colonial Georgia*, 161–62.

7. Minutes of the Trustees, March 21, 1750, *Col. Recs.*, 33:489 (unpublished, GDAH). More would be known about Ottolenghe's activities teaching the slaves but for the fact that many of his personal papers were lost in the Savannah fire of 1759 which destroyed the filature, and many of his letters from the late 1750s never arrived in England. See Ottolenghe to the SPG, October 4, 1759, Box 5, Folder 109, Christ Church Savannah Records, GHS.

8. Bartholomew Zouberbuhler to Benjamin Martyn, December 20, 1750, CO 5/643, 98.

9. Joseph Ottolenghe to the Board of Trade, September 11, 1753, CO 5/644, 63. Ottolenghe later confirmed that he had designed his new house expressly "to have more room for the instruction of white and black" (Ottolenghe to John Waring, November 19, 1753, in Van Horne, ed., *Religious Philanthropy,* 113).

10. Joseph Ottolenghe to Samuel Smith, December 4, 1751, ibid., 104–6.

11. Joseph Ottolenghe to John Waring, November 19, 1753, ibid., 113.

12. Joseph Ottolenghe to John Waring, July 12, 1758, ibid., 128.

13. Minutes of the SPG, October 18, 1771, vol. 19, Box 5, Folder 110, Christ Church Savannah Records, GHS. The actual figures were as follows: Anglican, 180 families, 664 men, 521 blacks, total 1,185; Lutherans, 35 families, 134 men, 59 blacks, total 193; Presbyterians 92 families, 327 men, 172 blacks, total 499; Jews, 6 families, 27 men, 22 blacks, total 49; no religion, 11 families, 23 men, 7 blacks, total 30. Sylvia Frey and Betty Wood argue that many Africans in the eighteenth century chose to reject Christianity in favor of their traditional beliefs (*Come Shouting to Zion,* 63–79).

14. This church had migrated as a complete unit from Dorchester in South Carolina shortly after the institution of royal government in Georgia and had its first black members, Scipio and Judy, by mid-1756 (Records of the Midway Congregational Church, June 26, 1756, vol. 1, typewritten copies of the originals, GHS).

15. Betty Wood has established that these particular South Carolina immigrants brought with them more than fifteen hundred bondspeople, strongly suggesting that the black members of the church were the property of the white members (*Slavery in Colonial Georgia,* 92).

16. Osgood, *Letter of Prudent Advice,* 5, Evans Bibliography of Early American Imprints, Microprint 10115, University of Cambridge Library.

17. Osgood, *Letter of Prudent Advice,* 8. Osgood's attitude toward slavery did not prevent him owning slaves himself. At his death in 1773, he left ten slaves to his wife, Mary, as well as substantial amounts of other property (*Abstracts of Colonial Wills,* 103–4).

18. Hawkins, *Historical Notices,* 104.

19. On the problems finding white preachers, see William Donaldson and John Moore to the Bishop of London, March 30, September 17, 1762, Correspondence, vol. 2, microfilm reel 2, Fulham Papers at Lambeth Palace Library, University of Cambridge Library; James Habersham to William Knox, November 26, 1770, Habersham to Rev. Thomas Broughton, December 1, 1770, December 10, 1770, Habersham to the Countess of Huntingdon, April 19, 1775. On the problems of David, see Habersham to the Countess of Huntingdon, April 19, 1775, and Habersham to Robert Keen, May 11, 1775, all in Habersham, "Letters," 95–96, 99–102, 102–9, 238–43, 243–44. See also Frey and Wood, *Come Shouting to Zion,* 112–13, and the several letters of William Piercy to the Countess of Huntingdon in the American Papers of the Countess of Huntingdon, Westminster College, University of Cambridge.

20. On the history of the First African Baptist Church in Savannah, see Simms, *First Colored Baptist Church;* Love, *History of the First African Baptist Church;* and Thomas, *First African Baptist Church.*

21. *Sketches of the Black Baptist Church at Savannah, in Georgia, and of Their Minister Andrew Bryan, Extracted from Several Letters,* Savannah, July 19, 1790, in "Letters Showing the Rise and Progress of the Early Negro Churches of Georgia and the West Indies," *Journal of Negro History* 1 (1916): 77. See also Presentments of the Grand Jury, Chatham County, Superior Court, Minutes, October Term 1788, vol. 1, 1782–89, GDAH, and Little, "George Leile," 193.

22. Jonathan Clarke to John Rippon, December 22, 1792, in Gardner, "Primary Sources," 99–100.

23. Jonathan Clarke to John Rippon, December 22, 1792, in "Letters Showing the Rise and Progress of the Early Negro Churches," 83.

24. Andrew Bryan to Jonathan Rippon, December 23, 1800, ibid., 87.

25. Holcombe, *First Fruits,* 61.

26. Members of the First Baptist Church, 1800–1830, La Far Papers, GHS. Peter Robert was described as a shopkeeper when he defaulted in the 1798 tax digest (Telfair Papers, GHS). Elizabeth Stone (formerly Clubb) was named as the widow of Thomas Clubb, a carpenter from Glynn County, in *Early Deaths in Savannah,* 149. Elias Roberts was named as a justice of the peace in the death record of his wife, Mary (who was also a member of the church), May 18, 1815 (*RoD,* 3:117). Eunice Hogg owned ten slaves, according to the 1793 tax digest for Chatham County, one of whom, Kate, had been one of the first Africans baptized in Savannah in the 1770s and was subsequently freed (Chatham County Tax Digest, 1793, GDAH); see also Jones, *Religious Instruction of the Negroes,* 50; *Georgia Analytical Repository* 1 (September–October 1802): 185–88.

27. Members of the First Baptist Church, 1800–1830, La Far Papers, GHS. Ten of the first fifteen members of the First Baptist Church were women. Of four who died in Savannah, their average age on joining the church was fifty-seven. See death records of Rachel Hamilton, Martha Stephens, Mary Roberts, and Eunice Hogg in *RoD,* 2:62, 3:61, 117, 129.

28. White, *Historical Collections,* 316. The couples were Henry and Frances Holcombe, George and Phoebe Moore, Elias and Mary Roberts, and Joseph and Mary Hawthorne. The first members of the First Baptist Church had previously belonged to South Carolina Baptist churches at Charleston, Black-Swamp, Sandy-Hill, and Euhaw. Mary Jones, "venerable relict of the late Lieutenant Governor Jones," was the first white Savannahian immersed by Holcombe (*Georgia Analytical Repository* 1 [September–October 1802]: 179).

29. See Presentments of the Grand Jury, Chatham County; CCM, March 4, 1794. See also *Georgia Gazette,* October 18, 1787, October 23, December 11, 1788, September 6, 1792. Similar restrictions operated in St. Marys; see St. Marys Town Council Minutes, July 24, 1843, July 11, August 26, 1844, GDAH.

30. "The Petition of Sundry of the Citizens humbly sheweth," quoted in Simms, *First Colored Baptist Church,* 26–29. As early as 1788 Andrew Bryan reported 225 full members and 350 "converted followers" who did not have their owners' permission to attend services ("Letters Showing the Rise and Progress of the Early Negro Churches," 79).

31. Permission for Andrew and his society to preach on Sundays, March 19, 1790, quoted in Simms, *First Colored Baptist Church,* 46–50. Although the religious affiliation of most signatories cannot be determined, Thomas F. Williams later became a member of

the First Baptist Church and Mordecai Sheftall was a leading member of the Michaeve Israel Synagogue.

32. Similar problems were encountered during the establishment of the African Methodist Episcopal Church in Charleston in the 1810s. See Petition of the African Methodist Episcopal Church in Charleston, ca. 1815, General Assembly Papers, 0010 003 ND 01893, SCDAH.

33. Morgan J. Rees to Richard Furman, February 7, 1795 in Gardner, "Primary Sources," 109. In 1794 the City Council rejected a petition from Andrew Bryan to open his chapel in St. Gall (CCM, June 27, 1794).

34. Henry Kollock was pastor of the Independent Presbyterian Church, and his meetings for bondspeople could go on until 10 P.M. See the account of William Grimes, "Life," 95. In 1810 the City Council instructed that all religious meetings held at night were to be prohibited because they "have been found to be productive of no good purpose." Similar restrictions were repeated in 1825 (CCM, April 13, 1810, September 15, November 1, 1825).

35. The three were Ebenezer Hills, John Millene, and Dr. Moses Vollaton, each of whom had signed the 1790 petition giving their slaves permission to attend services (*Sketches of the Black Baptist Church at Savannah in Georgia,* in "Letters Showing the Rise and Progress of the Early Negro Churches," 80).

36. Morgan J. Rees to Richard Furman, February 7, 1795, in Gardner, "Primary Sources," 105.

37. Holcombe, *First Fruits,* 115–16.

38. Simms, *First Colored Baptist Church,* 51; Thomas, *First African Baptist Church,* 38. David Fox died at the age of thirty-four in 1799 at his home in Little Ogechee "after a long and painful illness, which he bore with Christian fortitude" (*Early Deaths in Savannah,* 107, December 10, 1799). William Matthew was a member of the First Baptist Church from October 10, 1802, until 1805, when he received a letter of dismissal.

39. David Fox possessed no slaves while Josiah Fox owned seven slaves in 1793. William Matthew possessed ten slaves in 1793 but was registered as a nonslaveholding carpenter in the list of defaulters in 1798 (Chatham County, Tax Digest, 1793, 1798, GDAH; Telfair Papers, 1798, GHS). Thomas Polhill was not listed in either digest.

40. By 1800 as many as one in ten African Americans in Chatham County were Baptists. The stated reports of full members to the Baptist Associations continuously understated the real number of members at African churches, most likely making a distinction between those with and those without permission to attend (Frey, "'The Year of Jubilee Has Come,'" 97).

41. When trying to convert plantation slaves in the 1840s, Charles Colcock Jones argued that using black preachers was most effective method (Jones, *Suggestions on the Religious Instruction of the Negroes,* 18–19; *10th Annual Report of the Society for the Religious Instruction of the Negroes in Liberty County, Georgia,* 6–9). See also Frey, "Shaking the Dry Bones," 25–29; Frey, "'The Year of Jubilee Has Come,'" 116; Boles, "Slaves in Biracial Protestant Churches," 95; Raboteau, *Slave Religion,* 255.

42. Gardner et al., *History of the Georgia Baptist Association,* 33.

43. Georgia Baptist Association, Minutes, October 18, 1788, October 16, 1790,

October 19, 1793, MU. The official membership of the church was 198 in 1788, 250 in 1790, and 381 in 1793. Andrew Bryan reported a much higher total of 575 attendees in 1788, and, according to the Chatham County Grand Jury, "five and six hundred" bonds-people attended the church in 1794 ("Letters Showing the Rise and Progress of the Early Negro Churches," 79; Chatham County, Superior Court, Minutes, January Term 1794, vol. 3, 1793–96, GDAH). In 1803 the Savannah River Baptist Association reported that First African had 400 members; three years previously Bryan had informally counted more than 700 (SRBAM, 1803); Letter from the Negro Baptist church in Savannah, addressed to the Reverend Doctor Rippon, Savannah, December 23, 1800, in "Letters Showing the Rise and Progress of the Early Negro Churches," 86. William Capers noticed that many slaves from South Carolina preferred the African churches in Savannah to their own white Baptist churches (Box 22, Folder 306, p. 217, Waring Papers, GHS).

44. Chatham County Deed Book G, 215, GDAH; Thomas, *First African Baptist Church,* 37; Holcombe, *First Fruits,* 115–16. Eight of the thirty-one deacons to represent an African congregation at Baptist Association meetings were also free (SRBAM; SBAM, 1803–1830; Register of Free People of Color, GHS; *Daily Georgian,* March 10, 1828). One historian argues that the example set by free African Americans in running the First African Baptist Church was an important role model for enslaved city residents (Johnson, *Black Savannah,* 25).

45. Diary of Mrs. Smith from Newburyport, Massachusetts, March 17, 1793, DU.

46. Diary of Mrs. Smith, March 24, 1793, DU. In 1812 the First Baptist Church recorded similar occurrences when baptisms in the Savannah River were attended by a "great number of the members of this and of our sister churches," as well as a "large concourse of people" (First Baptist Church Minutes, April 19, July 19, 1812, MU; Love, *History of the First African Baptist Church,* 217). Mary was apparently aged 117 at the time of this recollection. Bull Island is about fifteen miles from Savannah by sea. After the construction of the Ogeechee Canal in the late 1830s, it was also used for baptisms by the African churches (Harden, *Recollections,* 38).

47. Diary of Mrs. Smith, March 24, April 14, 1793, DU. For similar descriptions, see Bodichon, *American Diary,* 125, March 7, 1857; Bremer, *Homes of the New World,* 360–63.

48. First Baptist Church, Minutes, August 9, 1812, MU; Holcombe, *First Fruits,* 115–16; Bryant, *Letters of a Traveller,* 95. When the Negro cemetery in Savannah was built on in the antebellum period, Bryan's was one of the few graves to be moved to the new site at Laurel Grove. In 1856 Andrew Marshall's funeral was attended by "an immense throng, without respect to color or condition" (*Savannah Republican,* December 15, 1856. See also Bodichon, *American Diary,* 119, February 28, 1857). William Harden recalled that Marshall "had the confidence and respect of all the white people of Savannah" (*Recollections,* 32).

49. SBAM, November 11, 1825. Andrew Marshall was pastor at the First African Baptist Church between 1812 and 1856.

50. Lyell, *Second Visit,* 2:2–3. John Hale remarked that the afternoon sermon he heard from Andrew Marshall one Sunday was far better than the one he had heard that morning in the Independent Presbyterian Church (Hale Family Paper, GHS).

51. Apart from the First African Baptist Church, African American Baptists attended the Second African Church (founded 1802), the Great Ogechee Colored Church (1803), Abercorn African Church (1820), White Bluff African Church (1820), Third African Church (1832), Darien Baptist Church (1834), Drakey African Church (1836), Wilmington African Church, (1836), White Oak African Church (1840), Oakland African Church (1846), St. Mary's African Church (1846 as a branch of Second African), St. Catherine's African Church (1846), Cumberland African Church (1847), Skidaway African Church (1848 as a branch of White Bluff), Clifton African Church (1849), and Bethlehem African Church (1860). See SRBAM, 1803–17; SBAM, 1818–60.

52. SRBAM, November 24–27, 1804. Henry Holcombe and John Goldwire were pastors at the First Baptist and Newington churches respectively.

53. SRBAM, November 16–18, 1805.

54. SRBAM, November 21, 1812.

55. First Baptist Church Minutes, August 9, 1812, MU. This was not the first time Holcombe had done this. In 1802 he had helped Andrew Bryan in the ordination of Henry Francis by giving "a solemn charge to faithfulness" while the "imposition of hands was made by Andrew Bryan" (Georgia Analytical Repository 1 [May–June, 1802]: 22).

56. SRBAM, November 27, 1813. This is presumably a reference to fears of a repeat of the tactic used by the British during the Revolution promising slaves freedom if they fought on the British side.

57. See Sobel, Trabelin' On, 357–62.

58. SBAM, 1818; only 64 (2.4%) of the 2,774 founding members of this association were white.

59. SRBAM, October 25, 1817.

60. SBAM, 1832, 1837; First Baptist Church Minutes, December 24, 1832, January 4, July 22, 1833, MU; Johnson, Black Savannah, 28–31; Raboteau, Slave Religion, 189–94.

61. The peak was in 1831 when 94.5% of lowcountry Baptists were black; throughout the 1850s and until the dissolution of the association in 1866 an average of 90% of Baptists were black (SBAM, 1818–64.) Baptists in South Carolina were also predominantly black (SRBAM, 1830).

62. In 1803 he was appointed to this position (First Baptist Church, Membership Roll, April 1802, MU).

63. First Baptist Church Minutes, May 24, 31, 1805, MU. This committee investigated the behavior of two African American women, one of whom was later expelled. The personal association of Cunningham with white members of the First Baptist Church clearly influenced his choice of guardian following his emancipation. Originally a lawyer, James Morrison, had acted as his legal representative, but in 1820 he was replaced by a member of the First Baptist Church, Josiah Penfield (Register of Free People of Color, 1817, 1823, GHS; Chatham County, Court of Ordinary, Inferior Court, Issue Docket, 1812–23, List of Guardians, 1820, GDAH). Josiah Penfield was a member of the First Baptist Church between July 17, 1818, and his death in 1829 (First Baptist Church Membership Records, MU). Guardians did not always share a denominational affiliation with their wards. Andrew Bryan's guardian, the Presbyterian lawyer Richard M. Stites, was not a Baptist. See Bryan's tax return filed by Stites in 1806, Chatham County Tax Digest, 1806, and the Communion Roll of the Independent Presbyterian Church, 1808, GHS.

64. The four were Richard Houstoun, Charlotte Wall, Jackson Lloyd, and Hetty Lloyd (First Baptist Church Minutes, August 9, 1808, MU).

65. First Baptist Church Minutes, January 5, 12, 1816, MU. Shave was restored on June 16, 1816. Shave had joined the church on April 21, 1811, and died on July 31, 1817. Thomas Williams joined on April 19, 1807, and, according to Mabel La Far, was expelled on July 5, 1817, though this is not noted in the minutes (First Baptist Church Membership Records, La Far Papers, GHS). Aaron Samuel Shave married Mary Ihly in 1808, but he does not appear in other civic records (*Marriages in Chatham County,* 1:181, August 8, 1808). Thomas F. Williams married Sarah Hills in 1798; she also became a member of the First Baptist Church. Their son died at his father's plantation in 1805 (*Marriages in Chatham County,* 1:45, April 27, 1798; *RoD,* 1:36, October 16, 1805). See also Wood, "'For Their Satisfaction or Redress,'" 109–23; Mathews, *Religion in the Old South,* 70–72.

66. Two individuals had their rents refunded in 1808, Healy and Lambert, who rented gallery pews 13 and 14 and paid rents of $8 and $12 respectively. It is possible that these people were free African Americans, Charles Haley and Delia Limbert, who were registered as free blacks living in the city in 1817 (Book 18, Pew Sales, November 26, 1807, Independent Presbyterian Church Records, GHS; Register of Free People of Color, 1817, GHS).

67. Trustees Minutes Book, January 23, 1808, Independent Presbyterian Church Records, GHS. See also Owen, "By Design," 230–31; Frey and Wood, *Come Shouting to Zion,* 179; Owen, *Sacred Flame,* 20, 70–72, 80–81.

68. Book 18, Pew Sales, November 26, 1807, Independent Presbyterian Church Records, GHS; Chatham County, Tax Digest, 1806, GDAH. Those who rented large pews and who were listed in the 1806 tax digest paid an average tax of $61. Comparable figures for small pews and gallery pews were $24 and $19 respectively. Those paying any of these amounts would have counted among the top quarter of taxpayers in Chatham County at the time. Pew renting was a common fund-raising method for lowcountry churches. See advertisements for Christ Church Episcopal, *Georgia Gazette,* April 21, 1791, April 11, 1793, December 18, 1794. For Independent Presbyterian Church, see *Georgia Gazette,* March 19, 1801; *Columbian Museum and Savannah Advertiser,* March 4, 1803. For First Baptist Church, see *Columbian Museum and Savannah Advertiser,* July 5, 1799, March 21, August 15, 1800; *Daily Savannah Republican,* January 4, 1820. In 1824 the First Baptist Church set its pews at $30, $25, and $15, the latter being "end pews" (Minutes, March 6, 1824, GHS).

69. Advertisement for Christ Church pews, *Daily Georgian,* December 23, 1827. It was for this reason that the Methodist church abolished pew renting in 1820 (Owen, *Sacred Flame,* 19). Only 4 (10.2%) of the 39 pew renters at the Independent Presbyterian Church listed in the 1806 tax digest paid less than $1 in tax. They were Ebenezer Parker, 93.75¢; William Moore and Robert Habersham, both 62.5¢; and Charles Howard, 31.25¢ (Book 18, Pew Sales November 26, 1807, Independent Presbyterian Church Records, GHS; Chatham County, Tax Digest, 1806, GDAH).

70. Quoted in Donald G. Mathews, *Slavery and Methodism: A Chapter in American Morality, 1780–1845* (Princeton, 1965), 295. Methodists would split into a Northern and a Southern conference over the slavery issue in 1844 (Burke, ed., *History of American Methodism,* 47–85; Owen, *Sacred Flame,* 23–24).

71. Stephen Cooke to John Rippon, November 26, 1791, "Letters Showing the Rise and Progress of the Early Negro Churches," 75–76. One such enemy was John Macpherson Berrien, who later became a United States senator. In a letter to the *Georgia Gazette,* Berrien stated that itinerant Methodist preachers in the lowcountry upset "the peace and good order of society" by preaching to slaves who left their work to listen (*Georgia Gazette,* January 27, 1791). For an excellent study of early Southern Methodists and their problem with slavery, see Lyerly, *Methodism and the Southern Mind,* esp. pp. 47–72, 119–45.

72. Minutes of the Annual Conference of the Methodist Episcopal Church, 1773–1851, Emory University; White, *Historical Collections of Georgia,* 306–7. The membership of the Methodist church in Savannah during the 1790s peaked in 1791 with 323 white members and 4 black. See also Andrew, "Rise and Progress of Methodism in Charleston," 22.

73. Of the five members, three were white and two black. See also Godley, *Centennial Story of Trinity Methodist Church,* 14–17. The Methodist congregation had been officially incorporated in 1802; see the Petition of the Methodist Congregation in Savannah, February 15, 1802, Box 45, Folder—Georgia Governors' Papers, Josiah Tattnall Jr., December 10, 1801–May 4, 1802, Cuyler Collection, UGa; Clark, Potts, and Ryan, eds., *Journals and Letters of Francis Asbury,* 2:746.

74. December 14, 1820, G. F. Greene Paper, GHS.

75. Life of William Capers, Box 22, Folder 306, pp. 211, 215–16, Waring Papers, GHS. See also Bowden, *History of Savannah Methodism,* 45–57. This was also true in upcountry South Carolina. See Ford, *Origins of Southern Radicalism,* 22–32.

76. Quoted in Mathews, *Slavery and Methodism,* 301–2. According to Christopher Owen, it was a deliberate policy of Methodists to separate sacred and secular matters (*Sacred Flame,* 33–40).

77. Loveland, *Southern Evangelicals,* 188–94; Gallay, "Planters and Slaves in the Great Awakening," 35–36.

78. By 1816 more than four thousand African American Methodists lived in the South Carolina lowcountry, mainly in Charleston and Georgetown (Andrew, "Rise and Progress of Methodism," 18, 22).

79. James Osgood Andrew to the editor of the *Southern Intelligencer,* January 21, 1822, reprinted in the *Columbian Star,* February 16, 1822. This claim is given substance by the annual reports to the Georgia Conference by the Savannah church. In 1821 it enumerated 56 whites and 110 blacks. By 1822 these numbers had grown to 143 whites and 174 blacks, an increase of 151 (Owen, *Sacred Flame,* 29).

80. In 1810 from a total population of 33,692 there were 159 Methodists in the lowcountry (0.4%). By 1830 from a population 38,642, 1,141 (2.9%) people were members of Methodist churches. Comparable figures for Baptist churches were, for 1810, 4,031 people (11.9%) and, for 1830, 6,834 (17.6%) (Minutes of the Annual Conference of the Methodist Episcopal Church, 1773–1851, Emory University; figures for 1811 and 1829 are the most complete; SRBAM, 1810; SBAM; Piedmont Baptist Association Minutes, 1829, available on microfilm at Mercer University).

81. Trinity Methodist Episcopal Church, Quarterly Conference Minutes, 1846–69, GHS. See entries for April 20, September 21, 1846, April 24, 1847; Bowden, *History of*

Savannah Methodism, 73. In contrast to Baptist churches, black members of Andrew Chapel had to make do with white preachers (Johnson, *Black Savannah,* 15).

82. Apparently a similar relationship developed in St. Mary's Catholic Church in Charleston between French émigrés and African Americans from San Domingo. See Moffat and Carrière, eds., "A Frenchman Visits Charleston," 139. Ira Berlin argues that throughout the South, free African Americans belonged to Catholic and Episcopal churches in far greater numbers than did bondspeople ("Structure of the Free Negro Caste," 112). See also Miller, "Failed Mission," 37–54; Shoemaker, "Strangers and Citizens," 202–12. The only monograph on black Catholicism totally ignores the biracial interactions in St. John's before the Civil War; see Gary Wray McDonogh, *Black and Catholic in Savannah, Georgia* (Knoxville, Tenn., 1993), 26–36.

83. The four men were Mr. Thomasson, Mr. Perrier, Mr. Jean Baptist du Bergier, and Joseph Joly. See St. John the Baptist Catholic Church, Savannah. Parish Register, 1796– 1816, GDAH, entry for August 30, 1804. See also marriages on June 23, 1808, April 20, 1809.

84. For examples of white people acting as godparents for African American children see entries for March 8, 31, 1808, July 20, September 23, 1808, January 10, 1811, January 12, 1812, January 6, 1816, ibid.

85. Ibid., February 5, 1805.

86. See the Sacramental Register, February 12, 1828, September 3, 1831, October 27, 1833, January 19, November 5, 1834, Church of St. John the Baptist, 1816–1838, Catholic Pastoral Center; Box 27, Folder 408, Hartridge Collection, GHS; Baptisms at St. John the Baptist, August 10, July 17, 1843, April 15, 1844, ibid.

87. Burke, *Pleasure and Pain,* 49. See also the description of the Macedonia Baptist Church in Harn, "Old Canoochee-Ogeechee Chronicles," 51. At Midway, baptisms of black and white were usually undertaken together (Mallard, *Montevideo-Maybank,* 54). See also Rousey, "From Whence They Came to Savannah," 334–335.

88. Clark, Potts, and Ryan, eds., *Journals and Letters of Francis Asbury,* 2:43, February 25, 1795.

89. Wood, *Slavery in Colonial Georgia,* 159–65; Wood, *Women's Work, Men's Work,* 160–76; Frey, *Water from the Rock,* 241–325; Frey and Wood, *Come Shouting to Zion,* 123–24, 143, 172–74.

90. Clark, Potts, and Ryan, eds., *Journal and Letters of Francis Asbury,* 1:593, March 1, 1789.

91. Bremer, *Homes of the New World,* 297.

92. Rules and directions for my Thorn island plantation, June 11, 1832, Box 5, Folder 51, Item 209, Rule 13, Telfair Papers, GHS.

93. Kemble, *Journal,* 66–67. On the same plantation in 1804 the overseers organized dances for the slaves on Sundays to deter them from going to church (Bell, *Major Butler's Legacy,* 150–51). See also Harn, "Old Canoochee-Ogeechee Chronicles," 148.

94. Narrative of George Lewis in Lane, ed., *Rambler in Georgia,* 181.

95. In 1826 the First African Baptist Church held services at 7 P.M. on Saturdays, presumably to enable members to worship and trade during the same visit (*Daily Georgian,* March 28, 1826).

96. On the dilemma African Americans had over how to spend their Sundays, see

Wood, "'Never on a Sunday?,'" 79–96. Edward Thomas recalled that slaves on his parents' South Newport River plantation in Liberty County both went to church and engaged in informal economic activity on Sundays (*Memoirs of a Southerner*, 9). Charles Parsons, in contrast, believed that slaves were usually too drunk on Saturdays and Sundays to attend church (*Inside View of Slavery*, 194–95).

97. Evans, ed., *Journal*, 7. In 1819 the Savannah marshal was instructed by the City Council to arrest all African American children "acting in a noisy and tumultuous manner" on the Sabbath (*Daily Savannah Republican*, October 15, 1819; Chatham County, Superior Court, Minutes, January Term 1802, vol. 5, 1799–1804; January Term 1808, April Term 1808, vol. 7, 1804–8; January Term 1819, vol. 10, 1818–22, GDAH).

98. This estimate was obtained by cross-referencing the returns of the churches made to their respective associations with the federal census. In 1820 10,733 African Americans resided in Chatham County. Of those, 3,449 (32.1%) attended First African Baptist, Second African Baptist, Great Ogechee Baptist, Abercorn Baptist, White Bluff Baptist, Independent Presbyterian Church, or the Methodist church. Figures for Liberty County permit different conclusions to be drawn. Of 5,100 African Americans resident in 1820, 562 (11%) attended Sunbury Baptist, Jones's Creek Baptist, or Liberty and Darien Methodist Churches (SBAM, 1820; Piedmont Baptist Association Minutes, 1820, MU; Record of Members of Jones's Creek Baptist Church, MU; Independent Presbyterian Church Records, GHS; Minutes of the Annual Conference of the Methodist Episcopal Church, 1820–23, Emory University). Nehemiah Adams thought that a third of all slaves attended church (*South Side View of Slavery*. 42). All census statistics were taken from http://fisher.lib .virginia.edu/census in 1999.

99. In 1831 the Sunbury Baptist Association enumerated 6,537 members of the black Baptist churches. The 1830 census of Chatham County counted only 4,409 slaves over the age of twenty-four, whereas there were 13,703 similarly aged slaves in Beaufort District (SBAM, 1831; Wood, "'Never on a Sunday?,'" 90). In 1849 the Euhaw, Beaufort, and St. Helena Baptist churches boasted having 5,000 black members (SRBAM, 1849, 13). In its March 7, 1860, issue the *Savannah Republican* confirmed that only about half the members of the First African Baptist Church lived in the city.

100. Exact figures for 1860 are 6,255 black Baptists, 14,807 slaves (SBAM, 1860).

101. Although only 867 (18.9%) of the 4,569 white people resident in Chatham County in 1820 are listed in the records of the First Baptist Church, Independent Presbyterian Church, and Methodist church, unknown numbers also attended the Lutheran and Episcopal denominations in the city. Of 1,641 white people resident in Liberty County, 182 (11%) were members of Jones's Creek Baptist, Salem Baptist, or Liberty and Darien Methodist Church (SBAM, 1820; Piedmont Baptist Association Minutes, 1820, MU; Record of Members of Jones's Creek Baptist Church, MU [minutes from this church, along with those from Salem and Little Ogechee, are available on microfilm at Mercer University]; Independent Presbyterian Church Records, GHS; Minutes of the Annual Conference of the Methodist Episcopal Church, 1820–23, Emory University). In 1860 there were only 585 white Baptists out of a total white population of 15,511 (SBAM, 1860; Owen, *Sacred Flame*, 85).

102. Mrs. E. H. Steele Paper, April 1, 1830, GHS.

103. Wood, "'For Their Satisfaction or Redress,'" 109–23; Frey and Wood, *Come*

Shouting to Zion, 183–206. On the inclusivity of evangelical churches, see Fronsman, *Common Whites,* 180–85; McCurry, *Masters of Small Worlds,* 158.

104. Independent Presbyterian Church Minutes of Session, June 5, 1830, Book 1, 1828–51, GHS. Equally, if African Americans and white people were cited at the same meeting for the same offense, they often received the same punishment. See, for example, the excommunication of Elizabeth Hurst and Hope for illicit pregnancies (Little Ogechee Baptist Church, Minutes, June 1829, MU).

105. Presentments of Chatham County, Grand Jury, March 2–5, 1784, Record Group 1-1-5, Box 1A, Executive Department, Incoming Correspondence, 1781–1802, GDAH. See also *Georgia Gazette,* January 5, 1774; Owen, *Sacred Flame,* 17, 79.

106. John Lambert observed the effect of a Methodist sermon in a Savannah church in 1808. According to him, the "terrible imprecation upon sinners" was so realistically put across to the congregation that they "were groaning in the most pitiable manner" (Lane, ed., *Rambler in Georgia,* 46). See also Creel, *Peculiar People,* 102, 145–48, 174; Ford, *Origins of Southern Radicalism,* 34.

107. That rural evangelicals were usually the nonelite is attested to by a Scottish exile named William Mylne, who observed that the poor residents of his locality were "mostly all babtists" (Ruddock, ed., *Travels in the Colonies,* 29. See also Mixon, "Georgia," 82–83; Owen, *Sacred Flame,* 15).

108. Darien Presbyterian Church Minutes, December 12, 1831, October 13, 1832, GDAH. See also ibid., May 15, 1844. For more on the civil rights of blacks in antebellum churches, see Sparks, *On Jordan's Stormy Banks,* 132–45.

109. Jones's Creek Baptist Church, Minutes, February 21, 1824, MU. Fanny was later "expelled for whoredom" (ibid., April 24, 1824). For similar cases of citing, see Little Ogechee Baptist Church, May 1811, June 1829, MU; Independent Presbyterian Church Minutes, July 14, 1831, GHS.

110. McCurry, *Masters of Small Worlds,* 141, 160, 171–95; Owen, *Sacred Flame,* 20; Frey and Wood, *Come Shouting to Zion,* 163–66.

111. See, for example, the Rules of the Black Creek Baptist Church, No. 9, 1828, USC.

112. See, for example, Powers Baptist, which "appointed March to look after our color'd brethren" (Powers Baptist Church Record Book, September 23, 1825, GHS; Rules and Regulations of the Colored Ministers, Elders and Members of the Baptist Church in Charleston, July 1819, USC). Jones's Creek Baptist Church established an entirely separate "negro conference" to determine cases of discipline involving slaves.

113. In 1829 the Independent Presbyterian Church accepted three black members of the Midway Church as full members (Independent Presbyterian Church Minutes of Session, Book 1, 1828–51, July 7, August 10, 1829, June 2, 1831. GHS). See also Darien Presbyterian Church Records, March 27, 1824, GDAH.

114. Little Ogechee Baptist Church Minutes, July 1823, MU. See also the letter of dismissal for Brutus, Sally, and Sue written by Adam Dolly, clerk at the First African Church, for them to attend Powers Baptist (loose paper in middle of Powers Baptist Church Record Book, GHS).

115. Boles, "Evangelical Protestantism in the South," 27–28; Owen, *Sacred Flame,* 82.

116. For example, in 1840 only four Baptist churches had been biracial, and the

874 members constituted only 16.4% of the 5,314 black lowcountry Baptists. By 1860 of twenty-seven Baptist churches in the lowcountry, ten were biracial, fourteen were black, and only three were white. The 1,824 black members of biracial churches constituted 32.5% of the 5,607 black lowcountry Baptists (SBAM, 1840, SRBAM, 1860).

117. In other words, Christianity permitted African Americans to retain a significant portion of their African heritage. See Frey, "Shaking the Dry Bones," 31; Frey, *Water from the Rock*, 31; Frey, "'The Year of Jubilee Has Come,'" 124; Frey and Wood, *Come Shouting to Zion*, 118–206. See also Janet Duitsman Cornelius, "'Praying Ground': The Sacred Landscape in the Antebellum Mission in the Lowcountry," paper presented to From Revolution to Revolution: New Directions in Antebellum Lowcountry Studies, 1775–1860, College of Charleston, May 1996, 11–16.

118. Silva, *Early Reminiscence of Camden County*, paper 11; Owen, *Sacred Flame*, 80–81.

119. Owen, "By Design," 226–30; Owen, *Sacred Flame*, 20; Jones's Creek Baptist Church Minutes, July 17, 1839, February 2, 1854, MU; Darien Presbyterian Church Minutes, May 11, 1861, GDAH; Jones, *Tenth Annual Report on the Religious Instruction of the Negroes*, 7.

120. Frey, "Shaking the Dry Bones," 35–42. See also Frey, "'The Year of Jubilee Has Come,'" 112–13; Frey and Wood, *Come Shouting to Zion*, 123–24. When Fredericka Bremer visited a lowcountry camp meeting in the 1850s she observed "a quieter scene among the whites" in comparison to the "great tumult" among African Americans (*Homes of the New World*, 316–17). In contrast, Mary Sharpe Jones was far more familiar with the emotional "shouting" of African American Christianity than some of her slaves, though she did not participate herself (Mary Sharpe Jones to Rev. and Mrs. C. C. Jones, January 2, 1856, in Myers, ed., *Children of Pride*, 181).

121. Plantation Journal for 1858, in Clifton, *Life and Labor on Argyle Island*, 250.

122. Evans, ed., *Journal of the Life, Travels, and Religious Labours of William Savery*, 9. Of 117 male members of the First Baptist Church between 1800 and 1830, 43 were listed in the tax digests of 1806 and 1809–30. Of those 43, 21 (48.8%) were nonslaveholders. Those not listed in city tax digests may have lacked property to be taxed on or were resident in South Carolina.

123. Thirty-one of the eighty-seven members of Jones's Creek between 1810 and 1830 were identified in parallel sources. Of the thirty-one, twenty-five (80.6%) were nonslaveholders, and six (19.4%) were slaveholders (listed in Parker, *History of Jones's Creek Baptist Church*, 75–114). This account is not complete as it included only white members. See Liberty County Tax Digests, 1812–15, 1830, GDAH. Long County was originally part of Liberty County.

124. Quoted in Sobel, *Trabelin' On*, 360. In 1845, Charles Colcock Jones stated that he expressly fought for all members, black and white, to attend the same churches, seeing any other arrangement as allowing white pastors to forget about black members (Jones, *Tenth Annual Report of the Association for the Religious Instruction of the Negroes in Liberty County, Georgia*, 38). See also Clay, *Detail of a Plan*, 9–10.

125. According to Independent Presbyterian Church Records, GHS, 81% of members were black or white women. Similar but less extreme statistics are obtained from other evangelical churches in the lowcountry, for example, Jones's Creek Baptist (67% female),

Powers Baptist (65% female), Darien Presbyterian (62% female), and Georgetown Methodist (58% female).

126. Mathews, *Religion in the Old South,* 102–20; Frey and Wood, *Come Shouting to Zion,* 163–66.

127. See, for example, Midway Congregational Church Minutes, December 21, 1798, GHS; St. Mary's Presbyterian Church Minutes, January 4, 1830, GDAH; Jones's Creek Baptist Church Minutes, October 25, 1834, MU; Salem Baptist Church Minutes, March 19, 1842, MU; First Baptist Church Savannah Minutes, January 27, February 28, 1859, MU. All the delegates to the Baptist Associations were men, as were all the elders of the Darien and Independent Presbyterian churches (SRBAM, 1803–17; SBAM, 1818–64; Darien Presbyterian Church Membership Roll, GDAH; Independent Presbyterian Church Communion Roll, GHS). Men also held all the offices at the African churches in the lowcountry (Frey and Wood, *Come Shouting to Zion,* 166).

128. *By-Laws of the Second Presbyterian Church* (Charleston, 1811), Rule 1, Shaw and Shoemaker Bibliography of Early American Imprints, Microprint No. 23739, University of Cambridge Library. See also *Rules for the Spiritual and Temporal Government of the First Presbyterian Church,* Rules 2, 3, and 14. Frederick Bode makes the point that giving white women any power in church affairs was seen as a threat by white men ("Common Sphere," 783–84, 801).

129. See Bruce, *And They All Sang Hallelujah,* 123–24.

130. Holcombe, *First Fruits,* 59–60.

131. Melish, *Travels.* 44.

132. For an excellent discussion of the significance of discipline councils, see Wood, "For Their Satisfaction or Redress"; McCurry, *Masters of Small Worlds,* 178–95. See also Friedman, *Enclosed Garden,* 78; Cornelius, "Slave Marriages," 128; Frey and Wood, *Come Shouting to Zion,* 183–206.

133. Covenant of the Salem Baptist Church, 1823, MU.

134. Circular Letter, Piedmont Baptist Association Minutes, October 1–12, 1829, MU.

135. First Baptist Church Minutes, July 6, 1822, September 1, 1859, GHS.

136. See the dismissal of Grace for an illegitimate pregnancy, Independent Presbyterian Church Minutes, July 14, 1831, GHS, and the dismissal of a free black woman, Kate Wall, for a similar offense, First Baptist Church Minutes, June 7, 1805, GHS.

137. First Baptist Church Minutes, February 9, March 6, 20, May 15, 1823, GHS.

138. Ann Lillibridge was a member of the church from 1812 until her death in 1838. She lived four miles from Savannah and was accustomed to provide "for travellers and strangers on Sunday" (First Baptist Church Minutes, February 5, March 5, 1825, October 1, December 13, 1830, Membership Records, June 21, 1812, October 1, 1838, GHS). For a similar case, see Trinity Methodist Church, Quarterly Conference Minutes, August 13, 1849, GHS. See also Loveland, *Southern Evangelicals,* 136.

139. For example, Willis Spears approached the Little Ogechee church to inquire how he should recover a debt from another member (Little Ogechee Baptist Church Minutes, June 1805, MU). See also ibid., August 1814, when Sister Vauters was examined by the church for failing to make a tax return.

140. First Baptist Church Minutes, February 16, 21, 28, 1812, GHS. For a similar

case, see Independent Presbyterian Church Minutes, May 21, 1849, November 24, 1853, GHS. Most churches had some connections with charitable institutions, for example, the Sisters of Mercy were attached to the Catholic church, and there was an orphanage associated with the Episcopal Church.

141. Darien Presbyterian Church, Membership Roll, McIntosh County Tax Digest 1825, GDAH. John Kell owned sixty slaves in 1825. The elders of the Independent Presbyterian Church included merchants Moses Cleland and Benjamin Buroughs and the physician John Cumming (Independent Presbyterian Church Communion Roll, GHS).

142. Twenty-five white men were expelled by the First Baptist Church between 1800 and 1830. Of those, seven were nonslaveholders, and three were slaveholders (City of Savannah, Tax Digests, 1806, 1809–30, GDAH). For similar conclusions, see Bode, "Formation of Evangelical Communities in Middle Georgia," 736.

143. See, for examples of men apologizing for their conduct, First Baptist Church Minutes, February 1, 1805, August 15, 1806, GHS; Jones's Creek Baptist Church Minutes, January 26, 1822, December 27, 1823, June 27, 1857, June 22, 1861, MU; Salem Baptist Church Minutes, July 2, 1825, July 1852, MU; St. Mary's Presbyterian Church, July 11, 1851, GDAH.

144. First Baptist Church Minutes, September 2, 12, November 28, 1831, January 23, 1832, GHS. George Ash was a slaveholding merchant and speculator (1860 Census for Chatham County, Georgia).

145. Salem Baptist Church Minutes, August 20, 1843, July 1852, MU.

146. White men constituted 152 (51.5%) and white women 63 (21.3%) of the 295 cases of discipline brought before Midway Congregational Church, First Baptist Church, Little Ogechee Baptist Church, Jones's Creek Baptist Church, Salem Baptist Church, Beaver Dam Baptist Church, Black Creek Baptist Church, Darien Presbyterian Church, and Independent Presbyterian Church. These figures do not include those expelled from the African churches as only raw numbers were reported to the association, with no breakdown by gender or offense (SBAM, 1818–64). For similar conclusions, see Sparks, On Jordan's Stormy Banks, 145–73.

147. Exact figures are white men 85 (55.9%) out of 152 cases, white women 13 (20.6%) out of 63 cases, black men 9 (17.6%) out of 51 cases, and black women no cases. Julia Harn recalled that although "a strong temperance sentiment prevailed in Taylor's Creek, there were some lapses among the men" ("Old Canoochee-Ogeechee Chronicles," 238).

148. Narrative of George Lewis in Lane, ed., Rambler in Georgia, 182. See also Clay, Detail of a Plan, 11.

149. SBAM 1830. In 1831 Second African reported that the membership of its temperance society had increased from 138 to 513. By 1832 the number had risen to 667; additionally, Great Ogeechee church reported a temperance society of more than 300 members (SBAM, 1831, 1832). Thomas Clay reported that his local African Baptist Temperance Society in Bryan County had a membership of more than 400 (Detail of a Plan, 11). See also Savannah Republican, November 26, 1859.

150. First Baptist Church Minutes, October 8, 1832, GHS. How effective this society was is questionable. On April 10, 1852, the Temperance Banner named Savannah as "the head quarters of King Alcohol."

151. Circular Letter, SRBAM, 1816, 8–9. See also the biography of John Rice in the *Georgia Analytical Repository* 1 (May–June 1802): 34.

152. See the resolution of Harmony Presbytery to "deliver public discourses as often as circumstances may render it expedient, on the sin and mischiefs of intemperate drinking" (Minutes of Harmony Presbytery, November 11, 1812, Columbia Theological Seminary). See also First Baptist Church Minutes, October 8, 1832, February 24, 1835, GHS.

153. Exact figures are black men, 17 (33.3%) of 51 cases; black women 15 (51.7%) of 29 cases. These figures do not take into account any African Americans cited for sexual offenses at the African churches, for which we have no evidence. There is, however, evidence that not all of the offenses of bondspeople actually reached the discipline councils of larger biracial urban churches. In 1819, the Charleston Baptist church authorized its African American ministers to examine bondspeople in all except "weighty matters . . . so as to prevent much uneasiness and trouble to the church." See Rules and Regulations of the Colored Ministers, Elders and Members of the Baptist Church in Charleston, South Carolina, USC. In smaller biracial rural churches, however, bondspeople were still brought before white discipline councils.

154. Circular Letter on Practical Godliness, SBAM, November 4, 1826.

155. Letter to Colored Members, Little Ogechee Baptist Church Minutes 1823, MU. In Savannah, the First African church implemented similar regulations. See Covenant of the Anabaptist Church, begun in America, December 1777 and in Jamaica, December 1783, in Gardner, "Primary Sources," 104–5.

156. SRBAM, 1849, 9

157. Of 414 members listed before 1830, 263 (63.6%) shared a surname with another member. For similar conclusions, see McCurry, *Masters of Small Worlds,* 171–77.

158. Exact figures are 26 (41.2%) of 63 cases.

159. First Baptist Church Minutes, June 19, 21, 1812, GHS.

160. Blauvelt, "Women and Revivalism," 1–2. See also Mathews, *Religion in the Old South,* 102; F. Cott, "Passionlessness."

161. Exact figures for expulsions were white men 34%, white women 42%, black men 39%, and black women 41%.

162. White men were forgiven in 27% of cases and black men in 21% of cases, whereas white women were forgiven in only 9% of cases and black women in just 3% of cases. See especially the case of boatman Thomas Eden, who was cited five times over nine years for drunkenness at First Baptist before finally being excommunicated (First Baptist Church Minutes, May 5, 1821, July 6, 1822, February 9, 1824, December 5, 1828, March 12, 1830, GHS). For other cases, see Charles Ulmor, Salem Baptist Church Minutes, July 12, 1823, July 2, 1825, March 4, December 3, 1826, MU; John Peacock, Jones's Creek Baptist Church Minutes, December 27, 1823, May 21, 1825, MU.

163. Minutes of the Congregational Church at Midway, August 26, 1770. Joseph Baker was suspended for "gitting in liquor and abusing his wife." Baker had paid more than £2,000 for 560 acres from his brother Benjamin in 1759 (Colonial Book C-1, Conveyances, 201, April 23, 1759, GDAH). John Goulding was suspended for "suspicion of keeping his own wench and living in adultery with another man's wife." Goulding had been granted 700 acres in St. John's Parish between 1759 and 1767 (Hemperly, *English Crown Grants in St. John Parish,* 46–47). Adley Maxwell was suspended for "unlawfully

keeping his own wench in adultery." Maxwell was a planter who owned substantial property in land and slaves on his death in 1776. In his will he left property to his wife and four sons, though three of his sons evidently had different mothers (*Abstracts of Colonial Wills*, 91–92, November 22, 1776).

164. Little Ogechee Baptist Church Minutes, October 1829, MU.

165. McCurry, *Masters of Small Worlds*, 130–34, 192–93.

166. First Baptist Church Minutes, December 1, 1827, GHS.

167. Cott, "Passionlessness," 220–28.

168. Case of Morning Shepherd, Little Ogechee Baptist Church Minutes, June 1, 1797, MU; Case of Mrs. Jenkinson, First Baptist Church Minutes, May 1, 1829, GHS. Mrs. Jenkinson was most likely the wife of the propertyless G. Jenkinson (City of Savannah, Tax Digest, 1828, GDAH). For similar cases, see Jane Caldwell expelled from Darien Presbyterian Church for fornication, March 6, 1836; Lucy Ann Prescott expelled from Independent Presbyterian for prostitution, April 26, 1843; and Mary Frances Gary suspended from Darien Presbyterian for fornication, January 4, 1858. On the sexual double standards of the South see Wyatt-Brown, *Southern Honor*, 292–324.

169. Independent Presbyterian Church Minutes of Session, September 22, 1828, May 11, 1829, GHS.

170. Report of the Committee of Bills and Overtures, Minutes of the Synod of South Carolina and Georgia, November 17, 1815, Columbia Theological Seminary.

171. Circular Letter, SRBAM, 1816, 11.

172. First Baptist Church, Membership Records, May 21, 1809, GHS. Hannah was most likely married to house carpenter Robert Jordan. He was the only male Jordan resident in Savannah in 1806, and he died on January 7, 1813, aged forty-two, and leaving a widow and a child (City of Savannah, Tax Digest, 1806, GDAH; *RoD*, 3:41). They are not listed in the marriage records of Chatham County.

173. First Baptist Church Minutes, October 12, December 21, 1810, January 11, 1811, GHS. See also the case of Brother and Sister Hutchinson; Brother Hutchinson was suspended after admitting that "he had on one or two occasions slapped her on the face" (First Baptist Church Minutes, April 25, 1836, GHS).

174. McCurry, *Masters of Small Worlds*, 178–95.

175. Circular Letter, SRBAM, November 1807.

176. McCurry, *Masters of Small Worlds*, 171–212.

177. SBAM, 1845, 11–12.

178. Piedmont Baptist Association Minutes, 1852, 5–7, MU.

179. Circular Letter, SRBAM, November 27, 1813, 14.

180. In 1785, Joseph Cook testified that he saw "a shaking among the dry bones" encompassing both whites and blacks in the Euhaw district (Cook to Lady Huntingdon, March 24, 1785, Cook Letters, UGa).

181. Richard Furman to William Rogers, April 22, 1802, USC.

182. Bowden, *History of Savannah Methodism*, 48; Lee, *Short History of the Methodists*, 290; *Charleston City Gazette and Daily Advertiser*, December 10, 1803, quoted in McCurry, *Masters of Small Worlds*, 148. This conclusion is supported by Boles, *Great Revival*, 82.

183. Ramsay, *History of South Carolina*, 2:33, 36; Melish, *Travels*, 43–44. Camp

meetings did eventually become popular in the lowcountry. See Harn, "Old Canoochee-Ogeechee Chronicles," 52, 237–38; Bremer, *Homes of the New World*, 313–25.

184. Lee, *Short History of the Methodists*, 291; Rousey, "From Whence They Came to Savannah," 334–35.

185. *Georgia Analytical Repository* 3 (September–October 1802): 124–28.

186. Ibid. Many churches found it hard to sustain the revival. By 1805 Cowpen Branch Baptist Church was reporting "very few additions" (History of Corinth Baptist Church, 2, Box 1, Folder 10, La Far Papers, GHS).

187. See, for example, the description of two churches in Bryan County as "not quite so magnificent as was Solomon's temple," Herman Stebbins to Eliza Diggins, October 23, 1815, Stebbins Papers, DU.

188. Minutes of the Charleston Baptist Association, October 21, 1818, USC. See also Minutes of the Savannah River Baptist Association, November 23, 1811, when the association agreed to "encourage itinerant preaching (and establish) a missionary fund." Two years later the association appointed Thomas Trowel as its first itinerant priest (SRBAM, November 27, 1813).

189. SBAM, October 21, 1818.

190. SBAM, 1825. The collection for domestic missions amounted to $83.93, with $6 coming from the four African churches. The African churches were not necessarily short of money. In 1832 the First African Baptist Church purchased the building of the First Baptist Church in Savannah for $1,000, with the money presumably coming from congregational donations (Thomas, *First African Baptist Church*, 49; Wood, *Women's Work, Men's Work*, 169–73).

191. Minutes of Harmony Presbytery, April 8, 1811, Columbia Theological Seminary.

192. Ibid., December 23, 1811. Thomas Clay argued that all Christians should "devote at least one evening in the week to visiting the Negroes on the plantations around him, destitute of religious instruction" (*Detail of a Plan*, 6).

193. Minutes of Harmony Presbytery, April 13, 1812, Columbia Theological Seminary. See also ibid., October 30, 1813.

194. George Lewis stated that in Savannah, "the Presbyterian church is doing little for the colored population . . . the Methodist and Baptist seem to have done almost all that has been done" (Narrative of George Lewis in Lane, ed., *Rambler in Georgia*, 183).

195. Journal of the Georgia Conference of Methodists, January 7, 1832, Emory University.

196. Corresponding Letter, SBAM, November 13, 1819; Circular Letter, SBAM, 1820.

197. Corresponding Letter, SBAM, November 8, 1822.

198. Darien Presbyterian Church Minutes, May 12, June 19, 1824, GDAH.

199. SBAM, November 11, 1825.

200. See, for example, Diary of William P. Hill, June 1, July 1, 1846, Hill Papers, SHC. Presbyterian missionaries named Fisk and Storrs stated that between December 1, 1810, and April 5, 1811, they had traveled more than 1,100 miles on their circuit in southern Georgia (Minutes of Harmony Presbytery, April 5, 1811, Columbia Theological Seminary).

201. Hill Diary, May 24, 1846, Hill Papers, SHC. On June 14, 1846, while visiting

the Welsh Neck Baptist Church, Hill "preached for the benefit of the colored congregation, at which time a goodly number of whites attended." Some less scrupulous individuals took advantage of the itinerant preaching system to pose as preachers and collect money for their own uses. See the caution issued by the Annual Conference of the Methodist Episcopal Church in 1793, Emory University.

202. Ramsay, *History of South Carolina,* 2:31–32.

203. Bremer, *Homes of the New World,* 314–15.

204. Report of Messrs. Fisk and Storrs, Minutes of Harmony Presbytery, April 5, 1811, Columbia Theological Seminary.

205. Mary W. Howard to Rev. A. Peters, May 3, July 7, 1828, American Home Missionary Society Papers, Emory University. See also the Constitution of the Domestic Female Missionary Society, Emory University. The twelve directresses were Mrs. Postell (Baptist), Mrs. Anderson (Presbyterian), Mrs. S. Lord (Presbyterian), Mrs. Nicole (Presbyterian), Miss Germaine (Baptist), Miss Robertson (Presbyterian), Mrs. Lloyd, Miss Barrou, Miss M. Howard (Presbyterian), Miss Mears (Presbyterian), Miss Goldwire, and Mrs. L. Roberts (Baptist). The religious affiliation of those not indicated could not be determined, but it is likely that several attended the Methodist church in Savannah. Burke and Screven Counties are between fifty and a hundred miles north of Savannah along the Savannah River.

206. American Home Missionary Society Papers, June 26, 1830, Emory University.

207. Raboteau, *Slave Religion,* 152–80.

208. Jones, *Suggestions on the Religious Instruction,* 28. Despite these restrictions, many owners were unimpressed with the missionary system, especially when missionaries began to talk of the duties of slaveholders rather than the duties of slaves. See Clay, *Detail of a Plan,* 5–8, 12–15; Bryan County, Superior Court, Minutes, December Term 1832, GDAH.

209. Raboteau, *Slave Religion,* 212–88; Frey and Wood, *Come Shouting to Zion,* 64.

210. Silva, *Early Reminiscences,* paper 11; St. Marys Town Council Minutes, July 11, 24, 1843, August 26, 1845, December 14, 1859, GDAH.

211. Jones, *Tenth Annual Report of the Association for the Religious Instruction of the Negroes in Liberty County,* 24.

212. Jones, *Thirteenth Annual Report of the Association for the Religious Instruction of the Negroes,* 21.

213. SBAM, 1845, 1846.

214. SBAM, 1852, 1853. See also Johnson, *Black Savannah,* 33–35.

215. Jones, *Religious Instruction of the Negroes,* 24.

216. Settled Claims, RG 217, Camden County, Georgia, Case 15215 (Furgus Wilson), Southern Claims Commission, GHS.

217. Boles, "Slaves in Biracial Protestant Churches," 104.

218. Boles, "Evangelical Protestantism," 26–28; Loveland, *Southern Evangelicals,* 51–53; Owen, *Sacred Flame,* 82; Frey and Wood, *Come Shouting to Zion,* 176; Morgan, *Slave Counterpoint,* 420–56.

219. See, for example, *Christian Index,* January 30, May 8, 15, 22, 1861. The vocal support of white Baptists was in marked contrast to the muted position of white Method-

ists. See Burke, ed., *History of American Methodism,* 208; Owen, *Sacred Flame,* 70–92. Baptists, like Methodists, had split into Northern and Southern divisions in 1844. See Robert Andrew Baker, *Relations Between Northern and Southern Baptists* (New York, 1980), 66–91; Richard J. Carwardine, *Evangelicals and Politics in Antebellum America* (Knoxville, Tenn., 1997), 153–69. For a discussion of the ultimately unsuccessful attempt to create a biracial Methodist Church in Georgia following the war, see Daniel W. Stowell, "'The Negroes Cannot Navigate Alone': Religious Scalawags and the Biracial Methodist Episcopal Church in Georgia, 1866–1876," in *Georgia in Black and White: Explorations in the Race Relations of the Southern State, 1865–1950,* ed. John C. Inscoe (Athens, 1997).

CONCLUSION

1. Phillips, *American Negro Slavery;* Phillips, "Central Theme of Southern History"; Buck, "Poor Whites," 52; Flynt, *Dixie's Forgotten People,* 11; Roediger, *Wages of Whiteness,* 12.

2. Brown, "Role of Poor Whites," 259; Genovese, *Roll, Jordan, Roll,* 23.

3. Bellows, *Benevolence Among Slaveholders,* 78–79, 108–11; Bolton, *Poor Whites,* 8–9; Ford, *Origins of Southern Radicalism,* 66; Hahn, *Roots of Southern Populism,* 16–17.

4. Griffen, "Poor White Laborers," 28.

5. Bellows, *Benevolence Among Slaveholders,* 161–87.

6. Quoted in Siegel, "Artisans and Immigrants," 229.

7. On lukewarm support for secession among some backcountry areas, see Fronsman, *Common Whites,* 202–17; Bolton, *Poor Whites,* 119–85; Hahn, *Roots of Southern Populism,* 112–16. In contrast, upcountry South Carolina strongly supported secession. See Ford, *Origins of Southern Radicalism,* 338–77. On the importance of independence to nonelite people, see Hahn, "Yeomanry of the Non-Plantation South," 31.

8. William Capers to Louis Manigault, October 21, 1860, in Clifton, *Life and Labor on Argyle Island,* 309.

9. Rev. C. C. Jones to Mrs. Mary S. Mallard, December 12, 1860, in Myers, ed., *Children of Pride,* 634. The misspelling of Father O'Neill's speech by Rev. Jones was intended for comedic effect.

10. All six coastal counties voted for secession in 1861, failing to elect a single co-operationsist delegate to the secession convention (Doyon and Hodler, "Secessionist Sentiment and Slavery," 340, 346).

11. McCurry, *Masters of Small Worlds,* 259–301; Harris, *Plain Folk and Gentry,* 18, 113; Fronsman, *Common Whites,* 185; Loveland, *Southern Evangelicals,* 202. For the success of this strategy, see Gillespie, "World of William Garland."

12. See Mooney, "History of the Legal Regulation of Slave Hire," 56–71; Mohr, *On the Threshold of Freedom,* 6–8.

13. Hodes, "Sex Across the Color Line," 2, 186–87. For an interesting discussion of the postbellum continuation of miscegenation in central Georgia, see Mark R. Schultz,

"Interracial Kinship Ties and the Emergence of a Rural Black Middle Class: Hancock County, Georgia, 1865–1920," in *Georgia in Black and White: Explorations in the Race Relations of the Southern State, 1865–1950*, ed. John C. Inscoe (Athens, 1997), 141–72. See also Hodes, *White Women, Black Men*, 123–208; Bolster, *Black Jacks*, 216–19; Hahn, *Roots of Southern Populism*, 206–16; W. Fitzhugh Brundage, ed., *Under Sentence of Death: Lynching in the South* (Chapel Hill, 1997), 1–20.

BIBLIOGRAPHY

MANUSCRIPT COLLECTIONS

Catholic Pastoral Center, Savannah, Georgia: Sacramental Register, Church of St. John the Baptist, 1816–38

Charleston Library Society, Charleston, South Carolina: James Cumming Receipt; Thomas Elfe Account Book; Charles Fraser Letter; J. B. Grimball Diary

Columbia Theological Seminary, John Bulow Campbell Library, Decatur, Georgia: Minutes of Harmony Presbytery, 1810–55; Minutes of the General Assembly of the Presbyterian Church in the United States of America, 1822; Minutes of the Synod of South Carolina and Georgia, 1813–44

Duke University, Special Collections, Perkins Library, Durham, North Carolina: Anonymous Diary, Savannah, Ga., 1820; Benjamin Burroughs Papers; U. Dart Papers; Thomas P. Jackson Papers; Mrs. Smith Diary; Herman Stebbins Papers

Emory University, Pitt Theology Library, Atlanta, Georgia: American Home Missionary Society Papers, 1773–1851; Minutes of the Annual Conference of the Methodist Episcopal Church, 1828–30; Minutes of the Georgia Conference of Methodists, 1831–33

Georgia Department of Archives and History, Atlanta: Acts and Resolutions of the State of Georgia, 1820; Ascension Lutheran Church Records, 1824–29; W. C. Blott Account Book; Bryan County (Road Commissioners Minutes, 1819–72; Superior Court Minutes, 1810–61); Camden County (Board of Education, Camden County Academy, 1801–2; Grand Jury Presentments, 1797–1859; Inferior Court Minutes, 1794–1815; Inferior and Superior Court, Miscellaneous Records, 1790–1924; Miscellaneous Records, 1800–1819; Register of Free People of Color, 1819–43; Road Duty Records, 1804–5; Superior Court Minutes, 1797–1842; Tax Digests, 1794, 1809, 1819–60); Chatham County (Aliens' Declarations, 1823–44; Deed Book G, 1789–90; Deed Book H, 1790–91; Deed Book N, 1824–26 ; Grand Jury Presentments, 1782–85; Inferior Court, Issue Docket, 1812–23; Inferior Court, Minutes, 1790–1802; Inferior Court, Trial Docket, 1813–27; Mayor's Court, Fine and Information Docket, 1836–38; Superior Court, Criminal Testimony, 1824–26, 1851–60; Superior Court, Criminal Docket, 1820–30; Superior Court, Minutes, 1782–1866; Tax Digests, 1793,

1806–65); Christ Church Savannah Records; City of Savannah, Tax Digests, 1809–60; Archibald Clark Journal; Colonial Book C-1, Conveyances, 1750–61; Colonial Book S, Conveyances, 1766–69; Colonial Book U, Conveyances, 1769; Colonial Book V, Conveyances, 1769–71; Colonial Book J, Miscellaneous Bonds, Deeds of Gift, Sales, 1755–62; Colonial Book O, Miscellaneous Bonds, Deeds of Gift, Sales, 1762–65; Colonial Book CCC, Miscellaneous Bonds, Deeds of Gift, Sales, 1783–92; Colonial Book DDD, Miscellaneous Bonds, Deeds of Gift, Sales, 1792–1813; Colonial Book H, Proclamations, 1754–94; Colonial Book AAA, Proclamations, 1782–1823; Colonial Book A, Wills, 1754–72; Colonial Book AA, Wills, 1772–77; Darien Presbyterian Church Records, 1822–64; Executive Department (Incoming Correspondence; Letterbooks, 1814–21; Minutes, 1819–21); File Group II, County Documents; Georgia, Colony, Letters of John Reynolds, 1756–57; Glynn County (Inferior Court Minutes, 1814–70; Superior Court Minutes, 1787–90; Tax Digests, 1790, 1794); Great Britain, Public Record Office, Board of Trade, Correspondence with the Colony of Georgia; Great Britain, Public Record Office, Secretary of State, Correspondence with the Colony of Georgia; Liberty County (Inferior Court Minutes, 1800–1802; Miscellaneous Collection; Superior Court Minutes, 1784–1808, 1822–59; Tax Digests, 1800, 1819–61; Wills and Inventories); McIntosh County (Tax List, 1825); Pleasant Grove Methodist Church Records, 1813–35; St. John the Baptist Catholic Church Records, 1796–1816; St. Mary's Methodist Church Records, 1788–64; St. Marys Presbyterian Church Records, 1807, 1830–58; St. Marys Town Council Minutes, 1841–61; State of Georgia, Board of Corrections, Inmate Administration Division, Central Register of Convicts, Vol. 1, 1817–68, Vol. 2, 1817–71; United States Department of Veterans Administration, Revolutionary War Pension and Bounty Land Warrant Application Files

Georgia Historical Society, Savannah: Wayne Stites Anderson Papers; Anonymous Carpenters Book, 1853–54; Joseph Vallence Bevan Papers; Margaret Davis Cate Collection; Chatham County, Superior Court, Criminal Testimony, 1837–40; Chatham County, Tax Digest, 1793; Christ Church Savannah Records; Darien Presbyterian Church Records, 1823–62; Jeremiah Evarts Diary, 1822; Federal Manuscript Census of Manufacturing, 1820; Federal Manuscript Census for Georgia, 1820, 1830; Federal Manuscript Census for South Carolina, 1830; First Baptist Church Savannah Records; Mabel Freeman La Far Papers; Gilbert Isaac Germond Papers; Robert S. Goff Letterbook; Grand Jury Presentment, 1737; G. F. Greene Paper, 1820; Hale Family Paper; Walter C. Hartridge Collection; Independent Presbyterian Church Records, 1808–61; Jones Family Papers; Mayor's Court Minutes, Petitions, 1806–7, 1821; Midway Congregational Church Records, 1754–1822; Daniel Mulford Papers, 1809; Powers Baptist Church Records, 1823–53; Register of Free People of Color, 1817–35; Savannah Board of Health, Minute Books, 1834–38, 1850–55; Savannah City Council Minutes, 1790–96, 1800–1861; Savannah City Marshal, Fine Docket Book, 1853; Savannah Clerk of Council, Liquor License Books, 1850–51; Savannah Mayor's Recorders Court, 1858–60; Savannah Mayor's Office Letterbook, 1817–51; Savannah Ordinance, 1810; Savannah Police Department, Jail Register, 1809–15, 1855–58; Savannah Port Society Minutes, 1843–73; Savannah Recorder's Court; Southern Claims Commission, Settled Claims, Record Group 217, Camden County and Chatham

County, Georgia; Mrs. E. H. Steele Paper, 1830; Telfair Papers; Trinity Methodist Episcopal Church Records, 1837–69; N. S. Tyler Paper; Joseph Frederick Waring Papers; Works Progress Administration, Savannah Writers' Project

Mercer University, Special Collections Department, Main Library, Macon, Georgia: *Columbian Star/Christian Index;* First Baptist Church Savannah Minutes; Georgia Baptist Association Minutes; Jones's Creek Baptist Church Minutes; Little Ogechee Baptist Church Minutes; Piedmont Baptist Association Minutes; Salem Baptist Church Minutes; Savannah River Baptist Association Minutes; Southern Baptist Convention Minutes; Sunbury Baptist Association Minutes

South Carolina Department of Archives and History, Columbia: Charleston District, Court of Common Pleas, Information, 1816–36; Charleston District, Court of General Sessions, Bills of Indictment, 1800–1816; Charleston District, Court of General Sessions, Records, 1758–75; Charleston District, Court of General Sessions, Session Journals, 1769–76; Commissioners of the Roads, St. Paul's Parish, 1783–1839; General Assembly Papers, 1790–1865; Peter Horry's Justice Book, 1783; State Free Negro Capitation Tax Book, 1822; St. Luke's Parish Tax Digest, 1798

South Carolina Historical Society, Charleston: Anonymous Journal, 1824–25; Baker-Grimké Papers; Ball Family Papers; Allard Belin Plantation Journal; Charles Caleb Cotton Letters; Alexander Crawford Daybook; William Dagliesh Workbook; Frederick Fraser Papers; Peter Gaillard Planting Book; Georgetown Methodist Church Records; Benjamin Pittman Papers; Henry Ravenel Papers; Harriet S. Simons Papers; Trinity Methodist Episcopal Church Records

University of Cambridge, University Library: American Papers of the Society for the Propagation of the Gospel; Fulham Papers at Lambeth Palace Library; Records of the States of the United States [Microfilm Series 15] (Acts of the Province of Georgia, 1735–74, 1780–81; Acts of the State of Georgia, 1778–1832)

University of Georgia, Hargrett Rare Book and Manuscript Library, Athens: Nathan Atkinson Brown Papers; Brunswick and Florida Railroad Survey, 1836–37; Thomas Carr Collection; Joseph Cook Letters; E. Merton Coulter Manuscripts; Telamon Cuyler Collection; Denison Family Papers; Egmont Manuscripts, Phillips Collection; Georgia–Liberty County Paper; Glynn County Tax Digest, 1786; Charles Colock Jones Jr. Collection; Liberty County Tax Digest, 1785; John Newton Diary; James Pelot Paper; Keith Read Collection; Records of the Antebellum Southern Plantations (Series F, Part II, William Gibbons Papers; Series H, Reel 28, Orme Letterbook 1821–25; Series J, Part 4, Richard James Arnold Papers); Savannah Cash Book, 1806–10

University of North Carolina at Chapel Hill, Southern Historical Collection, Manuscripts Department, Wilson Library: Alexander-Hillhouse Papers; Arnold-Screven Papers; Bulloch Family Papers; William A. Cooper Papers; Marianne Bull Cozens Paper; Michael Gaffney Paper; William Harris Garland Papers; Hentz Family Papers; William P. Hill Papers; Jackson-Prince Papers; Thomas Butler King Papers; Kollock Plantation Papers; Mackay-Stiles Papers; John Morel Paper; Josiah Smith Papers; Ella Barrow Spalding Papers; Courtlandt Van Rensselaer Paper

University of South Carolina, South Caroliniana Library, Columbia: Black Creek Baptist Church Papers; Charleston Baptist Association Minutes; Charleston Baptist Church Rules; Charleston House Bill; William John Connors Farm Journal; Paul Cross

Papers; John H. Eiffert Paper; Richard Francis Paper; Richard Furman Papers; Robert
Wilson Gibbes Papers; John Hampton Paper; William Joyner Papers; Captain Keown
Papers; Lawton Family Papers; John Wroughton Mitchell Papers; Oswald Family Pa-
pers; John O'Rawe Paper; Lemuel Reid Diary; John M. Roberts Papers; St. Andrew's
Parish Petition; Savannah Baptist Association Papers; Savannah River Anti–Slave
Traffic Association Papers; South Carolina Regulators Report; Thomas Waites
Papers
University of Warwick, University Library: Butler Plantation Papers; Colonial Records of
Georgia, vols. 1–39; Manuscripts of the Earl of Egmont
Westminster College, Cambridge: American Papers of the Countess of Huntingdon

NEWSPAPERS AND PERIODICALS

Brunswick Advocate, 1837–39
Columbian Museum and Savannah Advertiser, 1796–1821
Daily Georgian, 1820–56
Daily Morning News, 1850–61
Daily Savannah Republican, 1818–20
Darien Gazette, 1818–28
Darien Telegraph, 1835
Gazette of the State of Georgia, 1783–88
Georgia Analytical Repository, 1802–3
Georgia Gazette, 1763–76, 1788–96, 1798–1802
McIntosh County Herald and Darien Commercial Register, 1839–40
Republican and Savannah Evening Ledger, 1811
Royal Georgia Gazette, 1779–82
Savannah Republican, 1825, 1856–60
Southern Agriculturalist and Register of Rural Affairs, 1828–32
Temperance Banner, 1852–55

ARTICLES, BOOKS, AND DISSERTATIONS

Abstracts of Colonial Wills of the State of Georgia, 1733–1777. Atlanta, 1962.
Acts of the General Assembly of the State of Georgia. Milledgeville, Ga., 1809.
Acts of the General Assembly of the State of Georgia. Milledgeville, Ga., 1810.
Adams, Nehemiah. *A South Side View of Slavery*. Savannah, 1974.
Alexander, Adele Logan. *Ambiguous Lives: Free Women of Color in Rural Georgia,
1789–1879*. Fayetteville, Ark., 1991.
Andrew, Rev. James Osgood. "Rise and Progress of Methodism in Charleston, South
Carolina." *Methodist Magazine and Quarterly Review* 12 (1830): 17–28.
Armstrong, Thomas F. "From Task Labor to Free Labor: The Transition Along Georgia's
Rice Coast." *Georgia Historical Quarterly* 64 (1980): 432–47.
Ash, Stephen V. "Poor Whites in the Occupied South, 1861–5." *Journal of Southern His-
tory* 57 (1991): 39–62.
Atherton, Lewis E. *The Southern Country Store, 1800–1860*. Baton Rouge, 1949.

Ayers, Edward L. *Vengeance and Justice: Crime and Punishment in the Nineteenth-Century American South*. Oxford, 1984.

Baker, Robert A. *The Southern Baptist Convention and Its People, 1607–1972*. Nashville, Tenn., 1974.

Ball, Charles. *Fifty Years in Chains*. 1858. Reprint. New York, 1970.

———. *The Life of a Negro Slave*. Norwich, Conn., 1846.

Bancroft, Joseph. *Census of the City of Savannah*. Savannah, 1848.

Bartram, William. *Travels Through North and South Carolina, Georgia, East and West Florida*. 1792. Reprint. Savannah, 1973.

Beckemeyer, Frances Howell. *Abstracts of Georgia Colonial Conveyance Book C-1, 1750–1761*. Atlanta, 1975.

Bell, Malcolm. *Major Butler's Legacy: Five Generations of a Slaveholding Family*. Athens, Ga., 1987.

Bellamy, Donnie D. "The Legal Status of Black Georgians During the Colonial and Revolutionary Eras." *Journal of Negro History* 74 (1989): 1–10.

———. "Macon, Georgia, 1823–1860: A Study in Urban Slavery." *Phylon* 45 (1984): 298–310.

Bellamy, Donnie D., and Diane E. Walker. "Slaveholding in Antebellum Augusta and Richmond County, Georgia." *Phylon* 48 (1987): 165–77.

Bellows, Barbara L. *Benevolence Among Slaveholders: Assisting the Poor in Charleston, 1670–1860*. Baton Rouge, 1993.

———. "'My Children, Gentlemen, Are My Own': Poor Women, the Urban Elite, and the Bonds of Obligation in Antebellum Charleston." In Walter J. Fraser Jr., R. Frank Saunders Jr., and Jon L. Wakelyn, eds., *The Web of Southern Social Relations: Women, Family, and Education*. Athens, Ga., 1985, 52–71.

Berlin, Ira. "The Structure of the Free Negro Caste in the Antebellum United States." In Edward Magdol and Jon L. Wakelyn, eds., *The Southern Common People: Studies in Nineteenth-Century Social History*. Westport, Conn., 1980, 95–118.

———. "Time, Space, and the Evolution of Afro-American Society on British Mainland North America." *American Historical Review* 85 (1980): 44–78.

Berlin, Ira, and Herbert Gutman. "Natives and Immigrants, Free Men and Slaves: Urban Workingmen in the Antebellum American South." *American Historical Review* 88 (1983): 1175–1200.

Berlin, Ira, and Philip D. Morgan. *Cultivation and Culture: Labor and the Shaping of Slave Life in the Americas*. Charlottesville, Va., 1993.

———. *The Slaves' Economy: Independent Production by Slaves in the Americas*. London, 1991.

Beveridge, Charles E., and Charles Capen McLaughlin, eds. *The Papers of Frederick Law Olmsted*. Vol. 2, *Slavery and the South, 1852–1857*. Baltimore, 1981.

Bibb, Henry. *Narrative of the Life and Adventures of Henry Bibb, an American Slave*. New York, 1849.

Blair, Ruth, ed. *Some Early Tax Lists of Georgia*. Atlanta, 1926.

Blassingame, John W. *The Slave Community: Plantation Life in the Antebellum South*. New York, 1972.

———. "Status and Social Structure in the Slave Community: Evidence from New

Sources." In Harry P. Owens, ed., *Perspectives and Irony in American Slavery*. Jackson, Miss., 1976, 137–51.

Blassingame, John W., ed. *Slave Testimony: Two Centuries of Letters, Speeches, Interviews and Autobiographies*. Baton Rouge, 1977.

Blauvelt, Martha Tomhave. "Women and Revivalism." In Rosemary Radford Ruether and Rosemary Skinner Keller, eds., *Women and Religion in America*. Vol. 1, *The Nineteenth Century*. San Francisco, 1981, 1–45.

Boatwright, Eleanor M. "The Political and Civil Status of Women in Georgia, 1783–1860." *Georgia Historical Quarterly* 25 (1941): 301–24.

Bode, Frederick A. "A Common Sphere: White Evangelicals and Gender in Antebellum Georgia." *Georgia Historical Quarterly* 79 (1995): 775–809.

———. "The Formation of Evangelical Communities in Middle Georgia, Twiggs County, 1820–1861." *Journal of Southern History* 60 (1994): 711–48.

Bode, Frederick A., and Donald E. Ginter. *Farm Tenancy and the Census in Antebellum Georgia*. Athens, Ga., 1986.

Bodichon, Barbara Leigh Smith. *An American Diary, 1857–8*. London, 1972.

Boles, John B. *Black Southerners, 1619–1869*. Lexington, Ky., 1983.

———. "Evangelical Protestantism in the South." In Charles Reagan Wilson, ed., *Religion in the South*. Jackson, Miss., 1985, 13–35.

———. *The Great Revival, 1787–1805*. Lexington, Ky., 1972.

———. "Henry Holcombe, a Southern Baptist Reformer in the Age of Jefferson." *Georgia Historical Quarterly* 54 (1970): 381–407.

———. "Slaves in Bi-Racial Protestant Churches." In Samuel S. Hill, ed., *Varieties of Southern Religious Experience*. Baton Rouge, 1988, 95–114.

Boles, John B., ed. *Masters and Slaves in the House of the Lord: Race and Religion in the American South, 1740–1870*. Lexington, Ky., 1988.

Bolster, W. Jeffrey. *Black Jacks: African American Seamen in the Age of Sail*. Cambridge, Mass., 1997.

Bolton, Charles C. *Poor Whites of the Antebellum South: Tenants and Labourers in Central North Carolina and Northeast Mississippi*. Durham, N.C., 1994.

Bolton, Charles C., and Scott P. Culclasure, eds. *The Confessions of Edward Isham: A Poor White Life of the South*. Athens, Ga., 1998.

Boney, F. N., ed. *Slave Life in Georgia: A Narrative of the Life, Sufferings, and Escape of John Brown, a Fugitive Slave*. Savannah, 1972.

Bonner, James C., *A History of Georgia Agriculture*. Athens, Ga., 1964.

———. "Plantation and Farm: The Agricultural South." In Arthur S. Link, and Rembert W. Patrick, eds., *Writing Southern History: Essays in Historiography in Honour of Fletcher M. Green*. Baton Rouge, 1965, 147–74.

———. "The Plantation Overseer and Southern Nationalism." *Agricultural History* 19 (1945): 1–11.

———. "Profile of a Late Ante-Bellum Community." *American Historical Review* 49 (1944): 663–80.

Bontemps, Arna, ed. *Five Black Lives*. Middletown, Conn., 1971.

———. *Great Slave Narratives*. Boston, 1969.

Boorstein, Daniel. *The Americans: The Colonial Experience*. Suffolk, 1988.

Botkin, B. A. *Lay My Burden Down: A Folk History of Slavery.* Athens, Ga., 1945.

Bowden, Haygood S. *History of Savannah Methodism from John Wesley to Silas Johnson.* Macon, 1929.

Bremer, Fredericka. *The Homes of the New World: Impressions of America.* London, 1853.

Bridenbaugh, Carl. *Cities in Revolt: Urban Life in America, 1742–1776.* New York, 1955.

———. *Cities in the Wilderness: The First Century of Urban Life in America, 1625–1742.* London, 1971.

———. *The Colonial Craftsman.* London, 1950.

———. *Myths and Realities: Societies of the Colonial South.* Baton Rouge, 1952.

Brooks, Walter H. "The Priority of the Silver Bluff Church and Its Promoters." *Journal of Negro History* 7 (1922): 172–96.

Brown, W. O. "The Role of Poor Whites in Race Contacts in the South." *Social Forces* 19 (1940): 258–68.

Bruce, Dickson D. *And They All Sang Hallelujah: Plain-Folk Camp-Meeting Religion, 1800–1845.* Knoxville, Tenn., 1974.

Bryant, William Cullen. *Letters of a Traveller or Notes of Things Seen in Europe and America.* New York and London, 1850.

Buck, Paul H. "Poor Whites of the Ante-Bellum South." *American Historical Review* 31 (1925): 41–54.

Buckingham, James Silk. *The Slave States of America.* London, N.d.

Burke, Emily. *Pleasure and Pain: Reminiscences of Georgia in the 1840s.* Savannah, 1991.

Burke, Emory Stevens, ed. *The History of American Methodism.* Vol. 2. New York, 1964.

Burnwell, Joseph W., ed. "The Diary of Timothy Ford, 1785–1786." *South Carolina Historical and Genealogical Magazine* 13 (1912): 132–47, 181–204.

Butler, Jon. "Enlarging the Bonds of Christ: Slavery, Evangelism, and The Christianisation of the White South, 1690–1790." In Leonard L. Sweet, ed., *The Evangelical Tradition in America.* Macon, 1984, 87–112.

———. "Enthusiasm Described and Decried: The Great Awakening as Interpretative Fiction." *Journal of American History* 69 (1982): 305–25.

Bynum, Victoria E. *Unruly Women: The Politics of Social and Sexual Control.* Chapel Hill, 1992.

Byrne, William A. "The Burden and the Heat of the Day: Slavery and Servitude in Savannah, 1733–1865." Ph.D. dissertation, Florida State University, 1979.

Caldwell, Lee Ann. "Women Landholders of Colonial Georgia." In Harvey H. Jackson and Phinizy Spalding, eds., *Forty Years of Diversity.* Athens, Ga., 1984, 183–98.

Callaway, James Etheridge. *The Early Settlement of Georgia.* Athens, Ga., 1948.

Campbell, J. H. *Georgia Baptists: Historical and Biographical.* Macon, Ga., 1874.

Campbell, John. "As 'a Kind of Freeman'?: Slaves' Market Related Activities in the South Carolina Upcountry, 1800–1860." In Ira Berlin and Philip Morgan, eds., *The Slaves' Economy: Independent Production by Slaves in the Americas.* London, 1991, 131–69.

Campbell, Randolph B. "Planters and Plain Folks: The Social Structure of the Antebellum South." In John B. Boles and Evelyn Thomas Nolen, eds., *Interpreting Southern History: Historiographical Essays in Honor of Sanford W. Higginbotham.* Baton Rouge, 1987, 48–77.

Candler, Allen D., ed. *The Colonial Records of the State of Georgia*. Vols. 1–32. New York, 1970, and Athens, Ga., 1988–95.

Cates, Gerald L. "'The Seasoning': Disease and Death Among the First Colonists of Georgia." *Georgia Historical Quarterly* 64 (1980): 146–58.

Catterall, Helen Tunncliff, ed. *Judicial Cases Concerning American Slavery and the Negro*. Vol. 3, *Georgia*. Shannon, Ireland, 1968.

Censuses for Georgia Counties. Atlanta, 1979.

Chaplin, Joyce E. *An Anxious Pursuit: Agricultural Innovation and Modernity in the Lower South, 1730–1815*. Chapel Hill, 1993.

———. "Creating a Cotton South in Georgia and South Carolina, 1760–1815." *Journal of Southern History* 57 (1991): 171–200.

———. "Slavery and the Principle of Humanity: A Modern Idea in the Early Lower South." *Journal of Social History* 24 (1990): 299–316.

———. "Tidal Rice Cultivation and the Problem of Slavery in South Carolina and Georgia, 1760–1815." *William and Mary Quarterly* 49 (1992): 29–62.

City Directory for Savannah, 1849. Savannah, 1849.

Charles, Allan D. "Black and White Relations in an Antebellum Church in the Carolina Upcountry." *South Carolina Historical Magazine* 89 (1988): 218–26.

Chesnutt, David Rogers. "South Carolina's Expansion into Colonial Georgia, 1720–1765." Ph.D. dissertation, University of Georgia, 1973.

Clark, Dennis. *Hibernia America: The Irish and Regional Culture*. Westport, Conn., 1986.

Clark, Elmer T., J. Manning Potts, and Jacob S. Ryan, eds. *The Journal and Letters of Francis Asbury*. 3 vols. London, 1958.

Clay, Thomas. *Detail of a Plan for the Moral Improvement of Negroes on Plantations*. N.p, 1833.

Clifton, James M. *Life and Labor on Argyle Island: Letters and Documents of a Savannah River Rice Plantation, 1833–1867*. Savannah, 1978.

———. "The Rice Driver: His Role in Slave Management." *South Carolina Historical Magazine* 82 (1981): 331–53.

Clinton, Catherine. "'Southern Dishonor': Flesh, Blood, Race and Bondage." In Carol Bleser, ed., *In Joy and Sorrow: Women, Family, and Marriage in the Victorian South*. New York, 1991, 52–68.

Coclanis, Peter A. *The Shadow of a Dream: Economic Life and Death in the South Carolina Lowcountry, 1670–1920*. New York, 1989.

Cody, Cheryll Ann. "Naming, Kinship and Estate Dispersal: Notes on Slave Family Life on a South Carolina Plantation, 1786–1833." *William and Mary Quarterly* 39 (1982): 192–211.

———. "There Was No 'Absalom' on the Ball Plantations: Slave Naming Practices in the South Carolina Lowcountry, 1720–1865." *American Historical Review* 92 (1987): 563–96.

Coleman, Kenneth. *A History of Georgia*. Athens, Ga., 1971.

Collins, Bruce. *White Society in the Antebellum South*. London, 1985.

Commons, John R., et al., eds. *A Documentary History of American Industrial Society*. Vols. 1 and 2, *Plantation and Frontier*. Cleveland, Ohio, 1910.

Conrad, Georgia Bryan. *Reminiscences of a Southern Woman.* Hampton, Va., N.d.

Corbin, Gavin L. "The First List of Pew-Holders of Christ-Church, Savannah." *Georgia Historical Quarterly* 50 (1966): 74–86.

Cornelius, Janet. "Slave Marriages in a Georgia Congregation." In Orville Vernon Burton and Robert C. McMath, eds., *Class, Conflict, and Consensus: Antebellum Southern Community Studies.* Westport, Conn., 1985, 128–45.

Cott, Nancy F. "Passionlessness: An Interpretation of Victorian Sexual Ideology, 1790–1850." *Signs* 1 (1978): 219–36.

Coulter, E. Merton. "The Great Savannah Fire of 1820." *Georgia Historical Quarterly* 23 (1939): 1–27.

————. "A List of the First Shipload of Georgia Settlers." *Georgia Historical Quarterly* 31 (1947): 282–88.

Coulter, E. Merton, and Albert B. Saye. *A List of the Early Settlers of Georgia.* Athens, Ga., 1949.

Craft, William. *Running a Thousand Miles for Freedom; or, The Escape of William and Ellen Craft from Slavery.* London, 1860.

Crane, Verner W. "Dr. Thomas Bray and the Charitable Colony Project, 1730." *William and Mary Quarterly* 19 (1962): 49–63.

Craven, Avery O. "Poor Whites and Negroes in the Ante-Bellum South." *Journal of Negro History* 15 (1930): 14–25.

Creel, Margaret Washington. *"A Peculiar People": Slave Religion and Community-Culture Among the Gullahs.* New York, 1988.

Crowley, John E. "The Importance of Kinship: Testamentary Evidence from South Carolina." *Journal of Interdisciplinary History* 16 (1986): 559–77.

Davis, Angela. *Women, Race, and Class.* New York, 1981.

Davis, Harold E. *The Fledgling Province: Social and Cultural Life in Colonial Georgia, 1733–1776.* Chapel Hill, 1976.

Davis, Richard Beale. "The Ball Papers: A Pattern of Life in the Lowcountry, 1800–1825." *South Carolina Historical Magazine* 65 (1964): 1–15.

Debats, Donald A. *Elites and Masses: Political Structure, Communication, and Behaviour in Ante-Bellum Georgia.* New York, 1990.

Degler, Carl N. "Slavery and the Genesis of American Race Prejudice." In Peter Charles Hoffer, ed., *Africans Become Afro-Americans: Selected Articles on Slavery in the American Colonies.* New York, 1988, 46–63.

De Vorsey, Louis, Jr., ed. *De Brahm's Report of the General Survey in the Southern District of North America.* Columbia, S.C., 1971.

Dexter, Elizabeth Anthony. *Career Women of America, 1776–1840.* 2d ed. Clifton, N.J., 1972.

Diner, Hasia R. *Erin's Daughters in America: Irish Immigrant Women in the Nineteenth Century.* Baltimore, 1983.

"The Dirt Eaters." *Southern Literary Journal* 1 (1837): 9–14.

Doyon, Roy R., and Thomas W. Hodler. "Secessionist Sentiment and Slavery: A Geographic Analysis." *Georgia Historical Quarterly* 73 (1989): 323–48.

Dunn, Richard S. "The Trustees of Georgia and the House of Commons, 1732–1752." *William and Mary Quarterly* 11 (1954): 551–65.

Dusinberre, William. *Them Dark Days: Slavery in the American Rice Swamps*. New York, 1996.

Earle, Carville, and Ronald Hoffman. "The Foundation of the Modern Economy: Agriculture and the Costs of Labour in the United States and England, 1800–1860." *American Historical Review* 85 (1980): 1055–94.

Early Deaths in Savannah, Georgia, 1763–1803. Atlanta, 1993.

Easterby, J. H., ed. *The South Carolina Rice Plantation as Revealed in the Papers of Robert F. W. Allston*. Chicago, 1945.

Eaton, Clement. "Class Differences in the Old South." *Virginia Quarterly Review* 33 (1957): 357–70.

Edwards, Alexander, comp. *Ordinances of the City Council of Charleston, 1784–1802*. Charleston, 1802.

Egmont, Earl of. *Diary of the First Earl of Egmont*. Vol. 3, 1739–1747. London, 1923.

The 1860 Census of Chatham County, Georgia. Easley, S.C., 1980.

Endy, Melvin B., Jr. "Just War, Holy War, and Millenialism in Revolutionary America." *William and Mary Quarterly* 42 (1985): 3–25.

Escott, Paul D. "The Art and Science of Reading WPA Slave Narratives." In Charles T. Davis and Henry Louis Gates Jr., eds., *The Slave's Narrative*. Oxford, 1985, 40–48.

Evans, Jonathan, ed. *A Journal of the Life, Travels, and Religious Labours of William Savery, Late of Philadelphia, a Minister of the Gospel of Christ, in the Society of Friends*. London, 1844.

Fairbanks, Charles H. "Spaniards, Planters, Ships and Slaves: Historical Archaeology in Florida and Georgia." *Archaeology* 29 (1976): 165–72.

Ferguson, T. Reed. *The John Couper Family at Cannon's Point*. Macon, Ga., 1994.

Fields, Barbara J. "Ideology and Race in American History." In J. Morgan Kousser and James M. McPherson, eds., *Region, Race and Reconstruction: Essays in Honor of C. Vann Woodward*. New York, 1982, 143–77.

Flanders, Ralph B. "The Free Negro in Ante-Bellum Georgia." *North Carolina Historical Review* 9 (1932): 250–72.

———. *Plantation Slavery in Georgia*. 2d ed. Chapel Hill, 1968.

Flynt, J. Wayne, *Dixie's Forgotten People: The South's Poor Whites*. Bloomington, 1979.

———. *Southern Poor Whites: A Selected Bibliography of Printed Sources*. New York, 1981.

Ford, Lacy K., Jr. *The Origins of Southern Radicalism: The South Carolina Upcountry, 1800–1860*. New York, 1988.

———. "Popular Ideology of the South's Plain Folk: The Limits of Egalitarianism in a Slaveholding Society." In Samuel C. Hyde, ed., *Plain Folk of the South Revisited*. Baton Rouge, 1997, 205–27.

Fox-Genovese, Elizabeth. *Within the Plantation Household: Black and White Women of the Old South*. Chapel Hill, 1988.

Fraser, Walter J., Jr. "The City Elite, 'Disorder,' and the Poor Children of Pre-Revolutionary Charleston." *South Carolina Historical Magazine* 84 (1983): 167–79.

Frederickson, G. M. *The Black Image in the White Mind*. New York, 1971.

Frey, Sylvia F. "Between Two Wars: The Rise and Fall of Chattel Slavery in Georgia." *Slavery and Abolition* 8 (1987): 216–25.

———. "Shaking the Dry Bones: The Dialectic of Conversion." In Ted Ownby, ed., *Black and White Cultural Interaction in the Antebellum South*. Jackson, Miss., 1993, 23–54.

———. *Water from the Rock: Black Resistance in a Revolutionary Age*. Princeton, 1991.

———. "'The Year of Jubilee Has Come': Black Christianity in the Plantation South in Post-Revolutionary America." In Ronald Hoffman and Peter J. Albert, eds., *Religion in a Revolutionary Age*. Charlottesville, Va., 1994.

Frey, Sylvia R., and Betty Wood. *Come Shouting to Zion: African American Protestantism in the American South and British Caribbean to 1830*. Chapel Hill, 1998.

Friedman, Jean E. *The Enclosed Garden: Women and Community in the Evangelical South, 1830–1900*. Chapel Hill, 1985.

Fronsman, Bill Cecil. *Common Whites: Class and Culture in Antebellum North Carolina*. Lexington, Ky., 1992.

Gallay, Alan. *The Formation of a Planter Elite: Jonathan Bryan and the Southern Colonial Frontier*. Athens, Ga., 1989.

———. "Jonathan Bryan's Plantation Empire: Land, Politics, and the Formation of a Ruling Class in Colonial Georgia." *William and Mary Quarterly* 45 (1988): 253–79.

———. "Planters and Slaves in the Great Awakening." In John B. Boles, ed., *Masters and Slaves in the House of the Lord: Race and Religion in the American South, 1740–1870*. Lexington, Ky., 1988, 19–36.

Gardner, Robert G. "Primary Sources in the Study of Eighteenth-Century Georgia Baptist History." *Viewpoints: Georgia Baptist History* 7 (1980): 59–118.

Gardner, Robert G., Charles O. Walker, J. R. Huddleston, and J. Waldo Harris III. *A History of the Georgia Baptist Association, 1784–1984*. Atlanta, 1988.

Gaspar, David Barry. "Slavery, Amelioration and Sunday Markets in Antigua, 1823–1831." *Slavery and Abolition*, 9 (1988): 1–28.

———. "Sugar Cultivation and Slave Life in Antigua Before 1800." In Ira Berlin and Philip Morgan, eds., *Cultivation and Culture: Labor and the Shaping of Slave Life in the Americas*. Charlottesville, Va., 1993, 101–23.

General Index to the Keeper's Record Books at Laurel Grove Cemetery, 1852–1938. Savannah, 1939.

Genovese, Eugene D. "Black Plantation Preachers in the Slave South." *Southern Studies* N.S., 2 (1991): 203–29.

———. "Marxian Interpretations of the Slave South." In J. Bernstein Barton, ed., *Towards a New Past: Dissenting Essays in American History*. London, 1970.

———. *The Political Economy of Slavery*. London, 1966.

———. "Race and Class in Southern History: An Appraisal of the Work of Ulrich Bonnell Phillips." *Agricultural History* 41 (1967): 345–58.

———. "'Rather Be a Nigger Than a Poor White Man': Slave Perceptions of Southern Yeomen and Poor Whites." In Hans L. Trefousse, ed., *Toward a New View of America: Essays in Honour of Arthur C. Cole*. New York, 1977, 79–96.

———. *Roll, Jordan, Roll: The World the Slaves Made*. New York, 1974.

———. *The World the Slaveholders Made: Two Essays in Interpretation*. London, 1970.

———. "Yeoman Farmers in a Slaveholders' Democracy." *Agricultural History* 49 (1975): 331–42.

Genovese, Eugene D., and Elizabeth Fox-Genovese. "The Religious Ideals of Southern Slave Society." *Georgia Historical Quarterly* 70 (1986): 1–16.

Gillespie, Michele. "Artisan Accommodation to the Slave South: The Case of William Talmage, a Blacksmith, 1834–1847." *Georgia Historical Quarterly* 81 (1997): 265–86.

———. "Artisans and Mechanics in the Political Economy of Georgia, 1790–1860." Ph.D. dissertation, Princeton University, 1990.

———. "Planters in the Making: Artisanal Opportunity in Georgia, 1790–1830." In Howard B. Rock, Paul A. Gilje, and Robert Asher, eds., *American Artisans: Crafting Social Identity, 1750–1850*. Baltimore, 1995, 33–47.

———. "The World of William Garland: Work and Community in Antebellum South Carolina and Georgia." Paper Presented to "From Rebellion to Revolution: New Directions in Antebellum Lowcountry Studies, 1775–1860," a Conference Held at the College of Charleston, May 9–11, 1996.

Glen, Robert Strudwick, Jr. "Slavery in Georgia, 1733–1793." Senior B.A. thesis, Princeton University, 1972.

Godley, Margaret. *The Centennial Story of Trinity Methodist Church.* Savannah, 1948.

Goldin, Claudia D. *Urban Slavery in the American South.* Chicago, 1976.

Gray, Ralph, and Betty Wood. "The Transformation from Indentured to Involuntary Servitude in Colonial Georgia." *Explorations on Economic History* 13 (1976): 353–70.

Green, E. R. R. "Queensborough Township: Scotch-Irish Emigration and the Expansion of Georgia, 1763–1776." *William and Mary Quarterly* 17 (1960): 183–99.

Green, Fletcher M. "Democracy in the Old South." *Journal of Southern History* 12 (1946): 3–23.

Green, Venus. "A Preliminary Investigation of Black Construction Artisans in Savannah from 1820 to 1860." M.A. thesis, Columbia University, 1982.

Greenberg, Kenneth S. *Honor and Slavery: Lies, Duels, Noses, Masks, Dressing as a Woman, Gifts, Strangers, Humanitarianism, Death, Slave Rebellions, the Proslavery Argument, Baseball, Hunting, and Gambling in the Old South.* Princeton, 1998.

Greene, Evarts B., and Virginia D. Harrington. *American Population Before the Federal Census of 1790.* New York, 1932.

Griffen, J. David. "Medical Assistance for the Sick Poor in Ante-Bellum Savannah." *Georgia Historical Quarterly* 53 (1969): 463–69.

Griffen, Richard W. "Poor White Labourers in Southern Cotton Factories, 1789–1865." *South Carolina Historical Magazine* 61 (1960): 26–38.

Griffen, William D. *The Irish in America, 550–1972: A Chronology and Fact Book.* Dobbs Ferry, N.Y., 1973.

Grimes, William. "Life of William Grimes the Runaway Slave, Brought Down to the Present Time." In Arna Bontemps, ed., *Five Black Lives*. Middletown, Conn., 1971.

Gutman, Herbert G. *The Black Family in Slavery and Freedom.* Oxford, 1976.

Habersham, James. "Letters of Hon. James Habersham." *Collections of the Georgia Historical Society.* Vol. 6. Savannah, 1904.

Hagler, D. Harland. "The Ideal Woman in the Antebellum South: Lady or Farmwife?" *Journal of Southern History* 46 (1980): 405–18.

Hagy, James W. *People and Professions of Charleston, South Carolina, 1782–1802.* Baltimore, 1992.

Hahn, Steven. *The Roots of Southern Populism: Yeoman Farmers and the Transformation of the Georgia Upcountry, 1850–1890*. Oxford, 1983.

———. "The Yeomanry of the Non-Plantation South: Upper Piedmont Georgia, 1850–1860." In Orville Vernon Burton and Robert C. McMath, eds., *Class, Conflict and Consensus: Antebellum Southern Community Studies*. Westport, Conn., 1985, 29–56.

Hall, Captain Basil. *Travels in North America in the Years 1827 and 1828*. Vol. 3. Edinburgh, 1829.

Hall, Neville. "Slaves' Use of Their 'Free Time' in the Danish Virgin Islands in the Later Eighteenth and Early Nineteenth Century." *Journal of Caribbean History* 13 (1980): 21–43.

Harden, William. *Recollections of a Long and Satisfactory Life*. New York, 1968.

Harn, Julia E. "Old Canoochee-Ogeechee Chronicles." *Georgia Historical Quarterly* 16 (1932): 47–55, 146–51, 232–39.

Harrell, David Edwin, Jr. "The Evolution of Plain-Folk Religion in the South, 1835–1920." In Samuel S. Hill, ed., *Varieties of Southern Religious Experience*. Baton Rouge, 1988, 24–51.

Harris, J. William. *Plain Folk and Gentry in a Slave Society: White Liberty and Black Slavery in Augusta's Hinterlands*. Middletown, Conn., 1985.

———. "The Organisation of Work on a Yeoman Slaveholder's Farm." *Agricultural History* 64 (1990): 39–52.

———. "Portrait of a Small Slaveholder: The Journal of Benton Miller." *Georgia Historical Quarterly* 74 (1990): 1–19.

Harris, J. William, ed. *Society and Culture in the Slave South*. London, 1992.

Harris, Robert L. "Charleston's Free Afro-American Elite: The Brown Fellowship Society and the Humane Brotherhood." *South Carolina Historical Magazine* 82 (1981): 289–310.

Harrold, Frances. "Colonial Siblings: Georgia's Relationship with South Carolina During the Pre-Revolutionary Period." *Georgia Historical Quarterly* 73 (1989): 707–44.

Hatch, Nathan O. "Millennialism and Popular Religion in the Early Republic." In Leonard I. Sweet, ed., *The Evangelical Tradition in America*. Macon, Ga., 1984, 113–30.

Haunton, Richard H. "Law and Order in Savannah, 1850–1860." *Georgia Historical Quarterly* 56 (1972): 1–24.

———. "Savannah in the 1850s." Ph.D. dissertation, Emory University, 1968.

Hawkins, Ernest. *Historical Notices of the Missions of the Church of England in the North American Colonies, Previous to the Independence of the United States*. London, 1845.

Helper, Hinton Rowan. *The Impending Crisis of the South: How to Meet It*. 1860. Reprint. Cambridge, Mass., 1968.

Hemperly, Marion R. *English Crown Grants for Islands in Georgia, 1755–1775*. Atlanta, 1973.

———. *English Crown Grants in Christ Church Parish in Georgia, 1755–1775*. Atlanta, 1973.

———. *English Crown Grants in St. Andrew Parish in Georgia, 1755–1775*. Atlanta, 1973.

———. *English Crown Grants in St. John Parish in Georgia, 1755–1775*. Atlanta, 1973.

———. *English Crown Grants in St. Matthew Parish in Georgia, 1755–1775.* Atlanta, 1973.

———. *English Crown Grants in St. Philip Parish in Georgia, 1755–1775.* Atlanta, 1973.

———. *English Crown Grants in the Parishes of St. David, St. Patrick, St. Thomas, and St. Mary in Georgia, 1755–1775.* Atlanta, 1973.

———. "Federal Naturalization Oaths: Savannah, Georgia, 1790–1860." *Georgia Historical Quarterly* 51 (1967): 454–87.

Henry, Charles S., comp. *A Digest of All the Ordinances of the City of Savannah Which Were in Force on the 1st July 1854.* Savannah, 1854.

Hewat, Alexander. *An Historical Account of the Rise and Progress of the Colonies of South Carolina and Georgia.* London, 1779.

Hilliard, Sam B. "Antebellum Tidewater Rice Culture in South Carolina and Georgia." In James R. Gibson, ed., *European Settlement and Development in North America: Essays in Honour and Memory of Andrew Hill Clark.* London, 1978, 91–115.

Hindus, Michael S. "Black Justice Under White Law: Criminal Prosecutions of Blacks in Antebellum South Carolina." *Journal of American History* 63 (1976): 575–99.

Hodes, Martha Elizabeth. "Sex Across the Color Line: White Women and Black Men in the Nineteenth-Century American South." Ph.D. dissertation, Princeton University, 1991.

———. *White Women, Black Men: Illicit Sex in the Nineteenth Century South.* New Haven, 1997.

Hodgson, Adam. *Letters from North America, Written During a Tour in the United States and Canada.* London, 1824.

Hoetink, H. *Slavery and Race Relations in the Americas.* London, 1973.

Hoffmann, Charles, and Tess Hoffmann. "The Limits of Paternalism: Driver-Master Relations on a Bryan County Plantation." *Georgia Historical Quarterly* 67 (1983): 321–35.

Hofstadter, Richard. "U. B. Phillips and the Plantation Legend." *Journal of Negro History* 29 (1944): 109–24.

Holcombe, Henry. *The First Fruits in a Series of Letters.* Philadelphia, 1812.

Hollander, A. N. J. Den. "The Tradition of Poor Whites." In W. T. Couch, ed., *Culture in the South.* Westport, Conn., 1970, 403–31.

Hornsby, Alton, Jr. *The Negro in Revolutionary Georgia.* N.p., 1977.

Hoskins, Charles Lwanga. *Black Episcopalians in Savannah.* Savannah, 1983.

House, Albert Virgil. *Planter Management and Capitalism in Ante-Bellum Georgia: The Journal of Hugh Fraser Grant, Ricegrower.* New York, 1954.

Hudson, Larry E. "'All That Cash': Work and Status in the Slave Quarters." In Larry Hudson, ed., *Working Toward Freedom: Slave Society and Domestic Economy in the American South.* Rochester, N.Y., 1994, 77–94.

Hundley, Daniel R. *Social Relations in Our Southern States.* 1860. Reprint. Baton Rouge, 1979.

Hyde, Samuel C., ed., *Plain Folk of the South Revisited.* Baton Rouge, 1997.

Jackman, Mary R., and Robert W. Jackman. *Class Awareness in the United States.* London, 1983.

Jackson, E. "Letter." *Georgia Historical Quarterly* 8 (1924): 325–26.

Jaher, Frederick Cople. "Antebellum Charleston: Anatomy of an Economic Failure." In Orville Vernon Burton and Robert C. McMath, eds., *Class, Conflict, and Consensus: Antebellum Southern Community Studies.* Westport, Conn., 1985, 207–31.

Jervey, Theo D. "The White Indentured Servants of South Carolina." *South Carolina Historical and Genealogical Magazine* 12 (1911): 163–71.

Johnson, Elmer D., and Kathleen Lewis Sloan, eds. *South Carolina: A Documentary Profile of the Palmetto State.* Columbia, S.C., 1971.

Johnson, Michael P. "Planters and Patriarchy: Charleston, 1800–1860." *Journal of Southern History* 46 (1980): 45–72.

———. "Runaway Slaves and the Slave Communities in South Carolina, 1799–1830." *William and Mary Quarterly* 38 (1981): 418–41.

———. "Work, Culture and the Slave Community: Slave Occupations in the Cotton Belt in 1860." *Labor History* 27 (1986): 325–55.

Johnson, Michael P., and James L. Roark. *Black Masters: A Free Family of Colour in the Old South.* New York, 1984.

Johnson, Whittington B. *Black Savannah, 1788–1864.* Fayetteville, Ark., 1996.

———. "Free African-American Women in Savannah, 1800–1860: Affluence and Autonomy Amid Adversity." *Georgia Historical Quarterly* 76 (1992): 260–83.

———. "Free Blacks in Antebellum Savannah: An Economic Profile." *Georgia Historical Quarterly* 64 (1980): 418–31.

Johnston, Edith Duncan, ed. "The Kollock Letters, 1799–1850." *Georgia Historical Quarterly* 30 (1946): 218–58.

Johnston, Elizabeth Lichtenstein. *Recollections of a Georgia Loyalist.* New York, 1901.

Johnston, James Hugo. "The Participation of White Men in Virginia Negro Insurrections." *Journal of Negro History* 16 (1932): 158–67.

Jones, Charles Colcock. *Religious Instruction of the Negroes: An Address Delivered Before the General Assembly of the Presbyterian Church at Augusta, Georgia, December 10, 1861.* Savannah, 1861.

———. *The Religious Instruction of the Negroes in the United States.* Savannah, 1842.

———. *Suggestions on the Religious Instruction of the Negroes in the Southern States.* Philadelphia, 1847.

———. *Tenth Annual Report of the Association for the Religious Instruction of the Negroes in Liberty County, Georgia.* Savannah, 1845.

———. *Thirteenth Annual Report of the Association for the Religious Instruction of the Negroes in Liberty County, Georgia.* Savannah, 1848.

Jones, George Fenwick. "Von Reck's Second Report from Georgia." *William and Mary Quarterly* 22 (1965): 319–33.

Jones, George Fenwick, ed. "Report of Mr. Ettwein's Journey to Georgia and South Carolina, 1765." *South Carolina Historical Magazine* 91 (1990): 247–60.

Jones, George Fenwick, and Renatte Wilson, eds. *Detailed Reports on the Salzburger Emigrants Who Settled in America Edited by Samuel Urlsperger.* 18 vols. Athens, Ga., 1968–95.

Jones, Jacqueline. "Encounters, Likely and Unlikely, Between Black and Poor White Women in the Rural South, 1865–1940." *Georgia Historical Quarterly* 76 (1992): 333–53.

———. *Labor of Love, Labor of Sorrow: Black Women, Work, and the Family from Slavery to the Present.* New York, 1985.

———. "Race, Sex, and Self-Evident Truths: The Status of Slave Women During the Era of the American Revolution." In Ronald Hoffman and Peter J. Albert, eds., *Women in the Age of the American Revolution.* Charlottesville, Va., 1989, 293–337.

Jones, Norrece T. *Born a Child of Freedom, Yet a Slave: Mechanisms of Control and Strategies of Resistance in Antebellum South Carolina.* Hanover, N.H., 1968.

Jordan, Winthrop D. *White over Black: American Attitudes Toward the Negro.* Chapel Hill, 1968.

Joseph, J. W. "White Columns and Black Hands: Class and Classification in the Plantation Ideology of the Georgia and South Carolina Lowcountry." *Historical Archaeology* 27 (1993): 57–73.

Joyner, Charles. *Down by the Riverside: A South Carolina Slave Community.* Chicago, 1984.

Kaplanoff, Mark Dementi. "Making the South Solid: Politics and the Structure of Society in South Carolina, 1790–1815." Ph.D. dissertation, Cambridge University, 1980.

Kemble, Frances Anne. *Journal of a Residence on a Georgian Plantation in 1838–1839.* London, 1863.

Kenzer, Robert C. *Kinship and Neighborhood in a Southern Community: Orange County, North Carolina, 1849–1881.* Knoxville, Tenn., 1987.

King, Boston. "Memoirs of the Life of Boston King, a Black Preacher." *Methodist Magazine* 21 (1798): 105–10.

Kirwan, A. D. *The Civilization of the Old South: Essays in Honour of Clement Eaton.* Lexington, Ky., 1968.

Klebaner, Benjamin Joseph. "Public Poor Relief in Charleston, 1800–1860." *South Carolina Historical Magazine* 55 (1954): 210–27.

Klein, Rachel N. *Unification of a Slave State: The Rise of the Planter Class in the South Carolina Backcountry, 1760–1808.* Chapel Hill, 1990.

Koger, Larry. *Black Slaveowners: Free Black Slave Masters in South Carolina, 1790–1860.* London, 1985.

Kollock, Susie M. "Letters of the Kollock and Allied Families, 1826–1884." *Georgia Historical Quarterly* 34 (1950): 36–62.

La Far, Mabel Freeman. "The Baptist Church of Savannah, Georgia." Manuscript. 3 vols. Savannah, 1941.

———. "Henry Holcombe, D.D. (1762–1824): Minister, Humanitarian and Man of Letters." *Georgia Historical Quarterly* 28 (1944): 157–75.

Lambert, Frank. "'Peddlar in Divinity': George Whitefield and the Great Awakening, 1737–1745." *Journal of American History* 77 (1990): 812–37.

Lambert, Robert Stansbury. *South Carolina Loyalists in the American Revolution.* Columbia, S.C., 1987.

Land, Aubrey Christian. *Bases of the Plantation Society.* Columbia, S.C., 1969.

Lane, Mills, ed. *The Rambler in Georgia.* Savannah, 1973.

Lauder, E. M. "Slave Labor in South Carolina Cotton Mills." *Journal of Negro History* 38 (1953): 161–73.

Laurel Grove Cemetery, Savannah, Georgia. Vol. 1, 12 Oct 1852–30 Nov 1861. Savannah, 1996.

Lee, Jesse. *A Short History of the Methodists in the USA Beginning in 1766 and Continued Till 1809.* Baltimore, 1810.

"Letters Showing the Rise and Progress of the Early Negro Churches of Georgia and the West Indies." *Journal of Negro History* 1 (1916): 69–92.

Levine, Lawrence W. *Black Culture and Black Consciousness: Afro-American Thought from Slavery to Freedom.* Oxford, 1977.

Levy, B. H. "The Early History of Georgia's Jews." In Harvey H. Jackson and Phinizy Spalding, eds., *Forty Years of Diversity.* Athens, Ga., 1984, 163–78.

Lewis, Johanna Miller. *Artisans in the North Carolina Backcountry.* Lexington, Ky., 1995.

Lichtenstein, Alex. "That Disposition to Theft, with Which They Have Been Branded: Moral Economy, Slave Management and the Law." *Journal of Social History* 21 (1988): 413–40.

Lincoln, C. Eric. "The Black Church in the Context of American Religion." In Samuel S. Hill, ed., *Varieties of Southern Religious Experience.* Baton Rouge, 1988, 52–75.

Linden, Fabian. "Economic Democracy in the Slave South: An Appraisal of Some Recent Views." *Journal of Negro History* 31 (1946): 140–89.

Little, Thomas J. "George Liele and the Rise of Independent Black Baptist Churches in the Lower South and Jamaica." *Slavery and Abolition* 16 (1995): 188–204.

Littlefield, Dan C. *Rice and Slaves: Ethnicity and the Slave Trade in Colonial South Carolina.* Baton Rouge, 1981.

Lockley, Timothy J. "Crossing the Race Divide: Inter-Racial Sex in Antebellum Savannah." *Slavery and Abolition* 18 (1997): 159–73.

———. "Encounters Between Afro-Americans and Non-Slaveholding Whites in Lowcountry Georgia, 1750–1830." Ph.D. dissertation, Cambridge University, 1996.

———. "Partners in Crime: African-Americans and Non-Slaveholding Whites in Antebellum Georgia." In Matt Wray and Annalee Newitz, eds., *White Trash: Race and Class in America.* New York, 1997, 57–72.

———. "Spheres of Influence: Working Black and White Women in Antebellum Savannah." In Susanna Delfino and Michele Gillespie, eds., *Neither Lady, Nor Slave: Working Women of the Old South.* Forthcoming.

———. "A Struggle for Survival: Non-Elite White Women in Lowcountry Georgia, 1790–1830." In Christie Anne Farnham, ed., *Women of the American South: A Multicultural Reader.* New York, 1997, 26–42.

Loewald, Klaus G., Beverly Staricka, and Paul S. Taylor, eds. "Johann Martin Bolzius Answers a Questionnaire on Carolina and Georgia." *William and Mary Quarterly* 14 (1957): 218–61; 15 (1958): 228–52.

Longstreet, Augustus Baldwin. *Georgia Scenes, Characters, Incidents Etc., in the First Half Century of the Republic by a Native Georgian.* Augusta, 1835.

Love, E. K. *History of the First African Baptist Church, from Its Organisation on January 20, 1788 to July 1, 1888.* Savannah, 1888.

Loveland, Anne C. *Southern Evangelicals and the Social Order, 1800–1860.* Baton Rouge, 1980.

Lyell, Sir Charles. *A Second Visit to the United States of North America.* 2 vols. London, 1850.

Lyerly, Cynthia Lynn. *Methodism and the Southern Mind.* Oxford, 1998.

Main, Jackson Turner. *The Social Structure of Revolutionary America.* Princeton, 1965.

Mallard, John B. *A Short Account of the Congregational Church at Midway Georgia.* Savannah, 1840.

Mallard, R. Q. *Montevideo-Maybank, Some Memoirs of a Southern Christian Household in the Olden Time.* Richmond, Va., 1898.

———. *Plantation Life Before Emancipation.* Richmond, Va., 1892.

Marriages of Chatham County, Georgia. Vol. 1, *1748–1852*; Vol. 2, *1852–1877.* Savannah, 1993.

Marshall, Woodville K. "Provision Ground and Plantation Labor in Four Windward Islands: Competition for Resources During Slavery." In Ira Berlin and Philip Morgan, eds., *Cultivation and Culture: Labor and the Shaping of Slave Life in the Americas.* Charlottesville, Va., 1993, 203–20.

Martin, Sidney Walter, ed. "Ebenezer Kellogg's Visit to Charleston, 1817." *South Carolina Historical and Genealogical Magazine* 49 (1948): 1–14.

———. "A New Englander's Impressions of Georgia in 1817–1818: Extracts from the Diary of Ebenezer Kellogg." *Journal of Southern History* 12 (1946): 247–62.

Mason, Jonathan. *Extracts from a Diary Kept by the Hon. Jonathan Mason of a Journey from Boston to Savannah in the Year 1804.* Cambridge, Mass., 1885.

Mathews, Donald G. "Charles Colcock Jones and the Southern Evangelical Crusade to Form a Bi-Racial Community." *Journal of Southern History* 41 (1975): 297–320.

———. *Religion in the Old South.* Chicago, 1977.

McCall, Hugh. *The History of Georgia: Containing Brief Sketches of the Most Remarkable Events up to the Present Day.* 1784. Reprint. Atlanta, 1909.

McCurry, Stephanie. "Defense of Their World: Gender, Class, and the Yeomanry of the South Carolina Lowcountry, 1820–1860." Ph.D. dissertation, State University of New York at Binghamton, 1988.

———. *Masters of Small Worlds: Yeoman Households, Gender Relations and the Political Culture of the Antebellum South Carolina Lowcountry.* New York, 1995.

McDonald, Forrest, and Grady McWhiney. "The Antebellum Southern Herdsman: A Reinterpretation." *Journal of Southern History* 41 (1975): 147–66.

McDonald, Roderic A. *The Economy and Material Culture of Slaves: Goods and Chattels on the Sugar Plantations of Jamaica and Louisiana.* Baton Rouge, 1993.

McDonnell, Lawrence T. "Money Knows No Master: Market Relations and the American Slave Community." In Winfred B. Moore, Joseph F. Tripp, and Lyon G. Tyler, eds., *Developing Dixie: Modernization in a Traditional Society.* London, 1988, 31–44.

———. "Work, Culture, and Society in the Slave South, 1790–1861." In Ted Ownby, ed., *Black and White Cultural Interaction in the Antebellum South.* Jackson, Miss., 1993, 125–47.

McElligott, Carroll Ainsworth. *Charleston Residents, 1782–1794.* Bowie, Md., 1988.

McIllwaine, Shields. *The Southern Poor White from Lubberland to Tobacco Road*. New York, 1970.

McMillen, Sally G. *Southern Women: Black and White in the Old South*. Arlington Heights, Ill., 1992.

McWhiney, Grady. *Cracker Culture: Celtic Ways in the Old South*. Tuscaloosa, Ala., 1988.

Meaders, Daniel E. "South Carolina Fugitives as Viewed Through Local Colonial Newspapers with Emphasis on Runaway Notices, 1732–1801." *Journal of Negro History* 40 (1975): 288–317.

Melish, John. *Travels Through the United States of America in the Years 1806 and 1807 and 1809, 1810 and 1811*. London, 1818.

Mell, Mildred Rutherford. "A Definitive Study of the Poor Whites of the South." Ph.D. dissertation, University of North Carolina at Chapel Hill, 1938.

———. "Poor Whites of the South." *Social Forces* 17 (1938): 153–67.

Merrens, H. Roy. *The Colonial South Carolina Scene: Contemporary Views, 1697–1774*. Columbia, S.C., 1977.

———. "A View of Coastal South Carolina in 1778: The Journal of Ebenezer Hazard." *South Carolina Historical Magazine* 73 (1972): 177–93.

Miller, Randall M. "The Enemy Within: Some Effects of Foreign Immigrants on Antebellum Southern Cities." *Southern Studies* 24 (1985): 30–53.

———. "The Failed Mission: The Catholic Church and Black Catholics in the Old South." In Edward Magdol and Jon L. Wakelyn, eds., *The Southern Common People: Studies in Nineteenth-Century Social History*. Westport, Conn., 1980, 37–54.

Minutes of the Union Society: Being an Abstract of Existing Records from 1750 to 1858. Savannah, 1860.

Mintz, Sidney W., and Douglas Hall. *The Origins of the Jamaican Internal Marketing System*. New Haven, 1970.

Mixon, Wayne. "Georgia." In Samuel S. Hill, ed., *Religion in the Southern States*. Macon, Ga., 1983, 77–100.

Moffatt, Lucius Gaston, and Joseph Medard Carrière, eds. "A Frenchman Visits Charleston, 1817." *South Carolina Historical and Genealogical Magazine* 49 (1948): 131–54.

Mohl, Raymond, A. "A Scotsman Visits Georgia in 1811." *Georgia Historical Quarterly* 55 (1971): 259–74.

Mohr, Clarence L. *On the Threshold of Freedom: Masters and Slaves in Civil War Georgia*. Athens, Ga., 1986.

Mooney, Sean. "A History of the Legal Regulation of Slave Hire in Georgia." M.Phil. in Historical Studies thesis, Cambridge University, 1996.

Moore, Sue Mullins. "Social and Economic Status on the Coastal Plantation: An Archaeological Perspective." In Theresa A. Singleton, ed., *The Archaeology of Slavery and Plantation Life*. Orlando, Fla., 1985, 141–60.

Moore, Wilbert E., and Robin M. Williams. "Social Stratification in the Antebellum South." *American Sociological Review* 7 (1942): 343–51.

Morgan, David T. "The Great Awakening in South Carolina, 1740–1775." *South Atlantic Quarterly* 70 (1971): 595–606.

———. "John Wesley's Sojourn in Georgia Revisited." *Georgia Historical Quarterly* 64 (1980): 253–62.

Morgan, Philip D. "Black Life in Eighteenth-Century Charleston." *Perspectives in American History* 1 (1984): 187–232.

———. "Black Society in the Lowcountry, 1760–1810." In Ira Berlin and Ronald Hoffman, eds., *Slavery and Freedom in the American Revolution*. Charlottesville, Va., 1983, 83–142.

———. "Colonial South Carolina Runaways: Their Significance for Slave Culture." *Slavery and Abolition* 6 (1985): 57–78.

———. "The Ownership of Property by Slaves in the Mid–Nineteenth Century Lowcountry." *Journal of Southern History* 49 (1983): 399–420.

———. "A Profile of a Mid–Eighteenth Century South Carolina Parish: The Tax Return of Saint James, Goose Creek." *South Carolina Historical Magazine* 81 (1980): 51–65.

———. *Slave Counterpoint: Black Culture in the Eighteenth Century Chesapeake and Lowcountry*. Chapel Hill, 1998.

———. "Work and Culture: The Task System and the World of Lowcountry Blacks, 1700–1880." *William and Mary Quarterly* 39 (1982): 563–99.

Morris, Richard B. *Government and Labor in Early America*. New York, 1946.

———. "White Bondage in Ante-Bellum South Carolina." *South Carolina Historical and Genealogical Magazine* 49 (1948): 191–207.

Morris, Thomas D. *Southern Slavery and the Law, 1619–1860*. Chapel Hill, 1996.

Mullin, Michael, ed. *American Negro Slavery: A Documentary History*. New York, 1976.

Murdoch, Richard K. "Letters and Papers of Dr. Daniel Turner: A Rhode Islander in South Georgia." *Georgia Historical Quarterly* 53 (1969): 341–93, 476–509; 54 (1970): 91–122, 244–82.

Murray, Hon. Amelia M. *Letters from the United States, Cuba and Canada*. New York, 1856.

Murray, Gail S. "Charity Within the Bounds of Race and Class: Female Benevolence in the Old South." *South Carolina Historical Magazine* 96 (1995): 54–70.

Murrin, John M. "No Awakening, No Revolution? More Counterfactual Speculations." *Reviews in American History* 11 (1983): 161–71.

Myers, Robert Manson, ed. *The Children of Pride: A True Story of Georgia and the Civil War*. New Haven, 1972.

Nash, Gary B. *Class and Society in Early America*. Englewood Cliffs, N.J., 1970.

Newby, I. A. *Plain Folk in the New South: Social Change and Cultural Persistence, 1880–1915*. London, 1989.

Noll, Mark A. "The American Revolution and Protestant Evangelism." *Journal of Interdisciplinary History* 23 (1993): 615–38.

Oakes, James. *The Ruling Race: A History of American Slaveholders*. New York, 1982.

———. *Slavery and Freedom: An Interpretation of the Old South*. New York, 1990.

O'Brien, Susan. "A Transatlantic Community of Saints: The Great Awakening and the First Evangelical Network, 1735–1755." *American Historical Review* 91 (1986): 811–32.

O'Hara, Arthur J. *Hibernian Society, Savannah, Georgia, 1812–1912: The Story of a Century*. Savannah, N.d.

Olmstead, Charles H. "Savannah in the '40s." *Georgia Historical Quarterly* 1 (1917): 243–52.

Olwell, Robert. "Loose, Idle and Disorderly: Slave Women in the Eighteenth Century Charleston Marketplace." In David Barry Gaspar and Darlene Clark Hine, eds., *More Than Chattel: Black Women and Slavery in the Americas*. Indianapolis, 1996, 97–110.

———. *Masters, Slaves, and Subjects: The Culture of Power in the South Carolina Low Country, 1740–1790*. Ithaca, N.Y., 1998.

———. "A Reckoning of Accounts: Patriarchy, Market Relations and Control on Henry Laurens's Lowcountry Plantations, 1762–1785." In Larry Hudson, ed., *Working Toward Freedom: Slave Society and Domestic Economy in the American South*. Rochester, N.Y., 1994, 33–52.

One Hundred Years of the First Baptist Church, Brunswick, Georgia, 1855–1955. Brunswick, Ga., 1955.

Orser, Charles E., Jr. "The Archaeological Analysis of Plantation Society: Replacing Status and Caste with Economics and Power." *American Antiquity* 53 (1988): 135–51.

———. "The Archaeology of African-American Slave Religion in the Antebellum South." *Cambridge Archaeological Journal* 4 (1994): 33–45.

Osgood, John. *A Letter of Prudent Advice and Religious Counsels Given to His Children by a Very Affectionate Father. Dated Midway, January 1, 1756*. Savannah, 1774.

Otto, John Solomon. *Cannon's Point Plantation, 1794–1860: Living Conditions and Status Patterns in the Old South*. London, 1984.

———. "A New Look at Slave Life." *Natural History* 88 (1979): 8–30.

———. "Race and Class on Antebellum Plantations." In Robert L. Schuyler, ed., *Archaeological Perspectives on Ethnicity in America*. New York, 1980, 3–13.

———. "Slavery in a Coastal Community, Glynn County (1790–1860)." *Georgia Historical Quarterly* 63 (1979): 461–68.

Otto, John Solomon, and Augustus Marion Burns III. "Black Folks and Poor Buckras: Archaeological Evidence of Slave and Overseer Living Conditions on an Antebellum Plantation." *Journal of Black Studies* 14 (1983): 185–200.

Owen, Christopher H. "By Design: The Social Meaning of Methodist Church Architecture in Nineteenth Century Georgia." *Georgia Historical Quarterly* 75 (1991): 221–53.

———. *The Sacred Flame of Love: Methodism and Society in Nineteenth Century Georgia*. Athens, Ga., 1998.

Owens, Leslie Howard. *This Species of Property: Slave Life and Culture in the Old South*. Oxford, 1977.

Owsley, Frank L., and Harriet C. Owsley. "The Economic Basis of Society in the Late Antebellum South." *Journal of Southern History* 6 (1940): 24–45.

Owsley, Frank Lawrence. *Plain Folk of the Old South*. Chicago, 1949.

Pace, Antonio, ed. *Luigi Castiglioni's Viaggio: Travels in the United States of North America, 1785–1787*. Syracuse, N.Y., 1983.

Padgett, James A. "Journal of Daniel Walker Lord, Kept While on a Southern Trip." *Georgia Historical Quarterly* 26 (1942): 166–95.

Painter, Nell Irvin. "Of Lily, Linda Brent and Freud: A Non-Exceptionalist Approach to Race, Class and Gender in the Slave South." *Georgia Historical Quarterly* 76 (1992): 258–59.

Palmer, Bryan D. "Social Formation and Class Formation in North America, 1800–1900." In David Levine, ed., *Proletarianisation and Family History.* London, 1984, 229–88.

Parker, Elmer Oris. *A History of Jones's Creek Baptist Church, Long County, Georgia, 1810–1985.* Greenville, S.C., 1985.

Parsons, Charles G. *An Inside View of Slavery.* Savannah, 1974.

Penal Code of the State of Georgia as Enacted December 19, 1816, with Reflections on the Same and on Imprisonment for Debt. Philadelphia, 1817.

Phillips, Ulrich Bonnell. *American Negro Slavery.* London, 1918.

———. "The Central Theme of Southern History." *American Historical Review* 34 (1928): 30–43.

———. *Life and Labour in the Old South.* Boston, 1937.

———. "The Slave Labour Problem in Charleston District." In Elinor Miller and Eugene D. Genovese, eds., *Plantation, Town and County.* London, 1974, 7–28.

Pierre, C. E. "The Work of the Society for the Propagation of the Gospel in Foreign Parts Among Negroes in the Colonies." *Journal of Negro History* 1 (1916): 349–60.

"The Pine Woods." *Southern Literary Journal* 1 (1837): 306–14.

Pope-Hennessey, Una, ed. *The Aristocratic Journey: Being the Outspoken Letters of Mrs. Basil Hall Written During a Fourteen Months' Sojourn in America, 1827–1828.* New York, 1931.

Power, Tyrone. *Impressions of America During the Years 1833, 1834 and 1835.* Vol. 2. London, 1836.

Powers, Bernard E. *Black Charlestonians: A Social History, 1822–1885.* Fayetteville, Ark., 1994.

Price, Jacob M. "Economic Function and the Growth of American Port Towns in the Eighteenth Century." *Perspectives in American History* 8 (1974): 123–86.

Prince, Oliver H., ed. *A Digest of the Laws of the State of Georgia.* Athens, Ga., 1837.

Quincy, Josiah. "Journal of Josiah Quincy, 1773." *Proceedings of the Massachusetts Historical Society* 49 (1916): 424–81.

Raboteau, Albert J. *Slave Religion: The Invisible Institution in the Antebellum South.* New York, 1978.

Ramsay, David. *History of South Carolina.* 2 vols. Charleston, 1809.

Rawick, George P., ed. *The American Slave: A Composite Autobiography.* Vol. 12, Pts. 1 and 2. Westport, Conn., 1972.

Reed, John Shelton. *Southern Folk, Plain and Fancy: Native White Social Types.* Athens, Ga., 1986.

Register of Deaths in Savannah, Georgia. 6 vols., 1803–53. Savannah, 1989.

Reidy, Joseph P. *From Slavery to Agrarian Capitalism in the Cotton Plantation South: Central Georgia, 1800–1880.* Chapel Hill, 1992.

————. "Obligation and Right: Patterns of Labor, Subsistence and Exchange in the Cotton Belt of Georgia, 1790–1860." In Ira Berlin and Philip Morgan, eds., *Cultivation and Culture: Labor and the Shaping of Slave Life in the Americas*. Charlottesville, Va., 1993, 138–54.

Report of John E. Ward, Mayor of the City of Savannah for the Year Ending 31st October 1854. Savannah, 1854.

Report of R. D. Arnold, Mayor of the City of Savannah. Savannah, 1860.

Report of Thomas M. Turner, Mayor of the City of Savannah. Savannah, 1858.

Roediger, David R. *The Wages of Whiteness: Race and the Making of the American Working Class*. London, 1991.

Rogers, George C., Jr., David R. Chesnutt, Peggy J. Clark, et al., eds. *The Papers of Henry Laurens*. 14 vols. to date. Columbia, S.C., 1968–.

Rogers, W. McDowell. "Free Negro Legislation in Georgia Before 1865." *Georgia Historical Quarterly* 16 (1932): 27–37.

Rolinson, Garry L. "An Exploration of the Term Underclass as It Relates to African Americans." *Journal of Black Studies* 21 (1991): 287–301.

Roper, Moses. *A Narrative of the Adventures and Escape of Moses Roper from American Slavery*. Philadelphia, 1838.

Rousey, Dennis C. "From Whence They Came to Savannah: The Origins of an Urban Population in the Old South." *Georgia Historical Quarterly* 79 (1995): 306–36.

Ruddock, Ted, ed. *Travels in the Colonies in 1733–1775, Described in the Letters of William Mylne*. Athens, Ga., 1993.

Rules for the Spiritual and Temporal Government of the First Presbyterian Church, Savannah, Georgia, May 13, 1840. Savannah, 1840.

Russel, Robert R. "The Effects of Slavery upon Non-Slaveholders." In Edward Magdol and Jon L. Wakelyn, eds., *The Southern Common People: Studies in Nineteenth-Century Social History*. Westport, Conn., 1980, 139–53.

Ryan, Mary P. *Womanhood in America: From Colonial Times to the Present*. New York, 1975.

Salley, A. S. "Diary of William Dillwyn During a Visit to Charles Town in 1772." *South Carolina Historical and Genealogical Magazine* 36 (1935): 1–16, 29–35, 73–78, 107–10.

————. *Minutes of the Vestry of St. Helena's Parish, South Carolina, 1726–1812*. Columbia, S.C., 1919.

Savannah Unit, Federal Writers' Project, Works Progress Administration of Georgia. "Plantation Development in Chatham County." *Georgia Historical Quarterly* 22 (1938): 305–30.

Saye, Albert Berry. "Was Georgia a Debtor Colony?" *Georgia Historical Quarterly* 24 (1940): 323–41.

Scarborough, Ruth. *The Opposition to Slavery in Georgia Prior to 1860*. Nashville, Tenn., 1933.

Scarborough, William Kauffman. *The Overseer: Plantation Management in the Old South*. Baton Rouge, 1966.

Schlotterbeck, John T. "The 'Social Economy' of an Upper South Community: Orange and

Greene Counties, Virginia, 1815–1860." In Orville Vernon Burton and Robert C. McMath, eds., *Class, Conflict, and Consensus: Antebellum Southern Community Studies*. Westport, Conn., 1985, 3–28.

Schwarz, Philip J. *Slave Laws in Virginia*. Athens, Ga., 1996.

Schweninger, Loren. "The Free-Slave Phenomenon: James P. Thomas and the Black Community in Ante-Bellum Nashville." *Civil War History* 22 (1976): 293–307

———. "Prosperous Blacks in the South, 1790–1880." *American Historical Review* 95 (1990): 31–56.

———. "Slave Independence and Enterprise in South Carolina, 1780–1865." *South Carolina Historical Magazine* 93 (1992): 101–25.

———. "The Underside of Slavery: The Internal Economy, Self Hire and Quasi Freedom in Virginia." *Slavery and Abolition* 12 (1991): 1–22.

Scomp, Henry Anselm. *King Alcohol in the Realm of King Cotton or a History of the Liquor Traffic and of the Temperance Movement in Georgia from 1733 to 1887*. N.p., 1888.

Scott, Joan Wallach. *Gender and the Politics of History*. New York, 1988.

Shalhope, Robert E. "Race, Class, Slavery and the Antebellum Southern Mind." *Journal of Southern History* 38 (1971): 557–74.

Shapiro, Herbert. "Historiography and Slave Revolt and Rebelliousness in the United States: A Class Approach." In Gary Y. Okihiro, ed., *In Resistance: Studies in African Caribbean and Afro-American History*. Amherst, Mass., 1986, 133–42.

Shelly, Fred. "The Journal of Ebenezer Hazard in Georgia, 1778." *Georgia Historical Quarterly* 41 (1957): 316–19.

Shick, Tom W. "Healing and Race in the South Carolina Low-Country." In Paul E. Lovejoy, ed., *Africans in Bondage: Studies in Slavery and the Slave Trade*. Madison, Wisc., 1986, 107–24.

Shoemaker, Edward M. "Strangers and Citizens: The Irish Immigrant Community of Savannah, 1837–1861." Ph.D. dissertation, Emory University, 1990.

Shryock, Richard H., ed. *Letters of Richard D. Arnold M.D.* Durham, N.C., 1929.

Sidbury, James. "Slave Artisans in Richmond, Virginia, 1780–1810." In Howard B. Rock, Paul A. Filje, and Robert Asher, eds., *American Artisans: Crafting Social Identity, 1750–1850*. Baltimore, 1995, 48–62.

Siegel, Fred. "Artisans and Immigrants in the Politics of Late Antebellum Georgia." *Civil War History* 27 (1981): 221–30.

Silva, James S. *Early Reminiscence of Camden County, Georgia*. Kingsland, Ga., 1975.

Simmonds, Lorna. "Slave Higglering in Jamaica, 1780–1834." *Jamaica Journal* 20 (1987): 31–38.

Simms, James M. *The First Colored Baptist Church in North America*. Philadelphia, 1888.

Sirmans, M. Eugene. *Colonial South Carolina: A Political History, 1663–1763*. Chapel Hill, 1966.

———. "The Legal Status of the Slave in South Carolina, 1670–1740." *Journal of Southern History* 28 (1962): 462–73.

Sixth Annual Report of the Board of Managers of the Savannah Port Society. Savannah, 1849.

Smith, Julia Floyd. *Slavery and Rice Culture in Low Country Georgia, 1750–1860.* Knoxville, Tenn., 1985.

Smith, Mark M. *Mastered by the Clock: Time, Slavery and Freedom in the American South.* Chapel Hill, 1997.

Smith, Warren B. *White Servitude in Colonial South Carolina.* Columbia, S.C., 1962.

Smith-Rosenberg, Carroll. "The Female World of Love and Ritual: Relations Between Women in Nineteenth-Century America." *Signs* 1 (1975): 1–30.

Smyth, John Ferdinand Dalziel. *A Tour in the United States of America.* London, 1784. Facsimile ed. New York, 1968.

Sobel, Mechal. *Trabelin' On: The Slave Journey to an Afro-Baptist Faith.* Westport, Conn., 1979.

———. "Whatever You Do, Treat People Right: Personal Ethics in a Slave Society." In Ted Ownby, ed., *Black and White Cultural Interaction in the Antebellum South.* Jackson, Miss., 1993, 55–82.

Soltow, Lee, and Aubrey C. Land. "Housing and Social Standing in Georgia, 1798." *Georgia Historical Quarterly* 64 (1980): 448–58.

Sommerville, Diane Miller. "The Rape Myth in the Old South Reconsidered." *Journal of Southern History* 61 (1995): 481–518.

Spalding, Phinizy. "South Carolina and Georgia: The Early Days." *South Carolina Historical Magazine* 69 (1968): 83–96.

Sparks, Randy J. *On Jordan's Stormy Banks: Evangelicalism in Mississippi, 1773–1876.* Athens, Ga., 1994.

Spindel, Donna J. "The Administration of Criminal Justice in North Carolina, 1720–1740." *American Journal of Legal History* 25 (1981): 141–62.

———. *Crime and Society in North Carolina, 1663–1776.* Baton Rouge, 1989.

Spruill, Julia Cherry. *Women's Life and Work in the Southern Colonies.* Chapel Hill, 1938.

Stewart, Mart A. *"What Nature Suffers to Groe": Land, Labor and Landscape on the Georgia Coast, 1680–1920.* Athens, Ga., 1996.

Stickland, Reba Carolyn. *Religion and the State in Georgia in the Eighteenth Century.* New York, 1939.

Stokes, Durward T. "The Baptist and Methodist Clergy in South Carolina and the American Revolution." *South Carolina Historical Magazine* 73 (1972): 87–96.

Swann, Lee Ann Caldwell. "Landgrants to Georgia Women, 1755–1775." *Georgia Historical Quarterly* 61 (1977): 23–34.

Takaki, Ronald T. *Iron Cages: Race and Culture in Nineteenth-Century America.* London, 1979.

Tappert, Theodore G., and John W. Doberstein, trans. *The Journals of Melchior Muhlenberg.* Camden, Maine, 1982.

Taylor, Paul S. "Colonizing Georgia, 1732–1752: A Statistical Note." *William and Mary Quarterly* 22 (1965): 119–27.

———. "The Plantation Laborer Before the Civil War." *Agricultural History* 28 (1954): 1–20.

Taylor, Susie King. *Reminiscences of My Life in Camp.* Boston, 1902.

Thayer, Theodore. "Nathaniel Pendleton's 'Short Account of the Sea Coast of Georgia in

Respect to Agriculture, Ship-Building, Navigation and the Timber Trade.'" *Georgia Historical Quarterly* 41 (1957): 70–81.

Thomas, Rev. Edgar Garfield. *The First African Baptist Church of North America*. Savannah, 1925.

Thomas, Edward J. *Memoirs of a Southerner, 1840–1923*. Savannah, 1923.

Thompson, Edgar T. *Plantation Societies, Race Relations and the South: The Regimentation of Societies*. Durham, N.C., 1975.

Toplin, Robert Brent. "Between Black and White: Attitudes Toward Southern Mulattos, 1830–1861." *Journal of Southern History* 45 (1979): 185–200.

Twyman, Robert W. "The Clay Eater: A New Look at an Old Southern Enigma." *Journal of Southern History* 37 (1971): 439–48.

Van Horne, John C., ed. *Religious Philanthropy and Colonial Slavery: The American Correspondence of the Associates of Dr. Bray, 1717–1777*. Chicago, 1985.

Ver Steeg, Clarence L. *Origins of a Southern Mosaic: Studies of Early Carolina and Georgia*. Athens, Ga., 1975.

Vibert, Faith. "The Society for the Propagation of the Gospel in Foreign Parts: Its Work for the Negroes in North America Before 1783." *Journal of Negro History* 18 (1933): 171–212.

Wade, Richard C. *Slavery in the Cities: The South, 1820–1860*. New York, 1964.

Walker, George Fuller. *Abstracts of Georgia Colonial Book J, 1755–1762*. Atlanta, 1978.

Walsh, Richard. "The Charleston Mechanics: A Brief Study, 1760–1776." *South Carolina Historical Magazine* 60 (1959): 123–44.

———. *Charleston's Sons of Liberty: A Study of the Artisans, 1763–1789*. Columbia, S.C., 1959.

Waring, William R. *Report to the City Council of Savannah on the Epidemic Disease of 1820*. Savannah, 1821.

Waterhouse, Richard. "Economic Growth and Changing Patterns of Wealth Distribution in Colonial Lowcountry South Carolina." *South Carolina Historical Magazine* 89 (1988): 203–17.

Watkins, Robert, and George Watkins. *A Digest of the Laws of the State of Georgia to 1798*. Philadelphia, 1800.

Watson, Harry L. "Conflict and Collaboration: Yeomen, Slaveholders, and Politics in the Antebellum South." *Social History* 10 (1985): 273–98.

Wax, Darold D. "'New Negroes Are Always in Demand': The Slave Trade in Eighteenth-Century Georgia." *Georgia Historical Quarterly* 68 (1984): 193–220.

Weaver, Herbert. "Foreigners in Antebellum Savannah." *Georgia Historical Quarterly* 27 (1953): 1–17.

———. "Foreigners in Antebellum Towns of the Lower South." *Journal of Southern History* 13 (1947): 62–73.

Weiman, Robert M. "The Economic Emancipation of the Non-Slaveholding Class: Upcountry Farmers in the Georgia Cotton Country." *Journal of Economic History* 45 (1960): 71–93.

Weir, Robert M. *Colonial South Carolina: A History*. Millwood, N.Y., 1983.

Wertheimer, Barbara Mayer. *We Were There: The Story of Working Women in America*. New York, 1977.

White, Deborah. *Ar'n't I a Woman?: Female Slaves in the Plantation South*. New York, 1985.

White, George. *Historical Collections of Georgia*. New York, 1854.

Whitefield, George. *A Letter to James Wright*. Savannah, 1768.

Wikramanayake, Marina. *A World in Shadow: The Free Black in Antebellum South Carolina*. Columbia, S.C., 1973.

Williams, Jack K. "Travel in Antebellum Georgia as Recorded by English Visitors." *Georgia Historical Quarterly* 33 (1949): 191–205.

Wilson, Edward G. *A Digest of All the Ordinances of the City of Savannah*. Savannah, 1858.

Windley, Lathan A. *Runaway Slave Advertisements from the 1730s to 1790*. Vol. 4, *Georgia*. London, 1983.

Wittke, Carl. *The Irish in America*. Baton Rouge, 1956.

Wolfe, Samuel M. *Helper's Impending Crisis Dissected*. Philadelphia, 1860.

Wood, Betty. "'Never on a Sunday?': Slavery and the Sabbath in Lowcountry Georgia, 1750–1830." In Mary Turner, ed., *From Chattel Slaves to Wage Slaves: The Dynamics of Labour Bargaining in the Americas*. London, 1995, 79–96.

———. "A Note on the Georgia Malcontents." *Georgia Historical Quarterly* 63 (1979): 264–78.

———. "'The One Thing Needful': The Slavery Debate in Georgia, 1732–1750." Ph.D. dissertation, University of Pennsylvania, 1975.

———. "Prisons, Workhouses and the Control of Slave Labour in Lowcountry Georgia, 1763–1815." *Slavery and Abolition* 8 (1987): 247–71.

———. *Slavery in Colonial Georgia*. Athens, Ga., 1983.

———. "Some Aspects of Female Resistance to Chattel Slavery in Lowcountry Georgia, 1763–1815." *Historical Journal* 30 (1987): 603–22.

———. "'Until He Shall Be Dead, Dead, Dead': The Judicial Treatment of Slaves in Eighteenth-Century Georgia." *Georgia Historical Quarterly* 62 (1987): 377–99.

———. "'White Society' and the 'Informal' Economies of Lowcountry Georgia, c. 1763–1830." *Slavery and Abolition* 11 (1990): 313–31.

———. "White Women, Black Slaves and the Law in Early National Georgia: The Sunbury Petition of 1791." *Historical Journal* 35 (1992): 611–22.

———. *Women's Work, Men's Work: The Informal Slave Economies of Lowcountry Georgia, 1750–1830*. Athens, Ga., 1995.

Wood, Peter. *Black Majority: Negroes in Colonial South Carolina from 1670 Through the Stono Rebellion*. New York, 1974.

Wood, Virginia Steele, ed. *Robert Durfee's Journal and Recollections of Newport, Rhode Island; Freetown, Massachusetts, New York City and Long Island, Jamaica and Cuba, West Indies and Saint Simons Island, Georgia, ca. 1785–1810*. Marion, Mass., 1990.

Wood, Virginia Steele, and Ralph Van Wood, eds. "The Reuben King Journal, 1800–1806." *Collections of the Georgia Historical Society*. Vol. 15. Savannah, 1971.

Wright, Gavin. "'Economic Democracy' and the Concentration of Agricultural Wealth in the Cotton South, 1850–1860." *Agricultural History* 44 (1970): 63–93.

Wyatt-Brown, Bertram. "The Antimission Movement in the Jacksonian South: A Study in Regional Folk Culture." *Journal of Southern History* 36 (1970): 501–29.

———. "Community, Class, and Snopesian Crime: Local Justice in the Old South." In Orville Vernon Burton and Robert C. McMath, eds., *Class, Conflict, and Consensus: Antebellum Southern Community Studies*. Westport, Conn., 1985, 173–99.

———. "Religion and the Formation of Folk Culture: The Poor Whites of the South." In Lucius F. Ellsworth, ed., *The Americanization of the Gulf Coast, 1803–1850*. Pensacola, Fla., 1972, 20–33.

———. *Southern Honor: Ethics and Behaviour in the Old South*. Oxford, 1982.

Young, Jeffrey R. "Ideology and Death on a Savannah River Rice Plantation, 1835–1867: Paternalism Amidst 'a Good Supply of Disease and Pain.'" *Journal of Southern History* 59 (1993): 673–706.

INDEX

Abercorn, landholding around, 8

adultery, 152, 154

African American women: adultery of, 152; competition with white women, 34–35; employment of, 30, 62–63, 67, 74, 83, 120; hiring by, 82; preaching of, 149; in prison, 224 (n. 191); runaway slaves, 119–21; sexual relations of, 54; theft committed by, 111; trading by, 62–63; violence against, 104–5

African Americans, free. *See* free African Americans

African Methodist Episcopal Church, 228 (n. 32)

alcohol: African Americans paid with, 81; licenses to sell, 12, 80–81, 82–83, 86, 113; sold by shopkeepers, 44–45, 78–87, 89–90, 94, 95, 96, 113, 114, 164; violence caused by, 102, 103, 105, 108. *See also* drunkenness; taverns; temperance societies

American Home Missionary Society, 159

Andrew Chapel, 143

Anglicans, and slavery, 132, 133

Arnold, Richard James, 31, 59, 61, 94–96

artisans, 8, 9–11, 12–13, 14–16, 18, 24, 35, 62, 73–74, 203 (n. 118); competition between black and white,

5, 6–7, 67–74, 96; difficulty in classifying, xv–xvi; employed by planters, 31; free black, 70–74; land purchased by, 21–22; occupational flexibility of, 10, 13; regulations governing, 64, 67–70; slaves owned by, xvi, 7, 14, 22; slaves trained as, 5, 6, 61, 64, 67–74, 120, 164, 199 (n. 54); supervisory experience of, 31; wages of, 9–10, 31, 38. *See also entries for specific occupations*

assaults. *See* violence

Association for the Religious Instruction of the Negroes in Liberty County, Georgia, 159–60

Augusta, employment in, 69

badge system. *See* ticket/pass/badge systems

Ball, Charles, 28, 43, 60, 61, 65–66, 77–78, 115

Baptist Associations, 138–40, 152, 155–56, 157, 158, 228 (n. 40), 229 (n. 44), 234 (n. 99), 237 (n. 127)

Baptist churches: discipline meetings in, 140–41, 147, 150–55; influence of, 160–61; membership of, 140, 145, 228 (n. 40), 232 (n. 80), 236 (n. 116), 236–37 (n. 125); missionary work by, 157,

Methodists attempt to create, 243
(n. 219); number of, 235–36 (n. 116);
racial segregation in, 132, 141–42,
144, 148, 161–62; social hierarchies
reinforced by, 155–56, 161–62, 167;
women in, 135, 148–49, 151, 153–56
churches, black, 132, 144; first
established, 135; influence of, 160–61;
membership of, 140, 145; number of,
236 (n. 116); white involvement in,
138–40. *See also* African Methodist
Episcopal Church; First African Baptist
Church; Second African Baptist
Church; Third African Baptist Church
Civil War, 53, 56, 65, 93, 117, 161, 162;
racism following, 168
cloth producers, 24, 35, 62
clothing and footwear manufacturers, 12–
13, 35
construction workers, 9–11
Craft, William, 42–43, 54, 61, 75, 122
crime. *See entries for specific crimes*
Cunningham, Henry, 140

dances, biracial, 48–51
Darien: anti-slavery views in, 3–4;
churches in, 144, 147, 150, 237
(n. 125); employment in, 30, 34;
jailbreak in, 127; lynchings in, 126;
missionaries in, 158; population of,
2; self-hire in, 64; Sunday trading in,
76, 91
Denmark Vesey rebellion (1822), 128–
29
dock workers, 74
Domestic Female Missionary Society, 159
domestic work, employment in, 12, 24,
34–35, 62, 67, 74, 83, 120, 165
drunkenness, 44–45, 81, 87, 122, 127;
churches' views on, 151–52, 153

Ebenezer: anti-slavery views in, 3–4;
artisans in, 10, 13, 69; indentured
servants in, 16–17, 18–19;
landholding around, 7

Elfe, Thomas, 14
Ellis, Governor Henry, 15, 20, 69, 174
(n. 39)
Episcopalian church, 91, 132–33, 238
(n. 140)

fire duty, 39–40
fires, in Savannah, 36, 39–40, 45, 225
(n. 7)
First African Baptist Church: dismissal to
other churches from, 147; dissolved
(1832–1836), 140; early history
of, 135–37; financial support for,
136–37; firefighting assistance by
congregation of, 39–40; founded
(1788), 135; influence of, 161;
links with white Baptists, 138–40;
membership of, 137; preachers in, 135,
136–38, 140; runaway slaves concealed
in, 120; testimony by members of, 53;
views on drunkenness, 152
First Baptist Church (Savannah), 137;
black members of, 140–41; discipline
meetings in, 140–41, 150, 151, 153,
154–55; founded (1800), 135; links
with First African Baptist Church,
138–40; social composition of
members of, 148; and Sunday trading,
91
Flyming, George, 52–53
Forsyth, Henry E., 109–10, 125
Frederica, employment in, 69
free African Americans: concentrated in
cities, 2, 24; guardians of, 230 (n. 63);
houses rented to, 46–47; legal rights
of, 106; occupations of, 67, 70–73,
127; population of, 39, 70, 171 (n. 3),
172 (n. 5), 195 (n. 190), 201 (n. 80),
202 (n. 102); property owned by, 108,
137; runaway slaves assisted by, 120–
21; sexual relationships of, 54
freedom, purchase of, 61, 65; by black
preachers, 137–38; by women, 149
fugitive slaves. *See* runaway slaves
Furman, Richard, 136, 156

gambling, 44, 45, 95
gender: church attitudes toward, 147,
    149–151, 153–155, 159; prejudices
    about, 53
Georgetown, 1; churches in, 237 (n. 125);
    illegal trading in, 80, 116; slave revolt
    in, 129; slave stealing in, 125
Georgetown Grand Jury, 116
Georgia Baptist Association, 137
Georgia Grand Jury, 127
Georgia State Penitentiary, 98, 101, 125
Glynn County: landholdings in, 25–26;
    population of, 171 (n. 3); wealth
    distribution in, 181 (n. 163)
Gowrie plantation, 148
Great Ogechee African Church, 139
Great Revival (1800–1805), 156
Grimes, William, 43–44, 65, 112

Habersham, James, 6, 7, 70, 134, 203
    (n. 106)
Hall, Basil, 36, 59, 61
Helper, Hinton Rowan, xii
Hibernian Society, 37
Holcombe, Henry, 135–36, 139, 149,
    157
honor, personal, 102, 104, 106
Hundley, Daniel R., xi–xii
Huntingdon, Countess of, 134

illegitimacy, 152, 154
indentured servants: landholdings of, 22;
    number of, 20; problems caused by,
    16–19
Independent Presbyterian Church, 85,
    131; civil rights in, 146; discipline
    meetings in, 154; elders of, 237
    (n. 127), 238 (n. 141); late night prayer
    meetings at, 136; racial segregation
    in, 141–42; and Sunday trading, 91;
    women members of, 236 (n. 125)
industrial businesses: employment in, 23,
    30–31, 166; wages in, 31
informal slave economy: independent
    production in, 57–62; marketing in,

63, 67; self-hire in, 24, 64–66, 70, 79,
    164–65
inns. See taverns
Irish immigrants, 24; assaults by, 100,
    102; church attendance of, 143;
    employment of, 35, 36–38, 40, 166;
    female, 35; illegal trading by, 84, 85–
    86; support Confederacy, 166

jails. See prisons
Jones, Rev. Charles Colcock, 148, 159,
    161, 228 (n. 41)
Jones, Charles Colcock, Jr., 47, 95, 96,
    166
Jones's Creek Baptist Church, 147, 148,
    234 (n. 101), 236 (n. 125)

Kemble, Frances Anne ("Fanny"), 26–27,
    29–30, 37, 59, 62, 74, 116, 144
King, Reuben, 30, 38, 39, 66, 76, 78,
    113–14

labor: attitudes toward manual, 17–19,
    29–30; and gang system, 58; and
    strikes, 74; task system of, 58–59;
    yeoman farmers perform, 36
larceny. See stolen goods, trading in; theft
Laurens, Henry, 11, 13, 20, 33, 61
Lee, Jesse, 156
Liberty County: church members in, 234
    (n. 98, n. 101); execution in, 105–6;
    Grand Jury members in, 204–5
    (n. 134); illegal trading in, 79, 86, 204–
    5 (n. 134); incitement of slaves in, 129;
    jail in, 127; missionaries in, 158, 159–
    60; population of, 24–25, 171 (n. 3);
    social mobility in, 25
liquor licenses, 12, 80–81, 82–83, 86,
    113; revenue from, 83. See also
    alcohol; drunkenness; taverns
Little Ogechee Baptist Church, 147, 152
Lowcountry, definition of, 1
lumbermen, 203 (n. 118)
Lutheran church, 133
luxury-good makers, 14

manufacturing. *See* industrial businesses

market trading, 12, 62–63, 78, 87–89, 91–93

Marshall, Andrew, 138, 140, 147, 151–52

McIntosh County: free African Americans in, 39; missionaries in, 158; runaway slaves in, 121; slave population of, 171 (n. 4); slave revolt in, 224 (n. 199)

Methodists, 131; biracial church attempted by, 243 (n. 219); elite opposition to, 142–43, 228 (n. 32); missionaries, 156, 158; number of, 143, 234 (n. 101); racial segregation in churches of, 148; Wesley Chapel founded by, 147; women, 237 (n. 125)

Midway Congregational Church, 134, 147, 153–54, 233 (n. 87)

migrants, white, 4, 6, 8–9, 24, 25, 47–48; grants to aid, 20; as planters, 21, 26; poverty suffered by, 20–21; as servants, 17–20. *See also* Irish immigrants

missionaries, 156–61

mulattos, 51, 54

murders: capital punishment for, 100, 103, 105–6; lynchings, 126; of overseers, 33–34; of slaves, 100, 103–4, 105, 140–41

Nevill's Creek Baptist Church, 155

nonslaveholders: definitions of, xv–xvi; descriptions of 26–28; illiteracy of, 2, 122; kinship ties with elite, xiii–xiv; population size of, 2, 22–26, 66–67; racial concepts of, 35–36, 56, 96–97, 129–30, 163–65; and residential proximity with slaves, 46–48; support Confederacy, xii; work alongside slaves, 29–44. *See also* artisans; sexual contacts; violence

Oglethorpe, General James, xvii, 3, 4, 9

Oglethorpe ward: African American population of, 195 (n. 190); brothels in, 54; Methodist chapel in, 143; residences in, 46, 48, 101, 118

Olmsted, Frederick Law, 59, 75, 80

Ottolenghe, Joseph, 19, 133

overseers, 2, 5; contracts of, 205 (n. 139); denied right to raise chickens, 60; in industrial businesses, 31; on patrol duty, 40–41; planters' relations with, 34; religious sentiment of, 148; on road duty, 38–39; and sexual contact with slaves, 54; slaves hired by, 66; social status of, 13, 32–33; stolen goods received by, 112; violence against, 33–34; violence by, 33, 39, 40, 103, 140–41; wages of, 184 (n. 23)

passes. *See* ticket/pass/badge systems

paternalism, xiv–xv, 33, 105, 165

patrols, 56; areas covered by, 46; houses entered by, 48–51, 118–19; membership of, 40–41, 117; payment of, 41; and relations with slaves, 43–44; religious meetings disrupted by, 135, 136; violence by, 40–43, 105, 135

Petition for Negroes (1738), 4–5

pine barrens, 26–27, 124

poor relief, 21, 238 (n. 140)

poor whites: clay eating by, 27; economically marginalized by slavery, 7–9, 25–26; employment of, 9–16; enthusiasm for slavery in colonial period, 4–6

population: expansion of, 10–11; free black, 39, 70, 171 (n. 3), 172 (n. 5), 195 (n. 190), 201 (n. 80), 202 (n. 102); geographical distribution of, 2, 23–24; nonslaveholding, 22–26; of Savannah, 2, 37, 180 (n. 149), 195 (n. 190); slave distribution among owners, 22, 23, 24; slave vs. white, 2, 6, 11, 171 (n. 28); of slaves in Beaufort District, 145, 171 (n. 28); of slaves in Chatham County, 145, 171 (n. 3); of slaves in Georgia, 18, 180 (n. 145), 202 (n. 102); of whites in Georgia, 177 (n. 99)

poverty, growth of, 20–21

ticket/pass/badge systems: for slave hire, 64–65, 70; for trading by slaves, 75, 77, 79, 112; for travel, 42, 43, 49, 121–22

trading: in chickens, 60–61, 63, 111, 122; control of, 76–96 *passim*, 167; of cotton, 77, 111, 114–15; evening, 75, 76, 82; in moss, 58, 62; offenses, 75–77; profitability of, 84–86, 92; in rice, 7, 77, 111–12; social status of persons, 83–84; in tobacco, 111. *See also* stolen goods, trading in

trading licenses, 87, 88; for slaves as vendors, 63, 67. *See also* liquor licenses

Trinity Methodist Church, 143

Trustees' Gardens, 55, 87

Union Society, 21, 150, 193 (n. 157)

Vesey, Denmark, rebellion (1822), 128–29

violence: by African Americans against whites, 33–34, 101, 105–8; alcohol-induced, 102, 103, 105, 108; fines for, 99, 100, 103; jail sentences for, 99, 100; against Methodists, 142; ordered by owner/employer, 106–8; against overseers, 33–34; by overseers, 33, 39, 40, 103, 140–41; against patrols, 43; by patrols, 40, 41–43, 105, 135; by poor whites against blacks, 99–105, 140–41; prosecutions for, 101; by slave owners, 103; by white women, 104. *See also* murders

Virginia: artisans in, 199 (n. 54); lynchings in, 126; rape cases in, 194 (n. 178); runaway slaves in, 221 (n. 141); slave revolts in, 128

wages: artisans', 9–10, 31, 38; black compared to white, 30–32, 37; overseers', 184 (n. 23); for patrol duty, 41; from self-hire, 65–66; for Sunday working, 66

Wesley Chapel, Savannah, 147

white women: in churches, 135, 149, 151, 153–56; employment of, 11–12, 15–16, 24, 30, 34–36, 74; illegal trading by, 83–84, 113; missionary work supported by, 159; runaway slaves assisted by, 123; sexual relations of, 52–54, 56; violence by, 104; as wet-nurses, 34

women. *See* African American women; white women

workers' associations, 101

Wright, James (Governor), 12–13, 15–16, 179 (n. 138), 191 (n. 123)

yellow fever epidemic (1854), 94–95

yeoman farmers: definitions of, xv–xvi; farms of, 2; marginal existence of, 8; relative prosperity of, xii–xiii; trading with slaves, 78–79; violence by, 43; working alongside slaves, 36

Zouberbuhler, Bartholomew, 17, 132, 133